The Material Fall
of Roman Britain,
300–525 CE

THE MATERIAL FALL OF ROMAN BRITAIN, 300–525 CE

Robin Fleming

UNIVERSITY OF PENNSYLVANIA PRESS

PHILADELPHIA

Copyright © 2021 University of Pennsylvania Press

All rights reserved. Except for brief quotations used for purposes of review or scholarly citation, none of this book may be reproduced in any form by any means without written permission from the publisher.

Published by
University of Pennsylvania Press
Philadelphia, Pennsylvania 19104-4112
www.upenn.edu/pennpress

Printed in the United States of America on acid-free paper

10 9 8 7 6 5 4 3 2 1

Library of Congress Cataloging-in-Publication Data

Names: Fleming, Robin, author.
Title: The material fall of Roman Britain, 300–525 CE / Robin Fleming.
Description: 1st edition. | Philadelphia : University of Pennsylvania Press, [2021] | Includes bibliographical references and index.
Identifiers: LCCN 2020044286 | ISBN 978-0-8122-5244-6 (hardcover)
Subjects: LCSH: Material culture—Great Britain—History—To 1500. | Great Britain—Antiquities, Roman. | Great Britain—Antiquities. | Great Britain—Civilization—To 1066. | Great Britain—History—Roman period, 55 B.C.–449 A.D. | Great Britain—History—Anglo-Saxon period, 449–1066.
Classification: LCC DA145 .F58 2021 | DDC 936.2/04—dc23
LC record available at https://lccn.loc.gov/2020044286

For Susan Reynolds,
who taught medieval historians—
especially me—to mind our language

What we are being offered is a chronicle of changing perceptions, at family level, by people who may or may not have been aware of their future role as historical actors. This might be a disappointing conclusion for students of history, but is an exciting prospect for students of people.
—Martin Carver, Catherine Hills, and Jonathan Scheschkewitz,
Wasperton: A Roman, British, and Anglo-Saxon Community in Central England

CONTENTS

Introduction. Down a Rabbit Hole? — 1

Chapter 1. The World the *Annona* Made — 10

Chapter 2. The Rise and Fall of Plants, Animals, and Places — 34

Chapter 3. Why Pots Matter — 51

Chapter 4. The Afterlife of Roman Ceramic and Glass Vessels — 73

Chapter 5. Pragmatic, Symbolic, and Ritual Use of Roman Brick and Quarried Stone — 95

Chapter 6. Metal Production Under and After Rome — 119

Chapter 7. Living with Little Corpses — 138

Chapter 8. Who Was Buried in Early Anglo-Saxon Cemeteries? — 157

Chapter 9. The Great Disentanglement — 176

Notes — 193

Index — 295

Acknowledgments — 301

The Bibliography appears online at the following address: https://repository.upenn.edu/fleming_material-fall

The Material Fall
of Roman Britain,
300–525 CE

INTRODUCTION

Down a Rabbit Hole?

> But, when the Rabbit actually took a watch out of its waistcoat-pocket, and looked at it, and then hurried on, Alice started to her feet, for it flashed across her mind that she had never before seen a rabbit with either a waistcoat-pocket, or a watch to take out of it, and burning with curiosity, she ran across the field after it, and was just in time to see it pop down a large rabbit-hole under the hedge. In another moment down went Alice after it, never once considering how in the world she was to get out again.
> —Lewis Carroll, *Alice's Adventures in Wonderland*

I am a historian, not an archaeologist, but almost two decades ago, as I settled into a new book project—I was writing the early medieval volume of the *Penguin History of Britain*—I began reading archaeology seriously for the first time in my career.[1] Like most early medieval historians, until this point I had spent the bulk of my time wrestling with the shortcomings of texts written in the early Middle Ages. Almost all the sources describing Britain's first hundred years after Rome were written not in the fourth or fifth centuries, but rather in the eighth century and beyond.[2] The authors of these retrospective texts framed the past in ways that would have made sense to contemporary audiences, especially their twin assumptions that Anglo-Saxon kings and their war bands were the period's only historical actors and that these men had rapidly taken power in lowland Britain after Rome's withdrawal. Three consecutive entries in the *Anglo-Saxon Chronicle* will suffice to illustrate how this plays out in our sources:

> In the year 495, two chieftains, Cerdic and his son Cynric, came with five ships to Britain at the place which is called *Cerdicesora*, and they fought against the Britons on the same day. In the year 501, Port and his two sons Bieda and Mægla came to Britain with two ships at the place which is called Portsmouth, and there they killed a British man of very high rank. In the year 508 Cerdic and Cynric killed a British king, whose name was Natanleod, and 5,000 men with him; and the land right up to Charford was called Netley after him.[3]

Although the *Chronicle*'s portrayal of the past doubtless rang true to the better sorts of people living at the time of its compilation, there are good reasons for thinking that we should be more skeptical. One of the things I learned, as I plowed through the stacks of excavation reports on my desk, is that the mass of contemporary evidence—which is material rather than textual—strongly argues that people in lowland Britain in the fifth century were much more concerned with subsistence agriculture than warfare, and that almost all of them lived in highly circumscribed worlds in ranked rather than steeply hierarchical communities.[4] My reading also brought home the fact that most individuals and households during the first four or five generations after Rome's fall were closer to poor than rich, not something one gleans from a close reading of Bede or the *Anglo-Saxon Chronicle*. This fundamental fact is missing from our interpretations of the period, not only because we historians often limit ourselves to the study of texts produced by and for elite men, but because most of us are not fully aware of the material prosperity found in Britain before Rome's fall.

I came to learn from my reading of archaeology that the people living in this period who were not weapon-bearing men engaged with the world and its problems in ways that would be fundamental in Britain's eventual transformation from Roman to early medieval, but that most of the important work they undertook never appears in annals, histories, or saints' lives. As I puzzled my way through the archaeology, I was surprised by how much evidence there was for those great crowds of people mostly missing from our texts—women, children, farm families, part-time craftspeople—in other words, the kinds of individuals who actually made up the overwhelming majority of all those living in lowland Britain. It was the collective actions of these people, that is, the ones who generally have no place in either our early medieval texts or our modern historical treatments of the period, that stood behind many of the period's most crucial transformations.

My reading of the material evidence also suggested that on the whole historians and archaeologists of Anglo-Saxon England have not thought hard enough about Britain's large, indigenous population once the "Anglo-Saxons" arrive on the scene. In most treatments, the indigenous population either rapidly exits stage left or is cast as the losers in an epic saga of one ethnic group's triumph over another. As a result, native British peoples' part in the story of the making of early medieval England has not been well served, in spite of the fact that several million of them lived through the generations of transition. The day these various realizations finally sank in marks the day that I threw myself headfirst into the archaeological literature and what I feared to be a great, gaping rabbit hole. What I learned, instead, was that it was not a rabbit hole at all, but rather an immensely complicated and revelatory space. Indeed, as I finished this book on the late Roman material culture regime in Britain at its end, it is clear that I am never going to claw my way back out of the evidentiary world into which I have fallen. Not only have I established permanent residence down here, but I hope that my book and I can lure other historians down the rabbit hole with us, so that we can show them the kinds of things one can see down here that one cannot see anywhere else.

Romanists and Medievalists/Historians and Archaeologists

Reading works in archaeology brought home the profound structural and conceptual divisions between scholars specializing in Roman Britain and those who study early medieval Britain. The two groups, for the most part, inhabit different intellectual worlds, each one with its own historiography, period-specific journals, and professional conferences, as well as separate bodies of evidence, burning questions, and enemy camps. Exacerbating this divide is the fact that most scholars working on Roman Britain concentrate their efforts on the earlier part of their period, while those studying Anglo-Saxon England labor, for the most part, in the latter half of theirs. And few specialists are sufficiently familiar with both the before and the after to think constructively across the two periods.[5] Because 400 CE marks both the beginning and the end of a period, questions for scholars working on one side of the divide are rarely carried over by scholars laboring on the other side.

For example, many Roman-period archaeologists have participated in a productive, decades-long discussion of a constellation of issues that fall under the much-contested term "Romanization," that is, the impact of Roman material culture on Britain's native population in its four hundred years under empire.[6] Questions revolving around ways Roman objects were made, distributed, and used, and how Roman-style material culture affected identity and lifeways in Britain sit at the heart of much of what has been written in the field. And yet the impact of the disappearance of Roman-style material culture in the later fourth and fifth centuries is virtually absent in the scholarship. Indeed, with the change of period comes a change of personnel. Early medieval archaeologists are much more interested in questions revolving around migration and ethnicity. Because of this, many of the material changes we see in the period are attributed to the arrival of new people with new ideas. On the other hand, questions related to the effects of what one might call "de-Romanization" are rarely asked.[7]

That evidence actually dating from the long fifth century challenges the picture painted by our retrospective written sources will come as no surprise to historians. But if Roman and early medieval specialists inhabit different planets, historians and archaeologists live in different galaxies. With a few happy exceptions,[8] most historians are not as familiar as they should be with the large amounts of evidence unearthed by archaeologists, especially that explicated in the more technical and scientific portions of site reports.[9] And hardly any are aware of the riches buried in gray literature—the tens of thousands of unpublished reports that few historians know exist, much less read.[10] So, although a few historians have made good use of the data unearthed and explicated by archaeologists, most have not, and the fifth century, with its few late and lapidary written sources, has yet to receive sufficient attention from historians. At the same time, many archaeologists have incorporated older historical paradigms or treatments of texts long abandoned by historians into their interpretations, and they have used them to build the interpretive scaffolding on which to hang the archaeological evidence.[11]

This book attempts to bridge the intellectual and academic barriers just described. Histories of Britain with a date range of 300 CE–525 CE are rarely written. The years 300–400 are dealt with in histories of Roman Britain, and those falling after 400 are found in volumes on early medieval history, although most histories of the early medieval period, in actual fact, begin in 500 rather than 400.[12] Historians of the period do not write books based on material culture. That is what archaeologists do. Finally, the bulk of scholars working on early medieval Britain in this period concentrate their efforts on either "Anglo-Saxons" or "Britons." I, however, am not particularly interested in either, because I do not think that there were large enough affinities of people knocking up against one another in this early period for ethnic identities to have been driving historical developments. Indeed, I believe that giving ethnic labels to people and things in the immediate generations after the Roman state's collapse in Britain is not only anachronistic and misleading, but also hinders our attempts to uncover what happened in the past. Both historians' and archaeologists' habitual use of the term "Anglo-Saxon" makes it difficult for us to think about the people of fifth-century Britain and their things as something other than "Anglo-Saxon," and the new forms of material culture developing at that time as something other than "intrusive." I want to see what the period looks like when we push discussions of ethnicity to the side, and when 400 CE stands in the middle of our period, rather than at its end or its beginning.

In spite of my turn toward archaeology and my firm belief that contemporary things surviving from the period should be given primacy over texts written long after the fact, I remain a historian. Nor am I the only historian who studies things and object worlds. Living in the particular moment we do, when some of the things in our lives—smart phones, plastic, carbon-based fuel, handguns, automobiles—have major impacts on our daily experience of the world, our culture, and our planet, it is hardly surprising that so many of us have gravitated toward a study of human entanglements with objects.[13] Those of us working on material culture have come to understand how much the things in our lives make us *us*. If this is indeed the case, then it follows that losing whole categories of things in a relatively short period of time—which is what happened in Britain in the half century between c. 375 and c. 425—would have meant not only that the people living through this period experienced crippling economic and political dislocations, but that these losses would have had a profound impact on the people living through them, and would be foundational in the making of a brand-new early medieval world.

Although my interests have drifted away from texts, I also continue to write like a historian, and I still maintain, like most historians, that the past is best made legible through narratives. The genre constraints of the excavation report often leave their authors little room for thinking through the lived experience of the past.[14] As a result, details often swamp analysis, making some reports intractable for the uninitiated and very tough going for scholars in other fields. I was reminded, a few years ago, of some of the archaeology I have read, when I viewed the Walid Raad exhibit at the Institute of Contemporary Art in Boston. One of its installations was a series of photographs, taken during the Lebanese civil wars, of the engines of cars that had been used as car bombs.[15] The point of the piece was to expose the futile study of these engines. It was always the case that the block of the car's engine was the only thing that had survived the blast. But the cars used in the bombings had always been stolen, so a maniacally thorough examination of them told investigators exactly nothing about the questions they most wanted answered. The piece serves as a fitting metaphor for how whole categories of archaeological remains often appear in print. We have a lot of partially blown-up car engines, and we have thousands of painstaking investigations of their remains. But they rarely tell us what we really want to know.

This is a long-winded way of saying that my work continues to lean heavily on narrative. Although I understand that a narrative is, in reality, a rhetorical device constituted by words on a page and that it is not human experience reconstituted, I have long appreciated its power because of its hardwired-into-the-form insistence that history is about flesh-and-blood people as well as abstract, impersonal forces. A well-constructed story, moreover, can have a kind of explanatory force, which simultaneously underscores both individuals' agency and the way their actions are constrained by the particular material circumstances in which they live.

Material Collapse

So why should we be interested in the late Roman material culture regime and its end? Although Britain in 300 CE had been as Roman as any province in the empire, in the generations on either side of 400, urban life, industrial-scale manufacturing of basic goods, the money economy, and the state collapsed. One of the consequences of these dislocations is that many of the most ubiquitous, quotidian, and fundamental categories of Roman-style material culture ceased to be manufactured and used in Britain. Skills related to iron and copper smelting, wooden board and plank making, stone quarrying, commercial butchery, horticulture, and tanning were disappearing, as was the knowledge standing behind the production of wheel-thrown, kiln-fired pottery and building in stone. The material losses that resulted were severe. No other period in Britain's prehistory or history witnessed the loss of so many classes of once-common objects,[16] and these disappearances triggered fundamental changes in the structures of everyday life.

In the Roman period, ordinary people in most of lowland Britain had access to and were relatively heavy users of Roman-style objects. Given the ubiquity of things such as wheel-thrown, kiln-fired pottery, hobnailed shoes, and low-value coins, it is clear that these and other objects had been incorporated into the lifeways of large numbers of humble people by the fourth century. Still, it is clear that different communities in different parts of lowland Britain adopted and adapted different suites of objects and deployed Roman-style objects in different ways. Roman material culture also had important roles to play in western Britain and in Britain north of Hadrian's Wall. Nonetheless, it was in lowland Britain—essentially the lands that would come to constitute what we have come to think of as Anglo-Saxon England—where Roman-style material culture was omnipresent and where it shaped lifeways. And it was in this zone where the collapse of its production would have a profound impact on everyone living through the aftermath. Because of this, this book concentrates its efforts here, in order to tease out the impact of the dramatic restructuring of material culture on the ordinary and the everyday.

Each material dislocation that resulted from Britain's half-century-long material collapse would have required some new material go-round and would have given rise not just to new ways of making and doing, but to new ways of being in the world. The end of mass-produced, Roman-style pottery, for example, triggered radical dislocations in foodways and death rituals and reshaped patterns of domestic labor in very profound ways.[17] The end of large-scale iron smelting required a rethinking of the ways one acquired metal, built, and farmed, and it would have forced households to establish quite different rhythms of work.[18] And the collapse of masonry architecture would have led to the disappearance of what had been one of the primary ways in the Roman period of structuring and experiencing social difference.[19]

Historians, though, rarely think about the material losses precipitated by the fall of Rome in Britain, because it not something the authors of our surviving texts considered worth writing about. As a result, the Big Story for Britain in this period is the story of the fall of the Roman Empire in an institutional sense and the rise of a new Britain of petty kingdoms and warlords, because that is what we can see in texts. If, however, one believes, as I do, that people and things are entangled in such a way that that people are dependent on things that are dependent on people who in turn are dependent on things, and if one holds, as I do, not just that people make things, but that things make people, and that material culture plays a profound role both in making the world seem to its inhabitants like the way the world ought to be and in its social reproduction,[20] then it is certain that an investigation of the post-Roman material collapse is crucial for gauging and understanding the period's *real* Big Story, which, so it seems to me, is about the creation, over the course of a single century, of a startlingly different material Britain.

I hold that the transformations in lowland Britain's material culture over the course of the long fifth century can serve as proxies for the tectonic shifts taking place in the ways people lived their lives and in their perceptions of how the world ought to be. In thinking about the transition from Roman to not-Roman in Britain, I find that I want to know what people living through this period did when faced with such profound material dislocations.

- How, materially, did lifeways, identity, burial, and status marking change in Britain as the Roman state and economy receded and as connections to the wider Roman world-of-things unraveled?
- What did people in Britain do when confronted with the material losses that accompanied the rapid deskilling of the population? And more importantly, what can their responses tell us about transformations of society, culture, and identity in this particular time and place?
- What happened when individuals whose parents' lives had been shaped by Roman material culture, and whose working lives were determined in important ways by the needs of the Roman state, no longer had access to the same kinds of objects and were no longer living within the constraints of the imperial political economy?
- What lengths did people go to get hold of everyday Roman-style objects once they started to disappear? And when people found such objects, did they use them as they had always been used, or did they deploy them in novel ways?
- Material dislocations were compounded by settlement collapse and the widespread abandonment of traditional cemeteries and ritual sites. What happened to ancient places, buildings, and landscapes during this period? And what did this mean for people abandoning old places and founding new ones?
- What accounts for the new forms of material culture found in many places in Britain by the last quarter of the fifth century? Were these foreign objects brought to lowland Britain by "Anglo-Saxon" settlers—the standard explanation—or is the genesis of the new material culture package more complicated?

The people living through these changes—whoever they were and wherever they came from—were occupied, above all else, with building a startlingly new material reality, and they were doing it with their bare hands. Although there are few sword-wielding warriors in the pages that follow, the story I tell is no less heroic. Periods of radical material loss are hard on the people living through them, but in lowland Britain, both natives and newcomers did the best they could, and over the course of a few generations, they were able to piece together a brave new material world. It is this story that animates my book.

The book is organized as follows. The first chapter sets the scene and puts Britain's Roman-period material production in the context of its political economy. All the chapters that follow, save the last, explore particular kinds of things or sets of material practices. In each chapter we look at both the before and the after, tracing the fate of a class of objects or material practices across the divide of 400. In these chapters we examine the history of Roman plant and animal introductions under and after Rome. We will do the same for pottery, for vessels more broadly, for metal, and for masonry building material. We will then turn to the material practices that accompanied burial and think about infant burials before and after 400 and look at the kinds of things women chose to wear and place in graves. The final chapter will pick out the themes that have emerged from the proceeding chapters and use them to recast the history of fifth-century lowland Britain. A lengthy bibliography for the book, available at https://repository.upenn.edu/fleming_material-fall, closes this work, not only to acknowledge its and my intellectual debts, but to provide those unfamiliar with the period's archaeology with an entrée into the literature.

A final note: The production of this book was delayed by the Covid-19 pandemic. The manuscript was sent to the press in the summer of 2019. Thus, in spite of its 2021 publication date, nothing published after August 2019 is reflected in the notes and bibliography.

CHAPTER 1

The World the *Annona* Made

> The most crucial result of this for the question of how and why Roman Britain ceased to exist was the removal of the revenue/payment cycle and its associated activities.
> —Simon Esmonde Cleary, *The Ending of Roman Britain*

We need to understand the broad contours of wealth and power in the late Roman period and the ways in which the state and elite actors together shaped the world in which everyone else operated in order to understand how, why, and for whom the period's material culture was produced, a subject that will concern us for much of the rest of this book. The success of the imperial enterprise depended on the state's ability to collect for itself much of the surplus created by those living within the empire. Its ability to extract wealth rested, in turn, on the cooperation of elite actors, who played a central role in agricultural production, extraction, and collection, and who, alongside the state, were entitled to a generous share of the spoils generated by these activities. To get a sense of how many people profited from this system and how many supported it with their labor, this chapter begins by laying out evidence concerning the broad demographic contours of late Roman Britain. The chapter also explores the ways people and things moved to and from Britain, and how its people and things were connected to the broader Roman world. As we will see, Rome's political economy and its dizzying inequalities were critical in the creation of Roman Britain's material culture. Because of this, the withdrawal of the Roman state from Britain in the early fifth century, and the difficulties experienced by those people whose livelihoods had been most closely bound to it, had profound ramifications for the production of whole categories of material culture. This overview will serve as a backdrop for investigating how the material culture dealt with in the rest of the book was made and consumed, and how and why it disappeared after Britain lost its place within the empire.

The Haves and the Have-Nots in Late Roman Britain

All population statistics for late Roman Britain are derived from piecemeal evidence cobbled together from texts written elsewhere in the empire, so even the best are really just back-of-the-envelope estimates. Still, there is broad consensus that a reasonable figure for Roman Britain's population in the fourth century lies somewhere between two million and three million.[1] Perhaps seventy-five thousand were soldiers and their dependents, most of whom could be found in the northern frontier zone. Another 150,000 or so lived in urban or semiurban communities, making up a very broad middling group of members of the households of craftsmen, peddlers, merchants, builders, minor functionaries, and low-status state employees, people such as teamsters and warehousemen. Another fifteen thousand or so could be counted among the fortunate few, members of the households of high-ranking imperial administrators or major landholders. By the fourth century, most of the people just described, even villa owners, administrators, and soldiers, would have descended from local British families. In total these groups—numbering under a quarter of a million and encompassing very wide economic and social spectra—had two things in common: they dined daily on food raised for the most part by people other than themselves, and they lived above subsistence and relied on the market or the state for many of their basic needs. It was this group that produced and consumed a good portion of the Roman-style objects found in Britain, and it was these people whose worlds were most shaped by and whose lives most benefitted from Rome's presences in Britain. The remaining 85 percent of the population were farmers, agricultural laborers, and rural specialists such as woodcutters and reapers.[2] Most would have been free and lived on somewhere between one and two times minimum subsistence,[3] and their daily needs, for the most part, were met without engaging in the market economy.[4] There is evidence to suggest that this segment of the population may have been considerably less healthy than those in the 15 percent, an indication of the price of the period's high levels of inequality.[5] Although these bald generalizations paint a picture of a homogeneous agrarian mass, in reality rural populations on the ground were as socially and economically variegated as urban ones—wealthy villa proprietors, semi-industrial salt workers and potters, village headmen, and landless laborers all resided in the countryside and helped to constitute one another's worlds. They would have been linked by many of the same "small politics," enmities, and obligations described in texts that survive from elsewhere in the Roman world, but that are impossible to reconstruct from archaeology alone.[6] And different rural communities in different regions within Britain, although obliged in various ways to the Roman state and their social betters, developed quite different engagements with and attitudes toward Roman-style pottery, architectural forms, coinage, and foodways, as well as burial and other ritual practices.[7]

Wherever they were and whatever their relationship was to Roman material culture, the late Roman tax system systematically disadvantaged this 85 percent. Although together these people created the bulk of Roman Britain's wealth, something on the order of two-thirds of what they produced would have been taken from them by the state or their landlords for taxes, tributes, and rents.[8] Most taxes, after the reforms of Diocletian and Constantine—which were paid in kind, in labor levies, and in cash—were land taxes assessed by skilled professionals;[9] and the bulk of the land tax was paid one way or another by the bottom 85 percent.[10] A number of the people included among the more fortunate 15 percent, moreover—retired state officials, veterans, and members of the senatorial order—were exempted from various taxes, making the tax-paying burdens of the poor all the heavier.[11]

Not only did various individuals in the 15 percent of the population whose well-being was most closely bound to the Roman state implement, maintain, and reinforce the social and economic inequalities of imperial society, but they increased such inequalities over time. By the turn of the fourth century, local elites and agents of the state (two often-inseparable groups) controlled production, because by this time, they exercised considerable power over labor, transportation, and information, which helped them shape the world in which the 85 percent worked to feed their families and meet their obligations. Members of low-status rural communities, particularly in Britain's "South East" and "central zone,"[12] where provincial elites, urban communities, and state administrators were thickest on the ground, were disadvantaged by these asymmetrical relationships, and they owed a significant share of their labor and surplus to the colonial regime and its facilitators, who together built, rebuilt, and improved on a culture of social inequality that both molded labor regimes and habitually reminded rural people of their powerlessness to do much about them.[13] As Michael Given reminds us: "The most direct involvement of ordinary people with imperial rule is when their hard-won food is removed from in front of them and taken right out of their family, their community, and often their country. As well as the loss of livelihood, there is the personal humiliation, the knowledge that they are being cheated, if not by the tithe collector then certainly by the regime."[14] The annual tax cycle and the seasonal accountings by landlords, their bailiffs, and state functionaries would have reminded many in the bottom 85 percent that life was not fair and never would be, and that each year part of what they produced would be taken from them.

Still, most rural households in lowland Britain had not only enough after harvest to meet their obligations and hold back enough seed and stock for next year's farming, but a little to spare for pots, iron tools, shoes, or brooches made by craft workers. Economies of scale were such in the fourth century that low-value, mass-produced goods were within the reach of quite humble people. The proliferation of durable material culture on rural sites in fourth-century Britain mirrors a similar development in North Africa, where rural settlement sites are much more visible in the archaeological record at just this time because their inhabitants, too, were now regularly using coins and wheel-thrown pottery.[15] Because of the availability and ubiquity of a wide array of such objects, many rural, low-status households acquired these goods and incorporated them into their daily practices of life.

Although the institutions and individuals standing behind taxes and rents were inefficient and wasteful, they were nonetheless able to collect astonishing amounts of revenue each year. Many landlords in Britain would have spent their cut on extending their landed interests and bankrolling conspicuously grand lives, propped up by expensive Mediterranean-style material culture—things such as mosaics, bath houses, and plastered interiors. The state for its part used what it collected to fund an array of eye-wateringly expensive undertakings—a large, professional standing army; patronage of a new religion; a new imperial capital; and guaranteed low-cost food for the empire's most important urban populations.[16] Taxes also paid for the staff, bureaucratic machinery, and enforcement mechanisms needed to collect and keep account of state revenues, and to oversee the transportation of its in-kind bounty to the imperial court, the army, and the empire's hungry capitals. State bureaucrats received salaries of foodstuffs, fodder, and clothing as well as cash, so their cut of the annual in-kind tax had to be accounted for, moved, and distributed as well.[17]

The empire's monetary system also worked against the interests of the bottom 85 percent. There were essentially two parallel monetary systems operating within the empire in the fourth century. One, a low-value currency, was made up of small bronze coins, sometimes called *nummi*, and was widely used by the lower orders in the late Roman period. Its value was eaten away by inflation, a curse of the period, with annual rates hovering around 13 percent. At the same time, however, there were precious-metal coins, and their value was extremely stable.[18] The best guess for the relative value of these currencies in c. 364 is that a gold *solidus* was worth eighty silver *siliquae*, and a *siliqua* was valued at thirty-six bronze *nummi*.[19] The high-value, precious-metal, inflation-proof coinage was the only currency accepted by the state for taxes, and it was used to pay the salaries of imperial officials. Gold and silver were also distributed by the state to groups whose loyalties it deemed essential (Figure 1).

Soldiers were one such group. Although they got most of their wages in kind, they received gold donatives from the state fairly regularly.[20] Between 364 and 378 they might have been due as many as eight donatives, totaling fifty-two *solidi* over the course of fourteen years. Because the late antique state was rife with corruption and freely made exaggerated promises, it is unlikely that soldiers were given all that was pledged to them, but even if most during these years only received forty-two *solidi*, their gold payouts would have averaged almost three *solidi* a year.[21] In the mid-fourth century, thirty-five *modii* of wheat—considerably more than three hundred liters—cost a single *solidus*, so such donatives were significant.[22]

High-ranking military and civilian officeholders also had salaries paid in part in these precious-metal currencies, and like the soldiers, these officeholders benefited from gifts of gold and silver medallions, silver presentation dishes, and official belt sets and brooches that emperors distributed when marking important milestones in their own careers.[23] Large numbers of precious-metal hoards have been found across the Roman world, especially in Britain, secreted away by men of this class in the fourth and early fifth centuries, and these hoards give an indication of the capital that those closely allied with the state might accumulate over the course of their careers. One such hoard, which dates to c. 350 and was found east of the Rhine near Hannover at Lengerich, includes a magnificent gold crossbow brooch, the kind worn by men in the highest ranks of imperial service, as well as a number of elaborate gold finger and arm rings and pendants, dishes of silver and bronze, at least ten gold *solidi*, and about seventy silver coins (now lost), probably *siliquae*.[24] Another hoard, one that might have belonged to a high-ranking official working in Britain, was found at Durobrivae (Water Newton). It included thirty gold *solidi* and two different pieces of silver plate folded into squares, one weighing two Roman pounds and the other one Roman pound: cut, folded silver plate such as this was a common form of donative.[25]

High-ranking military and civilian administrators could put together impressive collections of precious metal objects and coins over the course of their

FIGURE 1. An illustration of the insignia of a senior fiscal official, the Count of the Sacred Largesses, that shows the gold and silver coins, belt fittings, and precious-metal plate used by the Roman state to buy the loyalty of constituents whose fidelity was most important to its preservation. The image is found in a fifteenth-century copy of a Carolingian copy of the late antique *Notitia dignitatum omnium tam ciuilium quam militarium*. (Oxford, Bodleian Library MS. Canon. Misc 378, fo. 142v. By kind permission of Bodleian Libraries.)

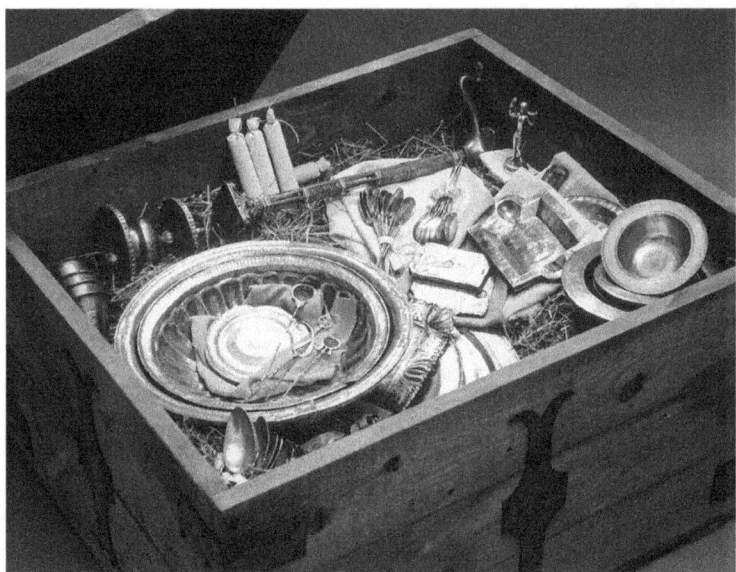

Figure 2. The large silver hoard discovered in Kaiseraugst, Switzerland, dating to 337–52. It likely represents the silver donatives, private gifts, and inherited valuable metalwork amassed by a late Roman military officer. (Roman Museum, Augusta Raurica, Basel, Switzerland. By kind permission of the Roman Museum, Augusta Raurica.)

careers. The monstrous silver hoard recovered from the Roman fort at Kaiseraugst (Castrum Rauracense) in Switzerland, for example, was amassed between 337 and 352 and likely belonged to a military officer, who received some of the eighty-four silver objects and 186 silver coins directly from the emperor as donatives at various times and places during his career: some of the objects in the hoard had been made in the East and some in the West, evidence of the extraordinary mobility of men in imperial service. The older silver pieces in the hoard, however, might have come to its owner not from the emperor's largess, but through inheritance. And those objects inscribed with different personal names may represent gifts from fellow officers. By the time this hoard was buried, there were almost sixty kilograms of silver, a heavy but easily transportable cache of capital (Figure 2).[26]

With their hefty collections of gold and silver, men compensated in this way could amass considerable fortunes. The anonymous author of the mid-fourth-century tract *De rebus bellicis* wrote despairingly that "the houses of the powerful were stuffed [with gold] and their splendor enhanced to the destruction of the poor."[27] Many, no doubt, used their precious metal to extend their landed interests.[28] That looks to have been happening in Milan's hinterland, where imperial bureaucrats working at the new imperial capital seem to have been using their wealth to buy up or buy out small and medium landowners in its hinterland.[29] Something similar might have been taking place in and around the villa at S. Giovanni di Ruoti, in Campania: its wealthy proprietor was gobbling up smallholdings within the villa's orbit.[30] Such consolidation, from the mid-fourth century on, was of concern to the state, and there was considerable legislation aimed at stopping imperial administrators and military officers from expanding their landed interests at the expense of the smallholders around them.[31] Across the fourth century, laws were also promulgated to put the brakes on some of the most egregious land grabs standing behind the period's mega-estates.[32]

A few villa estates built in this period had very large footprints. One of the most notable is what was probably an imperial estate at Langmauer, just north of Trier. A seventy-two-kilometer-long wall encircled its territory.[33] Most estates of the period, however, were likely piecemeal affairs, patchworks of discontinuous demesne holdings, subtenancies, and small industrial zones, as well, of course, as comfortable domestic quarters, all carefully and directly managed by the staffs of wealthy families and run with an eye toward the markets generated by the needs of the 15 percent and by the demands of the state.[34]

Because no surviving estate records or boundaries survive from Britain, we cannot identify the outlines of a single estate here, nor estimate the yields of such agglomerations. An interesting attempt, however, has been made with a hypothetical reconstruction of the estate centered on Maddle Farm villa in the Berkshire Downs. It is based on the scatter of Roman pottery found on the surface of many fields there, which had likely spread as the result of manuring regimes, that is, the fertilizing of the more intensively cultivated fields with household waste and night soil carefully collected from estate workers and their families as well as those living in the big house. In all, it has been postulated that the estate extended approximately 850 hectares. Of these, 211 hectares—the zone that was regularly manured—would have been under arable production. Another thirty-nine hectares—land close by the villa center without evidence of manuring—could have provided summer pasture for some thirty-two head of cattle. In total, such an estate would have required between forty and eighty workers. If these estimates are remotely correct, the estate could have produced enough food to feed one hundred people (workers, children, nonworking members of the villa-owning family), and a surplus to feed another fifty.[35] Such modest (by modern standards) but hard-won surpluses would have been the focus of landlords' and state agents' relentless efforts.

Elites during this period were also using their riches to improve and monumentalize their domestic quarters. Villas in provinces across the empire were larger and more luxurious in the fourth century than they had been a century earlier.[36] The years between c. 320 and c. 380 were especially frenetic decades for the construction of villas for families of rank,[37] luxury accommodations with increasing attention lavished on reception and dining rooms. These villas not only announced the wealth of their proprietors but are evidence of the intense competition between military and administrative parvenus and older landholding families, all of whom displayed and proclaimed their power via their feverish programs of construction, remodeling, and redecorating.[38]

This was certainly happening in Britain. Here some fifteen hundred villas have been identified, although the standard working definition of "villa" covers an unusefully broad range of housing types. Generally, a villa is defined as any rural domestic building built from stone and comprising more than two rooms. At the bottom end of the range were small, stone-built houses, often without window glass or underfloor heating. At the top were a handful of luxurious country houses the size of Blenheim Palace.[39] Many villas—both modest and grand—were constructed in the last decades of the third and the first decades of the fourth century; indeed, many hundreds were improved or built from scratch during this period.[40] A few were massive complexes—with grand entrances, garden features, multiple stories, large numbers of heated rooms, elegant summer and winter dining rooms, and sophisticated programs of mosaic floors and painted plaster interiors.[41] More often, they were buildings of eight or ten rooms, a couple of which would have been enhanced with mosaic floors or underfloor heating or both, and a couple devoted to bathing and dining.[42] By c. 360, however, many of Britain's middling villas were in distress or had been abandoned, although some establishments, including some very grand houses, continued to be enlarged, improved, and redecorated into the 380s and sometimes beyond, hinting that the very rich were getting richer at the end of the century, even as the less wealthy were falling on hard times.[43]

Imperial Connections and Infrastructure

As both the *Fields of Britannia* and the *New Visions of the Countryside of Roman Britain* projects have made clear, late Roman Britain comprised a number of distinct regions, each of which could be broadly characterized by a particular agricultural regime. Although the two projects' regions do not map perfectly onto one another, the *Fields of Britannia*'s "South East" and "central zone,"[44] and the *Rural Economy*'s "South," "Central Belt," "North East," and the southern and eastern edges of the "East" are of particular interest here (Figure 3). Farmers, not just at Maddle Farm villa, but across these regions had moved decisively, by the late Roman period, in the direction of specialist production of cattle and wheat; and it was here that villas and bulk crop-processing facilities such as corn driers and mills were most often found.[45] Because the state was never able to collect all it required each year through in-kind taxes, it depended on *coemptiones*, or large cash purchases at set prices, to fulfill some of its needs.[46] In this way, well-connected landholders could profit mightily by supplying the state and its army with grain, animals, and other necessities.[47]

The increased emphasis on cattle and wheat in these regions was likely driven by the needs of the state.[48] Indeed, the agricultural bounty produced in Britain would have been of keen interest to imperial administrators, who, from the end of the third century up until 388, often ruled Britain, Gaul, and the Rhineland from the imperial capital at Trier.[49] In the early fourth century, the defenses along the lower Rhine and the Meuse were dramatically reorganized. An important component of this reorganization may have included an extension and re-jiggering of a logistical system used to supply military communities now responsible for this region's defenses, which took advantage of Britain's agricultural bounty. This is because the regular provisioning of troops in the lower Rhine had been complicated by the fact that much of the productive landscape of the region, by the early fourth century, had collapsed,[50] a state of affairs that would have required the bringing in of foodstuffs and other supplies from elsewhere. A variety of infrastructure would have facilitated the movement of these goods from Britain to the lower Rhine. The towns and roads of Britain, northern Gaul, and the Rhineland shared a dense series of connections, which show high levels of connectivity within this region.[51] At the same time, the so-called Saxon Shore forts along Britain's east coast may have been built, in part, to aid in the organization, processing, guarding, and transporting of goods collected in Britain by the *annona* system that were now destined for the Rhineland.[52] Finally, the construction of new granaries in the lower Rhineland and in and around Trier suggests that the region's military and administrative communities were now living off stores of foodstuffs collected from beyond their immediate hinterlands.[53]

Contemporary accounts of the transshipment of British grain to the Rhineland supports this view. Two historians, Zosimus and Ammianus Marcellinus, and the orator Libanius all record large shipments of grain from Britain to military depots on the Rhine in the second half of the fourth century.[54] Although

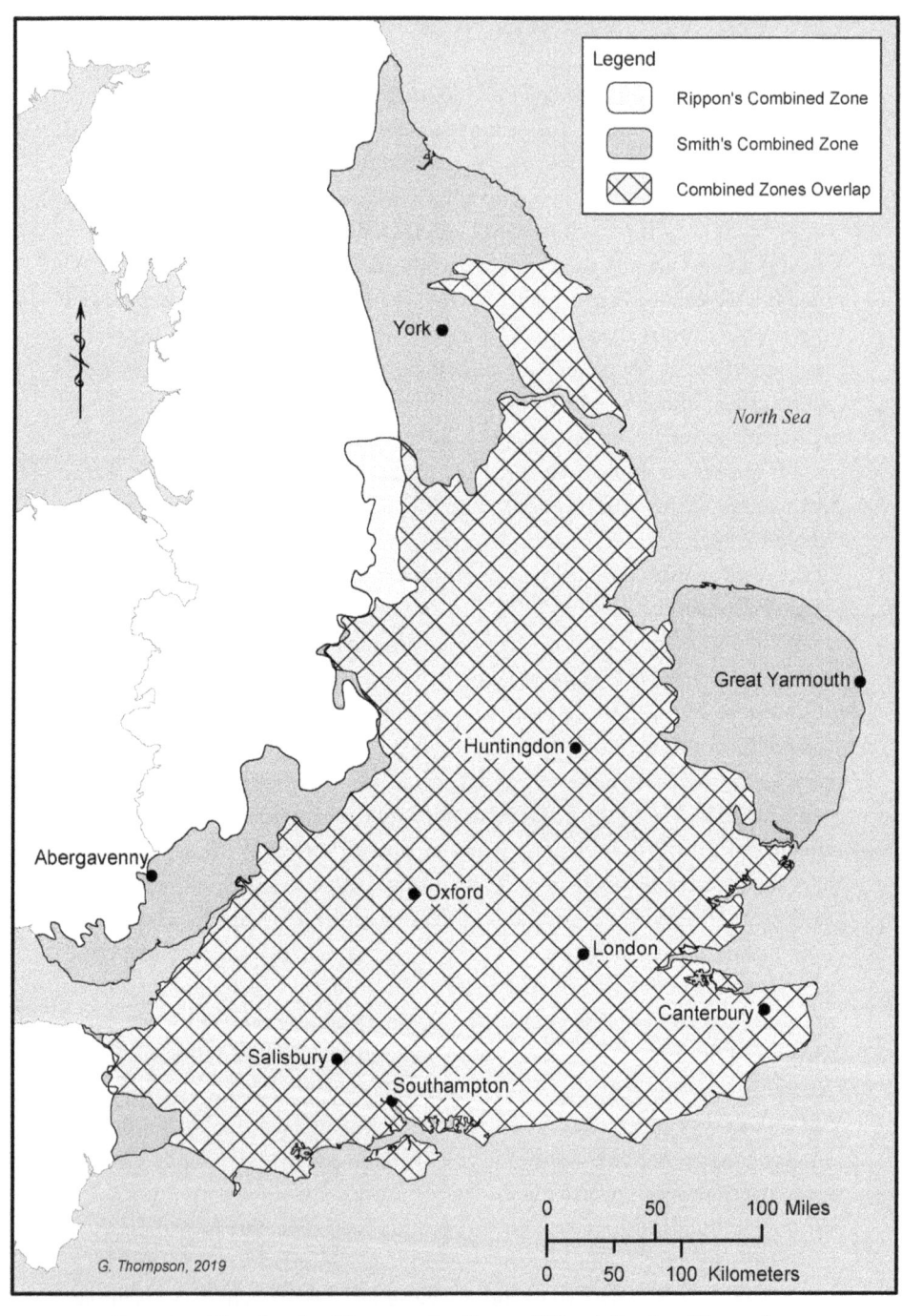

FIGURE 3. Map showing Rippon and colleagues' "South East" and "central zone" (*Fields of Britannia*) and Smith and colleagues' "South," "Central Belt," "North East," and "East" (*Rural Settlement of Roman Britain*). This was the heart of Britain's wheat and cattle belt. (Map drawn by Gordon Thompson.)

one way to interpret these notices is that the shipments were mentioned because they were unusual, another way to understand them is that the movement of grain from Britain to the Rhineland was now a regular event.[55] Cargo ships embarking from the mouth of the Thames were only a two-day sail away from the mouth of the Rhine;[56] so shipping bulk goods from Britain to Trier would have been faster and cheaper than bringing them from many seemingly closer regions in Gaul.[57] The transshipment of grain from Britain to the continent, moreover, was a practice of long standing. A population of stowaway British grain pests has been recovered from a late second-century shipwreck found off the coast of the Netherlands, which had probably been making its way to one of the army supply depots along the Rhine before its untimely sinking.[58] Another collection of British grain pests, similarly dated to the second century, has been found in Amiens, in modern-day France.[59]

Coins and ceramics also point to the movements of goods in the late Roman period between Britain and other of the empire's northwest provinces. Coin finds from the first half of the fourth century suggest that Britain, northern Gaul, and parts of the Rhineland formed a single, integrated economic region centering on the channel. In the early fourth century, when imperial mints in London and Trier were operating, coins from both cities were distributed equally on either side of the channel.[60] Large numbers of silver *siliquae*, moreover, are found in Britain. The distribution of both single *siliqua* accidentally lost by their owners (more than sixteen hundred of which have been recovered and reported through the Portable Antiquities Scheme since 1997), and large numbers of *siliquae* hoards (which range in size from a couple of coins to over fourteen thousand), are concentrated in the heart of Britain's rural cereal belt.[61] These coins arrived in their greatest numbers between 316 and 363, but they continued to flow into Britain after 363 until 402.[62] One explanation for their ubiquity here is that they reflect the relationship between the region's agricultural production and the late Roman state, because these coins were the means by which the state paid for the bulk purchase of basic goods needed to make up for the shortfalls not covered by the *annona*.[63] At the same time, important east coast ports such as Richborough have higher percentages of coins struck in the Rhineland than other British sites, again hinting that these coins might have something to do with the procurement of British grain for the Rhineland.[64]

Ceramics produced in northern Gaul and in Britain, which archaeologists have recovered on both sides of the channel, also help us piece together the ways the economies of the northwest provinces were connected. In the fourth century, ceramics made by a number of regional continental producers were available in parts of Britain, especially around the Thames and Solent estuaries, and at important military and administrative sites such as London, Colchester, Richborough, and Cunetio (Blackfield, Mildenhall).[65] At the same time, pottery produced in Britain in the late Roman period is also found in Gaul. Because the overwhelming majority of pottery used in both northern Gaul and Britain during this period was locally made, it appears that the transshipped pottery had moved because it was subsidiary cargo.[66] Thus, we can posit that some of the British-made wares found, for example, in Boulogne traveled southward toward London from kilns in Oxfordshire by piggybacking on carts and riverboats that were transporting grain and hides from the rich agricultural heartland of Britain. Some of these pots then moved across the channel in large shipments mostly destined for imperial use via Richborough to the port at Boulogne.[67] From there, the shipments moved on to military storehouses in the Rhineland, to the western imperial capital at Trier, or to the towns in the interior of northern Gaul where there were *fabricae*, military outposts, and imperial administrators, all of which were supported by the *annona*.[68] Thus, the drivers of the large-scale exchange of goods and money across the channel were what Chris Wickham has called "bulk product hegemonies."[69] Although some of these transported goods would have been purchased and sold in commercial transactions that had nothing to do with the state, many of them would have been collected, moved, and distributed on the orders of imperial officials.

Impressive amounts of infrastructure built along both sides of the channel made large-scale exchange possible. There must have been large grain stores in Britain where the *annona* was collected and organized before transshipment, although such structures are difficult to identify in the archaeological record, probably because cereal crops after harvest in Britain were more often stored in the lofts of agricultural buildings or stockpiled in rooms with cement, brick, or raised wooden floors than in granaries built with raised stone floors: such stone-floored granaries are rarely found in Britain outside military settlements.[70] Work on Roman Britain's grain pests, however, is suggestive. According to David Smith and Harry Kenward, in order for the mostly wingless insects to spread and establish the large, permanent populations found in Britain, there had to be "a constant and substantial movement of bulks of grain between very large, long-standing grains stores."[71] Evidence for infested grain stores in Britain is restricted to villas, roadside settlements, towns, and military settlements, suggesting that infestations were taking place in central stores that were serving as collection points for the surrounding countryside.[72] Once collected, some of this grain would have moved on to urban communities, and some would have been moved to military settlements in Wales and the North,[73] although by the fourth century it seems that the needs of military communities in Britain itself were more and more often being met by the *annona militaris* levied on civilians in the immediate neighborhood.[74]

The area around Richborough, in Kent, helps us see the kinds of investments the state made in order to facilitate the large-scale movement of goods. Richborough had long served as a military port and supply base, and it was the most important point of entry for goods into Britain for most of the Roman period. There was a major road leading directly from Rome to Boulogne, and with a short voyage from Boulogne one reached Richborough, which marked the start of the road network in Britain. Nearby sat the late Roman site at Ickham, where near industrial-scale metalworking, leather and textile manufacturing, and milling were undertaken.[75] A number of lead seals dated 317–63 have been recovered at both Ickham and Richborough. They were once attached to sacks or bales of goods, which had been packaged for the state.[76] Numerous villas in the neighborhood had large above-ground grain-storage facilities, in which the agricultural bounty of the countryside could be stored before shipment. Some, such as the recently excavated aisled hall at Hog Brook, Deerton Street, Faversham, Kent, not only are very large, but they were elaborately decorated display buildings.[77] Villa proprietors' storehouses were monuments to their power over the labor and surplus of others, and Nicolas Purcell has used them as evidence of villa owners' embrace of what he calls "the romance of storage."[78] Many villas in the region also had large-scale milling, parching, malting, and brewing facilities,[79] all of which point to significant levels of production, storage, and transportation, to feed not only the quarter of a million or so civilians and soldiers living in Britain who were not directly involved in growing their own food, but soldiers and administrators on the far side of the channel.

The systems of exchange and trade that stood behind the state's ability to collect and move what was owed it, and that allowed wealthy landholders to transport what they produced to market or to state officials, were facilitated by networks of specialist settlements, roads and waterways, fleets of transportation vehicles and ships, and huge numbers of oxen, wagons, and pack animals. Places such as London and York had well-developed wharves and warehouses to facilitate the gathering, storage, and further transshipment of whatever the state and other important traders collected. State actors were also transforming townscapes in late Roman Britain, to ensure the collection of all that was owed to the state. Within a decade or so of 350, for example, Cirencester's extramural amphitheater, probably derelict at the time, was transformed into a secure, enclosed area with controlled access and a large, paved workspace. During these alterations, the old northeast entrance of the amphitheater was enlarged considerably, a move that entailed the demolition of the entrance's vault and the hauling away of considerable amounts of building rubble. The new ingress was something on the order of eight meters wide, and to judge from its rutted and periodically repaved road surface, it witnessed years of use by heavily laden carts. We know, because of coins recovered from the various road surfaces at the amphitheater, that one paving, laid down and in use later than 383–87, was resurfaced again after 399–402.[80] The site's excavator has argued that these changes were made in order to transform the amphitheater into a central collection depot for the *annona*, where in-kind taxes could be accounted for and organized for distribution and transshipment.

Other construction projects, which involved the taking down of buildings and the creation of open paved yards with controlled access, took place in a number of late Roman towns.[81] Within Cirencester's town walls, for example, archaeologists have uncovered evidence for a hall-like structure, built in the last quarter of the fourth century, with an open graveled yard. There, they also recovered the remains of large numbers of butchered animals. It may have been a meat market, but it is equally likely that it operated as a state depot for livestock given over as tax, which had been driven into the city on the hoof.[82] Cunetio, in Wiltshire, was another grand, late Roman rebuilding project likely undertaken to facilitate the collection of the *annona*.[83] It was the beneficiary of several major building campaigns in the late Roman period, most notably the construction, after 360, of a freestanding circuit of stone walls around the settlement, replete with bastions and at least one monumental gate.[84] Their closest parallels can be found in the Rhineland at military sites such as Alzy and Bad Kreuznach.[85] After the walls were completed, two substantial stone buildings were constructed in the already-crowded area within the walls,[86] one over forty meters in length.[87] The settlement was positioned at the junction of a number of roads, which converged on a ford of the River Kennet and connected Cunetio to both other important administrative and cultural centers—Silchester, Bath, Alchester, Winchester, and Cirencester—and the rich agricultural lands of the region. Mark Corney has persuasively argued that the revamped site functioned as an imperial administrative and fiscal center—in short, a place from which the late Roman state's in-kind tax could be enforced, collected, and stored.[88]

Modest settlements with less ambitious infrastructure were also crucial for the transshipment of the *annona*. Some were places where oxen could be fed, watered, rested, or exchanged, critical facilities given the arduous multiday journeys that road travel often required. And little transshipment ports along navigable rivers and at inlets along the coast would have been equally critical—places where goods could be collected, warehoused, and disembarked, and where cargoes could be put on larger or smaller ships, depending on whether they were heading upriver or toward the coast and the open seas. Crandon Bridge, in Somerset, is likely one of the latter places, perfectly situated to help facilitate the transshipment of local pottery, salt, and agricultural goods both across the region and further afield to military forts and state supply depots via coastal shipping.[89] Elsewhere, at settlements in and around Stonea, in the Fenlands, which sat at the center of a region dedicated to salt production and perhaps the processing of salted meat, the presence of crossbow brooches and large numbers of very late issue Roman coins hint at hardworking imperial administrators and systems of production designed to feed the army along the Rhine.[90] And individual villas, such as the one at Littlecote, near Ramsbury, may have included as part of their infrastructure boat channels for shallow-draught barges, used to transport the villa's bounty.[91] Such major investments by the state, by landowners, and by private entrepreneurs made the large-scale movement of foodstuffs possible.

On the Move with the Late Roman State

The late Roman state also moved people from northern Gaul and the Rhine frontier to Britain and back. Mirroring evidence for the distribution of continental pottery and coins in Britain is evidence for mobile individuals in Britain's large administrative towns and its military settlements. One way to track the more cosmopolitan men living in late Roman Britain is through the fancy metalwork dress fasteners they wore. In the late Roman period, men closely associated with the state adopted a uniform style of dress. They wore crossbow brooches, fancy belt sets, and prick spurs, which helped mark them as men in imperial service whether they were soldiers, civilian administrators, or members of the local elite. This trio of objects is generally all that survives of this costume in Britain, but it would have also included long-sleeved tunics embellished with decorative vertical strips and patches, and short, military-style cloaks.[92] We have detailed knowledge of this dress and its wide adoption from visual representations, most of which were made outside Britain (Figure 4). But it is clear that elite men in the northwestern provinces adopted it, because some were buried with belt sets and crossbow brooches.[93]

Some of the crossbow brooches and belt sets found in Britain were made in state factories and had been given out to military men and administrators as

FIGURE 4. Details from a wall painting from a late Roman tomb in Silistra, Bulgaria, showing a great man's servants bringing him his trousers, belt, cloak, and crossbow brooch. (Georgi Atanasov, *The Roman Tomb in Durostorum—Silistra* [Silistra, 2014]. By kind permission of Georgi Atanasov.)

donatives on special occasions. Some had been manufactured in Britain, but others were fashioned in state workshops along the Danube frontier. Their variety of origins argues that these objects and the people who wore them could be highly mobile.[94]

Recent isotopic studies have revealed that late Roman cemeteries in Britain where crossbow brooches and belt sets have been recovered contained the skeletons of people who had spent their early childhoods outside Britain.[95] Extramural cemeteries at Winchester, York, Dorchester, Gloucester, and Scorton, near Catterick, in North Yorkshire, all include the remains of men buried with crossbow brooches or official belt sets or both. The oxygen and strontium isotopic ratios preserved in the tooth enamel of some of these men make it unlikely that they had been born in Britain, and, given their burial costumes, it is not unreasonable to argue that they had arrived there either as civilian servants of the state or as soldiers.[96] These foreigners came from a variety of regions from across the Roman world rather than a single point of origin.[97] Isotopic studies, though, also suggest that some of the locally born dead were buried in ways that made them look as if they had come from other parts of the empire, and that some of the foreign-born were buried in accordance with more local funerary rites. A recent DNA study of a man buried in the cemetery at Driffield Terrace, in York, has uncovered the fact that his closest genetic affiliation is with modern-day populations living in the Middle East.[98] All this evidence, taken together, argues that a number of people in Britain had wide experience within the empire, whether locally born or not.[99]

Studies of stable isotopes have also identified a number of foreign women—some with exotic grave goods, others without—in York's, London's, and Winchester's extramural cemeteries.[100] And fifth-century funerary inscriptions as far afield as southern Gaul and Pannonia commemorate dead women who had been born in Britain.[101] Impressive numbers of late Roman bracelets from Britain have also been recovered from the graves of women buried in the Rhineland. Distribution of these bracelets is limited to cemeteries closely associated with towns or military sites.[102] These bracelets, too, argue for the movement of people closely associated with the state—in this case women, who were accompanying their husbands, male relatives, or owners from Britain to new imperial postings.[103] There are almost one hundred graves with Romano-British bracelets at Krefeld-Gellep, a cemetery attached to a late Roman fortification on the lower Rhine, which are dated from the second half of the fourth century to the first decades of the fifth.[104] Some bracelet-wearing women were placed in the ground with more than one type of Romano-British bracelet, suggesting that they had collected them over some years, and that they had probably arrived in Gaul wearing them.[105] A number of men in the cemetery were buried with crossbow brooches or belt sets or both.[106] Not all women on the continent buried with Romano-British grave goods had traveled from the same communities in Britain. At a cemetery at the late Roman fort at Oudenburg, in Belgium, for example, the grave of one bracelet-wearing woman included a Much Hadham–ware face pot from Hertfordshire, and another a Dales-ware pot from Yorkshire.[107] Impressive numbers of brooches made in Britain have also been found along the Rhine, most probably traveling on the bodies of soldiers or discharged veterans returning home.[108] So people associated with the running and perpetuation of the late Roman state could be highly mobile, and some traveled, via the Rhineland, Boulogne, and Richborough, into Britain and back, in much the same way as the pots, bangles, and crossbow brooches did.

Some mobile servants of the state were very wealthy, and we know quite a lot about them from their houses. For example, in the first half of the fourth century, a number of lavish houses were built for men in charge of forts along Hadrian's Wall. At South Shields the old *praetorium*, or commander's house, was replaced with a grand courtyard house. It was very large, over one thousand square meters, if one includes its unroofed, internal courtyard,[109] and in its new incarnation, it was considerably larger than the fort's administrative and ritual headquarters. It included elegantly decorated spaces for entertaining—reception and dining rooms, and a lavishly appointed bath suite—as well as plenty of room for guests, servants, and horses. Courtyard houses were much favored in the fourth century by the rich in North Africa, Italy, and the Levant, but they are rare in Britain.[110] We know from textual evidence from elsewhere in the empire that commanding officers in charge of forts were drawn from an empire-wide aristocracy of service.[111] Although we do not know where the commissioner of the house at South Shields was born, according to the *Notitia Dignitatum* the man in charge of the fort at the very end of the Roman period commanded a unit of boatmen from modern-day Iraq, and this may reflect the situation earlier in the century. Whatever his origins, the South Shields commander commissioned the kind of house popular with cosmopolitan imperial administrators with wide experience in the Mediterranean world.[112] Sometime after its first rebuilding, the *praetorium* was improved with, among other refinements, a more efficient heating system, a more elaborate bathing facility, and an indoor latrine.[113]

The late Roman *praetorium* at the fort at Binchester was similarly aggrandized. Here, too, sometime between 335 and 345 (we know this because a coin of that date was sealed beneath one of the new building's floors), this fort's commander built a new courtyard house. It had a similar one-thousand-square-meter footprint, with the same collection of magnificent rooms as the one at South Shields. Different commanders would have lived in the house during the fourth century, and they improved it over the years: it was redecorated and further elaborated at least twice after its initial building, taking this luxury accommodation up, perhaps, to the last decade of the fourth century.[114] It is likely such domestic display helped commanders succeed in their duties. Their ability to compete socially and politically with other high-ranking imperial officers, and their ability to overawe the local population they ruled, required status-enhancing accommodations.[115] Indeed, such houses monumentalized social inequalities and the state's right to take what it needed.[116]

The surviving archive of a mid-fourth-century commander of a small fort in Egypt provides us with some insights into the social background of the men in charge of late Roman forts and details the nature of their everyday activities. The commander, Abinnaeus, may have been born in Syria,[117] but over the course of his career he served in posts across the eastern half of the empire.[118] As head of his fort, much of his time was spent working with civilian administrators on enormously complicated tasks related to the collection of the *annona*, and we can see him working tirelessly to inspect, move, store, and distribute it.[119] He was in constant negotiation with local communities, who were required to provide agricultural goods, cash, their labor, and the use of their animals. In one letter sent to Abinnaeus by a subordinate, we see the various in-kind taxes he was responsible for, and his difficulties in collecting them: "I wish you to know with reference to the schedule which you have given me, no one has paid me anything. In respect of the hay of Peeieus and Eulogius, they said, 'We have no hay. If, therefore, he is willing, we will give wheat instead of hay.' As to the *aroura* of Malites, they planted *helix*, but wild *helix*, and the villagers would not give it up, declaring that it was village property. Send me the sacks, that I may load the wheat, for it has been notified. If you are willing to give a little barley to our men as a harvest bonus, write to me at once."[120]

Commanders at South Shields and Binchester must have similarly labored to ensure that the communities in the hinterlands of their forts handed over the mountains of hides, grain, oxen, and cash that fed and clothed their men. Presenting oneself as a great man living in a grand house would have been crucial to this endeavor. At the same time, men commanding forts were also in competition with local landholders. The orator Libanius, writing from Antioch c. 390, was outraged that a local military commander was wooing away his tenants by supporting them in legal cases, and that in gratitude, they were bringing him grain, fodder, and ducks, things that should have gone, by rights, to Libanius.[121] Anecdotes such as this hint that the grandeur of the northern forts' Mediterranean-style courtyard houses was aimed, in part, at local elites with whom high-ranking military men were in competition for the hearts, minds, and surplus of local farmers.

The forts' courtyard houses also tell us something about the aspirations, loyalties, and connections of high-ranking military officials in late Roman Britain, at least some of whom hailed from elsewhere: but whether from Britain or not, they shared cosmopolitan tastes with others who moved in the same official circles as they.[122] The interests and duties of this group as a whole would have been focused on the preservation of the larger imperial state and of families like their own, both of which depended on the late Roman project of extracting the maximum surplus from the near-subsistence populations over whom they ruled. Their project, to perpetuate the late Roman world, was backed, of course, by the threat of violence.[123]

Other grand fourth-century villas not associated with the forts also hint at the connections wealthy landowners in Britain had to the broader imperial state and its needs, and they can be used to argue that people with imperial administrative or military experience could also be found settled comfortably in the countryside. Rudston villa in Yorkshire is one such place. A very fine bronze prick spur was recovered from the Rudston villa site.[124] A number have been found on late Roman military sites, but they have also been recovered at villas. They were likely, as we have seen, part of the standard dress, along with crossbow brooches and elaborate belts, of both high-ranking military officers and imperial administrators,[125] and most of the ones in Britain have been found in Yorkshire, along the east coast, and in and around the two important late Roman administrative towns of Winchester and Cirencester.[126] That at least one of Rudston's proprietors was a high-ranking administrative official is suggested by the presence of this spur.[127]

At its grandest, the villa at Rudston had buildings built along three sides of an open courtyard. A number of its rooms had mosaic floors. The most famous, its Venus mosaic (Figure 5), was long misunderstood as a crude example of unsophisticated native taste and incompetent workmanship. Its most recent commentators, however, have argued that it is a highly sophisticated work in its themes, if not in its execution.[128] At the center of the mosaic stands a short-legged, pear-shaped Venus attended by a Triton, a pairing that is quite often found in the mosaics of late Roman North Africa. Surrounding her are some of the human and animal combatants of the arena. A bull is accompanied by an inscription, which most likely translates as "The Bull Manslayer," and above him is an ox goad, symbolizing the *telegenii*, a family of animal fighters active in North Africa. Another beast, impaled on a spear and spurting blood, is identified in the mosaic with the words "fiery lion." The naming of circus beasts on mosaics is found nowhere else in Britain but was commonplace in North Africa.[129] So, the early fourth-century commissioner (and we assume owner) of the villa was interested in and knowledgeable about North African entertainments.[130] Another of Rudston's surviving mosaics, this one located in the changing room of the bath suite, features Oceanus surrounded by fish and dol-

FIGURE 5. The Venus mosaic from Rudston villa. (David S. Neal and Stephen R. Cosh, *Roman Mosaics of Britain: Northern Britain*, vol. 1 [London, 2002], fig. 353. Painting by David S. Neal. Reproduced with kind permission of David S. Neal.)

phins. This scene, too, was rarely found on British floors but was, again, popular in North Africa.[131] Another Rudston mosaic depicts a more classically fashioned Roman charioteer, a member of the Red Faction in his four-horse chariot. He is kitted out with the standard protective gear, including a leather helmet; and the plumes and ribbons decorating the horses are the same as those depicted in mosaics from Italy, Spain, North Africa, and in Trier. There is no evidence that four-horse chariot races took place in Britain, so the choice of the design may signal a well-heeled proprietor missing home.[132] The heads of the seasons, which accompany the triumphant charioteer, are, moreover, in an altogether different, more classical style than the pear-shaped Venus.[133]

Falling Out of the Late Roman Political Economy

There are stark differences between the material record of mid-fourth-century Britain, used as evidence in this chapter, and that of the mid-fifth century. Much of the archaeologically visible material culture of fourth-century Britain was produced, as we have seen, within a complex economy, structured around the needs of the state and the people most closely associated with it.[134] Agents of the state and local elites—both foreign and native born—worked hand in glove to build and perpetuate the social and economic inequalities that made possible the collection and redistribution of so many families' hard-won surpluses to their social betters and imperial masters. The state, the army, and local elites, in turn, made possible the lives of specialist producers, people who fashioned whole classes of objects—iron nails, ceramic pots, bricks, hobnail shoes—that were used not only by the rich, but by humble people as well. At the same time, the political economy made possible the pampered lives of the rich, the evidence of which is preserved in the most archaeologically visible sites of the period. In short, Britain's economic prosperity and its material culture were intimately connected to the Roman fiscal system.[135]

The withdrawal of the Roman state from Britain in the early fifth century precipitated the collapse of Roman-style material culture there, and yet we do not know exactly why, when, or how this uncoupling took place. James Gerrard and Simon Esmonde Cleary have both recently laid out a variety of political difficulties and military crises facing Britain's imperial masters in the second half of the fourth century that highlight our uncertainty about the meanings and outcomes of these events.[136] Gerrard, moreover, has aptly characterized the way Britain's few appearances in late Roman texts are habitually used to cobble together a political narrative of Roman Britain's end: "The methodology employed can be unkindly termed 'Britain spotting,' whereby a series of events in a historical source or sources are linked together to form a narrative: in this case a military or political crisis. The event that has been concocted by this process is a 'crisis.'"[137]

What is clear from our surviving written sources is that military and political difficulties mostly taking place outside Britain led to changes in the way the western empire was ruled, defended, and paid for; and that crises stemming from invasions elsewhere in the empire and from breakaway usurpers who needed troops, supplies, and taxes made Britain less crucial than other parts of the empire and stripped it of resources and troops. These things together dogged Britain and those who administered and defended it in the second half of the fourth century, and this series of unfortunate events seems to have come to a head early in the fifth century. But it is not at all clear when the imperial government ceased collecting taxes in Britain, when it stopped paying administrators and military men, and when it ceased to consider Britain part of the empire, although a variety of dates in the first decade of the fifth century have been suggested. Not only is Roman Britain's constitutional and institutional end unclear, but it is equally unclear if imperial disengagement from Britain was followed by a sharp break or a long, slow slide.[138] But whenever the break took place and however long the effects of the change took to take hold, the social and economic structures within which raw materials and objects had long been produced, transported, and used by all sorts of people in lowland Britain could no longer be sustained.

As the demands of the state disappeared, as the mechanisms standing behind elite handouts were no longer in operation, and when official political and economic links between Britain and the rest of the empire were severed, the production of a wide range of once-ubiquitous objects—mass-produced ceramics and glass, masonry buildings, freshly smelted iron billets, foodstuffs raised in market gardens, and many other things—went into steep decline. And within fifty years of 400, whole constellations of material objects had disappeared. Thus, the faltering and then the withdrawal of the Roman state from Britain triggered a kind of "systems collapse," accompanied by both the archaeological invisibility of the people who continued to live there as well as a rapid change in material culture.[139] This, in turn, both gave rise to and necessitated new ways of living in the world.

In the chapters that follow, we will examine various classes of objects and material practices both before and after the Roman state's withdrawal, in order to gauge the impact of the Roman state's political economy and the effects of its disappearance not just on just villa owners and cities dwellers, but on potters, smelters, and agricultural laborers as well.

CHAPTER 2

The Rise and Fall of Plants, Animals, and Places

> When human beings convert part of their environment into food, they create a peculiarly powerful semiotic device. In its tangible and material form, food presupposes and reifies technological arrangements, relations of production and exchange, conditions of field and market, and realities of plenty and want. It is therefore a highly condensed fact.
>
> —Arjun Appadurai, "Gastro-Politics in Hindu South Asia"

In this chapter, we will think through two large categories of things—plants and animals—and trace their histories across the Roman and post-Roman periods. Plants and animals will serve here as vehicles for helping us uncover some of the transformations in the lived experience of ordinary and not so ordinary people and the look of the world around them both under and after Rome. The introduction and disappearance of plants and animals precipitated radical material changes during this period. Plants and animals, moreover, are good to think with, because they help clarify the relationship between people and things. First, plants and animals, alongside their human collaborators, were (and still are) the makers of mealtimes and landscapes.[1] They are the things that made the world outside people's doorways look the way it ought to look, and made the smell of dinner inside their houses comforting and familiar. Second, plants and animals in our period sat at the center of what Tim Ingold has called "taskscapes," the activities that play out in the landscape as individuals move across the spaces they inhabit in order to make a living and through which they socially reproduce the world around them.[2] Third, humans, plants, and animals are connected in complex chains of mutual dependency, ones in which humans find themselves dependent on plants, which in turn are dependent on animals, which are dependent on humans, who are dependent on plants, and so on and so on.[3] Although these entanglements seem natural, eternal, and right to all those who are bound up within their webs, if links in these chains of dependency begin to fail or are reordered, whole systems of entanglements and material production can collapse or be renegotiated, profoundly altering landscapes, taskscapes, and mealtimes, and taking much of the material world down with them. In order both to illustrate and to argue these things, the first half of this chapter details the history of Britain's Roman-period plant and animal introductions and then identifies the ones that did not long survive imperial withdrawal. In the second half of the chapter, we will think through the ways these introductions and disappearances helped make Britain's Roman and post-Roman material realities so different.

Plant Introductions

There is a wealth of agricultural manuals, natural history tracts, cookbooks, and medical treatises written in Italy in the first centuries BCE and CE that describe in some detail the plants of the Roman world.[4] For tenth- and eleventh-century England, there are riddles, glosses, and leech books, which tell us about plant use and plant knowledge in English monastic communities.[5] But we are almost wholly dependent on material evidence for information on Britain's plants during the Roman and early post-Roman periods. Our knowledge of cereal plants rests, in part, on carbonized (that is, burned) plant remains and in part on pollen sequences. Evidence for fruits, vegetables, and flowering plants, on the other hand, is preserved, in large part, in either anaerobic, waterlogged archaeological contexts or in mineralized deposits, both of which are more frequently encountered on urban and military sites than on rural ones.[6] Although this kind of evidence does survive for the North and West of Britain, there is less of it than for the much more thoroughly excavated South and East.[7] So the data are far from perfect. Nonetheless, Marijke van der Veen, Alexandra Livarda, and Alistair Hill have systematically studied botanical evidence from over five hundred British sites dating to the Roman period and over six hundred medieval sites. The broad outlines of their findings give us a fairly clear picture of the introduction of new plants into Britain during this period and the kinds of sites on which they were cultivated or consumed, and some idea about the chronology of plant disappearances as well.[8]

So, what does their work tell us? First and foremost, it shows that there was a major influx of alien plants into Britain after the Roman conquest, one that precipitated the most profound diversification of the human diet in Britain since the arrival of wheat and barley in the Neolithic.[9] Foods that we consider quintessentially English—fruits and nuts such as apples (*Malus domestica*), pears (*Pyrus communis*), plums (*Prunus domestica*), damsons (*Prunus insititia*), cherries (*Prunus avium/cerasus*), and walnuts (*Juglans regia*); vegetables such as leeks (*Allium porrum*), cucumbers (*Cucumis sativus*), carrots (*Daucus carota*), cabbage (*Brassica oleracea*), lettuce (*Lactuca sativa*), turnips (*Brassica rapa*), and parsnips (*Pastinaca sativa*); and herbs such as dill (*Anethum graveolens*), parsley (*Petroselinum crispum*), coriander (*Coriandrum sativum*), mint (*Mentha* sp.), and summer savory (*Satureja Hortensis*)—started their careers in Britain in the first century CE as exotics. The plants in this list were also joined by several dozen others.[10] A few native plants not eaten in the Iron Age also came to be incorporated into local foodways during the Roman period.[11] It is possible that some of the new plant foods were familiar, before the Roman conquest, at a few high-status sites, but the archaeological contexts in which this kind of evidence might survive are rarely encountered on sites dating to the Iron Age.[12] Still, the overall impression is that large numbers of new plant foods were introduced and adapted in Britain in the Roman period.

In the first decades of Roman rule, these plants would have often been imported or grown for imperial administrators, soldiers, and merchants, people who came to Britain in the aftermath of the Roman conquest, and who arrived with culinary habits that could not be accommodated by the agricultural practices or climate of Britain.[13] Soon, though, these imports were being consumed, as well, by burgeoning urban populations. And by the late Roman period, many had spread, indigenized, and transformed into common kitchen staples in quite humble rural communities.[14]

The foodplants adopted in Britain during this period had diverse, individual histories. Coriander and cabbage, for example, were western Mediterranean staples at the time of their introduction in the early years of imperial rule. Cherry trees arrived in the first century as well,[15] but Romans at the time probably would have considered them eastern exotics rather than trees from home.[16] Strawberries (*Fragaria vesca*), on the other hand, were British natives, but like a number of wild species—both flora and fauna—they were not apparently considered edible until the Romans arrived.[17]

Not all these many plant foods were adopted across all site types or embraced with equal enthusiasm by all social groups.[18] Head cabbage (*Brassica oleracea*), for example, was cooked in towns and at military forts, but it never seems to have caught on in peasant communities.[19] Fennel (*Foeniculum vulgare*) and parsley were common in major towns but were not widely adopted outside them, and lettuce, so far as we can tell, was raised in the gardens of elites but not of peasants.[20] Crocuses (*Crocus sativus*), for their part, might have been grown near London to supply medical practitioners.[21] Many other plants, though, were transformed from exotic luxuries into everyday fare: carrots (white rather than orange), parsnips, turnip, beet leaf, leek, and celery (*Apium graveolens*); mint, poppy seeds, oilseed rape (*Brassica napus*), and coriander; and cherry, apple, plum, damson, and walnut took root and grew to be common on low-status rural sites, at least those south of York and east of the Severn.[22] And even on rural sites in northwest Britain, where the new introductions were not much taken up outside military communities, British people came to consume more native food plants—strawberries, blackberries (*Rubus fruticosus*), and raspberries (*Rubus idaeus*)—things they had not eaten before the Roman conquest.[23]

It is instructive to see the way these new plants were embraced at different kinds of sites. In the late Roman period, for example, the proprietors of Great Holts Farm, in Boreham, Essex, were prosperous, but their domestic buildings, which were pretentious in some ways, were quite modest in others. The main house was a winged-corridor villa, as many elite houses of the period were, with a small bathhouse as well, an amenity often found at elite residences. But the villa was built from timber, not stone; none of its walls were plastered; none of its rooms had underfloor heating; and none of the floors were tiled, mosaicked, or cemented. Instead, they were beaten earth, periodically covered with fresh straw. As a result, the domestic space was infested with dung beetles and other insects.[24] So this was hardly the villa Romana del Casale, and the villa's proprietors, even in the late Roman period, had not fully adopted Mediterranean domestic forms. But they had embraced Roman food plants with great enthusiasm. There is evidence that residents grew stone pine (*Pinea pinea*), walnut, cherry, and apple trees, and possibly grapes;[25] and they consumed other, even more exotic imported foodstuffs, including sweet chestnuts (*Castanea sativa*), olives, and Spanish mackerel, alongside wine and olive oil from central Italy, southern Spain, and Gaul. All this suggests that the villa's proprietors were committed cosmopolitan eaters.[26]

The patrons of a takeaway food shop in Leicester also had access to an impressive array of imported foodstuffs, including figs, dates, Spanish olive oil, wine from Gaul and Italy, and fish sauce from Spain. They could also purchase a range of fruit grown in Britain itself, including grapes, plums, apples, and wild strawberries, as well as the seeds of opium poppies.[27] Peasants at the much poorer rural settlement at Wavenden Gate, in Buckinghamshire, for their part, were living in traditional, timber-built roundhouses, so they had eschewed Roman-style rectangular buildings. Nonetheless, they enlivened their meals with black mustard, coriander, celery, and summer savory, and they were cultivating plum and cherry trees.[28] So the story written from individual sites, alongside an examination of aggregated data for the whole of Britain, gives us a sense of the range of places where once-exotic plants had settled in and become part of local landscapes, taskscapes, and "flavorscapes."[29] Indeed, the cultivation of these introductions and the growing of a diverse range of plants, according to the data gathered by the *New Visions of the Countryside of Roman Britain* project, developed into significant economic activities in lowland Britain,[30] much of it doubtless aimed at urban consumers.

In spite of the eventual embrace of many new fruits, herbs, and vegetables, which were now being raised in gardens and orchards across Britain, cereal cultivation (alongside other ubiquitous field crops such as Celtic beans [*Vicia faba var. minor*], peas, and flax) continued to be the main focus of farming after the coming of Rome. There is ample, diverse, and incontrovertible evidence to show that the major story of the Roman period in regards to cereal production was extensification. By the third and fourth centuries not only were the people farming in the central, southeastern, and northeast lowland zones of Britain growing very large amounts of wheat,[31] but estate owners in these regions had systematically extended cereal fields into clays and floodplains that had once been grassland and were now under the plow.[32] Across the Roman period, moreover, an impressive array of infrastructure was built, making large-scale production worthwhile;[33] indeed, storage and processing buildings on high-status sites often operated as display buildings and thus served not only as places to store surplus, but as a way of monumentalizing social disparity.[34] All this points toward significant levels of production, storage, and transportation, to feed not only the quarter of a million or so people living in Britain who were not directly involved in the growing of their own food, but also soldiers stationed along the Rhine frontier.

Animal Introductions

Britain's cereal fields, as important as they were, were not sites of plant introduction.[35] But the scale of cereal cultivation and the massive transportation efforts it demanded did precipitate a number of animal introductions. Some were highly *synanthropic* animals, creatures whose success depends on their close association with humans.[36] Granary weevils (*Sitophilus granarius*), saw-toothed grain beetles (*Oryzaephilus surinamensis*), and rust-red grain beetles (*Laemophloeus ferrugineus*) were the three most prolific and troublesome Roman animal introductions.[37] None were native, and there is no trace of any of them in Britain before the conquest. But by c. 100 CE, all three were firmly entrenched in military settlements and towns, and all were infecting grain supplies and causing trouble.[38] Today the granary weevil alone destroys 5 percent of the world's cereal harvest each year, which suggests that its introduction into Britain was not good news.[39] These and other pests (such as the *Blatta orientalis* cockroach found in late Roman Lincoln) hailed from warmer and drier parts of the empire, and none was capable of moving more than a few meters on their own. In order to cover ground and survive, they would have had to hitchhike in loads of grain carried by pack animals, wagons, and boats, and they had to find warm places to stay, because even Britain's summers are almost too chilly for them.[40] So they colonized a very specific (and very Roman) habitat in Britain—above-ground grain storage facilities, a building type unknown in Britain before the Roman conquest.[41] These buildings, in turn, were closely associated with other very Roman spaces—towns, military installations, and villa estates. The black rat (*Rattus rattus*) was another Roman introduction, and it was a well-established urban animal by the second century, living in many of the same spaces as the nonnative insects and occasionally found on villa sites.[42]

Mules were also new to Britain; and because they are hybrids, there had to have been donkeys in Britain as well. They are found in the early Roman period primarily on military sites, but by the fourth century, it looks as if some villa owners were actively breeding them, doubtless using them, alongside oxen, to plow, harvest, and haul, and they would have been useful animals for cereal producers and transporters.[43] Animals long in Britain were also used in different ways under Rome. Roman cavalry horses, for example, required new kinds of large-scale agricultural regimes in areas along Hadrian's Wall, where many thousands were maintained, and they needed constant supplies of fodder, bedding, and grazing.[44] Elites in the period also embraced pork-rich diets as a way of living and displaying status and to mark regular eaters of pork as different from other people.[45] And cattle were now bred for size and strength, and herds were managed to accommodate the period's nearly insatiable demands for plowing and hauling animals.[46]

The bulk of the remaining animal introductions was closely associated not with plowed fields, but with gardens and parks. A number of new bird introductions—in particular pheasants,[47] peacocks,[48] doves,[49] and guinea fowl[50]—functioned during the Roman period as walking garden features as well as objects of the hunt and high dining. Occasionally exotic birds were also used in structured deposits placed in wells or ritual shafts.[51] Their well-being required special know-how and infrastructure—fenced gardens, aviaries, dovecotes, coops, and cages.[52] Rabbits (*Oryctolagus cuniculus*), an import from Spain, were similarly found in a few *leporaria* situated in the parklands of the high and mighty, and they were raised both for the hunt and for elite dinners.[53] The same can be said for fallow deer (*Dama dama dama*), which were imported from the Mediterranean, and remained, throughout the Roman period, creatures of villa parkland.[54] Many of the animals just described were hothouse creatures, and they came to inhabit parklands, gardens, and ritual spaces. Their distribution mirrored new tree species such as the stone pine, which grew throughout the western Mediterranean; box (*Buxus semper virens L.*); and mulberry (*Morus nigra L.*), a Persian native. The range of these trees in Britain was highly circumscribed, limited to fancy urban townhouses and villa gardens, temple sites, and cemeteries,[55] where they were sometimes incorporated into funerary rituals,[56] and grown alongside newly introduced roses, lilies, corn marigolds, opium poppies, and columbine.[57] These animals hint at the increased control that the proud owners of such parkland had over local landscapes and the people who lived within them.[58] The remains of charismatic megafauna, such as those of a giraffe found in Kent and a few bears in London, hint that some of the exotic beasts use in entertainments elsewhere in the Roman world were occasionally on view in Britain as well.[59]

A few other species were introduced only for the kitchen. A handful of dormice and edible snails (*Helix pomatia*) have been found in Britain, brought there, no doubt, to meet the needs of the most discriminating palates, but they have been found only in large towns and military forts.[60] Domestic fowl (the technical name for chickens) sometimes also served as food animals, but they had an interestingly different trajectory from the other bird introductions. A few arrived in Britain as rare, feathered wonders before the Roman conquest, but only in limited numbers, and they were found on the kinds of sites that have produced Mediterranean amphorae and metalwork: elites probably acquired them as exotic curiosities, using them and other displays of Roman material culture to prop up their social positions. According to Caesar, they were used for cockfighting in Britain, but never eaten.[61] Yet, over the course of the Roman period, they came to be as common as coriander and apple trees. They were bred on some scale, and their flesh and their eggs were sold in market stalls in and around new towns and forts from very early in the Roman period.[62] Indeed, one of the Vindolanda tablets includes a request to buy "twenty chickens . . . and one or two hundred eggs, if they are for sale at a good price."[63] It also looks as if eggs were sold at the amphitheater at Chester as snack food.[64] Chickens are perfect little protein factories—both edible and egg producing, and because they are one-meal-sized animals there is no problem with preservation after slaughter. Like a lot of omnivores, they are also excellent subsistence animals, easy to maintain on household scraps and a little free-range foraging.[65] Chickens and their eggs, though, would always be more typical of urban meals than rural ones. And, they were never just food animals in the Roman period. Cockfighting remained an important pastime in Britain as well,[66] and roosters were also closely associated with the cults of Mercury and Mithras, and people may have considered them psychopomps.[67] They are regularly found in Roman-period graves, including in rural cemeteries.[68] Hundreds were also sacrificed or eaten or both during ritual meals at a number of Romano-British temples and cemeteries.[69]

One animal introduction—the brown hare—which was well established *before* the Roman conquest, came, like strawberries, to be thought of as food only in the Roman period, and only on certain kinds of sites.[70] Some were raised in the same parkland as fallow deer, where they were reared to enhance great men's reputations.[71] Hare at mealtime, though, was likely popularized by the introduction of hare farming, which had long been practiced in Italy.[72] By the late Roman period hares were being sold in food markets at military establishments and in Britain's larger towns, alongside chickens and rock doves, another animal introduction.[73]

Disappearances

It is clear, then, that Britain was awash with new plants and animals, many of which, by the late Roman period, were commonplace. Yet, within a few generations of 400, most of the Roman animal and plant introductions seem to have disappeared. The evidence for animals is relatively straightforward, based on bone assemblages from hundreds of sites, which allow us, with some confidence, to argue that Roman Britain's parkland and garden creatures—its exotic birds, fallow deer, and rabbits—did not survive the transition from Roman to medieval.[74] All these animals had been poured into very specific, circumscribed habitats. As a result, their ranges were not contiguous, so viable breeding populations never developed outside them. These animals were also highly susceptible to predators and poachers; and without powerful elites, estate managers, a punitive state, and gangs of laborers to maintain fences and ditches, they were doomed. No villas, no elites: no fallow deer, no peacocks.

The Roman introductions associated with cereal agriculture also faded away. Although cereal agriculture continued to be important in Britain after 400, without a taxing state or a market, there was now little point in producing or storing much surplus, and so the balance between cereal cultivation and pastoral farming shifted.[75] The grain pests, so it turns out, were absolutely dependent on long-distance cereal trade and large-scale cereal-storage buildings: they could not survive without them, and because both went away in Britain in the fifth century, so, too, did they.[76] Black rats are big-grain-stores, built-environment kinds of animals as well, and more likely than not they, too, disappeared.[77] And traction animals, such as mules, which required special breeding programs, died out. Thus, both the exotic, garden animals and the cereal-dependent species, although settled in Britain for many centuries by 400, were utterly dependent on the Roman political economy, social structures, and infrastructure. Once villas, towns, the money economy, and systems of imperial taxation were no longer viable, neither were they.

Many of the new plants also seem to have gone the way of grain weevils and peacocks. The evidence for their demise, however, is less clear-cut, because we are dependent, for most Roman plant introductions, on remains preserved in wet, anaerobic conditions or through mineralization, usually in human feces, and the circumstances that allowed for the formation of such contexts were much rarer after 400 than before. The plants we can see, moreover, are by and large herbs and fruits, because the seeds of these plants were often ingested; and it is only the seeds that can still be identified after a trip through the human gut. Although evidence is scare, it is probably correct to argue that many food plants that by 400 had been grown and eaten for hundreds of years by hundreds of thousands of people ceased to be cultivated in Britain.

We have evidence for the continued use of a few Roman plant introductions from cess (human waste) recovered at a handful of early medieval rural sites.[78] In the first couple of centuries after 400, for example, we know that people living at Lyminge, in Kent and Wolverton Mill, in Buckinghamshire, still seasoned their food with *Brassica* seeds (black mustard/cabbage).[79] At Stansted, in Essex, and Sutton Courtenay, in Oxfordshire, meals included the seeds of opium poppy.[80] At Abbots Worthy, near Winchester, people were using both poppy and mustard seeds.[81] The persistence of *Brassica* and poppy is not surprising, given that both are famously opportunistic self-sowers and had, in all likelihood, naturalized by the fifth century, and had come to grow outside garden contexts, without the help of humans.[82] So, they would not have to be cultivated to be available. At other sites where cess has been preserved, such as the Middle Saxon sites at West Fen Road, Ely, and Brandon, in Suffolk, no evidence for culinary herbs has been found.[83]

The dearth of Roman-period herbs at these early medieval rural sites is echoed in the finds from newly forming trading communities, which date to the later seventh and early eighth centuries. The earliest dated Hamwic cesspit contained no trace of culinary herbs, and neither did the cesspits in use there a couple of generations later.[84] Similarly, in Lundenwic, the earliest botanical evidence, dating from the late seventh to the mid-eighth century, includes no culinary herbs; at Fishergate, York, the only culinary herb recovered from the earliest deposits is poppy.[85] But at none of these sites is there any indication that other of the everyday condiments, so ubiquitous on Roman sites, had survived the transition from Roman to early medieval.[86] Unlike poppy and black mustard, plants such as coriander do not self-seed in the British climate,[87] and some, such as summer savory and marjoram, do not do well without human help, because British weeds out-compete them,[88] so it is unlikely that these plants had naturalized.[89]

People living in the earliest generations of Hamwic, Lundenwic, Ipswich, and York did, however, eat a wide range of *wild* plants. People at these sites were eating not only blackberries and hazelnuts (*Corylus avellane*), but elderberries (*Sambucus nigra*), rosehips, sloes (*Prunus spinosa*), hawthorn berries, rowanberries, and bilberries.[90] Archaeobotanical evidence from early medieval rural sites shows that these communities, too, were eating a lot of wild plants.[91] The presence of the remains of wild food sources in cess argues that one of the basic provisioning strategies both in Britain's early medieval trading centers and in its rural communities was the foraging of fruits and nuts from hedgerows, woodland edges, and bogs.[92] It might also be the case that wild greens such as vetch (*Vicia ervilia*), stinging nettles (*Urtica dioica*), dandelions (*Taraxacum* sp), and fat hen (*Chenopodium album*), the seeds of which are commonly found on early medieval sites, were gathered and eaten.[93] In short, what limited evidence we have suggests that people in the post-Roman period had more or less given up on gardening and instead were putting their energy into foraging. I am not arguing that this is a bad thing, or, for that matter, a good thing, but am simply pointing out that it is different. It looks to me as if much of the world that Roman horticulture had made—a world in which market gardens surrounded every town, where garden plots were tended on high- and low-status sites alike, and where many sold or shopped at vegetable stalls in markets[94]—had been replaced in large part by a parallel early medieval universe in which the collection of wild plants was a ubiquitous subsistence strategy and gardening was hardly practiced.

A World Without Gardens

So how might people without gardens live differently than people in a world overrun with them? How might they live in a world without villa estates, parkland, large-scale cereal infrastructure, and the myriad other ecosystems into which plant and animal introductions had been poured? In thinking about this, it is useful to begin with an insight from the anthropologist Daniel Miller: "Things do things to us, and not just the things we want them to do."[95] If we think carefully about the two quite different plant/animal/human worlds so far described, it is easy to come to the conclusion that humans are not always the masters of the things in their lives.[96] Indeed, while thinking about this myself, I am left with the unsettling notion that it is the plants and not the people that are the things driving our narrative. In late Roman Britain everyone would have had been entangled with at least some of the plant introductions, whether they were peasants, villa owners, imperial administrators, teamsters, or wives. It was these plants' biological needs that set the daily tasks and yearly calendars of everyone living in Britain during the Roman period, no matter who they were—and not the other way around. Grain was not harvested when humans felt like harvesting it: it was harvested when grain's own needs determined that it was ready. Humans did not heavily fertilize plants in the cabbage family because they felt like it, but because the plants demanded it. Plants also, in many ways, required people to create material culture appropriate to the plants' own needs—everything from hoes and mattocks, to iron-covered spades and pruning hooks, to threshing floors and corn driers. And plants' needs often dictate their human cultivators' animal husbandry practices, pushing them toward the selection of particular species, kill ages, and animal labor practices. People in late Roman Britain, for example, ate lots of four- and five-year-old steers. They may have been under the impression that they were doing this because they liked beef stew, but in reality their diet was beef heavy because there were hundreds of thousands of old, arthritic steers around, a result of the Roman state's and the Roman elites' heavy dependence on these animals for plowing cereal fields and hauling grain.[97] Plants' demands trapped their human helpers, as they found themselves weeding, fertilizing, loading their bounty into wagons, raising cattle, and haggling at markets, because their plants demanded that they do so. Plants needed all this done for them to successfully reproduce, and people in turn needed plants to succeed, because they would starve without them (or no longer be rich, or able to overwinter their cattle, or field an army, etc.). Both Roman-style extensification and horticulture entangled humans, plants, and animals in very particular chains of mutual dependency, and they created the taskscapes of everyone in Britain living under Roman rule.

Over time, plants' demands normalized the ways farmers in Roman Britain did things and made the daily and yearly rhythms of their lives seem like the way things ought to be: thus, plants' requirements played a central role in both making the world and socially reproducing it day after day, harvest after harvest. This means that the introduction of new plants and new agricultural regimes and their indigenization profoundly shaped the lived experience and lifeways of all of Britain's population. It also means that their disappearances similarly upended lifeways. As Andrew Gardner has observed, "highly routinized material practices are more ... likely to be an important element in the structuration of social relations. ... Disruptions to such practices will be correspondingly traumatic."[98]

The introduction and establishment of most of the plants (and indeed many of the animals) required a grand reworking of Britain's basic agricultural, dietary, and labor regimes. The main reason for this is that many of the new food plants and animals established under Rome inhabited gardens rather than plowed fields. This, as Marijke van der Veen has pointed out, means that, their very existence depended on the importation of a whole category of agriculture that had been unknown in Britain before the Roman conquest—horticulture.[99] Horticulture is agriculture based not on the plow, but on small, carefully controlled, man-made plots, which provide little ecosystems in which plants can grow and develop. Gardens are intensively cultivated plant habitats, where a mix of species, rather than a single crop, is grown. The plants grown in this way were watered, fertilized, weeded, divided, and otherwise intensively fussed over in ways that field crops such as wheat never were.[100] So the importation of new plants into Britain came as part of a cultural package. Not only did this include culinary preferences, seeds, recipes, and new styles of cooking pots, but the *idea* of horticulture and the technologies and resources necessary to practice it—things such as hoes, spades, and pruning hooks (all Roman introductions),[101] and grafting techniques, plant knowledge, and weed-, pest-, and animal-control strategies. Also part of the "horticulture package" were new categories of space in which to practice horticulture—zones of intensive agriculture found in and around urban and military markets, and in close proximity to the rural houses of both the high and mighty and the poor.[102]

A century of work by anthropologists has made clear that labor practices surrounding plants and animals are often highly gendered.[103] So the introduction of agricultural packages (such as horticulture or extensive wheat production) or animals (such as chickens), may well have altered standard gendered work in very profound ways.[104] Horticulture's retreat would have meant that the rhythms of many families' days in the fourth century were quite unlike those of the fifth century. And an increased emphasis on wool, dairy, or foraging may have redirected the labor of women and children quite noticeably.

Those farmers in Britain under Rome who came to practice horticulture (or, for that matter who ran extensive cereal-growing concerns) would not have been able to discern the larger forces that made their agricultural practices possible—things such as imperial ideologies, which were developed, upheld, and perfected far from the gardens and spelt fields of Britannia. Urban and military communities transplanted into Britain in the early days of Roman colonization were initially very dependent on imported food from home. But by the second half of the first century new, locally produced foods were available in towns such as Colchester and London. Demand for these foods—first by Roman soldiers and administrators and later by urban populations—made horticulture not only a possibility in the hinterlands around these settlements, but a necessity.[105] And imperial taxation demanded larger surpluses, pushing farmers, by the late Roman period, to concentrate heavily on cereal production. So, both horticulture and cereal extensification were not just made possible by the demands of imperial elites who had come to rule Britain, but they were now requirements.[106] While Romano-British market gardeners or villa owners may have believed themselves to be the masters of their own destinies, as they planted a few more cherry trees or extended their spelt fields, they were doing so to meet the needs of a political economy completely outside their control. In the words, once again, of Daniel Miller, "people are constructed by their material world, but they are often not themselves the agents behind that material world through which they must live."[107]

Of course, the whole thing came tumbling down for reasons completely outside the control of Romano-British agriculturalists and estate owners. All the imperial spaces—the towns, the villas, the forts, parks, gardens, kitchens, food markets, and grain-storage facilities—depended on a series of interlocking institutions—a taxing state, the mass transshipment of agricultural goods, a money economy, and elites who displayed their wealth in ways familiar elsewhere in the empire. These places, institutions, and cultural practices together created the ecosystems into which the new plants and animals settled, and from which they operated as they moved to change, in quite profound ways, the daily lives of their human collaborators, who for better or worse had become entangled with them. And when these spaces, institutions, and social customs collapsed, they took the plants and animals down with them. And when they did, ordinary peoples' everyday taskscapes unraveled.

It is fashionable, these days, to argue that the withdrawal of the Roman state in Britain affected elites but meant little to those who were still down on the farm, a thesis that could be articulated only by academics who acquire all their food from Whole Foods or Waitrose and who have never milked a cow! Farmers do not live outside of history, and farming is not an ahistorical practice unaffected by the world around it. If ordinary women no longer spent hours each day tending their gardens or preparing dinners with plants that came with empire; if communities now devoted considerable time to foraging rather than horticulture; if farmers' herds were now dominated by cows rather than steers, and they were spending more hours each year milking than driving oxen; if people now gave relatively more attention to their sheep and pigs and less to their cattle; and if they were now participating in small-scale subsistence agriculture, rather than growing for the market and the state,[108] then the rhythms of their lives and their entanglements with plants and animals were altogether different from those of the people in Britain who had farmed before the Roman state's withdrawal. Again, this is a statement of fact, not a value judgement, and there are no claims in it that these developments are either a "Bad Thing" or a "Good Thing." But things were different.

What Have the Romans Ever Done for Us?

Still, a handful of Roman plant and animal introductions did survive the immediate post-Roman period. Fruit trees persisted, and apple, plum, cherry, and pear continued to be cultivated and eaten on both early medieval rural and urban sites.[109] "Apple tree," moreover, is a very common place name element, and some of our earliest charters used these trees in their boundary clauses.[110] Some Roman-period fruit trees may have escaped into the hedgerows and gone feral,[111] but in order for the fruit of apples, pears, and plums to stay true, these trees have to be propagated by grafting.[112] So at least this one horticultural practice seems to have survived the fall in Britain. It is also likely that people continued to cultivate leeks.[113] Chickens, as Naomi Sykes and others have shown, also endured, although by the end of the fifth century they had lost their Big Magic and had become the most ordinary of farmyard animals. But their survival meant that one of the sounds of empire—the dawn crowing of the cockerel—continued to herald the beginning of each day for many people living in Britain.[114]

Almost all the other plant and animal introductions, though, went away. This stands in stark contrast to other places in the former Roman West. A number of excavations of early medieval sites in Italy, Spain, and Gaul, and along the Danube have produced evidence that suggests that although the range of cultivated plants had narrowed in the post-Roman period, gardens and orchards persisted nonetheless, and that a variety of vegetables, herbs, fruits, and nuts continued to be cultivated.[115] And we also have contemporary textual descriptions of a world of professional cooks and court cuisine.[116] For the Carolingian period, both textual and archaeological evidence suggests very long-standing and sophisticated horticultural practices and plant management regimes, and a whole world of plants and gardening practices the roots of which could be traced back in an unbroken line to the Roman period.[117] The *Capitulare de villis vel curtis imperii*, for example, lists the many fruit trees royal estates were to have in their orchards—apple, pear, plum, sorb, medlar, chestnut, peach, quince, hazel, almond, mulberry, and stone pine—almost all Roman trees. These royal orchards were to contain not only a mix of species, but a range of varieties: "They shall have . . . nut and cherry trees of various kinds. The names of the apples are *gozmaringa*, *geroldinga*, *crevedella*, *spirauca*. There are sweet and bitter apples, ones that should be eaten straightaway and early ones. There should be three or four kinds of pears—those that keep well, sweet ones, ones for cooking, and those that ripen late."[118]

Large numbers of herbs and vegetables, according to the text, were grown both on the royal demesne and on the lands of those owing tribute to the king.[119] And decorative birds such as peacocks, pheasants, and doves were kept in royal gardens as well.[120] This world of pleasure gardens, orchards, impractical display birds, and the self-conscious cultivation of not just one kind of plum or apple, but different varieties of them, although long vanished in Britain, was alive and well in Francia.[121]

Still, almost all the Roman plant and animal species that had failed to survive Britain's fifth century eventually made their way back. Horticulture and the plants associated with it were likely reintroduced by two quite different groups—monks and foreign merchants. The Italian, Frankish, and Greek churchmen who helped missionize and lead the early English church came from monastic traditions with well-entrenched notions of gardening as a central devotional practice and as an important source for both food and medicinal plants.[122] Besides evidence for a *hortulanus* in the early days of the monastery at Iona,[123] we know that texts associated with medicinal plants were read and copied at early English monasteries,[124] and churchmen, in their correspondence, worried over the fact that they did not always have access to all the plants called for in their herbals.[125] Material evidence, for its part, hints at the hand foreign merchants had in reintroducing horticulture into England's early trading communities. Frankish merchants hailed from a place where Roman-style horticulture had never gone away. It is hardly surprising that they, like the Roman soldiers, administrators, and merchants who had come before them, brought seeds, gardening practices, and culinary habits with them to England. Indeed, at the eastern edge of Lundenwic a unique collection of plants has been uncovered, which dates between the mid-eighth and the mid-ninth century, and it may offer us our earliest archaeological evidence for the return of more recognizably Roman-style horticulture to Britain. Here a wide variety of plants have been recovered, including white horehound (*Marrubium vulgare*), violets, verbena (*Verbena officinalis*), greater celandine (*Chelidonium majus*), and alexanders (*Smyrnium olusatrum*), all plants featured in Roman agricultural and medical texts.[126] These plants' presence suggests that there was a garden here, and that someone c. 800 was raising culinary and medicinal herbs. This evidence was recovered alongside a fairly large assemblage of imported pottery as well as figs and raisins from southern Europe.[127] The rarity of these plants and their cosmopolitan context argue that foreign traders used to these plants at home were propagating them for their own households abroad: perhaps they were even raising them for the market. From this time on, we find evidence that at least a few people in Hamwic were garnishing their food not only with mustard and poppy seeds, but with dill, fennel, caraway, lovage, and coriander. In addition, gooseberries, not native to Britain, were being eaten and probably grown there as well.[128]

By the mid-eleventh century, carrots, parsnips, beets, coriander, fennel, celery, and summer savory were once again available in English towns.[129] Perhaps some of these were grown in the market gardens and town orchards that enterprising landholders were increasingly setting up, and which we can see in Domesday Book.[130] Different varieties of fruit trees, moreover, were now being cultivated,[131] and monastic communities had vegetable gardens and orchards.[132] Some well-to-do thegns in the countryside were eating dishes garnished with cabbage or mustard seeds, and poppy and celery seeds.[133] Mules and donkeys came back, as well, and so, too, did rats,[134] and grain pests.[135] And over the course of the eleventh and twelfth centuries, aristocrats worked themselves into a lather to reestablish the vanity animals—the fallow deer, peacocks, pheasants, and rabbits—in the hunting parks and gardens that now, once again, were an important accoutrement of elite life.[136]

There are three things to take away from the story of the rise and fall and then the rise once again of Roman plants and animals. First, the collapse of plant and animal populations in Britain in the generations after c. 400—but nowhere else in the former western Empire—argues that the particular material dislocations precipitated by Rome's early withdrawal from Britain were especially severe—indeed more severe than almost everywhere else in the West, where Roman plants, animals, and horticulture survived. Second, when agricultural practices change, so, too, do lifeways, and when we wrestle with the meaning of the ending of Rome, we should think about its meaning for the vast majority of people living through it—the people who spent their days ministering to plants and animals. Third, and finally, if we think hard about the timing of the return of the majority of Roman plant and animal introductions, we are reminded that the pheasants and dill, and the parsley and the donkeys are not there because the Romans brought them there. They are there because people in the early Middle Ages worked hard to build a brand-new material world on the ruins of the old one, and eventually succeeded in creating the kind of place that could once again accommodate such wondrous and useful alien biodiversity.

CHAPTER 3

Why Pots Matter

> In current academic practice... the institutional structure is such that detailed, specialist artefact studies are kept separate from grand historical narratives. The idea is that one can talk about the latter by merely skimming over or summarizing the former.
> —Astrid Van Oyen, *How Things Make History*

In recent years, a number of archaeologists have produced maps of Roman Britain that plot the find spots of different categories of material evidence. When stacked one on top of another, they tell an interesting story, one that strongly suggests that the parts of Britain in the late Roman period most heavily implicated in cereal production, elite landholdings, specialist industrial production, and the *annona* were the same regions in which the lives of both rich and poor were most entangled with the abundant material culture we associate with Rome.

Philippa Walton's maps of the find spots of coins minted between the years 348 and 378, for example, show heavy, low-value coin use from the West Country through the East of Britain, extending as far north as the Vale of Pickering (Figure 6). Walton's maps also reveal large swaths of territory where coins were not much used by ordinary people. They include much of Wales, the west Midlands, and the Northwest and Southwest of England.[1] Maps put together by Roger Bland, Sam Moorhead, and Philippa Walton plot the find spots for silver *siliquae* minted in the same years, and they illustrate that this high-value currency's use was mostly limited to the same regions.[2] Data generated by the *New Visions of the Countryside of Roman Britain* project supports these maps and argues that people living in eastern Britain, the South of England, and the region they term

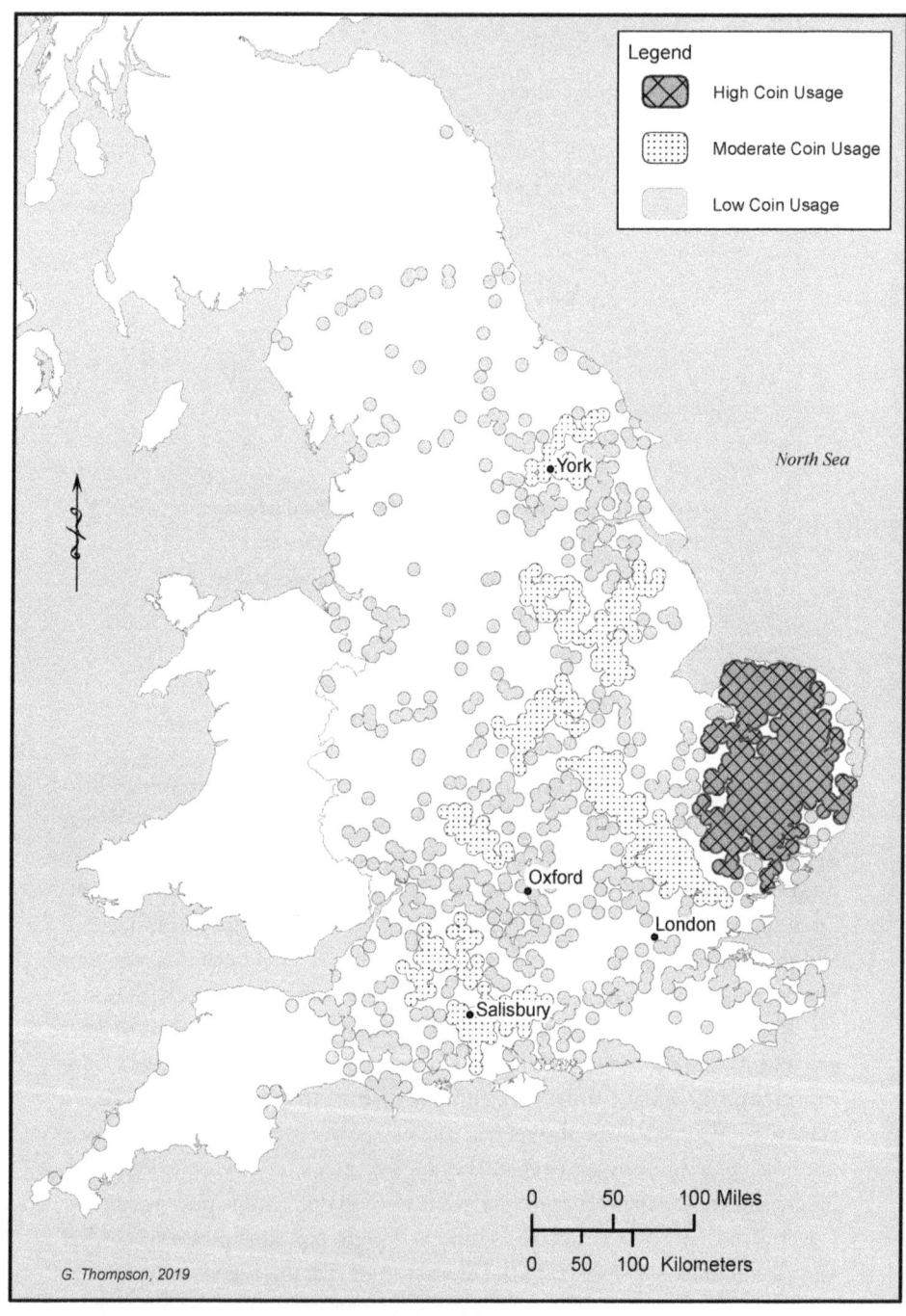

FIGURE 6. Map of coin finds, suggesting areas of coin use and non use in the late Roman period, based on the work of Philippa Walton (*Rethinking Roman Britain: Coinage and Archaeology*). (Map drawn by Gordon Thompson.)

"the Central Belt," regularly used coins and were engaged in quite profound ways with the Roman economy.[3] Similarly, maps published by the same project illustrate that the regions with the most corn driers, above-ground grain storage facilities, and villas are more or less coterminous with Walton's coin-using zone.[4] Walton's coin-using zone also shares the same broad contours as those found on Kevin Leahy's map plotting the distribution of late Roman belt fittings and Simon Esmonde Cleary's map of the find spots of crossbow brooches,[5] and these suggest that the kinds of people in the late Roman period involved in running and profiting from the imperial project were most active in areas with heavy coin use. Evidence in the late Roman period for the regular use of everyday, low-value objects also falls within the coin-using zone. Jeremy Evans's map showing where, in Britain, ceramics were common and where they were hardly used at all is similar to Walton's map of coin use and nonuse.[6] Data from the *Rural Settlement of Roman Britain* for burials in wooden coffins, which can serve as a rough proxy for areas where iron nails were abundant, produces more or less the same zones of use and nonuse.[7]

Although these maps are not perfect reflections of material practices in late Roman Britain—some regions have seen many more excavations and much more metal detecting than others, and this has shaped, in significant ways, the data standing behind them—they nonetheless provide useful approximations of where people, as a matter of course, consumed broad classes of durable Roman-style material culture.[8] When read together, they also argue that villas, large-scale cereal production, imperial administrators, and the movement and consumption of low-value manufactured goods were strongly correlated in the late Roman period.

In this chapter, we will focus on the people living in the region most heavily implicated in Roman-style material culture both before and after 400, paying particular attention to their engagement with ceramic vessels, that is pots. Not only does pottery survive better in the archaeological record than any other class of artifact, but it was a crucial category of thing in the Roman period, made by specialists and used daily in every household in Walton's coin-using zone to move, store, and prepare food. Pottery helped structure the ways people socialized at mealtimes and grieved during funerals; and it was often present when gods-fearing families performed small, ritual acts.[9] In 350 CE, kitchens and barns in Walton's coin-using zone would have had stacks of ceramics—fine and coarse wares, cooking pots, tableware, storage jars, beakers, and *mortaria* (a popular special-purpose mixing vessel)—almost all crafted by professional potters.[10] One hundred years later, though, pots in Britain were no longer fashioned by skilled craft workers using Roman technology, and the great variety of forms, wares, and finishes had mostly disappeared. Pots were much harder to come by than they had been in the Roman period, and people made do without pottery in areas of their lives where its use had once been common. The few pots people did possess in 450, moreover, often behaved differently from Roman-period pottery and required its users to accommodate themselves and their lifeways to its particular material characteristics. Given these dramatic changes, it is reasonable to ask what happened when one of the most basic, hard-used, and plentiful categories of things was so dramatically reconfigured in such a short period of time. How did life under the old pot regime differ from life in the new ceramic order? To answer these questions, we will begin with a discussion of the manufacturing, acquisition, and use of pottery during the late Roman period in Walton's coin-using zone and then trace the fate of ceramics, their makers, and their users across the period of the fall and beyond.

Making and Moving Pots in the Late Roman Countryside

In the early fourth century, there were a number of loosely organized, highly productive, rural pottery-production areas within Walton's coin-using zone. Although fewer centers were producing pottery than in earlier centuries, and although the range of different pots made at many sites was narrowing, professional potters working in, among other places, Oxfordshire, the Nene Valley, and in and around Alice Holt, Poole Harbor, and Crambeck, were churning out astonishing numbers of pots.[11] J. R. L. Allen and Michael Fulford have argued, for example, that something on the order of 750 potters at any one time were working at workshops around Poole Harbor, and that they were producing more than a million pots a year![12]

Some of the pottery used and made in the late Roman period was handmade and then finished on a slow-moving turntable, but most was produced on a fast wheel. After the pots were shaped but before they were fired, they were finished in a variety of ways. Some, especially coarse wares, were smoothed with a wet hand. Other, fancier pots were mica dusted, a process that after firing gave them something of the appearance of bronze. Other pots were polished with the aid of a smooth bone or stone burnisher. Many table wares were slip coated, that is, dipped in an iron-rich clay slurry, which gave them a glossy finish after a trip through the kiln. Some producers fired their ware in clamps, which were easy-to-build, one-time firing structures made from turf, earth, and logs, but the bulk of the period's pottery was fired in up-draught kilns, stone structures in which multiple pots could be stacked on perforated floors suspended about a firing chamber.[13]

The pots that professional potters produced in the late Roman period moved in a variety of ways from manufacturer to user. Some households purchased pots for cash, especially those in urban communities, where ceramics were heavily used, and where consumers could choose from a range of wares in shops and market stalls.[14] Roadside settlements also acted as crucial nodes of pottery distribution into the countryside, and they may have been the places where many rural households acquired the pots they needed.[15] Low-status rural workers in pottery-producing regions such as Oxfordshire had access not only to coarse wares, but to fine and specialist wares.[16] Here, pots may have been purchased at nearby roadside settlements or distributed by peddlers, but locals may have also gotten hold of them because of their personal connections with neighborhood potters. The distribution of ceramics outside immediate zones of production, on the other hand, would have been determined in some ways by the command economy: consignments of newly manufactured pottery likely piggybacked onto loads of grain, salt, or hides gathered and transported by the state. Such free or nearly free transportation would have kept the price of ceramics low in the areas through which the in-kind tax and large state purchases traveled.[17] Some of the pottery used in low-status communities might originally have served as packaging for salt or agricultural products, but after these goods had been transported and decanted from their ceramic containers, locals could repurpose the empties as storage vessels and cooking pots.[18] Finally, some pots may have been manufactured at the behest of and distributed by landlords or state agents, as in-kind payments for labor services,[19] or so that tribute- and tax-in-kind-owing farm families could return them filled with what they owed.[20] In all these ways and more, rich, poor, urban, and rural households in the heavily administered breadbasket of Britain had easy access to pottery and interacted with it daily as they cooked, ate, drank, stored, worked, mourned, and worshipped.[21]

Late Roman potters and their work practices were deeply enmeshed in local contexts and modes of production. We can see this clearly at the workshop of Nene Valley potters excavated at Stibbington, in Cambridgeshire.[22] The pottery-making complex here centered on a stone-footed building, which was equipped with a couple of clay preparation tanks, potter's wheels, and a well. It also had two kilns, one for firing coarse wares and the other for color-coated *mortaria* and fine wares. It was one of dozens of such establishments, operating in an industrialized zone of some forty hectares, where pottery workshops were interspersed with iron smelting and bloom-making concerns. Both ironworkers and potters required regular supplies of fuel (each firing at Stibbington would have consumed something on the order of fifty kilograms of wood), so there must have been extensive, carefully managed woodland in the region, given that both groups burned copious amounts of fuel here for more than a century.[23] As a consequence of these specialists' heavy fuel use, many people in the neighborhood would have spent at least part of each year coppicing, cutting, drying, and hauling wood to where it was needed.[24] Potters working at Stibbington also needed supplies of clay as well as tempering agents such as sand, crushed pottery, shell, or grog (pulverized ceramics), which, when added to the clay, made it easier to work, kept vessels from shrinking and cracking before they were fired, and made them more resistant to thermal shock during and after firing.[25] We know that potters at Stibbington sometimes tempered their clay with shell, because one of the excavated tanks contained crushed freshwater mussel shells.[26] We do not know if potters dug clay and collected tempers for themselves—perhaps this is what occupied them in the dark, wet months of winter, when drying pots and running kilns were difficult—or whether others procured these raw materials for them. What is clear is that some of the activities connected with potting were seasonal and that they were complementary with other occupations.[27] However self-sufficient the potters at Stibbington were, they certainly depended for some things on the labor and know-how of others. The workshop, for example, had a stone-lined well, which professional well diggers would have built, and a millstone there served as part of their potter's wheel: it was the handiwork of specialist stoneworkers.[28] Still other laborers would have raised, cared for, and driven the oxen used to move raw materials to the kilns and the finished pots away from them. And the carts onto which the pots were loaded and the harnesses used to yoke the teams of oxen that hauled them away were made by other specialists.[29]

Potters at Redcliff Farm, Worgret, and Bestwall Quarry, operating around the mouth of the River Frome, in Dorset, practiced their craft in yet another rural district thick with potteries.[30] The hand-built, black burnished ware, known as BB1, made along this stretch of coast, could be found as far away as London, Hadrian's Wall, and northern Gaul because imperial agents depended on it to move the Roman state's in-kind tax and military supply shipments. So the livelihoods of the hundreds of potters working at any one time in this corner of Dorset depended on the larger political economy.[31] Potters here burned chaff in their kilns, which helped give their pots a distinctive black matte finish. Chaff is a by-product of cereal processing, so potters in Dorset must have depended on local cereal producers for a steady supply for their kilns; and cereal producers, for their part, may have sometimes used the potters' kilns as corn driers.[32]

Malcolm Lyne has suggested that when pots at Redcliff Farm were fired, charcoal was sometimes made in the same firings, hinting that some potters were supplementing their livelihoods with secondary products, which would have entangled them in yet other relationships.[33] Potters at Worgret were grinding tempers with quern stones that had been traded onto the site.[34] They depended on boatmen operating along the River Frome to move their wares to more distant places and were thus beholden to the expertise of shipbuilders. And as we enter into the last quarter of the fourth century, more and more of the pots they made were being used locally, so potters would have increasingly depended on carters and the owners of pack animals to move their wares.[35]

Many Dorset and Nene Valley potters would have operated within villa estates, so their labor, raw materials, and pots were bound up in economic and tenurial relationships operating within and between elite estates.[36] Although the potters working in these two areas produced distinctively different pots in distinctly different environments, neither group could operate without the aid of dozens of specialist producers—farmers, foresters, peat cutters, ironworkers—and both groups labored within an economy in which different specialist workers were highly integrated and very much dependent on one another. As a result, potters and their wares bound together very particular fourth-century landscapes, joining places where the diverse raw materials they needed could be found, and binding the livelihoods of very different kinds of producers—some of whom controlled, produced, or supplied raw materials, others who provided the labor to make or moved the things potters needed in order to make pots and make a living. These patchworks of labor, raw materials, and transport were stitched into large-scale landscapes that were, in Ben Jervis's words, "fluid, dynamic bundles of relationships."[37] Potters making pots on the Dorset coast and in the Nene Valley were able to find takers for their wares because the political economy imposed by the state allowed for the cheap transportation of so many pots, helped create the kinds of communities that needed them, and provided an ecosystem in which people laboring in so many different ways could meet one another's needs.

The Winding Down of the Roman Pot-Manufacturing Regime

In the second half of the fourth century, British potters in some regions were astonishingly productive. Not only is this true of potters working in the Nene Valley and along the Dorset coast; it was also the case for the fine-ware potters in Oxfordshire; the shell-tempered and sand-tempered ware producers in and around Hadham, in Hertfordshire, and Harold, in Bedfordshire; the grog-tempered ware producers of Hampshire and Kent, and the makers of Alice Holt/Farnham and Portchester D/Overwey wares operating respectively along the Hampshire-Surrey border and in Surrey (Figure 7).[38] All were churning out increasing numbers of pots consumed by more and more people in ever expanding territories.[39] This same period, though, was a grimmer time for other regional potters and witnessed the collapse of long-standing, local pottery industries in Cambridgeshire, Gloucestershire, Hampshire, Kent, the Severn Valley, and the Midlands.[40] Like some of the iron producers we will meet in Chapter 6, some regional potters likely lost their ability to make a living because of transformations in the ways troops along Hadrian's Wall were provisioned midcentury.[41] BB1 production along the Dorset coast, for example, contracted in these decades because fewer supplies were now being moved north from the south coast; and producers in the Thames valley, whose pottery was used along Hadrian's Wall in the early fourth century, seem to have lost their market entirely.[42] But one potter's catastrophe was another's windfall: in Yorkshire, Crambeck- and Huntcliff-ware producers flourished under the new military-provisioning scheme.[43]

Let us look more closely at the interplay between failing regional potteries and the thriving and increasingly productive supraregional producers. The coarse-ware potters working in and around Horningsea, in Cambridgeshire, will serve as our example of members of a doomed local industry. With kilns in northeastern Cambridgeshire on either side of the River Cam, potters producing coarse wares here supplied people living in the region with the majority of their ceramics from the second century to the middle of the fourth.[44] But early in the mid-fourth century, shell-tempered wares from Bedfordshire and fine wares from the Nene Valley became much more common in the region around Horningsea, and the demand for local Horningsea wares declined.[45] Sometime in the 370s, Horningsea potters ceased running their kilns altogether.[46] In spite of this, people in the area continued to have access to ceramics, but from this point on none were local. The reasons for both the demise of the Horningsea potteries and the triumph of nonlocal wares are not entirely clear. It may be, though, that pots from outside the region, some of which had a kind of cachet as fine wares, were able to swamp the local pottery market because the cost of their transportation was now being absorbed by state transports associated with the *annona* and *coemptiones*, which may have been reorganized in these years. The frenetic hauling of bulk goods associated with the state could have rewired transportation networks and linked more closely regions through which official, imperial collections and transportation were taking place; and this may have triggered a reworking of supply networks.[47]

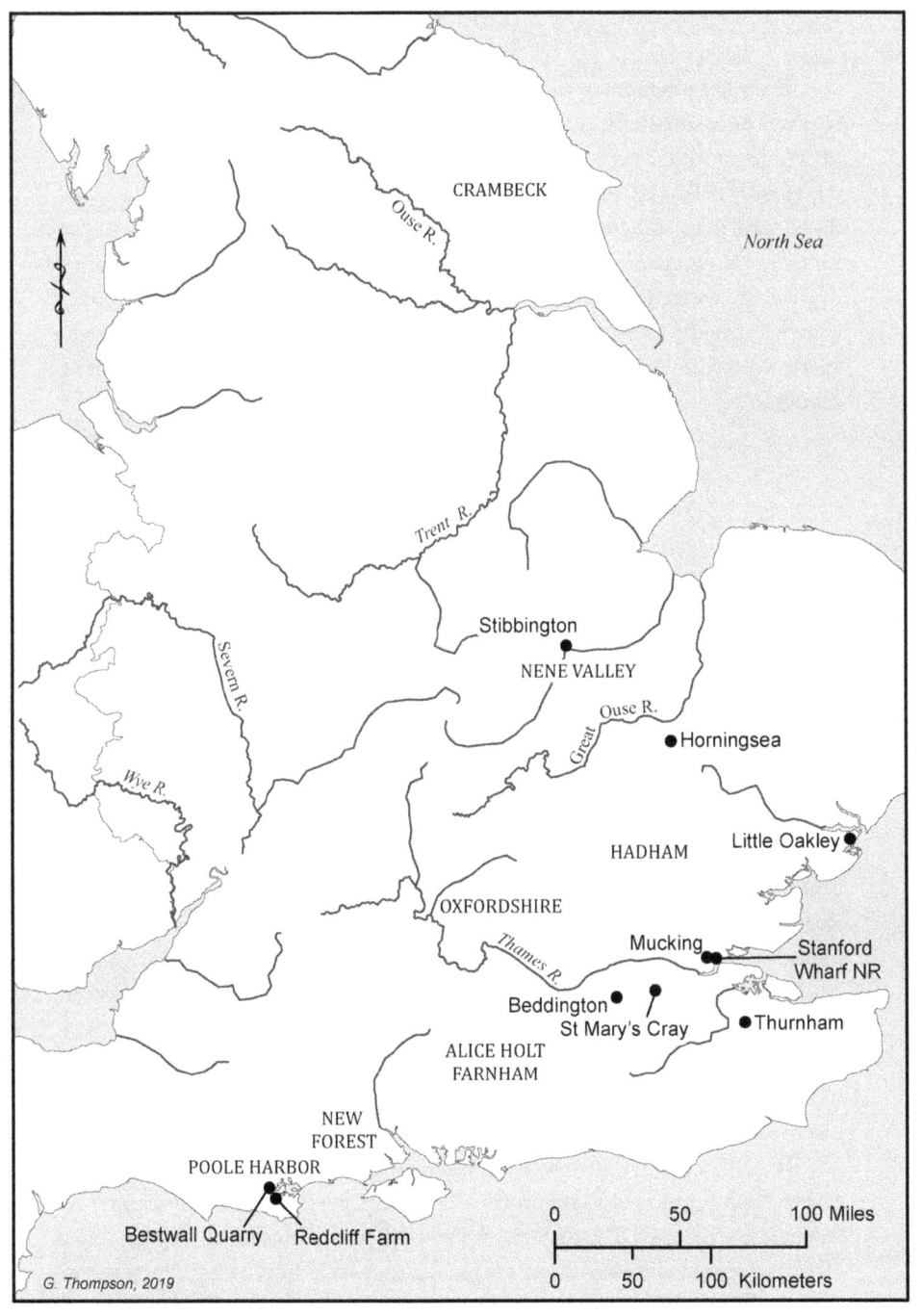

FIGURE 7. Areas in which some of the large-scale, late Roman pottery producers worked—in and around Poole Harbor, the New Forest, Alice Holt/Farnham, Oxfordshire, Hadham, the Nene Valley, and Crambeck. (Map drawn by Gordon Thompson.)

The wares produced outside of Cambridgeshire continued to make their way to places once supplied by Horningsea potters, probably through the first couple of decades of the fifth century. But when these long-lasting, supraregional industries finally collapsed, local potting families around Horningsea, who had produced local gray wares for a couple of centuries, had already been out of business for two or three generations. This meant that in 420 or 430, when communities in the region were losing access to wares made in the Nene Valley or Bedfordshire because the transportation systems on which potters depended had come apart, no one in the area remembered how to make wheel-thrown, kiln-fired ceramics.[48]

Old-Style and New-Style Pots in Daily Life

A number of late Roman pottery producers persisted in making and moving pottery in the early decades of the fifth century, and because of this, Roman-style pots and the people who had access to them continued to be entangled in everyday activities. It was long thought that the production of Roman-style pottery collapsed at the same time Britain fell out of the empire, and that it was closely connected to the collapse of the money economy, precipitated by the end of precious-metal currency supply to Britain by the Roman state. But in recent years, we have come to realize that some late Roman pottery producers continued to make and distribute ceramics in the first two or three decades of the fifth century.[49] A close chronology of the collapse of both the money economy and Romano-British pottery production is impossible to establish, because we do not know how soon after the imperial government ceased to supply Britain with new coinage that coins themselves stopped being used. We thus cannot say whether the pottery found alongside coins issued in the very late fourth century was used and disposed of in the same years as the coins were struck, or whether—if these older coins continued to circulate—the pottery had actually been produced or disposed of a decade or even two decades after the issuing of the latest coins.[50]

To further complicate matters, many families, even if they no longer had access to fresh supplies of Romano-British pottery, would have had stockpiles of older vessels, acquired in earlier decades and still perfectly useable.[51] And in some places, people in the fifth century look like they were scavenging kiln wasters, seconds that had been discarded at the time of manufacturing.[52] So old-style pottery would not have vanished overnight: instead, people continued to use and break it.[53] But where this happened, it is often impossible to distinguish the remains of vessels broken in the late Roman period from those being used and damaged after 400. Because of the problem of residuality, it is easier to catch glimpses of fifth-century people and their Roman-style pots on greenfield sites— that is, at new settlements established in the fifth century on ground where pottery had not been used and broken in the fourth century.

In spite of these difficulties, we do find small amounts of newly made, Roman-style pottery continuing to play some part in the lives of settlements situated along the Essex and Kentish coasts and in and around the mouth of the River Thames. Mucking, in Essex, founded about the same time the Roman state collapsed in Britain, is one such place.[54] In the seventh century, eight or ten households resided here, but in the first decades after 400, the number was more likely four or five.[55] Many of the objects and the building uncovered at the settlement and its two cemeteries are similar to objects and buildings encountered in the early Middle Ages in a broad zone around the North Sea, particularly in the lands between the Elbe and Weser Rivers and in Schleswig-Holstein, so it is a place where we can see the material culture and lifeways of new immigrants transforming the material world of Britain in the early fifth century.[56] Indeed, Mucking has become an iconic "Anglo-Saxon" settlement for both historians and archaeologists. Yet surprisingly large numbers of the settlement's earliest dateable artifacts are late Roman in style and originated in Britain.[57] This includes a high percentage of Mucking's earliest pottery.

The presence of Romano-British potsherds at post-Roman sites does not, in itself, prove that Roman-style pots were still in use. In the fifth century, people poking around deserted Roman-period sites sometimes collected pot sherds either as curiosities or to rework the bases as spindle whorls.[58] When the majority of Roman-period sherds recovered from an early medieval site are shiny, red pieces of color-coated ware, and when most of the sherds are derived from pot rims or bases, their presence is likely the result of this kind of activity.[59] At a few post-Roman sites, however, other wares besides color coats are well represented, and considerably more body sherds are found than rim and base sherds. This is true at Mucking, where Sam Lucy has shown that more than 70 percent of the site's Romano-British sherds are body sherds.[60] This mirrors the ratio of body/rim/base sherds found in Roman-period ceramic assemblages, and what it suggests is that Romano-British style vessels were arriving at the post-Roman settlement whole and used until broken.

The fill of an early fifth-century sunken-featured building (SFB) at Mucking preserves some of our best evidence for the supply and use of Roman-style pottery during the settlement's earliest years.[61] When the building went out of use sometime in the first half of the fifth century, the rubbish that had been accumulating around it was pushed into the hole left by its cellar.[62] The pottery in the fill argues that people living at Mucking in the early fifth century were able to get their hands on a little Oxfordshire and Nene Valley color-coated pottery, as well as Portchester D/Overwey ware, Hadham ware, and a few late shell-tempered vessels. Here, and in a growing number of early fifth-century settlements, we have evidence that potters making these wares were still in production, albeit on a much-reduced scale.

The same SFB fill also contained fragments of Roman belt fittings, a few Roman-period beads and shale bracelets, and twenty-two Roman coins, the latest of which date to 367–75. None of these objects would look out of place in a late Roman assemblage.[63] A couple of Mucking's earliest graves also contained late Roman jewelry, military belt sets, or belt buckles.[64] The woman buried in Grave 631 in Mucking's Cemetery 1, for example, was accompanied by a collection of four Roman-style bracelets,[65] and the woman in Grave 875 was wearing a bracelet, a finger ring, and a single, penannular brooch.[66] Both sets of grave goods are similar to those one would expect to find in late Roman cemeteries.[67] Another of Mucking's early dead, the man buried in Grave 117 in Mucking's Cemetery 1, wore one of the most beautiful Quoit Brooch-style belt sets ever found. It was made in Britain and comes out of a late Roman milieu.[68] And he is not the only person in the cemetery buried with late Roman metalwork.[69] The traditional explanation for why a handful of Mucking's earliest and most elaborately buried dead were put in the ground with official belt sets is that they were German *foederati*, hired by Romano-British communities to fight incoming "Anglo-Saxons" after the Roman state had abandoned them.[70] A simpler and more likely explanation, in light of Lucy's work on Mucking's pottery, is that these were the graves of British people of some standing, who continued to wear the kinds of metalwork members of their class had worn in the last decades of the fourth century.[71] A late, intrusive, high-status burial in a nearby defunct first-through third-century cremation cemetery may represent the first of the new phase of burials at the end of or after the Roman period at Mucking. There, the body of a young man lay, in late Roman fashion, covered in quicklime in a stone coffin, and he was accompanied in the ground by a late fourth-century glass bowl. His may be the earliest of the run of late or post-Roman burials that soon moved to Mucking's two brand-new cemeteries.[72]

Because Mucking, like many early medieval sites, has been labeled "Anglo-Saxon," it has been transformed in the literature and in our imaginations into an ethnic enclave, a place inhabited by "Anglo-Saxons." But the Roman-style artifacts encountered in some of Mucking's earliest graves and SFBs counter this narrative and argue that a household or two in the early fifth century included people whose families had long resided in the neighborhood. The early pottery, belt equipment, and bracelets, as well as the nearby stone-coffin-and-quicklime burial hint that at least a few people living and dying in Mucking in the first half of the fifth century were the children or grandchildren of people who had been in Britain all along.

The site's continuing supply of Roman-style pottery also suggests that at least one of Mucking's early households procured some of the things it needed using long-established exchange networks that were limping along in a much-diminished fashion after the Roman state's departure. Besides the remains of the Romano-British-style pottery, the fill of the early SFB also included the remains of a few continental-ware vessels known as *Céramique à l'éponge*, which show that in the first years of the settlement, there was some contact, albeit infrequent, with people on the continent still living under Rome, and that there was still a trickle of exchange along the routes that had, until recently, connected the Thames and the Rhine estuaries.[73] A little contemporary Mayen ware recovered in a ditch near the SFB further supports this argument.[74] What did Mucking have that might be worth trading for? Perhaps some of the people living there were descendants of those who had controlled or administered salt production in the area: salt making had long been undertaken in the neighborhood.[75] That at least one household proudly wore and buried their dead with heirloom metalwork and bracelets, like the ones worn in the Roman period by the kinds of people who had once helped administer the province, suggests some continuity in population and culture.

How similar were the wares available at early fifth-century Mucking to the ones found in the region in the late fourth century? Pottery assemblages from a variety of site types provide material for comparison. The one from the late Roman salt-making operation at Stanford Wharf Nature Reserve, just two kilometers from Mucking, is nearly identical. Here, archaeologists have recovered late shell-tempered wares, fine wares from the Nene Valley and Oxfordshire, and Portchester D/Overwey ware, as well as Mayen ware and *Céramique à l'éponge*.[76] The late fourth-century ceramics from the villa site at Great Holts Farm, Boreham, Essex, are also comparable: Oxfordshire and the Nene Valley, Alice Holt/Farnham, and Portchester D/Overwey wares were all well represented, as were small amounts of Mayen ware and *Céramique à l'éponge*.[77] Further afield, late Roman pottery assemblages in London and Southwark also included color-coated ware from Oxfordshire and the Nene Valley, Alice Holt/Farnham and Portchester D/Overwey wares, and small amounts of Mayen ware along with *Céramique à l'éponge*.[78] Thus, the sources of Roman-style pottery used at Mucking in the early fifth century are analogous to those used in the region in the late fourth century. The similarity in the compositions of these sites' pottery argues for a period of ceramic continuity in Essex and around the mouth of the Thames that stretched from c. 370 to c. 420 or 430, a period in which some people in the region continued to have at least some access to pots made outside of Essex by professional potters.[79]

One important difference between the pottery found at post-Roman Mucking and the Roman-period sites just mentioned is that at Mucking, alongside Romano-British vessels, people were also using new-style, hand-built, sand-tempered pots.[80] Pottery, for example, in the fill of the early Mucking SFB included hand-built wares. Of special interest are the contemporary, continental-style, faceted-carinated vessels, which are similar to the ones made and used in the Netherlands.[81] Over 90 percent of these vessels at Mucking were recovered from the southern part of the settlement, which constituted its original, early core.[82] So early Mucking was not a Romano-British enclave but looks, rather, like it may have been a place where newcomers and old-timers were working together to build a new material present.

Elsewhere in Essex people in the early fifth century were also using both old- and new-style pottery. This was happening at the villa at Little Oakley. Like Mucking, Little Oakley was very near the Essex coast and sat in salt-making country: during the late Roman period the villa likely had an interest in a cluster of Red Hill salt-production sites around Romney Creek, just below the villa.[83] The grand domestic quarters at Little Oakley, like so many others, were abandoned in the years just prior to or just after 400. The house was superseded by a framed, timber-built structure constructed atop a rubble platform. Sherds of late Roman wares from Hadham, Oxfordshire, and the Nene Valley as well as shell-tempered wares from Hertfordshire were incorporated into the rubble platform, as were the remains of organic- and quartz-tempered hand-built pots. Thus, both old-style and new-style vessels were being used and broken on the site at the same time as the timber building was being constructed.[84] In the last decades of the fourth century, people living at Little Oakley had had access to pottery produced outside the immediate neighborhood, in particular fine wares from Oxfordshire, the Nene Valley, and Hadham, as well as late Roman shell-tempered wares,[85] and it looks as if some of these wares continued to find their way to Little Oakley in the fifth century. Nonetheless, these sources could no longer meet all the needs of the people living in the timber hall, so they had begun making their own unlovely but functional hand-built pottery.[86]

If we travel south from Essex and cross the River Thames into Kent, we encounter other early fifth-century sites in which Romano-British pottery and hand-built wares were probably used at the same time. A corn-drying oven at Thurnham, in Kent, produced Alice Holt/Farnham, Portchester D/Overwey wares, and Oxfordshire wares in the material shoveled into it after it was decommissioned, which represent the vessels in use while the corn drier was in operation. But a couple of hand-built miniature pots, probably made in the early fifth century, were also recovered from the corn drier, helping us date the deposit to the post-Roman period.[87] Similarly, the fill of an early fifth-century SFB in St. Mary Cray, in Kent, contained sherds from both hand-built, mostly quartz-tempered pots, and Oxfordshire and Alice Holt/Farnham vessels.[88]

A careful trawl through the excavation reports of sites elsewhere in lowland Britain turns up many other examples of Romano-British style pottery used in the fifth century in conjunction with hand-built pots. At the villa site at Beddington, in Surrey, hand-built pedestal vessels (which are described in the excavation report as "Saxon") were being used in conjunction with very late Roman Pevensey ware. People living, in the early fifth century, at the villa sites at Bancroft, in Buckinghamshire; Eastington and Frocester, both in Gloucestershire; Redlands Farm, in Northamptonshire; and Shakenoak, in Oxfordshire, were also using late Roman-style pottery alongside hand-built sand- or organic-tempered wares. The contemporaneous use of Roman-style and hand-built wares could also be found in the immediate post-Roman period at rural shrines such as Uley, in Gloucestershire, dying urban and administrative settlements such as Alchester, in Oxfordshire, and Pevensey, in Sussex, and in the countryside at still-running corn driers and low-status settlement sites such as those at Burgess Hill, in West Sussex; High Post, near Salisbury, in Wiltshire; Crossgates and Wykeham, in Yorkshire; Lodge Field in Billingford, Norfolk; and Orpington, in Kent.[89]

The evidence just presented suggests that in the first half of the fifth century, Roman-style pottery and hand-built wares were often used side-by-side. Roman-period and Roman-style material culture continued to be available for several decades after the Roman state's withdrawal, allowing people who depended on it to make gradual accommodations to contend with its disappearance. Although the hand-built ceramics of the fifth century are habitually described as "Anglo-Saxon" in excavation reports, not only is this ethnic label misleading, but in many cases, it is wrong. Indigenous households, as professional potters disappeared and as their supplies of professionally produced pottery dwindled, began to make pots for themselves. Given that some of the new-style pots bore close affinities to pottery made in coastal communities across the channel, it is possible that some British people who had never potted were learning the craft from immigrants beginning to settle in Britain. But in some places, where there is no evidence for immigrants from the continent, it is clear that they were figuring things out on their own.

Shapes, Tempers, and Foodways

By the middle of the fifth century, Roman-style pottery and manufacturing techniques were no longer used in Britain, and Roman-period production sites had been abandoned. From this time forward, households could no longer count on acquiring a few pots from potters still making ceramics in traditional, Roman ways; and whatever stockpiles of old pots they once had were gone. If they were going to continue to use pottery, they would have to get hold of it in some new way. The potter's wheel and the kiln at this point were lost technologies, and slip coating was a forgotten technique. Now all pots would be built by hand and fired in clamps or bonfires. And because we have entered a world where there were no longer any fine wares, only coarse wares, and where the range of different sizes, shapes, finishes, and colors had narrowed so dramatically, people were going to have to accommodate themselves to these changes as well.

From the second third of the fifth century, most of the new-style ceramics would be used in one of two contexts: the grave or the cooking fire. Some pots were even used in both. The analysis of wear on the inner surfaces of a number of the period's undecorated cinerary urns suggests that they had started their careers as cooking pots. There is also some evidence that the fancier, highly decorated cremation urns increasingly used in the fifth century may have played a role in brewing before they moved on to second acts as receptacles for human ash.[90] In the fifth century, in communities where cremating families lived, plain, workaday pots continued to be vessels of choice for many, and a few people were even able to get hold of and use old, Roman-period, wheel-thrown cooking vessels in funerals.[91] Increasingly, though, especially in East Anglia, Lincolnshire, and East Yorkshire, cremators were selecting elaborately decorated, hand-built urns new to Britain. These pots, and the objects that sometimes accompanied them, were part of a package of material culture and material practices that find their closest parallels in the Elbe-Weser region and in Schleswig-Holstein.[92]

Many of the new-style cremation urns were wildly inventive in their shapes and decorative schemes, and they survive better in the archaeological record than do cooking pots. Both their abundance and their designs provide clues about their production. Their stamped decorations demonstrate that at least a few were fashioned by highly skilled, peripatetic potters, who ranged over relatively wide areas, making special pots for people other than themselves. The best-known example is the so-called Sancton-Baston potter, whose vessels, stamped with the same set of antler dies, have been found in cemeteries as far apart as the East Riding of Yorkshire and southern Lincolnshire. In spite of the common hand and stamps that stand behind their production, these pots were made with clays from near the cemeteries in which they were found, so we know that it was the potter who traveled, and not the pots.[93] Two elaborate cremation urns—one found in the Spong Hill cemetery, in Norfolk, and the other 160 kilometers to the northwest at the cemetery at Cleatham, in Lincolnshire, were also the work of a single potter.[94] These pots and a few others, however, represent only a tiny minority of the many thousands of surviving urns, most of which were not made to such high standards. Kevin Leahy's study of the 1,204 urns from the cemetery at Cleatham concludes that while the majority of pots were competently executed, only 3.5 percent (forty-two) were the work of potters who were "accomplished." There were also, in his judgment, seventy-one pots in the cemetery that were badly made, with the rest falling somewhere in between.[95] The facts that most urns look like the work of people who potted now and again rather than professionals, and that most cinerary urns were made with local clays, argue that the vast majority were produced by the communities in which the dead, themselves, had lived.[96] Indeed, the multiple groups of urns identified within both the Spong Hill and the Millgate cemeteries, stamped with the same sets of dies, suggest to Catherine Hills and Sam Lucy that these pots were the results of "small-scale family production."[97]

It is worth thinking through what, precisely, "small-scale family production" might have looked like in practice. Little has been written about the gender of early medieval household potters, but work by anthropologists has shown time and again that small-scale production of hand-built pots is more often women's work than men's.[98] As Cathy Costin argues, "in kin-based societies, gender, along with age, is often the primary factor in determining who does what."[99] But Diane Bolger cautions us against thinking of early potting as exclusively "women's work," because many disparate tasks went into making a pot.[100]

Ethnographic studies have shown that many people, including children, are often part of the *chaîne opératoire* (that it, the move from raw material to finished product) standing behind small-scale pottery production, and that a variety of people work to source and acquire clay, temper, and fuel, and to haul water, prepare pastes, and shape, decorate, and fire vessels.[101] So the small-scale, "domestic" production of the early Middle Ages would have necessitated cooperation, coordination, and negotiation. Although early medieval potting is often described as "household production," it might be better to think of it as "settlement production." Five or six households of light pottery users could probably meet all their settlement's needs with one or two bonfires' worth of new pottery each year.[102] Thus, many settlements' pottery may not have been produced by households on their own, but rather by coresidential groups, that is, households within a single community. Carol Kramer has also emphasized that "a single vessel can be the work of more than one individual.... Learning and production can occur in the context of potting 'bees' whose participants are linked by residential bonds that for some purposes supersede those based on kinship."[103]

The notion of a potting bee is an attractive one and suggests a gathering focused on sharing the burden of a periodic, labor-intensive task. A few individuals in the neighborhood might be more proficient than others and could, therefore, oversee the production of both ritual ceramics and workaday pots. Other members of the community during pot-making time could undertake the laborious task of digging and mixing clays, gathering wood, and so on. Such occasions would be an important context in which knowledge of skilled work practices and socialization into that training could take place.[104] At such events people across the settlement could decide, negotiate, and learn both what a proper pot was and the proper way to make it.[105] Tim Ingold has called this type of process "enskilment," and has emphasized that it is through processes of enskilment that lifeways are transmitted.[106] The pots made at such events, then, might not be independently authored, but rather produced through collaboration.[107]

A few cremation urns may preserve evidence of the initiation of novices into the craft by more experienced craftspeople. One urn from the cemetery at Lackford, in Suffolk, for example, was shaped by a relatively skilled potter, but its tentative, unsteady scored decorations look like the work of a child (Figure 8).[108] A similar scenario may stand behind a couple of urns at Millgate, in Nottinghamshire, and one from Sancton, in Yorkshire.[109] Other pots are ornamented with overlapping or competing decorative schemes,[110] which may preserve the work of more than one set of hands. That a crowd of people were involved in the clay preparation, and in the shaping, bossing, scoring, and stamping of such pots could have added to their sensory and mnemonic impact, things Ruth Nugent and Howard Williams have argued were fundamental to these vessels' purpose.[111] Because the size and shape of these urns were linked, in different but particular ways in each cemetery, to the ages or genders of the people whose ashes they contained, groups who actually knew the dead in life would have been especially suited to the job of making such vessels.[112]

FIGURE 8. A cremation urn from the early medieval cemetery at Lackford, Suffolk, which was perhaps decorated by a child. (Museum of Archaeology and Anthropology, Cambridge, 1950.170A. By kind permission of the Museum of Archaeology and Anthropology, Cambridge.)

At Cleatham and Spong Hill grains of barley were sometimes mixed into the clay before cremation urns were formed. This cannot have been an accident, and it may be related to the ritual of burning grain in the houses of the dead, a tradition much discouraged in later, Christian missionizing texts.[113] The mixing of barley into the clay of cremation pots is evocative, and like the notion of multiple hands making pots, it emphasizes the communal, social, and performative aspects of the production of special pots and fits well with the potting bee model. Perhaps pot making was an event as much as a task.

Unlike cremation urns, the new-style ceramics used for cooking, hauling, and storing were almost always plain and relatively small. The shapes of these pots and the different mixes of clays and tempers used in their making varied from one firing to the next, sure signs that they were the handiwork of amateurs who did not pot often enough to standardize their practices.[114] The only things most of these pots had in common were that they were heavily tempered, fired at relatively low temperatures, friable, and homely, and none look as if they had been crafted for the ages.[115] Experimental archaeologist have demonstrated how heating and cooling food in unglazed pots results in the rapid buildup of residues, rendering vessels, in relatively short order, rancid and foul smelling.[116] So pot makers may have spent little time on their appearance, because they were never considered more than short-lived objects. In spite of their obvious shortcomings, these pots were tools with jobs to do. The people who fashioned them had sufficient technical know-how to form and fire pots that could withstand the hostile environments of the clamp and the cook fire.[117]

The period's new-style pots behaved differently than those made in the Roman period. In part, this is because of their shape. Most Roman-period cooking pots had narrow mouths and flat bases. Pots shaped in this manner heat their contents faster than the globular, or round-bottomed, cooking pots that came to dominate in the second half of the fifth century.[118] Even more critical were the different tempers being used. Although many domestic pot makers continued, in the fifth century, to temper their pots with some of the same inorganic tempers that Roman-period potters had used,[119] by the early sixth century, more of them were more often reaching for organic tempers—everything from dung, to chaff, to chopped grass, to straw.[120] Archaeologists long thought that the idea of organic temper was introduced into Britain by early Germanic immigrants, but these tempers were not used in the fifth century in the areas on the continent thought to be the homelands of newcomers to Britain. Instead, the organic-temper habit seems to have gradually taken hold, by the sixth century, in a zone stretching from western Britain to Flanders.[121]

Organic-tempered, clamp- or bonfire-fired pots did not hold up as well as inorganic, kiln-fired wares. Experimental archaeology, moreover, has demonstrated that it is impossible to heat liquids to a boil in organic-tempered pots.[122] As a result, those who were now cooking with them would have had to develop new food-preparation strategies. Thus, as with the fall of Roman plants and animals, the fall of Roman-style pottery must have been accompanied by the disappearance of Roman-period foodways.

Although pots made with organic tempers handled themselves less well on the cooking fire, these tempers held a number of advantages for the episodic potter. First, unlike shell, grog, or calcite, organic tempers were on hand in every farmyard and required little effort to procure.[123] Second, clays tempered with organic material are more forgiving: they are easier to work, shrink less while drying, and react better to uneven firing, so they are perfectly suited to the needs of people who do not devote much time to potting and who do not have kilns.[124] So people making pottery in the centuries after Rome's withdrawal were making material choices with trade-offs—workability and tolerance for clamp and bonfire firing—at the expense of Roman-period pottery's particular cooking characteristics.[125] Different communities during this period were making different choices: for some, ease of firing may have been more important; for others, it may have been a pot's ability to stay longer on the fire.

The mineral-tempered, kiln-fired pots of the Roman period heated their contents much more efficiently than the organic-tempered pots that came to supersede them. Because of their tempering and high firing, Roman-style pots could withstand considerable thermal shock and could transition from cold, to hot, to cold again without breaking.[126] In the late Roman period, the people who used Roman-style pots anchored their foodways in their pottery's particular ability to stew. Both Crambeck gritted ware and BB1 jars were especially well suited for cooking in this way,[127] and both developed during the Roman period out of indigenous Iron Age potting traditions.[128] So, the households who cooked with these pots were participating in a centuries-long culinary tradition that had long appreciated this kind of pot's particular proficiencies.[129] As long as post-Roman communities still had access to a little late Roman or Roman-style pottery, they could carry on long-standing cooking practices that depended on the technological and morphological properties of Roman-period pots. But once the last of these pots had broken, meal preparation strategies would have to change.

The differences in cooking pots manufactured in c. 380 and those fashioned in c. 480 are stark. People using the earlier pots would have been able to deputized a standard cooking jar to take over the duties of making beef stew, a meal, judging from urban bone assemblages, that must have been common given the commercialized butchery practices found in towns and given the toughness of the cattle being slaughtered and eaten at the end of their working lives.[130] Such a jar, once filled with its contents, could have been placed on the hearth in the ash with its lid on, and it would have dutifully gone about its business of heating a stew's ingredients quickly, keeping the liquid within the jar, and holding its contents' temperature long after the pot was removed from the fire.[131] Organic residues found on the inside of Romano-British coarse-ware cooking jars and patterns of sooting found on their exteriors together tell us that cooking pots were typically placed on the hearth, with their bases embedded in the fire's ash. Sitting this way, their contents often heated to boiling.[132] In contrast, most hand-built, post-Roman pots, rather than having flat bottoms, had rounded bases, so they were not shaped to sit in the hearth's ashes in the same way, and they were probably suspended over the fire, instead. These pots, unlike their Roman-period predecessors, could not, because of their tempering, be used to boil their contents, and they often have carbonized (that is, burned) deposits on their *interiors*, often midway up the pot, and the interiors of the rounded bottoms of these pots are worn in ways that suggest that food was stirred while cooking. Jeremy Evans interprets this to mean that individual portions of meat were being cooked in fat.[133] Whatever the case, transformations in the physical capabilities of pots after 400 required people to change both their foodways and the ways they went about everyday tasks.[134]

By the middle of the fifth century, the role of pottery in daily life, even for those who continued to use it, would have been significantly smaller than in the fourth century. Less pottery was used, and it was used for fewer activities; and nonceramic objects such as wooden trenchers, leather vessels, and pot boilers were coming to be more central in everyday life.[135] Pottery's retreat was not limited to Britain. Even in Italy, where Roman pots and potting technology survived, the range of pots narrowed dramatically in the fifth and sixth centuries, a state of affairs reflected in contemporary cookbooks. A century later, in Francia, another place where the wheel and the kiln never disappeared, the preparation of many cooked dishes, according to a contemporary treatise on food preparation, did not require the use of any pottery at all.[136]

Sociability at the table would have changed during this period as well, at least for the kinds of people whose families had once used individual fine-ware place settings at dinnertime. And the more exotic silver and glass tableware of the rich was no longer available either. Once these objects had gone, mealtime hierarchies and habits would have to be refashioned.[137] Most people, regardless of the amount of surplus they had in their barns and no matter their place in the community or the household, would have now eaten communally out of the same hand-built pots and wooden trenchers as others gathered for the meal.

The very different modes of production that stand behind a pot made in 380 and a pot made in 480, as Roman-style techniques and technologies were lost, are clear evidence of first deskilling and then a low-level reskilling, as communities learned to make pottery for themselves. And the taskscapes across which craftspeople, raw materials, transporters, state agents, landlords, and the users of pots had been entangled in the Roman period, and through which mountains of pottery came into being, contracted sharply, once large-scale potting landscapes gave way to settlement-scale ones. Still it now seems clear that the transition from Roman to post-Roman pottery use and production was less abrupt than we once thought; and not just immigrants but people who had long resided in Britain were making and using the new-style, hand-built pots as well. But the increasing scarcity and finally disappearance of Roman pottery would spur people in Britain to use what little Roman-style pottery there was in new ways and to make new kinds of vessels on their own.

CHAPTER 4

The Afterlife of Roman Ceramic and Glass Vessels

> If this was history it did not feel like it.
> —George Orwell, *Homage to Catalonia*

This chapter details the ways people in different post-Roman communities engaged with old Roman glass vessels and wheel-thrown, kiln-fired pottery. We will learn a little bit about each of these groups—the kinds of people they were, the histories of the places in which they lived, and the strategies they developed for procuring still-useable Roman-period ceramics and glass. Their varied practices of reuse suggest that some groups marshaled surviving Roman-period material culture to help them continue traditional social or ritual practices, while others deployed it in ways that hint that they were interested in something other than perpetuating old ways. A study of the choices different groups made helps us uncover the lived experience of people who were having to figure out how to be in a period of radical material loss, and it highlights the ways different groups made radically different decisions during these years. The story of old pots and glass highlights the epic nature of everyday life and illustrates some of the challenges of living in a time in between, in the period in which the old material order had collapsed but the new early medieval material culture regime had yet to emerge.

Late Roman Glass and Pottery Production and Use

Before we investigate the way different communities deployed Roman-period ceramics and glass after c. 400, a few things need to be said about the scale of ceramic and glass production in Britain *during* the Roman period. In the first century under Rome, imported, workshop-produced, wheel-thrown, kiln-fired pots became staple, everyday objects within the zone, detailed in the last chapter, that would most heavily implicated in the Roman imperial economy and most engaged with Roman-style material culture. In the following centuries, pottery imports from other parts of the empire waned, but pottery production within Britain itself, with the aid of imported technology, expanded dramatically.[1] By c. 300, inexpensive pots from Romano-British kilns were widely available, and even peasants living in rural backwaters went about their lives with mass-produced, kiln-fired ceramics near to hand.[2] Pottery crucially affected the ways people cooked, ate, stored their surplus, socialized, interacted with their betters and inferiors, and practiced rituals associated with death. The fact that late Roman pottery was part of so many different kinds of people's daily routines is suggestive of the central role it played in shaping everyday life.[3] As we have seen, though, professional potters ceased making mass-produced pottery by c. 430. From this time forward, people who wished to use ceramic pots would have to procure them in new ways.

During the Roman period, glass containers and drinking equipment were not as widely available as pottery, but by c. 300 they were more common than they had been in earlier centuries. Small, thin-walled, free-blown, locally made cups fashioned from yellowish-green, bubble-filled glass would have been used in many fourth-century households of means. This was in part because changes in the kind of glass available and in glass-vessel-making techniques made glass beakers less expensive than they had been in earlier centuries.[4] Glassworkers in Britain, though, were now making more of their wares from recycled materials, because newly manufactured raw glass from the eastern Mediterranean was harder to come by.[5] In spite of the problems of supply, many late Roman households had access to glass tableware, hardly a surprise given that a single glassworker in London might produce as many as one hundred vessels a day.[6]

Still, the distribution of glass, even in the late Roman period, was far more restricted than pottery, because raw glass was less available than clay, because the glass industry was considerably smaller,[7] and because glassware, in spite of falling prices, remained relatively dear. Estimates based on Diocletian's Edict of Prices suggest that a glass vessel cost between ten and twenty times more than a ceramic one,[8] so glass's use was limited to those who either had extra cash or had the kinds of friends who might give glass as gifts. As a result, glass drinking equipment was common in towns, at villas, and on military sites, but, unlike mass-produced pottery, it was hardly present on low-status rural sites, or, indeed, on high-status rural sites in the North and the Southwest of Britain and in Wales.[9] There were also small numbers of luxury glass bowls engraved with mythological, biblical, or hunting scenes coming in from the continent in the late fourth century, but they had a very limited distribution and were only found on very grand sites.[10] Glass's use on the table doubtless signaled an individual's or a household's customs of living, dining, and socializing, and it would have marked its users' ways of being in the world as more grand than those who did not drink from glass at dinnertime.

Although glass was relatively plentiful in the middle of the fourth century, in later decades it grew harder to come by, and the range of qualities of glass began contracting as well.[11] It is not clear when glass production collapsed in Britain. A few craftspeople after 400 were still working glass in Roman ways; but "Anglo-Saxon"-style glass, which appears in the archaeological record in the second half of the fifth century, represents a clear break with Romano-British glassmaking techniques. Chemical analysis shows that very little of this later glass was made from recycled, fourth-century glass, and the shapes and styles of the vessels produced in Britain in the later fifth century are more akin to those fashioned in the Rhineland, northern France, and Belgium than to the ones once made in Britain.[12]

Finding people who continued to use Roman-period pottery and glass in the first generation after Rome's withdrawal can be challenging. Attempts are hampered by the fact that most very late and just post-Roman stratified sequences are gone because they have been ploughed out, built into, or excavated through. Where we have evidence of people continuing to use Roman-period pottery and glass after 400, it is often confined to negative features—the graves, pits, and wells that people living in the post-Roman period were digging or filling. Or, it can be found at newly established settlements, where pottery and glass had not been used or broken in the fourth century. Households using old pottery, which was always more common and heartier than glass, are easier to identify in the archaeology than those using glass. Still, there is always the danger that people after 400 who were using old pottery and glass will be identified as living in the Roman period. In this chapter, we will look at a number of communities that can be dated with some certainty to the fifth century and for which such evidence survives, and we will attempt to determine why they continued to have Roman-period pottery and glass, what kind of choices they made as they decided how to use it, and what those choices tell us about the problems confronting culturally Romano-British people in the fifth century, whose material world had collapsed.

Old Things and Old Ways

The first cache of pots we will examine is all that survives from a single event that took place in the decade on either side of c. 420, which culminated in someone or some group throwing large numbers of Roman-period pots down a well. The incident happened at Shadwell, which lay a kilometer east of the walls of the dying city of London, just beyond its now-abandoned suburban cemeteries.[13] Two or three generations earlier, in more prosperous times, the settlement at Shadwell had been graced with two monumental stone structures. The first was an imposing building known as "the Shadwell tower," probably an early Roman mausoleum.[14] The second was a popular bathhouse, founded in the mid-third century to serve a mixed clientele, some of whom were quite prosperous, if the hairpins, gold jewelry, and the remains of figs and grapes found in and around the bathhouse are anything to go by.[15] In spite of more than a century of successful operation, the bathhouse closed c. 375. It seems that the settlement's piped water system was failing, and that the long-standing procurement systems, which had supplied bathhouses with the large amounts of fuel they needed to operate, had started to come apart.[16] The bathhouse was left standing, but it was stripped of its precious lead piping, window glass, and iron building fittings.[17] In the same decade or so, the Shadwell tower was also demolished.[18] Although these two long-standing structures were now in ruins, at least one household continued to live at Shadwell, residing in a brand-new, partially mortared-stone building.[19] The household got its water from a new, poorly built, shallow well, the shaft of which was lined with recycled boards and a little roundwood, a far cry from the deep and beautifully engineered wells found in and around London in earlier years.[20]

Those living at Shadwell in this post-bathhouse phase were heavy users of ceramics, and they continued, for some decades, to have good access to the kinds of late Roman wares that we have seen in the last chapter used by other groups in London, Southwark, and Essex (see Figure 7). They carried on dining on British-made fine wares, mostly bowls and dishes produced by the Oxfordshire potteries, but they had a few Nene Valley wares as well. They also had access to Alice Holt/Farnham pottery, as well as smaller amounts of Portchester D/Overwey, and Much Hadham wares.[21] These ceramics would have arrived via some of the same system of transport used to move grain from the Thames valley, down the nearby River Lea, and into London in the last decades of Roman rule, and from there on to the forts of the Saxon Shore and other state installations.[22] There were also what Malcolm Lyne describes as "significant quantities" of very late Mayen ware and marbled flagons from the Rhineland,[23] evidence that people here were tied in not only to the networks that moved goods from Britain to the continent, but to the ones that ran in the opposite direction. So people in the new house continued to benefit from the state-sponsored movement of goods that linked the cereal- and cattle-producing estates of Britain to the army supply depots of the Rhineland.[24] North African amphorae also arrived on occasion, so these people had periodic access to imported olive oil, wine, or fish sauce.[25] Thus, while earlier high standards of construction and recreation had slipped, the impression given by the site's pottery is that some version of the good life continued in the new house. In the first couple of decades of the fifth century, though, things got tougher. The household's access to pottery narrowed. It managed to get hold of Alice Holt/Farnham ware, some of it quite badly made, and a little BB1, but in the end, it was using new-style, hand-built pottery as well.[26]

Those living in the house abandoned it about the same time as the networks still making and distributing Roman-style pottery failed. And yet the last of its residents marked the end of their life in the Shadwell house with an extravagant act. Although they no longer had access to new supplies of Roman-style wares, they deliberately deposited a large collection of complete or nearly complete Roman-style vessels in their poorly built well. A few of these vessels were cooking and storage pots, but most were pieces of Oxfordshire tableware. There were also a few sherds of North African amphorae and a copper bowl.[27] All these vessels were placed in the well in a single, purposeful act. Together, the collection looks like the remains of a feast or the symbolic representation of one. It is but one of dozens of known late and post-Roman well deposits, made when wells ceased to function as wells and apparently undertaken to mark the end of a nearby building or settlement. Many such deposits included impressive amounts of late Roman pottery, and occasionally bronze or pewter tableware.[28] The Shadwell deposit is, for example, similar to a contemporary well deposit at Worcester. Included in the Worcester well were very late cooking pots and tableware. They, too, look like the kind of ceramics that might have stood behind an evening of fine dining.[29]

What the pottery in the well at Shadwell seems to witness is a group of people who chose to use what may have been the last of their carefully husbanded Roman-style ceramics in a ritual that was essentially a funeral for a place, and, indeed, for a way of life. The decision they made, to use a stockpile of increasingly hard-to-find ceramics in this way, was not the least bit pragmatic and reminds us how crucial particular kinds of objects could be in the maintenance of proper relations between the unseen world and the world of the everyday. The effects of the pottery industry's collapse in Britain not only were felt at mealtimes and in storage sheds but would also require communities across lowland Britain to rethink special observances that had long had Roman material culture at their hearts.

Around the same time that the household at Shadwell was depositing the last of its pots down a well, we find two communities in northern Hertfordshire, just north and east of St. Albans, also deploying their diminishing supplies of pottery in ritualized acts, although in these cases, the acts were focused on the dead. In the early fifth century, a few people were still living in and around the former roadside settlement of Baldock, a once-lively place with a hardworking population of craftspeople and traders.[30] Others were residing a couple of kilometers away on the dead or dying Dicket Mead villa estate at Welwyn Hall.[31] At both places, people continued, in the fifth century, to bury their dead in cemeteries established during the Roman period. At Baldock, they were using a cemetery now known as the California cemetery, which had served as a burial site since the second century CE.[32] At Welwyn Hall, families were burying their dead at a cemetery that had probably been founded in the fourth century by estate workers laboring in the Dicket Mead villa's ironworking operation.[33]

Throughout the third and fourth centuries, mourners in this part of Hertfordshire had participated in a number of quintessentially Romano-British funerary rites.[34] Most of the dead, for example, were placed in the ground in wooden coffins,[35] and a few were decapitated postmortem or buried with hobnail boots.[36] Some were accompanied in their graves by domestic fowl and mass-produced, wheel-thrown pots, sometimes deliberately smashed in the grave.[37] Other households placed the recent dead in graves already occupied by others.[38] After 400, as pottery and iron production faltered in the region and as towns and villas disappeared,[39] people burying here carried on, as best they could, with time-honored funerary traditions.[40] Domestic fowl and coffins (although some now partially or wholly fastened with wooden dowels rather than increasingly scarce iron nails) continued to play a part in funerals;[41] postmortem decapitations and the sharing of graves persisted as well, and so, too, did the placing or breaking of pots in the grave.[42] It is the pottery that is of special interest here, because some of it was very old by the time mourners put it in the ground.

One of California's fifth-century burials, for example, was furnished with three pots. The first was a Samian dish in superb condition, despite the fact that it dates to the late first or early second century.[43] It looks like someone scavenged it, before its use in this California grave, from a long-abandoned cremation cemetery

FIGURE 9. A hard-worn, fourth-century Nene Valley color-coated beaker, placed in a fifth-century grave at the California cemetery, Baldock, Hertfordshire. (North Hertfordshire Museum, BAL1.3633.8872. Photo by author. By kind permission of the North Hertfordshire Museum.)

only a few hundred meters away, a cemetery where many cremations were accompanied by nearly identical dishes.[44] This is, however, the only vessel in the whole of the California cemetery that looks to have been looted from an earlier grave. Another pot in the same grave was an *extremely* worn fourth-century, color-coated ceramic beaker that had to have been at least a half-century old when buried (Figure 9). Unlike its Samian companion, this pot had not come from a closed context, that is, a place where delicate objects had been taken out of circulation for a time. Much of its slip coat had rubbed off from long years of use, and its rim and base were chipped and worn with age.[45] Although mourners burying at California and Welwyn Hall had often favored color-coated beakers in the fourth century,[46] pots as hard-worn as this were never used in fourth-century burials. It is an extraordinary survival, a carefully curated heirloom husbanded by people determined to carry on funerary practices that their families had participated in for generations. With the collapse of industrial-scale pottery production, these rituals must have required the careful husbanding of whatever pots they had left.[47]

Another late grave, this one at Welwyn Hall, included a flanged, rimmed, wheel-thrown fourth-century Nene Valley color-coated bowl (Figure 10).[48] Judging from its very worn condition, it, too, had been very hard-used by the time

FIGURE 10. A very worn fourth-century wheel-thrown, flanged dish buried in a fifth-century grave at Welwyn Hall, Hertfordshire. (Welwyn Hatfield Museum Service, HAT 165.70.1153. Photo by author. By kind permission of the Welwyn Hatfield Museum Service.)

someone repurposed it as a grave offering.[49] A post-400 grave at California contained a similar bowl, which, at first glance, looks much the same (Figure 11). The California bowl, however, is lopsided and hand built. The person who made it fashioned it to look like a fourth-century Nene Valley bowl and still knew how to slip coat a pot, but its lack of symmetry tells us that it was made without a potters' wheel. This pot, too, was so worn when placed in the ground that most of its color-coated slip had worn off.[50] It was likely produced in the fifth century, at a time when Nene Valley ware was no longer available, and when wheel-throwing techniques were being lost.

The same fifth-century California grave that contained the Samian dish and the very worn beaker also included another small bowl with a rimmed lip and a foot, made in this particular shape to give it the look of a wheel-thrown pot (Figure 12).[51] What its maker probably had in mind was a Hadham-ware bowl-jar, a ceramic type that had been locally mass-produced in the fourth century and had been placed in fourth-century graves in the area, including one at Welwyn Hall.[52]

FIGURE 11. A very worn, hand-built, fifth-century flanged, rimmed dish, made to look like a fourth-century, Nene Valley dish, placed in a fifth-century burial at the California cemetery, Baldock, Hertfordshire. (North Hertfordshire Museum: BAL1.1193. Photo by author. By kind permission of the North Hertfordshire Museum.)

Our fifth-century pot, though, was hand built and made by a person who had a very clear idea of what a pot should look like; that is, it should look as if it had been thrown on a wheel; but this person had not mastered the techniques that had been used by professional potters a few generations earlier. Thus, we can see people in the area moving, in their funerals, from recently purchased pots in the fourth century, to hard-worn, carefully husbanded ceramics by the fifth, and finally to hand-built facsimiles of fourth-century pots.

People living in northern Hertfordshire in the early years of the fifth century may have used the kinds of pots we see in their graves in their daily lives as well, but because we have not found where they lived, we cannot know whether they did or not. But the fact that they continued to use Roman-style ceramics in their burials shows how crucial these objects were to their ways of dying, death, and

FIGURE 12. A fifth-century hand-built pot, made to resemble a fourth-century wheel-thrown Hadham bowl-jar, placed in a post-Roman grave in the California cemetery, Baldock, Hertfordshire. (North Hertfordshire Museum: BAL1. 3633.8873. Photo by author. By kind permission of the North Hertfordshire Museum.)

burial. When Roman-style pottery was no longer available, people here would have to acclimate themselves to their new material reality and invent new material traditions for their dead.

A third fifth-century group using not just Roman-period ceramics, but Roman-period glass as well, lived in the West Country at Cadbury Congresbury, in Somerset. Here, as imperial institutions and structures collapsed in the early decades of the fifth century, a number of people abandoned their homes and moved to ancient hillforts. These had been built long before the Roman conquest, and although some served in the Roman period as sites for ritual activity, none continued on as settlements after the Roman conquest.[53] In the late fourth and early fifth-centuries, however, a number of them, including the one at Cadbury Congresbury, were reoccupied.[54] Within a generation of the hillfort's reoccupation c. 450, and quite possibly from its inception, some individual, family, or clique was in charge, and social stratification is clear in the site's archaeological remains. A number of structures, for example, were built during the earliest phase of reoccupation, some more elaborate than others. Many were roundhouses, a vernacular building style that had continued throughout the Roman period, often, but not exclusively, in rural backwaters.[55] Four of these roundhouses, excavated in the 1970s and shown to have been built in the post-Roman period, range in size from forty to ninety-five square meters.[56] Other buildings, though, were larger and rectangular, and one has been identified as a post-built timber hall of some 875 square meters.[57] By c. 500 serious refortification efforts were also underway at the site, and an impressive gatehouse, reminiscent of late Roman military architecture, was fashioned from timber and sod.[58] These things together argue that social stratification had survived the fall in this corner of Somerset, and that some at the site were in charge, while others did their bidding.

The people who first resettled the hillfort were culturally Romano-British, but they arrived with very little durable, Roman-period material culture. Nonetheless, in its initial decades some members of the community—especially those dining in the site's largest timber hall—were using mass-produced pottery: the remains of at least 170 Roman-period ceramic vessels have been found on the site.[59] Although these numbers may seem small, it is important to remember that only 5 percent of the site has been excavated. About half of these vessels were late Roman coarse wares, and almost a quarter were Oxfordshire color-coated vessels or *mortaria*.[60] But a few of the pots date to the first or second century.

People living at Cadbury Congresbury also had Roman-period glass bottles and beakers.[61] Archaeologists have recovered the remains of a minimum of ten. Of these, three date to the first or second century. There were three or four fourth-century jugs and at least four etched glass bowls from the continent, also dating to the fourth century.[62] The site's excavators, based on analyses of the break patterns and distribution of the glass and ceramic sherds, have convincingly argued that this material arrived on site whole, and that high-status people living in the great hall were dining on it.[63] It is important to note here that although the bulk of the pots and glass used at Cadbury Congresbury had been manufactured in the late fourth century and are similar to pottery used at nearby temples, villas, and roadside settlements, some of it was centuries old.[64] Where had all this material come from?

A few things may have been brought to the site as cherished family heirlooms.[65] The most likely candidates are the late Roman etched bowls. But the first- and second-century glass and pottery would not have survived two or three hundred years above ground, and it is likely that they were taken from closed contexts—and the most likely closed contexts for glass of this date are first- and second-century cremations.[66] The same is also true for the unusually old pots.[67]

Some of the other pottery, in particular, the Oxfordshire color-coated ware, may have come from late Roman inhumation graves.[68] The rest of the pottery could have been in active use when the hillfort was settled, but given that most of it would have been at least thirty years old, and given the large number of Roman-period pots uncovered in the excavation, it is likely that the community undertook systematic scavenging campaigns in search of still-useable vessels at deserted sites in the neighborhood. Certainly, two nearby Roman-period temple sites and a settlement had had access to the same types of pots in more or less the same proportions in the fourth century as people in mid-fifth-century Cadbury Congresbury were using.[69] So it seems that the most important people living at Cadbury Congresbury in the fifth century, those who dined—on special occasions—on Roman-period pottery and glass, were benefiting from systematic campaigns of scavenging. Interestingly, there was a contemporary cemetery only a couple of hundred meters from the hillfort at Henley Wood, the site of a defunct Roman-period temple. Some people living at the hillfort were probably burying their dead here. But none placed old, Roman-style pottery or glass in the graves of their loved ones.[70] Apparently, as far as members of this community were concerned, the most appropriate use of scavenged glass and ceramics was not in the upholding of traditional burial customs, but rather in continuing the customs of high-status dining. These objects were in very short supply, and choices had to be made.

Eventually, the hillfort's stockpiles of old glass and pots would have given out. Fortunately for those dedicated to dining on such tableware, the community began to engage, perhaps as early as 450, with foreign merchants, who traveled periodically to coastal western Britain with cargoes of wine, olive oil, and mass-produced, wheel-thrown ceramic tableware and glass still being produced in the Mediterranean world.[71] At Cadbury Congresbury as elsewhere in western Britain, archaeologists have recovered sherds of late fifth- and sixth-century tableware and amphorae from the Aegean, the eastern Mediterranean, North Africa, and perhaps southern Spain, some of which had been used as shipping containers for wine or olive oil.[72] Glass vessels from the Mediterranean also arrived at the site.[73] There is some evidence to suggest that a few of the foreigners involved in this trade died in Britain as well. Their skeletons have been tentatively identified in three early cemeteries in western Britain, because ratios of stable oxygen and strontium isotopes in their tooth enamel suggest that they had spent their childhoods somewhere in the Mediterranean basin.[74]

This handful of bodies, along with Mediterranean pottery and glass, are witnesses to the resumption of a small but significant long-distance trade in the late fifth century, which required merchants and sailors to work their way up the

Atlantic seaboard.[75] Whoever controlled the community at Cadbury Congresbury, in the wilds of the lost colony, must have had something foreign traders were interested in in return. What they probably had was tin, a rarity in Europe, and a commodity known in late antiquity as "the British metal."[76] Although levels of tin production in the fifth century were much lower than they had been in the Roman period,[77] early medieval tin ingots have turned up in western Britain.[78] In return for this, and whatever else they had worth trading, a thin trickle of Roman ceramics, glass, and luxury foodstuffs were available to some of the hillfort's inhabitants.

Infrequent though these contacts may have been, they enabled the most important members of the community to underscore their superior position within the society of the rebuilt hillfort with the aid of Roman-style ceramics and glass. During great feasts and celebrations held in their timber hall, they continued to dine on Roman tableware and drink rare Greek wine.[79] This was hardly the good life as described by Petronius, but it was the continuation of a political style centuries old by Roman Britain's fall, a social strategy of marking one's grand status by connecting oneself to Rome and things Roman. In this, Roman ceramics and glass played a central role. Feasting rituals dependent on Roman ceramics would not, however, have been perfect reenactments of late Roman high-status dining, which would had taken place in grand, heated, mosaic-floored rooms, at the semicircular dining couches on which the great shared special meals.[80] And the food served in late fifth-century Cadbury Congresbury would have been different from the dishes eaten at fourth-century dinner parties. The material culture of the cook fire at the hillfort, for some at least, would have been quite different from that of the dinner table. Locally produced, organic- and inorganic-tempered hand-built pots were recovered from Cadbury Congresbury, suggesting that at least some people at the hillfort had begun making their own pottery.[81] This pottery, as we saw in the last chapter, did not behave like Roman-period kitchen ceramics, and it would have necessitated new ways of cooking.

So, although status-enhancing foodways were carried out with the help of Roman-style objects, the events in which they were used were no longer Roman. Perhaps the people dining here imagined themselves to be participating in age-old traditions, but perhaps they did not. What the Roman vessels did do was allow meals to continue to define and make social status and mark high from low. Thus, some people at the site used Roman-period material culture strategically in a set of material practices that were about the performance of hierarchy and differentiated status, taken directly from the late Roman playbook. But the context and the rest of their foodways had shifted dramatically. Like those using Roman-period pottery at Shadwell and in northern Hertfordshire, people here showed themselves committed to upholding traditional ways that required the use of precious, indeed irreplaceable, Roman ceramics. But instead of throwing it down wells or placing it in graves, people at Cadbury Congresbury used it in the context of feasting. Different people in different places made different decisions about how to use their few remaining Roman-period objects, and different groups used it to maintain different material practices.

Old Things and New Ways

Other groups in Britain continued, in the post-Roman period, to be enthusiastic consumers of old Roman pots and glass, but they used them not to uphold old ways or the old order, but rather to create new customs and push new ideas about how the world should be. Take, for example, the people living in the first half of the fifth century at a site known as OD XII, on Overton Down, in Wiltshire.[82] The fourth-century complex of buildings discovered here—a workshop, a cereal-processing building, a two-roomed house, and a barn—were likely part of a larger late Roman settlement, which housed agricultural workers attached to a villa estate.[83] The fourth-century domestic quarters had stone foundations but were unassuming, and those who lived and worked here were the kinds of people who processed grain and reared sheep not for themselves, but for the period's astonishingly prosperous villa owners and its resource-hungry state.[84]

Although there were no high-status buildings at OD XII, there were several villa centers within three kilometers of the site.[85] They have not been excavated, but a few others in Wiltshire have, and a number of these had undergone substantial late Roman expansions and elaborations,[86] paid for, no doubt, by the extensification of farming much in evidence in the region during the first half of the fourth century.[87] The clearest manifestation of the fourth-century imperial state in this part of Wiltshire was the roadside settlement of Cunetio (Blackfield, Mildenhall, Wiltshire), eight kilometers east of OD XII.[88] Cunetio was the beneficiary of several major late Roman building campaigns.[89] Mark Corney has argued that the revamped site functioned as an imperial administrative center, and as a fortified center from which the *annona* could be enforced and collected.[90] But, as the state faltered in Britain, the places and institutions that depended on it began to fail as well. Cunetio was abandoned, as were the region's grand villas.

People continued to live at OD XII after Cunetio and villas in the area had gone into terminal decline, occupying at least one building on the site—Building 4A—until c. 440. As at Cadbury Congresbury, people here were using Roman-period pottery and glass.[91] We cannot tell what percentage of the potsherds recovered from the site had been broken in the generations leading up to 400, and what percentage represents fifth-century use of very late or even scavenged fourth-century ceramics. More certain, however, is that the people residing in Building 4A in the fifth century were using Roman-period glass.[92] There is no sign of glass at the settlement in earlier periods, which is hardly surprising, given that glass tableware on nonvilla rural sites was not at all common.[93] Most of the glass found in and around Building 4A was late Roman, thin-walled, yellowish-green cups and beakers, the same kind of glassware found on late villa and urban sites.[94] What makes the collection of glass at OD XII remarkable is that it constitutes the largest Romano-British glass assemblage from a low-status, rural site yet recovered.[95] The most likely source for all this late Roman glass was an abandoned villa in the neighborhood. Now that local high-status sites were derelict, rural people were helping themselves to abandoned objects. Alongside the glass, bits of painted wall plaster have been found near Building 4A. Because none of the buildings at OD XII had ever been embellished in such an elaborate manner, the site's excavator argues that someone living at OD XII had taken these decorative bits from an abandoned high-status building, perhaps as keepsakes. There would have been ample opportunity, as high-status sites fell into ruin, for the people at OD XII to help themselves to objects abandoned in once-grand houses.[96]

These descendants of villa farm workers, who were not the kind of people who had participated in late Roman dining practices that included glassware at mealtime,[97] seem, then, to have been living it up after 400 in ways that would have been unimaginable when Britain was an imperial possession and farm families were being bled dry by landlords and state officials. The glass hints at the ways people living here may now have been drinking for the first time in a manner that reflected something of what had gone on the dining rooms of their bosses and betters a generation or two earlier. So here, rather than upholding the status quo, this particular use of Roman glass reflected a world turned upside down.

Another group of users of Roman vessels were living far to the north, in the former military zone just south of Hadrian's Wall, at Crossgates, near Scarborough, in Yorkshire.[98] The people residing here during the late Roman period lived in stone-paved roundhouses, as members of lower-status communities often did in the West and North of Britain, even in the late Roman period.[99] A few fourth-century coins were recovered in and around the settlement, proof that it was connected to the broader economy, as were the remains of oysters, quern stones from the Rhineland, and a jet pendant, all of which had come from elsewhere.[100] It is, however, the surfeit of coarse-ware storage jars and cooking pots that provides the most compelling evidence for this community's connections to the outside world, particularly its entanglements with the redistributive late Roman economy.[101] People here, unlike those in Hertfordshire, did not have fine and specialist wares, either because they did not have access to such pots or because they had little interest in participating in the foodways and dining practices that required such wares.[102] Considerable quantities of Crambeck parchment ware and Huntcliff-type cookpots, both made in the East of Yorkshire and both typically found in assemblages dating after c. 360, were plentiful on the site, especially the latter, which made up three-quarters of the ceramics assemblage at Crossgates.[103] Impressive amounts of very late calcite gritted ware, produced sometime after 388, were also recovered from the site.[104] Jars tempered with this material had been in use in this part of Yorkshire since the Iron Age, so the continuities in use here are not only with the Roman period, but with very long-lived Iron Age traditions.

The community's heavy use of coarse-ware jars makes sense because late Roman rural communities needed not only to cook and store their own food, but also to transport surplus to those to whom they owed rents and taxes. The site's ubiquitous Huntcliff jars had hand-built bodies and wheel-made shoulders and rims.[105] These pots were especially common on military sites in the late Roman North, which suggests that they played a central role in military supply.[106] Large numbers have been found both at Crossgates and at a nearby military outpost, the so-called Scarborough signal station, built c. 370,[107] as well as at a site excavated in York, at Wellington Row.[108] Perhaps what we are seeing here is both the handing-over and the receiving ends of the late Roman in-kind tax.[109] Pottery like this is also found on villa sites in the North, and Mark Whyman has convincingly argued that low-status tenants used it to transport their in-kind rents.[110] Thus, the pottery at Crossgates is evidence that its inhabitants, especially after c. 360, were enmeshed in a tributary relationship with the late Roman state—locally manifest in the nearby coastal "signal station"—and with powerful landed interests hinted at by the recently discovered remains of a Roman-period limestone-and-timber villa building nearby.[111] The pottery found at Crossgates continued to be produced, but on a more diminished scale, in the first years of the fifth century, and it continued to be delivered, presumably full of agricultural rents and tributes, in the early decades of the fifth century to places such as

Wellington Row, in York.¹¹² But with the collapse of the state and traditional, late Roman surplus-extraction mechanisms in the decades after c. 400, potters stopped producing these ceramics.¹¹³

The people who had long made their homes at Crossgates shifted their settlement site sometime in the early fifth century, moving slightly to the west.¹¹⁴ Elsewhere in Britain we see settlements shifting during this period, sometimes, as here, by only a few hundred meters.¹¹⁵ It is clear that the people living on the newly shifted site, who the 1940s archaeologists working at Crossgates identified as "Anglo-Saxons," were indigenous, because the earliest of the so-called Anglian huts they were living in were, in actual fact, traditional, British roundhouses;¹¹⁶ and the people in them continued to use late Roman pottery, albeit alongside new, hand-built, mineral-tempered wares, which the excavators also labeled "Anglian."¹¹⁷ Two of the so-called Anglo-Saxon pots have shapes reminiscent of Romano-British globular beakers,¹¹⁸ and some of the pots continued to be heavily gritted and tempered with calcite, as much of the region's late Roman pottery had been, even though the technology standing behind their making had changed.¹¹⁹ Here, as in northern Hertfordshire, it seems that old, Romano-British ceramic forms continued to inform some pot makers, even though they had lost much of the technical expertise that had stood behind their models.¹²⁰

The ghosts of Roman pottery haunted Crossgates in other ways. An area just to the northeast of the late Roman settlement was transformed in the fifth century into the locus of periodic communal feasting. Here, the sites excavators uncovered several dozen fire pits.¹²¹ All were used (some more than once) to cook copious amounts of meat. The most common animals were cattle, but sheep, pigs, and horses were prepared in the pits.¹²² Some of these cooking pits also contained the remains of both hand-built pots and Huntcliff-type cook pots.¹²³ One explanation is that inhabitants were using stockpiles of late Roman ceramics, previously used for rendering agricultural rents and in-kind taxes, as well as new-style, hand-built wares at gatherings centered on communal feasting. The animals they ate on these occasions had been culled from the now unnecessarily large herds of horses and oxen, animals for which the late Roman state had had an insatiable appetite,¹²⁴ and which had had important roles as riding and draft animals in the old economy, an economy no longer in operation. Now that tax officials, bailiffs, and soldiers were either no longer in the neighborhood or unable to enforce the same tribute demands, local farmers may have been literally living high on the hog (or, sometimes, as at Crossgates, high on the horse), at feasts where repurposed late Roman ceramics no longer symbolized the tax collector or the rent man, but abundance.¹²⁵

Our last community of Roman pot users is the one at Barrow Hills, in Radley, Oxfordshire. People here, in the post-Roman period, scavenged for pots, but they were very particular about the kinds of pots they collected. They limited their collecting to smallish, late Roman color-coated wares.[126] They had many sources for such pottery. The ruins of a modest villa lay only three hundred meters from their settlement,[127] and the region in which they lived was thick with deserted Romano-British kilns, which had once produced copious amounts of color-coated ware, and would, in the fifth century, still be places marked by large dumps of pottery wasters.[128] One such dump, at nearby Lower Farm, in Nuneham Courtenay, when surveyed, measured something on the order of eighty meters by fifteen.[129] The Roman-period pottery in use in early medieval Barrow Hills, however, is in exceptional condition and may well have come from closed contexts, because so much of it maintains its polished surfaces and unbroken edges, a far cry from those worn vessels used in fifth-century Hertfordshire burials. Small, whole, color-coated drinking beakers accompanied some of the fourth-century Romano-British dead laid to rest in a cemetery located at the very edge of the Barrow Hills settlement,[130] and similar vessels could be found in many other late Roman cemeteries.[131] There were also a number of late Roman ritual deposits of color-coated vessels in the neighborhood.[132] So there were many promising places around Barrow Hills for people to poke around when they went looking for old Roman pots.

Unlike the other groups we have investigated, the people at Barrow Hills were not using the pots they collected for cooking or dining or in ritual practices; they were not even using them as pots. Instead, they were interested only in the bases of old Roman pots, which they collected already broken, or which they created by breaking off or chipping away the body of the pot from its footring base.[133] If the latter, they did this off site, because the body shards and rims that were once attached to these bases are nowhere to be found in the Barrow Hills settlement itself. Not all Roman pots had footed bases, but it is clear that the people of Barrow Hills were selecting for pots that did (Figure 13).[134] In total, the site's excavators recovered seventy-five modified Roman pot bases during their excavation of the Barrow Hills settlement, and they constitute the single most common artifact type by far recovered from the site.[135] This is all the more interesting when we consider that the people settled here never modified the bases of their own hand-built pottery in this way.[136] The curious pottery-collecting habits of the people of Barrow Hills were also shared by other groups living in the Thames valley and in eastern England.[137] So what were the people at Barrow Hills and elsewhere doing with Roman pot bases? In order to answer this question, we need to turn our attention to the kind of

FIGURE 13. A base of a fourth-century Romano-British pot from the post-Roman Barrow Hills, Radley settlement. (Formerly in the Ashmolean Museum, Oxford, Barrow Hills, Radley, 1225/B1 [acc. no. 1467]). Photo by author. Now lost.)

brooches women were beginning to wear a couple of generations after 400 in the region in which Barrow Hills lies.

Saucer brooches were the most common type of brooch worn by women in the Thames valley in the fifth and sixth centuries.[138] They were worn by women in matching pairs, one on each shoulder.[139] Although the craftspeople who made them worked hard to create identical sets, Tanya Dickinson has pointed out that judging from the small differences found in pair designs, it is likely that each brooch was cast from a different mold, most likely made using the lost-wax method.[140] Two wax blanks would be made, and then the metalworker, to the best of his ability, would carve the same relief design into each wax disc, which in turn would be covered with clay and fired, the wax poured out, and the melted copper alloy poured in to make two nearly identical cast brooches.

Although the relief decorations on each member of a pair of brooches differed slightly, the dimensions of the three diameters of each pair of brooches—the diameter of the decorative field, the measurement from rim to rim, and the diameter of the back base—so Dickinson has shown—differ hardly at all, usually by considerably less than a single millimeter,[141] and the angles of the rims of each pair are close to identical. In short, the wax templates included not only the decorative center of each brooch, but their rims as well, which come, essentially, in three forms: angular, flared, or "acutely upturned."[142] This suggests that the wax blanks for each pair had, themselves, been made with the same template. So how were metal smiths making their matched wax templates on which to carve two nearly identical brooches? I suspect that they were using at least some of the Roman-period pot bases they so assiduously collected to form the wax blanks, which they in turn used, using the lost-wax method, to create cast, copper-alloy saucer brooches, a brooch style new to England in the fifth century. These are exactly the same profiles as their curated and modified Roman pot bases, most of which have the same angular, flared, or acutely upturned profiles as saucer brooches. Most of the collected and modified bases, moreover, are saucer-brooch sized (Figure 14). Indeed, forty-two of Barrow Hill's modified bases have diameters measuring between 32 and 75 millimeters, appropriate dimensions for saucer-brooch templates.[143] One modified pot base from Market Lavington, in Wiltshire, helps clinch this argument. It was made from the base of a late Roman Oxfordshire color-coated pot. Not only has this base been chipped away from its body, but it was marked off into quadrants, and then further divided into segments of three, as if being prepared to act as some sort of design template.[144]

Each of our communities of Roman-period pot and glass users was responding differently to the disappearance of mass-produced Romano-British material culture, and they each treated residual Roman objects in their own way. The people living outside of the dying city of London at Shadwell and in northern Hertfordshire used pots made in the Roman period, choosing to consume their increasingly rare wheel-thrown pots in ritual practices that were important to them—traditional rites marking the deaths of buildings, settlements, and loved ones. Old Roman pots and glassware at Cadbury Congresbury were used by elites to maintain and underscore social distinctions, one of the hallmarks of late Roman society across the empire. By the looks of it, high-status members of the community were determined to invoke traditional, Roman-period material practices in the face of economic collapse by maintaining some of the dining practices of the late Roman period, with the help of Roman-period ceramics and glass. So all three communities, albeit in very different ways, deployed Roman-period material culture symbolically in projects of cultural continuity. Peasants living at OD XII, on the other hand, were collecting glass beakers—probably by helping themselves to what they found in deserted villas—putting glass drinking equipment in their

FIGURE 14. Roman pot bases from Barrow Hills, Radley. Their basic profiles can be compared with those of the saucer brooches shown here. Top row from left to right: a. An angular modified Roman pot base. (Formerly in the Ashmolean Museum, Oxford, Barrow Hills, Radley, 125/B1[(acc. no. 1467]. Photo by author. Now lost.) b. A flared modified Roman pot base. (Formerly in the Ashmolean Museum, Oxford, Barrow Hills, Radley, 3578/B2 [acc. no. 1484]). Photo by author. Now lost.) c. An "acutely upturned" modified Roman pot base. (Formerly in the Ashmolean Museum, Oxford, Barrow Hills, Radley, 3288/A1 [acc. no. 1479]). Photo by author. Now lost.) Bottom row from left to right: d. An angular-rimmed saucer brooch. (British Museum, London, 1964.0702.398. By kind permission of the British Museum.) e. A flared-rimmed saucer brooch. (Portable Antiquities Scheme, Tanner, A. (2017) WILT -7EA469t: https://finds.org.uk/database/artefacts/record/id/836180 [accessed: August 6, 2019. 6:35:11].) f. An acutely upturned-rim saucer brooch. (British Museum, London, 1875,0310.149. By kind permission of the British Museum.)

hands for the very first time. And at Crossgates, pots once used by the Roman state and elite landowners to extract surplus from low-status farming communities were sometimes used after the state's collapse for communal feasting. The activities at both OD XII and Crossgates, though, reflect a relatively brief post-Roman phase rather than a permanent revolution, as the supplies of late Roman pottery and glass were finite, and they eventually ran out. In the same period, we also encounter people such as the ones living at Barrow Hills, who never met a Roman pot they did not want to break, and they used these ceramics not to carry on old Roman ways, but to create brand-new, decidedly un-Roman material culture.

Some of the old pottery and glass still in use in the fifth century had had long and unexpected careers. One pot from Cadbury Congresbury, for example, had been thrown in the first century as a kitchen pot but was probably placed, early in its life, in a grave, where it acted for a couple of hundred years as a companion to a dead person. Found again in the fifth century and brought to a resettled hillfort, it may have been used at table during important meals. One of the California beakers, on the other hand, had an opposite trajectory. It started its life, in the fourth century, as a drinking companion for a middling inhabitant of a middling roadside settlement, but its exceptional longevity would have made it a cherished heirloom by the first couple of decades of the fifth century. It, alongside an even older Samian dish and a hand-built pot, would eventually be taken out of circulation for good, when placed in a baby's grave. The Cadbury Congresbury and California pots, like many of the vessels we have encountered in this chapter, survived much longer than ceramic vessels were meant to, and their longevity gave them special powers in the post-Roman period, when they were some of the last of their kind; and they enabled the last of their long lines of owners to evoke or preserve bits of Roman-period life that were dear to them in a rapidly evolving material reality.

An investigation of practices of reuse helps restore agency to people living through this period. We can see different groups, acting not in lockstep or like automatons, but rather making quite different choices as they decided what to do with their precious supplies of old Roman pots and glass; and from their decisions we learn interesting things about different groups' quite different priorities. For some, the maintenance of social distinction was crucial; for others, it was the continuation of ritual practices that mattered. For yet others, one suspects that the collapse of the Roman state in Britain, for all its many inconveniences, was embraced as good news. The range of responses in these communities complicates our understanding of the transition from Roman to post-Roman, and it requires us to reimagine the fifth century, not as a single story with a single narrative arc, but rather as the working out, sometimes on the fly, by thousands of different settlements, families, and individuals, of the confounding problem of how to move forward when many of the things around which daily life had long been structured were disappearing.

CHAPTER 5

Pragmatic, Symbolic, and Ritual Use of Roman Brick and Quarried Stone

> No maintenance, no building...
> —Stewart Brand, *How Buildings Learn: What Happens After They're Built*

This chapter investigates the rise and fall of two long-standing and ubiquitous material practices—the building, refurbishment, and repurposing of masonry buildings, walls, and foundations, and the recycling of stone, brick, and tile. Both were standard practices in Britain from the second century on, and both disappeared within a couple of generations of the Roman state's withdrawal from Britain. Masonry buildings were usually built for members of the same segments of society whose interests were most closely aligned with the Roman state— imperial administrators, landed elites, townspeople of means, and some craft workers.[1] Most households in Britain, however, had neither the means nor the inclination to indulge in stone-built architecture.[2] Thus, the use of stone for building was far from universal, and it is clear that timber continued to dominate the built environment. This was true even in the fourth century and even in towns.[3] In spite of their relatively small numbers, masonry buildings and the materials and skilled labor that made them possible are worth investigating, because they loomed large in the social imaginary of late Roman Britain.

In the first half of the fourth century, both recently built and newly remodeled masonry buildings were notable features in the same zone in Britain that was most heavily administered and in which people were most engaged with Roman material culture. As we have seen, the late empire was structured in ways that made landed families, imperial bureaucrats, and high-ranking military men very rich.[4] The reforms of the early Dominate, moreover, unleashed cutthroat rivalries between leading men across the empire. In Britain, not only had families caught up in this competition internalized a local version of imperial tastes and norms, but they had come to wield Roman material culture like a cudgel, using it to announce, underscore, and shore up their privilege. They were especially drawn to Roman-style domestic architecture as a way of furthering and monumentalizing their advantages as they competed for honors, power, clients, and social position. Many grand families in the generation on either side of 300 devoted considerable treasure to building and improving their country estates and townhouses.[5] That large numbers of British grandees were able to complete ambitious construction projects in so few years is a testimony to the efficiency of imperial building practices that had taken root in Britain in the centuries after conquest.[6]

The initial wave of high-end construction in the late third and early fourth centuries, however, constituted only the first of many building-related expenses. As Tim Ingold reminds us, the "serious work of building" begins *after* construction is completed, when proprietors "embark on their daily struggle to limit the damage inflicted by invasions of insects and rodents, the rot brought with fungal infestation and the corrosive effects of the elements. Rainwater drips through the roof where the wind has blown off a tile, feeding a mould that threatens to decompose the timbers."[7]

A direct consequence of the late Roman building boom was the thousands of renovation and refurbishment projects carried out in later years, some to keep high-status buildings up to date or up with the Joneses and others to keep them upright. One of the things this chapter sets out to do is to uncover the material practices standing behind the construction and upkeep of these buildings. Another is to trace the fate of these buildings and the materials and skill sets with which they were made across the second half of the fourth century and beyond. Because almost all these structures would cease to be maintained, improved, or refurbished by the middle of the fifth century, they represent yet another constellation of objects and material practices that did not long survive Rome's withdrawal from Britain. Thinking through the decline and fall of Roman-style masonry buildings and building material helps expose the increasingly difficult material landscape of the later fourth and early fifth centuries, as various interlocking systems of making, moving, and working began to fray: these buildings, the materials that went into their construction, and the final phases of their occupation expose some of the mechanics underlying such systemic breakdowns. A history of these buildings also allows us to consider the effects their demise had on materially based, Roman-style practices of social difference, which elevated and propped up elites, and which set social difference in stone.

Building in Stone Under Rome

The craftspeople described in Diocletian's Edict on Prices who labored in the building trades—stonemasons, joiners, woodworkers, lime burners, marble workers, mosaicists, *tesserae* makers, painters, and architects—were the kinds of skilled workers who could be found putting up villas, aisled halls, bathhouses, temples, fancy barns, and government buildings across Britain.[8] The impresarios of major building projects would have needed to hire most of these specialists, but it is likely that rather than engaging different categories of craft workers individually, they contracted professional construction crews that included the full range of skilled practitioners. Patrons in rural areas or in roadside settlements, where a new masonry structure might be constructed or refurbished only once every couple of generations, would have especially depended on itinerant construction crews, because their myriad specialists could not, under normal circumstances, have made a living locally. These crews' ability to complete major projects depended, in turn, on other groups of skilled workers—teamsters, metalsmiths, quarrymen, tile makers, and the like. The large gangs of unskilled laborers also needed for major building projects were, however, probably engaged closer to home: villa owners, for example, may have required their own tenants, farmhands, and slaves to perform the sweatiest work occasioned by their architectural ventures.[9]

Besides an abundance of skilled construction labor, there was an abundance of building material. In the first 250 years under Roman rule, much of the cut stone, brick, and tile used in Britain would have been newly fabricated.[10] But by 300 there were mountains of secondhand building materials, and the period's builders were exceptionally skilled in practices of reuse. Recycling was highly organized, and workers across the Roman world knowledgeable in controlled demolition regularly salvaged tile, brick, and building stone for reuse in everything from private dwellings and shops to major imperial infrastructure projects.[11] There is considerable evidence for this kind of activity in Britain. For example, archaeologists occasionally come across sorted, stacked, and stored tile, roofing slates, and stone that had been harvested from demolished buildings.[12] Excavation has also made clear that the crews putting up walls around London, Rochester, Lincoln, and Vindolanda used material salvaged from defunct monumental structures and cemeteries.[13] Those contracted to build private houses also built with reclaimed materials. In

London, brick and tile salvaged from the Huggin Hill baths complex could be found in many of the city's later structures;[14] and by the late fourth century, some of London's reused building material had been deployed more than once.[15] It also turns up in Roman-period well linings, hypocausts, and corn driers.[16]

Whole buildings were also extensively refurbished, repurposed, and rebuilt during this period. The large stone or stone-footed aisled hall at Quarry Farm, Ingleby Barwick,[17] and the magnificent basilica-style aisled barn at Hog Brook, in Deerton, Kent,[18] were originally built in the second century, and both were still in use at the end of the Roman period. Their longevity was made possible by regular maintenance and competent repairs.[19] Other buildings underwent thoroughgoing renovations as they changed functions over time. The villa house at Redlands Farm, Northamptonshire, originally constructed in the second century as a stone-built mill, was converted to domestic use in the early third century, and by the mid-fourth century it had been transformed into a winged-corridor villa with a hypocaust and mosaic floors.[20] An old flint-built barn at Littlecote, in Wiltshire, was similarly remodeled sometime after c. 360 into a deluxe, triple-apsed bathhouse with lavish Orpheus mosaics and a multistory tower;[21] and c. 370, the second-century aisled hall at Stanwick, Northamptonshire, was rebuilt as a comfortable winged corridor villa.[22] Many villas, moreover, underwent more than one fourth-century remodeling campaign. Bancroft, in Buckinghamshire, benefited from two, the first in the 330s and the second sometime after 350.[23] Barnsley Park, in Gloucestershire, was first built as a stone villa c. 360, but a new wing, hypocausts, and mosaics were installed in the 370s.[24] The villa at Frocester underwent major refurbishments c. 300, c. 340, and c. 360.[25]

Other buildings, by the late fourth century, had very old walls or foundations buried within them. One wall uncovered at the villa house at Great Weldon, in Northamptonshire, for example, dates to the Flavian period; but it was reused both in the house's rebuilding of c. 200 and in its elaboration and enlargement of c. 350.[26] The state also engaged in projects of reconstruction and repurposing. Builders working at forts along Hadrian's Wall in the late Roman period transformed granaries into living quarters, which required them to reengineer these structures' earlier suspended floors.[27] Such ambitious reworkings were possible because builders were skilled enough to confidently rethink and refashion older structures and features, bond new walls to old ones, and build new walls atop old foundations. The men in charge of projects such as these also regularly oversaw the insertion of new hypocausts into older rooms; the adding of new wings, towers, and second stories; and the moving of bath suites. Their ability to adapt whole and partial structures in these ways testifies to their mastery of complex skills and work practices as well as basic engineering knowledge.[28] The final outcomes of their labors were often impressive. Visitors approaching the palatial villa at Box, in Wiltshire, in 350, with its more than fifty rooms, its massive, buttressed hall, and a facade half again as long as an American football field, would not have been able to discern the much smaller third-century villa lurking at its heart.[29]

Like so many material practices in the later fourth century, both the systematic reuse of building material and the adaptive repurposing of older structures underwent a series of relatively abrupt transformations. Although both continued to the end of the Roman period and beyond, by c. 375 much less organized practices of reuse and less professional-looking refurbishments had become the new normal. In these decades, some villas were abandoned, and a few were expanded or expensively redecorated. Many, though, were neither deserted nor grandified: instead, their lavishly decorated domestic quarters were transformed into no-nonsense, heavily used workspaces. In short, these villas' *pars urbana*—the part originally built for elite comfort and display—was overtaken by their *pars rustica*—the productive components of an estate.[30] During the last decades of the fourth century and the first decades of the fifth, ovens used for iron and lead working[31] or corn drying and malting[32] were habitually installed in once-grand entertainment rooms, often ruining their mosaic floors. Entrances and interiors were sometimes retrofitted as well, to accommodate carts or livestock;[33] and rooms once devoted to bathing or dining were adapted to store agricultural surplus,[34] or to serve as sites where animals could be butchered.[35] Villas modified in these ways ceased to have tidy interiors, and we find animal bone, oyster shells, ash from ovens, and industrial waste strewn across their final-phase floors.[36] Town baths and basilicas underwent similar transformations.[37]

The demotions of once-grand buildings to workaday spaces, it should be emphasized, were limited neither to the late fourth century nor to Britain. In the third century, for example, the luxurious villas at Piddington and Thurnham were rebuilt as industrial workshops and living quarters for low-status workers,[38] reminding us that what we see happening so often in the late fourth century had a long history. What was new was that so many buildings were undergoing similar changes, and that so few opulent houses in Britain were being built or continuing on in their original use. Such reconfigurations were not much seen elsewhere in the Roman world in the fourth century aside from northern Gaul, but they would become common in southern Gaul, the Rhineland, and Italy in the fifth century, and in the eastern Mediterranean in the sixth century.[39] So, it is the earliness of the appearance of these practices in Britain and their ubiquity that are noteworthy.

It was once thought that these late, industrial phases were evidence that "squatters" had taken over abandoned villas. The existence of these supposed shiftless low-status workers or barbaric immigrants—who were blamed for ruining the splendid architectural heritage of upper-class Romans—has now been thoroughly debunked.[40] While it is true that the ostentatious dinner parties and pampered lives once so central to the spaces being repurposed no longer took place,[41] the people ordering these rebuildings—be they military authorities, elite landowners, or state officials—remained firmly in charge of the structures they were transforming. Those mandating these repurposings were the sorts of people who continued to control agricultural surplus and metalworking (hence their interest in bringing corn driers and forges into the interiors of villa buildings). They also continued to exercise power over other people, insisting, for example, that they help shift tons of previously used building material and help deploy it in new ways.[42] There is, however, no evidence in Britain, in the late fourth century or beyond, for the kinds of fairly standardized industrial installations at villa sites set up to recoup stone, glass, bronze, and lead for reuse in other places, which Beth Munro has identified operating on many fifth- and sixth-century Italian villa sites.[43] That similar organized efforts to process the wealth of materials that went into the making of these buildings for use elsewhere was not happening in Britain is a sign that demand for the scale and range of materials Munro's crews were recouping had collapsed. It also suggests that there were no longer crews with the skills to recover this material, networks of workers to move it to where it was needed, or craftsmen to rework it.

The dramatic reconfiguration of so many once-opulent spaces points to a sea change in elite life. Originally built as "machines of social competition," the domestic quarters of villas witnessed a startling change in function. They were no longer the locus of high-level social competition; instead, they had been transformed into the kinds of spaces where production could be closely supervised. Indeed, it may be that peasants were increasingly reluctant to meet labor demands if lords were not nearby, or that things such as grain—at one time threshed, dried, and stored at some distance for the big house—were no longer secure and needed to be kept closer to home, as the protective hand of state powers waned.

Deskilling

A close look at the floors and walls being inserted into masonry buildings during their final phases of occupation highlights the rapid and dramatic transformations in the ways building materials were being reused and in the level of skill with which construction was undertaken.[44] By the last couple of decades of the fourth century, many of the *opus signinum*[45] and mosaic floors of still-occupied buildings were badly in need of repair. A few of these floors were replaced with proper, mortared flagstones on top of newly constructed subfloors,[46] as had been the practice in earlier generations, when floors were invariably installed over subfloors made up of layers of sand, gravel, and cement. More typically, late replacement floors were simply covered over with recycled flagstones and seated without subfloors. We find instances, for example, of mosaic floors initially covered over with mortared flagstone floors, which in turn, after a period of hard ware, were covered over with even later floors made from reused, unmortared flagstones.[47] Other late floors were cobbled together not just from repurposed paving, but from salvaged material that had not previously served as flooring. A good example of this is found at the villa at Barnsley Park, in Gloucestershire. Sometime after 380, a number of the villa's rooms were paved over with mostly recycled stone flagging, taken from its now derelict west wing. But mixed in with the flagstones were hypocaust channel covers and architectural stonework, including two plinths, which in earlier years had embellished the villa's main entrance (Figure 15).[48]

Stone formerly used in facades, walls, or slate roofs was also repurposed as flooring in the temples of Sulis Minerva, in Bath, and Maiden Castle, in Dorset, and at the villas of Atworth, in Wiltshire, and Bucknowle, in Dorset.[49] The floor of a late post-Roman apsed building at Housesteads is especially telling (Figure 16). The people laying it used a collection of very large, mismatched stone blocks, salvaged from the walls of a derelict building, to create an extremely hummocky pavement.[50] In a practical sense the floor would not have functioned very well as a floor, which suggests that for the building's commissioners the idea of a stone floor was more important than a floor that actually worked.

Other late floors were made up of scavenged building material, perched atop loose, uneven, rubble-strewn surfaces, without subfloors, mortar, clay, or any other binding. Such floors look more like consolidation exercises than new floors. One was found at Redlands Farm, where sandstone flags were laid directly over a layer of masonry that had collapsed into a room.[51] A similar strategy was employed in the post-Roman period at Birdoswald, where mixes of unbonded, broken flagstones, reused roofing slates, and other flat stones were employed in the same way.[52] Elsewhere people refloored rooms with roofing tiles or roofing slates arranged in neat rows without mortar, and occasionally they dumped crushed Roman-period tile or limestone chips over badly worn floors.[53] A grab bag of

FIGURE 15. A floor at the villa at Barnsley Park, Gloucester, dated after 380 and made from recycled stone flagging, hypocaust channel covers, and architectural stonework. (G. Webster and L. Smith, "The Excavation of a Romano-British Rural Establishment at Barnsley Park, Gloucestershire, 1961–1979: Part II c. AD 260–400+," *Transactions of the Bristol and Gloucestershire Archaeological Society*, 100 [1982], 65–189, plate 1a. Photo reproduced with kind permission of the Bristol and Gloucestershire Archaeological Society.)

materials—random mixes of roofing slates and building rubble—was also collected during the final phase of occupation, and used for sloppy, stopgap repairs of failing floors.[54]

So, although a few late relaid floors were well crafted and built by craftsmen still fluent in Roman-period building practices, more often they look like amateur efforts, each one bad in its own way—installed either by people who had access to previously used stone and a desire to carry on having hard-surfaced, inorganic floors but did not know how such floors had been laid in the past, or by people who did know but no longer had the materials or the skilled labor to build floors in traditional ways. Late floors, then, expose fundamental changes in both reuse and

FIGURE 16. The uneven floor of a post-Roman apsed building at Housesteads, built from recycled building stone. (Photo reproduced with kind permission of the Tyne and Wear Archives and Museums.)

construction practices. They also highlight the disappearance of elegant, purpose-built, high-status spaces. The activities that once took place there were being overwritten by the new imperative to smelt or malt within the confines of estate centers.

Late-built walls tell a similar story. There were still builders in the late Roman and early post-Roman period constructing traditional stone-faced walls with strongly mortared rubble cores or bonded tile courses made from reused material.[55] The latest London riverside wall, for example, built in the last decade of the fourth century, had two mortared faces, and the space in between was filled with alternating layers of rubble and mortar.[56] Elsewhere, though, builders were putting up walls that no longer met traditional standards. Instead of filling the space between the faces with alternating layers of rubble and mortar, builders who continued to build traditional double-faced walls now sometimes filled them with earth. Other late builders bonded their walls not with mortar, but with mud or clay. Others still were constructing single-wythe walls, cobbled together from recycled building material that had not first been sorted by general size and shape, as would have been done a few decades earlier. Some were bonded with low-quality mortar, others with clay or mud. In the latest occupation phases of some buildings, we also come across newly built interior drystone walls made from scavenged rubble, facing stones, roofing material, and brick. Such walls often blocked no-longer-used doorways or served as wall sills for new timber or cob partitions put up to divide large rooms into smaller ones. Such partitions are standard features in the final occupation stages of once-grand spaces.[57]

During the same period, there is also evidence for the small-scale, opportunistic scavenging of building material to build or repair industrial features, including the corn driers, hearths, and bread ovens now operating in what had formerly been expensively decorated rooms. This was the case for a corn drier, probably dating to the early fifth century, inserted into the still partially occupied Roman-period aisled hall at Fullerton. Its main firing chamber was lined with eight courses of tile—a scrappy assortment of whole tiles, broken box tile, and square bricks, scavenged from defunct buildings on the site.[58] Similarly, a preexisting oven in Verulamium Insula XIV, Building 3 was amateurishly relined with an ill-assorted collection of scavenged tiles (Figure 17).[59]

The late floors and walls just described were built in ways that related to long-standing practices of reuse and construction. A few were ambitious in scope and used considerable supplies of finished stone, rubble, tile, or brick and were the work of skilled craftsmen. More often, though, late-stage construction efforts were small-scale, mend-and-make-do affairs, undertaken to shore up failing structures or to retrofit them with industrial features. Reused materials in the last couple of decades of the fourth century were rarely presorted by size or type or redeployed in the same ways that they had originally been used. And the builders of both masonry floors and walls used much less mortar than they had in earlier generations.[60]

The lack of proficiency with which late-phase construction was undertaken suggests a rapid deskilling within the building trades. It would be interesting to know more about the processes that stood behind this loss of craft knowledge. One contributing factor may have been that as smaller villas began to fail in the mid-fourth century, the demand for the services of construction crews waned as well, and because of this it became increasingly difficult, as the years went by, for them to make a living. As it became harder in Britain to sustain networks of skilled workers, those who still built or refurbished would have had to make do with less expertise, and while they might be able to do some things in traditional ways, for other tasks they would need to improvise or make do.

Four late construction projects illustrate how one set of building skills might persist in a place while others disappeared. The first was undertaken at the villa at Atworth, in Wiltshire, where we find evidence that skills associated with hypocaust construction were still alive and well at the end of the Roman

FIGURE 17. An oven in Verulamium Insula XIV, Building 3, both before and after it was unskillfully re-lined. (S. Frere, *Verulamium Excavations*, 2 vols. [London, 1972–84], vol. 2, plates Xa and Xb. Photos reproduced with kind permission of the London Society of Antiquaries.)

Figure 18. The reworked hypocaust at Atworth, made from recycled building stone and floor tiles. (A. S. Mellor and R. Goodchild. "The Roman Villa at Atworth, Wilts," *Wiltshire Archaeological and Natural History Magazine*, 49 [1940–2], 46–95, plate IX. Photo reproduced with kind permission of the Wiltshire Museum, Devizes.)

period and beyond. The villa's late Roman baths, built after 364,[61] were extensively modified at some later date. The furnace room was transformed into a stone-floored storeroom, a nearby room was remodeled to serve as the new furnace room, and the hypocaust was reconfigured to heat just two rooms.[62] At the same time, the bath's *caldarium* was refashioned into a corn drier.[63] This project was carried out entirely with reused building stone, architectural fragments, and large floor tiles stripped from other parts of the villa (Figure 18).[64] Although the site's earliest excavators opined that this remodeling had been executed in a "slovenly fashion,"[65] it is hard not to be impressed by the confidence of the person whose work it was, and the success of their undertaking. The dating of these changes, as is so often the case in Britain, is problematic, but the site has produced large numbers of fourth-century coins—the latest of which dates to the time of Theodosius (379–95)—as well as late fourth- or early fifth-century glass, metalwork, bracelets, and pottery.[66] So the hypocaust may well have been in use in the fifth century: it might have even been built then.

A second example is found at the villa site at Wortly, in Gloucestershire. In the mid-fifth century, although people here were no longer either capable of or interested in constructing mortared masonry buildings—they had moved on to timber—a small four-post structure was built, and remarkably, it was roofed in the old Roman way, with recycled Old Red Sandstone tiles and ceramic *imbrices*. So here, well into the fifth century, someone in the neighborhood still knew how to put up a masonry roof.[67] Our third example is from the roadside settlement at Heybridge, in Essex. A timber building with an alcove was built here, probably after 400, and someone installed a tessellated floor in the alcove. Although not a figurative mosaic, it was a floor laid with *tesserae* nonetheless, so someone here knew something about how to make such a floor.[68] Finally, in Litchfield, someone in the post-Roman period built a small, two-celled building from recycled stone, some of it still with traces of Roman-period mortar. The stone walls were bonded with clay, and the interior of the building was plastered.[69] These examples illustrate the way bits and pieces of expertise persisted in different places into the fifth century, but nowhere did the full package of Roman construction and reuse techniques endure. The interlocking webs of skill and knowledge that lay behind so much Roman-period production, which had been fully operational in many parts of lowland Britain a couple of generations earlier, had simply fallen apart. The result of such piecemeal deskilling was a terminal rupture in Roman-period ways of doing and making.[70]

The loss of networks of skilled labor meant not only that it would no longer be possible to build Roman-style masonry buildings, but that the people who had the skills to keep such buildings upright were disappearing as well. As indestructible and eternal as large stone structures appear, their survival is predicated on constant repair. Stewart Brand's catalogue of the things even the heartiest buildings are up against is worth quoting in full:

> The root of all evil is water. It dissolves buildings. Water is elixir to unwelcome life such as rot and insects. Water, the universal solvent, makes chemical reactions happen every place you don't want them. It consumes wood, erodes masonry, corrodes metals, peels paint, expands destructively when it freezes, and permeates everywhere when it evaporates. It warps, swells, discolors, rusts, loosens, mildews, and stinks...
>
> Because of water, houses deteriorate most from the bottom up and the top down. Damage comes from below thanks to what the British call, knowledgeably, "damp." Moisture from the ground rises by

capillary action into foundations and seeps into cellars and treats a building like a very large lump of sugar. Still, top-down is the main event. Water can rise only a few feet, but it can descend and branch out indefinitely. A building's most important organ of health is its roof.[71]

Without a ready pool of skilled labor, Britain's many thousands of masonry buildings were doomed.

A constellation of vernacular building practices, such as timber-framing techniques and the kinds of stone construction techniques communities had long used down on the farm or in roadside settlements—drystone construction; walls composed of rough stone, chalk blocks, or flints bonded in clay; or the use of unmortared stone, chalk, or clay in the footings of timber buildings—persisted into the immediate post-Roman period and beyond, because the skill sets that stood behind these activities were commonplace in the kinds of settlements where low-status people had always built for themselves.[72] That we find the construction techniques of low-status workers being used in very late and immediately post-Roman urban, military, and villa sites suggests that many of those with the power to build or remodel in this late period could no longer call on professional, itinerant construction crews, and had, instead, to depend on local labor. This may also explain why, as we move forward in time, less recycled building material was collected and used: not only were the people skilled in taking buildings apart hard to come by, but brick, tile, and building stone had never been of much use to most people in Britain. Indeed, there are hints that some late architectural salvage operations were not after stone, brick, or tile, but were, rather, collecting large, reusable timber beams.[73]

A few early post-Roman structures also took advantage of still-standing stone walls or stone from ruinous buildings. Timber structures, for example, were occasionally constructed as lean-tos against still-standing Roman-period masonry walls, as happened at Haddon and Uley.[74] At other sites, such as the villas at Latimer and Castle Copse, stone from abandoned buildings was used to make footings for the sleeper beams of new timber buildings.[75] Elsewhere still, scavenged building stone was used to create stone rafts for timber buildings, as found at Cirencester courtyard House VI.3, Frocester, and many other places.[76] And under exceptional circumstances, a few Roman-period buildings survived upright and in use. The aisled stone building at Deerton Street was one such building: it still had its masonry roof and continued to be remodeled in the late fifth century, when the people working on the site were using both handmade pots and imported, wheel-thrown wares from the continent.[77]

But these were exceptions. In spite of the many thousands of abandoned Roman-period masonry structures, few people after c. 450 availed themselves of their brick and stone.[78] Occasionally householders might use a few Roman bricks or tiles to make their hearths or furnaces;[79] and a handful of craftspeople in the early Middle Ages fashioned ingot molds out of Roman tiles.[80] Stone quarried in the Roman period was reused on early medieval settlement sites only slightly more often. Excavations have uncovered a little of this material at three of the hillforts reoccupied in the post-Roman period.[81] Roman stone and brick, however, were never used in the construction of new masonry buildings, the way they were elsewhere in the post-Roman West. Like literacy, Christianity, and Latinity, the skills needed to construct Roman-style masonry buildings were lost in this period and would be reintroduced into eastern Britain only in the early seventh century by foreign missionaries, who revived the practice. So, Roman quarried stone and Roman-period brick and tile—however omnipresent they might have been and however useful to builders from the seventh century on—were for the most part left untouched in the fifth and sixth centuries by those constructing new buildings.

Farewells Etched in Stone

Almost all of Britain's masonry buildings were deserted and in ruins by 450. The decline of some, such as Little Oakely, in Essex, and Frocester, in Gloucester, were gradual, as they first grew shabby and were then repurposed and transformed into industrial spaces. Later still, people on these sites abandoned their old masonry buildings completely and lived and labored instead in new-style timber buildings constructed atop rubble rafts next to the ruins. Eventually, though, not only were the stone buildings abandoned; so, too, were the settlement sites themselves.[82] Other villas had more abrupt ends. The people in charge of masonry buildings sometimes marked their abandonments with solemn acts that involved both building material and wells.[83] Again and again, during these events, people deposited large amounts of building material into nearby wells, obstructing and fouling them, and ending their careers as viable water sources. On these occasions jaw-dropping amounts of stone roofing shingles, *tegulae*, *imbrices*, *pilae*, worked stone, building rubble, wooden building fixtures, cement, and plaster were purposefully thrown down wells. Many of these well closures took place in the decades on either side of 400, which makes the well fills generated by them one of the period's most archaeologically visible sites of building-material repurposing. We have already examined one well-closure event at Shadwell,[84] but more than fifty others have been identified, which date to the period of Roman/medieval transition.[85]

Besides material stripped from buildings, people participating in well-closure events placed at least some of a standard assemblage of objects in their wells: partial or whole animals, including animal heads, notably dogs and deer but also cattle, sheep, goats, pigs, horses, and birds; human remains, especially skulls; coins, quern stones, and shoes (more often left than right!); complete or nearly complete ceramic pots and pewter or copper vessels; and oyster shells and hazelnuts. It was long held that mundane reasons stood behind these deposits—everything from cat-and-dog fights,[86] to dog population control measures,[87] to Pictish raiders,[88] building-site clearance schemes,[89] and accidental falls.[90] It is also true that people in the Roman period regularly used abandoned wells for rubbish disposal, especially for butchering waste.[91] But included among the kinds of objects repeatedly found in well deposits are things that were unlikely to have been considered rubbish—not just the human remains, but whole or nearly whole herbivore carcasses, the bodies of rare birds, undamaged pots, and pewter or bronze vessels—and this argues that these deposits were not the result of mundane, everyday activities.[92] They were also made in a specific context—a well—and they commemorated a particular event—an abandonment. Indeed, a similar complex of objects was also used during the Roman period to mark the decommissioning of corn driers,[93] pottery kilns,[94] watering holes,[95] shrines,[96] and ditches;[97] and many of the same objects can be found in structured deposits placed in purpose-built shafts.[98]

Structured deposits in wells have a very long history in Britain, so our late and immediately post-Roman well deposits should be seen not as a new tradition, but rather as the tail end of broader practices of deposition, which long marked the transition between use and abandonment and which had been a meaningful activity for large numbers of people in Britain since the pre-Roman Iron Age.[99] The predictable grammar of these depositions, the lack of what we might think of as a utilitarian explanation for their contents, and their repeated focus on wells help us interpret them as something more than accidental or routine. Indeed, they meet Catherine Bell's definition of a ritualized act: "a way of acting that is designed and orchestrated to distinguish what is being done in comparison to other, usually more quotidian practices."[100] It would be wrong, then, to view these depositions as irrational. The people who orchestrated and participated in these often labor- and resource-intensive acts must have believed in their efficacy. Besides marking an important rite of passage from use to nonuse, these acts may have been undertaken to ensure certain outcomes now lost to us.[101] So, although we may not be able to discern what the hoped-for results were, we can nonetheless detail the practice, especially as so many were so similar.[102]

Most of the scholarship on well deposits has focused on the pottery, small finds, and faunal and human remains recovered from them and ignores the Roman-period building material that often makes up the bulk of the fills. Many excavation reports fail to mention its presence at all, although it is often illustrated in their figures; and others note its existence only in passing with phrases such as "and the usual rubble." As a result, it is not possible to analyze this material systematically, because fills are often inadequately recorded.[103] Indeed, only a handful of people have speculated as to whether building stone was deliberately deposited in wells.[104] Nor is it always possible, based on excavation reports, to determine how many different depositing episodes stand behind each well fill. Some wells have distinctive layers within their backfills, which suggest the passing of time between multiple and discrete deposition episodes.[105] At other times, though, the distinction between layers is not at all clear.[106] Many also preserve evidence for what Ralph Merrifield identified as "commencement" deposits, often in the form of a whole pot or two placed in the well to mark the beginning of its life as a water source.[107] Some also include objects—such as buckets and ceramic water-carrying vessels—that had likely fallen in accidentally while the well served as a water source. And the fills of many wells slumped in the years after they were abandoned, and the depressions that resulted have filled with yet other deposits, formed long after the well had been abandoned.[108] Painstaking analyses of a few recently excavated wells, however, do suggest that these features were often backfilled in relatively short order,[109] and occasionally we can say with some certainty that the bulk of the fill was generated by a single event.[110] In short, although well fills may have formed over time, there is evidence for major, terminal depositing episodes in many, which would have marked their ends as functioning water sources.

We will examine the contents of just two wells in detail, both the results of closure events dating sometime after 370. The first is the impressively capacious well associated with the late Roman bathhouse at the villa of Rudston, in Yorkshire. The stone-lined well was thirty meters deep and 2.75 meters in diameter.[111] Its fill contained massive amounts of building debris, including building stone, *tesserae*, and wall plaster, much of it likely derived from the villa's dismantled bathhouse, as well as a limestone block carved with a figure of a deity and broken stone troughs.[112] At least two partially articulated red deer were also placed in the well, alongside nine lambs and the remains of cattle, horses, pigs, and chickens.[113]

There were large amounts of pottery as well, mostly late Huntcliff and Crambeck wares, much of it in a layer associated with three coins dated between 364 and 378, and at least some of the pots were likely deposited whole.[114] The pottery assemblage is comparable to one recovered from the collapsed Building 3 at Beadlam villa, and it dates this segment of the deposit to the very late fourth or early fifth century.[115]

A similar fill was found in another bathhouse well, this one at the villa at Dalton Parlours, in Yorkshire. Its sixteen-meter-deep shaft was packed with literally tons of building material. It included dressed stone, stone columns, and gritstone and limestone rubble, likely derived from the walls of the bathhouse. There were also large numbers of sandstone roofing shingles and ceramic roof tiles, *pilae*, *tesserae*, painted plaster, and structural timber. Like so many of the period's well fills, this one included large numbers of leather shoes, quern stones, and iron tools, including an anvil, a mason's pick, and a collection of ox goads. The remains of large numbers of animals were also in the fill, some whole or nearly whole when placed in the well, and there were more than a dozen skulls of cattle and horses as well as human remains. Finally, there were large amounts of pottery—almost all coarse-ware jars—including three pots made after c. 370, which allow us to date the event to the closing years of the Roman period. Shifting so much material across the site and down the shaft of the well would not have been a trivial matter. Wrestling not just the many cubic meters of manageable-sized material, but whole or nearly whole cattle carcasses and a threshold stone weighing some 900 kilograms into the well would have required gangs of supervised labor.[116]

The inexplicable (to us) individual components of these deposits are suggestive of some of the actions that stood behind them—the selection of still-useful vessels for deposition, the killing of animals, the retrieval of curated human remains, the hard work of dismantling masonry structures and the considerable manpower exerted to haul some portion of them—in some cases many tons of material—to the well. Behind the great events such as those that took place at Rudston and Dalton Parlours, we can sense the presence of powerful individuals who were able to press people into labor, who had the right to destroy property, who commanded the herds from which the slaughtered animals were taken, and who had the leisure time, the skills, or the staff to procure deer. The grander of these events must have been bloody, noisy, dramatic, costly, and monumental in scale. More modest closure events were less extravagant, but even when these wells were obstructed and fouled, animals were killed, shoes deposited, and pieces of buildings offered up to wells, because the people presiding over such doings shared the same basic understanding as grander people of what was proper and necessary at such events. Well closures could involve markedly different amounts of deposited material, and it looks as if the wealthiest sites often had the most notable events. Nonetheless, whether on grand sites or modest ones, these deposits shared a basic structure, which their participants must have deemed fundamental.[117] Marianne Hem Eriksen, writing about similar events accompanying the abandonment of houses in Iron Age and Viking Age Scandinavia, reminds us that "the house was an agglomerate of agencies, constituting an embodied *meshwork* of people, things, animals, and materials.... This meshwork—the *housebody*—was to some extent perceived as agential, capturing some of the essence of the household.... When the house was abandoned, this was understood as the death of the meshwork."[118] The highly choreographed well-closure events in Britain in the decades around 400, in the period that saw the death of such vital meshworks, capture some of the trauma that must have been associated with the abandonment of masonry buildings.

The more than fifty well deposits dating to the final decades of the fourth century and the first decades of the fifth argue that closure events were relatively common in these years, and that many people living in the period would have witnessed or heard about them.[119] The ubiquity of repurposed building material in them also suggests that well deposits were an important site for the reuse of building material during this period. Yet, in spite of evidence for a widespread agreement that repurposed building material was a necessary component in the activities undertaken to mark the death of buildings, settlements, and their wells, this practice did not survive much past the mid-fifth century. Although people in Britain in the late fifth century and beyond sometimes marked the abandonment of buildings with structured deposits,[120] wells ceased to be the site of such activity, and recycled building material no longer featured in them. So people in Britain not only abandoned, for the most part, the pragmatic redeployment of Roman building material in the early post-Roman period, but they ceased using it in traditional events that marked the abandonment of buildings and settlements, a sign that old ways and old ideas were losing their grip as Britain moved from Roman to medieval.

Although Roman building material ceased being considered a critical component of structured deposits, small amounts of scavenged Roman building material were occasionally included in post-Roman graves, suggesting that ideas about its ritual reuse survived in places.[121] In the early fifth century, for example, when the west wing of the partially demolished villa at Redlands Farm, in Northamptonshire, became the site of infant burial, the tessellated pavement originally laid in room 1114 was removed, and some of its *tesserae* were used to seal babies' graves.[122] More common, although still rare, was the repurposing of Roman-period building material for the making of cists. In the early Middle Ages, groups presiding over a cremation burial at Caistor-by-Norwich and a couple of inhumations at Irchester, in Northamptonshire, constructed cists out of Roman-period tile and slate roofing shingles.[123] A few graves excavated at the cemetery at Broughton Lodge, in Nottinghamshire, were lined with what look like cobbles from a nearby defunct Roman road, and another grave there included stones salvaged from a Roman building, including part of a column base.[124] At the early medieval cemetery at Butler's Field, Lechlade, a handful of graves included worked limestone, probably brought to the cemetery from the nearby ruined villa at Roughground Farm;[125] and reused Roman-period quarried stone (one piece with bits of plaster still adhering to it) lined one side of a grave at the cemetery at Wasperton, in Warwickshire.[126] At the Bainesse cemetery, in Yorkshire, one post-Roman grave had a cist partially constructed from stone armchair *voussoirs* from a bathhouse.[127] At Cleatham, a number of graves included pieces of worked stone in their fill, which had probably been scavenged from the villa at Mount Pleasant, a half kilometer from the cemetery. Interestingly, they were found in graves dated to both the fifth and the seventh centuries.[128] A few post-Roman cemeteries in Scotland also had cists made from recycled Roman stone, probably salvaged from nearby abandoned Roman forts.[129]

In a few instances, substantial rather than token amounts of repurposed Roman-period masonry were employed in this way. Impressive amounts of worked stone, including a pedestal and a limestone column, were used in a notably large fifth-century cist in a small cemetery founded next to the once grand temple-mausoleum at Bancroft, in Buckinghamshire (Figure 19). Another grave in the same small cemetery was lined with pieces of dressed limestone, *tegulae*, *imbrices*, and a chunk of *opus signinum*.[130] Still, this kind of reuse was rare, and with the exception of the Bancroft graves, these redeployments look more opportunistic than symbolic, and in reality, perhaps any close-to-hand stone would have done for most of these graves. After all, at cemeteries such as Broughton Lodge, where many graves included stones, only a fraction came from Roman-period structures.[131] So, although some of the reused material may have been significant to the rites being performed, their meanings were highly local or personal, rather than commonly understood symbolic moves undertaken by larger numbers of people.

Abandoned Roman sites were also occasionally used for post-Roman burial. The reuse of ancient monuments for burial is something we see a lot of between the fifth and seventh centuries, but the proclivity for this increased dramatically over time. And although Roman sites were, on occasion, used for

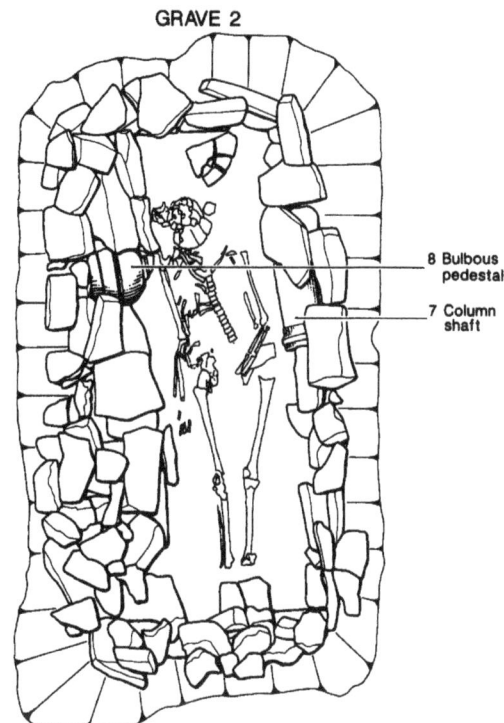

FIGURE 19. A post-Roman cist made from Roman-period *spolia* at Bancroft. (R. J. Williams and R. J. Zeepvat, *Bancroft: A Late Bronze/Iron Age Settlement, Roman Villa, and Temple Mausoleum*, 2 vols. [Milton Keynes, 1994], vol. 1, fig. 56. Illustration by David Williams. Figure reproduced with kind permission of the Buckinghamshire Archaeological Society.)

burial, Bronze Age barrows were much more commonly chosen by early medieval cemetery founders.[132]

Structuring Structures

By 500, people living in Britain might occasionally incorporate a still-standing Roman-period stone wall or floor into one of their new timber structures,[133] go looking for a few bricks or tiles to use for a hearth, or poke through a ruinous building in search of iron, lead, or old Roman pots. But most turned their backs resolutely on Roman buildings and the mountains of building materials harbored in their ruins. By the middle of the fifth century, the long-standing material practices related to the use and reuse of these buildings and the materials that made them were gone.

The decline and fall of masonry structures and the kinds of activities that took place within them, as well as the fate of the materials that went into their construction, are worth some thought, because the lives of both elites and those who hauled, worked, and sweated for them were entangled, during the late Roman period, with high-status buildings. In many parts of Britain, masonry buildings served as important markers of social and occupational difference. They were "structuring structures," not just for the people living within their walls, but for the people who helped build and maintain them and for all those who caught sight of them as they moved through the landscape.[134] Stone buildings monumentalized social difference,[135] and in the third and early fourth centuries, they created the illusion that the asymmetrical relationships and grossly unequal hierarchies of the late empire were set in stone. They also helped constitute both elite subjectivity and a kind of corporate identity for those who controlled and benefited from them.[136] Both the late-phase campaigns to keep stone buildings operating and the events that sometimes marked their ends are evidence that some, in the decades on either side of 400, continued to insist that the old social order was intact. But as these practices faded away, there must have been a dramatic reordering, especially when we enter a period when the ruined carapaces of so many stone buildings would have announced the end of the old order.

Much ink has been expended on detailing the role that villa residences played in the fourth century in elite social competition. Scholars often characterize these buildings as active participants in the tumultuous politics of the period and view them first and foremost as part of the "competitive discourse" between men of rank and substance, and as places where pecking orders and obligations could be established between the kinds of people who were invited into these buildings' most splendid rooms.[137] Considerable scholarship has also been devoted to considering the impact on the landscape of the most elaborate villa buildings, as viewed by the privileged visitors who traveled toward them.[138] We should, however, be equally attentive to their other, larger audience—the bottom 85 percent of Britain's population. Such villas' gleaming stone facades, smoke-billowing bathhouses, and massive barns were in direct conversation with Britain's laboring populations. For the people who worked in their shadows, villa compounds underscored social inequality: impressive domestic compounds, as Claude Lévi-Strauss put it, "naturalize differences in social status and competition for wealth."[139] In a similar way, the stone architecture of Roman forts reminded those living in their hinterlands of the permanence of the imperial regime. Thus, stone buildings served as the punch line for every winning argument about the timelessness of hierarchy and inequality, and they were proof that both the colonial regime and its highly unequal social structures were eternal.

I suspect, moreover, that these highly visible buildings also monumentalize privilege to labor,[140] because their construction was made possible, at least in part, by great men's ability to co-opt the labor, animals, fodder, and food stores of local dependents when they set about building or rebuilding in stone. Such architectural projects, then, would have been closely tied to the disciplining of labor. Although specialist construction crews, as we have seen, likely arrived on site with full complements of skilled workers, building in stone required huge amounts of backbreaking, unskilled work. Many hands and feet were needed to shift rubble, cut stone, and move roofing materials off wagons or around building sites; to haul punishing amounts of water, sand, and lime for mortar; to mix mountains of cement, and dig foundations.[141] Locals may have also been required to provide some of their precious surplus to feed skilled incomers and their animals. If this was indeed the case, it would never have been good news for ordinary people when the boss decided to build a new bathhouse or to grandify his living quarters.

So the episodic, once-a-generation villa refurbishments and aggrandizements so clear in the archaeological record not only enhanced and updated interiors, facades, and courtyard gardens and impressed a great man's familiars, but they disciplined the labor of his dependents, reminding them every few decades about how the world worked. These projects naturalized social inferiors' acquiescence to the demands of the colonial regime and their social betters.[142] Appropriated labor is almost always a central feature of colonialism and serves as an important medium for social control and domination.[143] Thus the impossibility, in the very late Roman and post-Roman period, of continuing repurposing and construction techniques related to masonry buildings both signaled and ushered in fundamental changes in the ways power and status would be expressed in the coming generations. When such campaigns were no longer possible, when elites could no longer call skilled work crews in, get hold of large amounts of building materials, and bully local laborers into work—it was then that the mechanisms for showing the world who was in charge could no longer be depended on to make social difference. And when these sites were in their final, dilapidated stages, or sat abandoned and ruinous, what a different statement they must have made in the landscape.

We have been conditioned by the tenth-century Old English poem *The Ruin* to imagine that the reactions Roman ruins elicited in the early Middle Ages were nostalgia and regret:

> Wondrous is this wall stone; disastrous events have shattered it;
> the fortified cities have broken apart, the work of giants decays.
> Roofs have fallen, towers are ruinous,

> The ring gate is destroyed, frost is on the mortar,
> The gaping protectors against storms are rent, have collapsed,
> Undermined by age . . .
> Bright were the city buildings, many bathing halls,
> An abundance of high gables, much martial noise,
> Many mead halls full of human joys,
> Until fate the mighty changed that.[144]

But the end stages of these buildings would have carried quite different cultural and political meanings for those who had been oppressed because of them, and they must have held an interpretive and explanatory power that carried an altogether different meaning from the message these buildings had telegraphed before Rome's fall.

CHAPTER 6

Metal Production Under and After Rome

> How the hell do some rocks become a toaster?
> —Thomas Thwaites, *The Toaster Project: Or a Heroic Attempt to Build a Simple Electric Appliance from Scratch*

This chapter recounts one of the major but forgotten stories of transition from Roman to early medieval in Britain—the collapse of Rome's metal economy. It first lays out the ways people went about producing and procuring metal in Britain in the Roman period and then traces the fate of metal production in the first couple of centuries after Rome. Finally, the chapter describes changes that began to take hold in England in the sixth century and argues that access to freshly smelted metal and the ability to produce it helped drive important economic and social transformations in the later sixth and seventh centuries, including the development of a steeply hierarchical society that is much in evidence in the eastern half of Britain by the time St. Augustine arrived in England. In short, metal supply sits at the center of two important developments in the years between c. 350 and c. 600. The first of these is the move from the highly stratified, surplus-producing society of the late Roman period to one marked by subsistence agriculture and only limited signs of social differentiation. The second is the move back toward hierarchy and surplus controlled by elites. Metal, in short, was implicated in both the move of many communities toward subsistence farming in the fifth century, and the eventual reestablishment of a surplus-generating, hierarchical society in the later sixth and seventh centuries.

Late Roman Britain's Metal Economy

Mining, metallurgy, and smithing stood at the heart of the Roman economy. Each year something on the order of one hundred thousand metric tons each of lead and iron and about fifteen thousand tons of copper were produced within imperial territory. Britain alone generated an estimated 2,250 tons of iron per annum.[1] The Greenland ice dramatically captures a record of the grand scale of Roman metal production, preserving evidence of a fourfold increase in tropospheric lead pollution in the first four centuries of the Common Era and an order of magnitude more copper-smelting pollution than found during the nineteenth century's Industrial Revolution.[2] By no means would all Roman-period objects, however, have been fabricated from freshly smelted metal. There is considerable evidence from across the Roman world for the recycling of a whole range of basic materials, including metals.[3] Scrap iron, lead, and bronze, for example, were regularly collected in Britain at military forts and rural sites, probably for smiths to rework.[4] Between large-scale mining and smelting on the one hand and systematic recycling on the other, the metal stock available within the empire increased dramatically over time.[5]

Experimental archaeologists have attempted to calculate the number of man-hours needed to transform ore in the ground into useable iron. Peter Crew managed to create a useable iron bar with one hundred kilograms of charcoal and twenty-five days of work, but Romans had to have produced iron more efficiently than this, given the metal's cheapness and its ubiquity, and given the fact that hundreds of thousands of tons of iron were produced within the empire under Rome. Indeed, David Sim, with the aid of a back-of-the-envelope calculation, has observed that if Crew's numbers are correct, the estimated 2,250 tons of finished, smithable iron produced in Britain each year would have require eighty-eight million man-hours per annum, proving, if nothing else, that Romans were better ironworkers than modern archaeologists are.[6] Whatever the actual figures, many steps and processes as well as much expertise, labor, and fuel stood behind the seemingly humble iron objects found on every Romano-British site in lowland Britain.

Both the scale and the success of smelters and smiths are illustrated by a find that is simultaneously quotidian and astonishing: at the short-lived first-century Roman fort at Inchtuthil, in Scotland, a cache of almost one million well-made nails has been recovered, fabricated in a variety of standard sizes and hardnesses: the longer nails contained more carbon steel, because they needed to withstand more hammering than shorter nails.[7] This outsized cache of nails is but one example of the astonishing success of iron producers and blacksmiths during the Roman period, something that would be unmatched after Rome's fall until the late Middle Ages.

One of the consequences of Rome's capacity to produce and reuse metal on the scale it did, is that wherever one went within the empire, including Britain, markets were brimming with inexpensive, ready-to-smith metal and impressive selections of finished metal goods; and rural settlements, even very modest ones, had good access to workable iron and to metal tools and fixtures.[8] This superabundance, in turn, helped metal insinuate itself into most facets of most people's lives. Shoes, loaves of bread, glass vessels, culinary herbs, stone-footed buildings, and carts, alongside hundreds of other everyday things, were created with its aid. Not only was metal implicated in the production of much of the period's material culture, but it made humans, their work animals, and the landscapes in which they made their livings more productive than they would otherwise have been.[9] Readily available metal was also crucial for imperial administrators and local elites, who, by the late Roman period, depended on the surplus wealth that metal helped create to maintain their positions and live the good life.

Behind the mountains of ready-to-use lead, copper, and iron stood a series of highly organized manufacturing processes, carefully marshaled resources, and crowds of specialist workers, some of whom may have engaged in this work only seasonally.[10] Three labor-intensive processes had to be undertaken in order to produce finished iron objects—the smelting of iron ore in a purpose-built furnace, which transformed the ore into a bloom of iron (a spongy lump of iron with many impurities); the reheating and repeated hammering of the bloom, which rid it of some of the impurities left by the smelting process, and welded together the iron particles of the bloom in order to make a workable billet or bar; and finally, the blacksmithing of the finished iron into useable objects. Each of these processes, in turn, required multiple intermediate steps—the mining and breaking up of iron ore; its roasting, further breaking up, washing, and sorting; the production of copious amounts of charcoal and all that that entailed (it took something on the order of eighty-two kilos of charcoal to produce a billet of iron);[11] the building, usually from clay, of smelting furnaces; the organizing of large amounts of the skilled labor and muscle to undertake all these associated tasks; and the marshaling of wagons, oxen, barges, and teamsters, first to move the various raw materials and then to transport the finished metal.[12] And, of course, there were institutions and individuals powerful enough to supervise highly managed landscapes, which allowed for the systematic husbanding of woodland resources so crucial for making the tens of thousands of tons of charcoal necessary each year for this scale of metal production, and powerful institutions that helped oversee policing, markets, and the distribution of capital.[13] The networks of institutions, raw-material providers, and skilled and unskilled workers, as well as the imperial economy in which they operated, knitted together the landscapes in which ironworkers were able to produce such copious amounts of iron and to which iron users had ready access. In short, iron fixtures and iron tools, like pots and building material, were widely available because of the complex networks of supply, production, and transportation that developed, extended, and flourished in Britain under Rome.

The Fall of the Metal Economy

In the middle of the fourth century, the metal economy in Britain began to unravel. There are signs, c. 350, that a few long-standing smelting sites and some of the small towns, so crucial for the distribution of iron and iron objects, had begun to decline.[14] Ariconium (Weston under Penyard) in Herefordshire, for example, a site of iron making and iron smithing since the Iron Age, lost most of its population, probably because smelting operations there ceased having an outlet for their iron because of the reorganization, midcentury, of the ways troops along Hadrian's Wall were supplied.[15] If ironworking concerns at Ariconium were, indeed, no longer provisioning military settlements, the settlement's abandonment exemplifies the critical role military provisioning within Britain sometimes played in even medium-scale industrial activities and the ways it helped to underwrite the prosperity of many communities and the specialist workers who lived within them, be they salters, potters, or iron smelters. Although Ariconium and other smelting sites were winding down midcentury, smelting continued unabated in other places. In the following decades, however, as more roadside settlements, villas, and finally the state itself failed in Britain, the production of freshly smelted metal became very much less common.

Across Britain, the collapse of new metal production would have required local communities to rethink the ways they went about procuring this most essential of materials. The strategy many seem to have adopted to compensate for disappearing supplies of fresh metal stock was scavenging. The collection and reuse of a wide variety of materials—not just metal, but glass and building materials— had taken place throughout the Roman period. Although this recycling under Rome was at times undertaken to make up for shortfalls during periods of scarcity,[16] recycling was practiced even when such materials were relatively plentiful. Behind Roman-period recycling—for metals as well as building materials—there were a constellation of practices that allowed for the relatively systematic collection of unwanted or damaged objects and their careful sorting by type and material. There were also systems in place to ensure that scrap was shipped to the specialists who could reuse the various materials being recouped. The massive scale on which recycling took place in the Roman world was facilitated by networks of collectors, brokers, sorters, and shippers.[17] As late as the fifth and sixth centuries in places such as Italy and Gaul, these systems remained intact. Indeed, fairly standardized, temporary industrial installations were regularly built in these centuries in abandoned masonry complexes across the western empire by specialist crews whose job it was to recuperate building materials, glass, bronze, iron, and lead. Given the commonness of this activity in late antiquity, those in the business of recycling must have had ready markets for their recovered materials.[18] No evidence, however, has been found for this kind of large-scale, organized recycling in fifth-century Britain.

What we find, instead, near the end of the fourth century, are groups of smiths beginning to lean very heavily on recycled scrap.[19] We can see them at work, for example, at two long-running Roman metalworking sites, one in Southwark and the other at Ickham, in Kent. Smiths at both places, in the last couple of decades of the fourth century, were reworking motley collections of previously used metal rather than forging items out of newly smelted metal, as had been their practice in earlier decades.[20] Their increasing dependence on scrap likely indicates that the production and supply of freshly smelted metal were breaking down in Britain; and by c. 420, both of these centuries-old metalworking sites had been abandoned. This was in part, no doubt, because of the problems associated with metal supply, but also perhaps because Britain could no longer sustain specialist communities of the skilled workers who had traditionally produced many of their wares for urban markets, villa estates, and the state: entities that were now faltering or extinct. And with the disappearance of specialist metalworking sites and workers, cheap necessities such as nails were harder to come by. Although historians rarely think about nails, it is clear that all our lives would be difficult, if we, or someone in our household or on our city block, had to first procure iron and then make all the nails we use in our lives.[21] In Britain what we see during the last couple of decades of the fourth century is the increasing scarcity of traditional, crucial, and once-common everyday objects that required the use of nails, such as hobnail boots and coffins.[22] Even those with power and status in the fifth century, such as the people in charge of the refortification of the Iron

Age hillfort at Cadbury Castle, in Somerset, no longer seem to have had access to many nails.[23]

Scavenging and recycling came to be the primary way those living in lowland Britain supplied themselves with workable metal. True, a few late Roman iron-smelting communities must have persisted into the fifth and early sixth centuries and passed their metalworking knowledge on to younger generations. The graves excavated at the East Yorkshire cemetery at Kelleythorpe, which lay very near the late Roman iron producing site at Elmswell, may be evidence of one such community: they contained an unusual number of high-quality iron artifacts, including iron brooches.[24] A plethora of iron grave goods was also recovered from the early medieval cemetery at Wakerley, in the Rockingham Forest, where many people in the Roman period had been involved in iron smelting.[25] And at Bestwall Quarry, in Dorset, the radiocarbon dating of charcoal used in a couple of small smelting ovens confirms that a little iron smelting was taking place in the fifth or early sixth century.[26] Similarly, one or two smelting events took place at Quarrington, in Lincolnshire, in the sixth or seventh century.[27] There is also the possibility that smelting in this period was undertaken at some distance from the period's settlements and because of this, post-Roman smelting sites have not been identified.[28] But given the relatively late dates for the forty-some early medieval smelting sites in Britain that have been investigated—generally active from the seventh century on—it seems likely that smelting is much more archaeologically visible for these later years because it had become a more common activity than in the preceding two centuries.

The amount of iron being produced at the few early medieval smelting sites that have been identified was miniscule. We know this, in part, because the process of making iron blooms produces copious amounts of a by-product known as slag—generally something on the order of three kilos of slag for every kilo of iron produced—and it survives well in the archaeological record.[29] Romano-British iron-producing enterprises, over the course of their long years in operation, especially those active before the third century, had often generated tens of thousands of tons of slag.[30] The slag heap covering the Beauport Park bathhouse, in Sussex, built for the people connected with an imperial ironworks there, once contained something on the order of one hundred thousand tons of slag. The slag, in turn, allows us to estimate that large imperial operations such as this one would have produced somewhere between thirty-two and forty-eight tons of workable iron each year. Medium-size, Roman-period operations, such as those at Bardown, Broadfields, and Ariconium, generated less slag and were probably producing ten or fifteen tons of finished iron annually.[31] But smelting also took place on a much smaller scale.[32] Some villa owners invested in iron-making facilities on their estates to produce for their own needs, but also, perhaps, in ways that supplied state actors.[33] The villa at Chesters, in Gloucestershire, for example (again, estimates are based in part on smithing slag), produced about a quarter of a ton of finished iron per annum.[34] All the necessary labor, skills, and natural resources needed for a complex smelting operation would have been available on such an estate.[35] Small-scale iron smelting took place on farmsteads as well, likely representing the part-time production of people who mostly farmed, but were diversifying what they produced, not only to supply themselves with the iron they needed for tools, but probably for the market and for cash.[36] There is some evidence as well to suggest that during the Roman period, itinerant smelting crews were available to produce iron for large construction projects: this, for example, may have happened at the villa at Frocester, in Gloucestershire.[37] Indeed, because smelting activity was so widespread, people did not always feel compelled to collect, recycle, and rework iron: spent iron implements and nails, as a result, were often thrown away.

Even the most modest Roman-period iron-production sites stand in stark contrast to the handful of fifth- and sixth-century sites where smelting continued to take place. At these later sites, archaeologists typically recover only a few kilos of smelting slag.[38] This radical diminution of slag is a direct reflection of the precipitous decline in iron production itself. More than forty dates before 900 have now been acquired for smelting activity in lowland Britain, mostly radiocarbon dates taken from charcoal preserved in early medieval slag heaps or smelting furnaces.[39] Only nine of these might witness smelting in the fifth century, but the date ranges here are very broad, and at all but two of these sites smelting is more likely to have taken place in the late sixth, seventh, or even eighth century than in the fifth. Eight others hint at episodic, small-scale smelting during the sixth century. So, although there is evidence for iron production in England between 400 and 900, very little of it can be assigned to the 150 years after the collapse of the Roman economy, and the little that was produced, made in small-batch bloomery ovens, was heterogeneous and full of impurities.[40]

The state of affairs in Britain is in direct contrast to the situation found elsewhere in the post-Roman West. In France, Italy, Switzerland, the Netherlands, Schleswig-Holstein, and Scandinavia there is unequivocal evidence for relatively large-scale fifth- and sixth-century iron-smelting operations. The magnitude of smelting at these sites was much reduced from the Roman period: the largest were producing something on the order of 10 percent of large-scale Roman concerns; in other words, tens of tons of iron rather than hundreds of tons.[41] Many early medieval smelting sites on the continent have, nonetheless, made impressive marks on the landscape. The remains, for example, of some eight thousand early medieval iron-smelting furnaces have been uncovered in a thirty-five-hectare area centered on Snorup, in Denmark.[42] Early medieval sites of similar scale in Britain, however, have not been found, and the few fifth- or early sixth-century British smelting sites that have been identified represent one-time or episodic operations that produced no more than ten or twenty kilos of iron. So it seems that in Britain—when the villa economy waned, towns lost their populations, and the money economy and the Roman state no longer functioned—it became nearly impossible for iron smelters to continue their specialist production. Once iron making ceased to be a viable way for most ironworkers to make a living, the knowledge of most of the skilled workers involved would disappear.

Thus, we should imagine that accompanying the collapse of the metal economy were a number of other economic dislocations, some the result of the scarcity of basic materials such as metal, others stemming from the deskilling of the population. The end result is clear in the archaeology of fifth-century lowland Britain. The former Roman diocese was now home to a society dependent on small-scale agriculture much reduced from the Roman period.[43] The diminution of surpluses may in part have been an active choice: now that farm families no longer had to hand over much of what they produced for rents and taxes, they were able to settle into more self-sufficient modes of production.[44] But the scarcity of metal must have also affected how much and how effectively people living in the period worked, and I suspect that metal's disappearance should be implicated in declining production.[45] Certainly, metal in this period was used in a much narrower range of tools and played a less central role in the production of material culture.

Scavenging and Subsistence

In spite of the collapse of the metal economy, people in Britain still had access to metal: evidence for the smithing, repairing, and reworking of iron artifacts is ubiquitous on early medieval sites, and in many places so, too, is lead- and copper-alloy working. So where were people in the century after Rome's withdrawal from Britain finding workable base metals? Their most likely source was abandoned Roman-period sites. By the second or third decade of the fifth century many of Britain's towns, manufacturing sites, forts, villas, and temple complexes had been abandoned.[46] But even in their ruinous states, tons of reusable material could be salvaged from them. Derelict stone buildings would have been good places to start, because Roman builders had been profligate in their use of metal. They often employed large iron clamps to hold stone walls together. Tens of thousands of Roman buildings also had iron door and shutter handles, hinges, and hooks; and grills, grates, structural beams, and nails; as well as lead window frames, gutters, and waterpipes.[47] Yet archaeologists rarely recover much architectural metalwork in their excavations of Romano-British structures, probably because scavengers had carted away so much of it over the centuries.

Salvage operations intent on removing Roman architectural metalwork could, of course, have taken place at any time between the late fourth century and the beginning of the twentieth. As a matter of fact, a nineteenth-century excavator at Bath famously sold all the lead he discovered in one of the Roman baths to a scrap-metal dealer.[48] There is evidence, however, to suggest that people at the very end of the Roman period and during the first two centuries of the Middle Ages were responsible for removing considerable quantities of metal from abandoned Roman buildings. A number of very late Roman metalwork hoards bear witness to this activity. One, discovered in Northamptonshire, represents a cache of lead weighing 11.5 kilograms. At least some of it was architectural and bears marks of having been cut free from buildings with a combination of axes and saws.[49] Another, this one found at Icklingham, in Essex, contained not only a collection of iron saw blades, but large numbers of iron hinges, nails, and rings that had been extracted from a building.[50] Standing behind these hoards are late Roman structures such as one of the buildings at the Roman villa at Little Oakley, in Essex, or the bathhouse at Shadwell, just outside Roman London. Both appear to have been stripped of all their iron and lead fixtures soon after they were decommissioned.[51]

Our best-dated example of fifth-century metal salvaging from a building comes from Bath. Sometime around 450, the monumental stone walls of the derelict Roman temple and bathing complex, once dedicated to Sulis Minerva, either fell down or were pulled down.[52] Before this happened, all the iron clamps with lead seatings used by its builders to connect the stone blocks together were hacked out of the walls in some kind of deliberate salvage operation.[53] We know that this had to have happened after c. 400 (because the building was in use until then), but before c. 450, when it collapsed, because once it fell, its rubble lay undisturbed for centuries. Yet the metalwork once housed in the stone building blocks of this structure, even that found at the bottom of the tumble of stones, had been removed, so the metal had to have been taken away before the building's collapse.[54] Considerable metal could be recovered from operations such as this. It has been estimated, for example, that the Roman Colisseum at one time contained three hundred tons of iron to bind its travertine facing to the body of the structure.[55] The temple of Sulis Minerva, although a much smaller building, would have provided considerable scrap metal to anyone with the tools and the patience to extract it. We know that metal was sometimes looted even from buildings in Francia in the post-Roman period, despite the fact that freshly smelted metal was still being produced there, albeit on a diminished scale. In his *History*, Gregory of Tours recounts that when one of Chilperic's men attacked Tours around 570, "he pulled apart the chapter house.... The building had been held together by nails [and] the men of Maine, who made up [his] army, put the nails into their pockets and took them away with them."[56]

More-portable iron, bronze, and brass objects were also being salvaged from deserted Roman-period sites. Everything from agricultural implements, to spoons, to cooking equipment would have been present on abandoned urban and rural sites, not only in and around deserted buildings, but in these settlements' former rubbish heaps. One interesting example of an object likely collected for recycling is the ridiculously luxurious elephant-ivory carpenter's plane found at Goodmanham in Yorkshire. In spite of its deluxe body, it has the standard iron rivets, iron bottom, and iron blade of more ordinary carpenter's planes. This extraordinary object was recovered from a very humble rural site some twenty kilometers from York in a late fourth-century context, and a likely explanation for its appearance there, alongside a late Roman copper-alloy lock plate that had been stripped from a door or chest, is that it had been scavenged from a deserted high-status residence.[57] Other late Roman metalwork finds also suggest that individuals in the years around 400 were collecting metal objects for recycling. One metalwork hoard found at Sibson, in Huntingdonshire, for example, included farm tools and bucket fittings; and although it might be a votive hoard, there is nothing in the context of this find to suggest this, so it may well represent someone's collection of scrap.[58]

Enterprising scavengers could also find caches of metal objects if they dug in and around abandoned Roman ritual sites, which were often surrounded by zones of pits filled with collections of metalwork originally placed in the ground both as votive offerings and for safekeeping; these deposits included everything from pot stands and woodworking tools to architectural metal and vessels.[59] We do not find Roman pot stands or woodworking tools on early medieval sites like the ones found in Roman metalwork hoards; but, then again, we rarely find *early medieval* pot stands or woodworking tools either, probably because old iron is easily reworked, and because of this, early medieval smiths could reforge mixed jumbles of scrap iron into just about anything except fine-edged tools.⁶⁰ As a matter of fact, archaeologists excavating settlement sites dating to the first few generations after Rome's fall generally recover little metalwork (certainly several orders of magnitude less than found in contemporary cemeteries), and this is probably because metal implements and dress fittings of use to neither the living nor the dead were carefully husbanded and reused in the crafting of new objects.⁶¹

Although archaeologists have not recovered Roman pot stands or door hinges from early medieval sites, they often encounter other Roman-period metalwork—things such as spoons, keys, balance arms from scales, brooches, coins, ear scoops, and rings from horse harnesses and bits.⁶² These particular objects regularly turn up in early medieval contexts because people in the fifth and sixth centuries had uses for them, and because of this, when they came upon them, they saved rather than reforged them. So, for example, Stanley West recovered an impressive number of Roman-period metalwork artifacts during his excavation of the early medieval settlement at West Stow, in Suffolk, including bronze spoons, bracelets, finger rings, ear scoops, and a steelyard, alongside almost three hundred Roman coins. These items look to have been scavenged from abandoned Roman sites in the neighborhood and brought home for reuse a they were or after some minor modifications.⁶³ Similarly, the women around Alton, in Hampshire, seem to have spent time poking around old Roman sites looking for metalwork, some of which they ended up saving as keepsakes, something that happened with a bronze Roman theater ticket kept with a collection of other trinkets in a bag worn on one Alton woman's hip.⁶⁴ So particular objects were sometimes held back from the jumble of metalwork being collected by scavengers. Once gathered, though, the items individuals or communities were not interested in reusing were sorted by metal type and reforged. We can actually see this happening at the seventh-century settlement at Bloodmore Hill, in Suffolk, where archaeologists have recovered a few identifiably Roman metal objects mixed in with deposits of undateable scrap, smithing slag, and the forging by-product known as hammerscale, so the Roman material here looks as if it had been deliberately collected for reworking.⁶⁵ This is interesting, indeed, because it tells us that even in the seventh century—when, as we shall see, some people were beginning to have better access to freshly smelted metal—metalwork produced in the Roman period continued to be an important source of raw material for smiths.

Early medieval people were interested in a range of Roman metalwork, which would have been present on most deserted Roman-period sites. Roman-period lead was certainly collected and reworked. Donut-shaped lead ingots, first identified by Helena Hamerow at Mucking, in Essex, have now been recovered from a number of fifth- and sixth-century settlement sites.[66] These ingots had to have been fashioned from recycled Roman lead, because there are no natural lead deposits in the parts of Britain where they have been found, and because there is no evidence that there was trade in this period between the people who were producing donut-shaped ingots and the people living in lead-producing areas far to the west or north.[67] Lead appears to have been more plentiful in the fifth and early sixth centuries than in the seventh, probably because easily recyclable Roman lead gutters and pipes had grown scarce after a hundred years of scavenging. Certainly, the people of Mucking used lead in a profligate fashion in the late fifth and early sixth centuries, even incorporating it into their funerary rites. Sometimes, for example, they poured molten lead onto the lids of coffins to seal them or fashioned it into vessels to accompany their dead. They even used it to plug holes in cremation urns that they had deliberately pierced before filling with human ash. Lead, however, was not much in evidence in Mucking by the late sixth century, probably because by this time all the Roman-period lead in the neighborhood had already been salvaged.[68]

A variety of copper alloys were also used in the fifth and sixth centuries to make the buckles, brooches, and girdle hangers that people wore both in life and in death. Many of these objects were fashioned from recycled Roman metalwork. Typically, early medieval dress fittings were fashioned from bronze contaminated with brass and quite heavily leaded, a sign that metal smiths were working with recycled scrap, including bronze, brass, gunmetal, and pewter objects, which they had not sorted very carefully by alloy type before reforging.[69] This mixing of alloy types was not something that happened much in the Roman period, when nonferrous metalworkers were careful to sort recycled scrap by alloy type.[70] There is some evidence that nonferrous metal objects in the fifth century were closer to standard alloys than they would be in the sixth, an indication that as we move forward in time, metal that had already been recycled at least once was being recycled with other metal yet again.[71] Some fifth- and sixth-century copper-alloy metalwork, moreover, contains minute traces of silver and gold. This suggests the recycling of debased late Roman silver coins, which often contain only tiny amounts of silver, as well as gilded Roman metalwork.[72] There is, moreover, no evidence to suggest that metalsmiths in Britain during this period had access to either pure copper or true brass, a fact that strongly argues that there were no new supplies of these metals available in Britain, and that nonferrous metalworkers used *only* scrap.[73] Even in the eighth century it seems that nonferrous metalsmiths working at Southampton and York were still collecting Roman scrap for reuse.[74] Thus, the composition of the metals used in early medieval copper-alloy objects was prepared in small batches, each of them often quite different in its composition from the last (although pairs of brooches and wrist clasps sometimes seem to have been made from the same melts), and each dependent on the particular collection of odds and ends being melted down.[75]

Similar arguments can be made for the metal used in the making of many early medieval iron artifacts. In light of the dearth of evidence for smelting already presented, it seems likely that much of the iron used by blacksmiths in the fifth and early sixth centuries was recycled. Scientific examinations of a number of iron objects confirm this. An iron bar recovered from a post-Roman coastal site at Gwithian, in Cornwall, where iron agricultural tools and knives were fashioned, looks, for example, to have been made from recycled iron; and some of the post-Roman knives made there were fashioned from recycled iron as well.[76] For many classes of objects—cooking equipment, shield bosses, bucket hoops, firedogs—recycled iron is perfectly serviceable. But it is a different matter for objects that require hard, sharp cutting edges.[77] It is worth thinking about sharp-edged objects, because in the couple of generations after c. 500 this particular class of objects was going to play a starring role in the reorientation of resources, in such a way that a minority of individuals and households were going to end up with more than their share of Britain's slowly but steadily increasing surplus.[78]

Metal and the Building of a New Political Order

Ironsmiths working in Britain in the early Middle Ages were often highly skilled,[79] but many of the bladed objects they crafted were not very serviceable. The period's best spearheads and knives had bodies fabricated from low-carbon iron (which is not brittle and, therefore, does not break easily) and blades edged with steel for a good cutting edge.[80] Scrap iron, however, when heated and re-forged, does not have the strength of freshly smelted metal; and it would not have been possible in the early Middle Ages to make steel from it.[81] Given the limitations of recycled iron, it is little wonder that metallurgical studies of the knives and spearheads excavated from early Anglo-Saxon cemeteries have identified many poor specimens. Thus, some of the spearheads examined from the cemeteries at Wasperton, Edix Hill, Empringham, Mucking, and Boss Hall were so poor that specialists have suggested that they are not actually "real" spearheads, but rather tokens made specially for burial.[82] It seems more likely that these objects were used in real life but were of poor quality because they had been made from recycled scrap by smiths who had little access to freshly smelted iron and steel. Supporting this argument is Andrew Welton's recent study of early medieval spearheads, a number of which, so his metallurgical analysis shows, were made from recycled iron.[83]

Early knives sometimes exhibit the same flaws as spearheads, and like spearheads, many were fabricated from low-quality iron and were innocent of steel.[84] High-quality, high-carbon steel knives were extremely rare in the fifth and sixth centuries.[85] Some knives were actually smithed from both low-carbon and high-carbon iron, but at times these different alloys, rather than being deployed strategically—with the softer iron forming the body of the knife and the stronger iron welded along its edge—had simply been hammered together to form a single bar, and then that bar, in turn, had been used to make knives.[86] All this suggests that during the period when there was little new iron being smelted in lowland Britain, smiths had ready access to recyclable Roman-period objects, certainly enough to allow most people, even children, to wear knives on their belts and for leading men in many households to possess spears.[87] At the same time, however, they had only very limited access to freshly smelted iron and steel, and because of this many early knives and spearheads were poor quality.

Given the limitations of recycled iron, it is useful to think about swords and their female cousins, iron weaving beaters (sometimes known as weaving swords), the most important iron status objects of the early Middle Ages. For our purpose, there are five important things to know about these objects. First, many more swords and iron weaving beaters were placed in graves during the sixth and the early seventh centuries than in the fifth,[88] so the vast majority date not from the first three or four generations after the withdrawal, but from the next period on. Second, some of but by no means all these objects, alongside other kinds of prestige weapons, are Frankish imports.[89] Third, almost as many have been found in Kent as in all other counties combined, with the bulk of the rest found along England's southern and eastern coasts or in the Thames valley.[90] Fourth, 90 percent of these swords and weaving beaters, especially those made after c. 500, are pattern welded.[91] Fifth and finally, blades made in the seventh century were generally crafted from higher-quality metal than were earlier blades.[92]

Pattern-welded swords and weaving beaters were often very beautiful, and it is clear that the complexity of their blades' designs was seen as an important measure not only of the blade, but of the person who owned it.[93] Although some specialists still argue that pattern welding served a functional purpose in sword blades, it is difficult to come up with a practical explanation for why weaving beaters, which women used to beat up the weft when weaving on a warp-weighted loom, should be pattern welded.[94] Instead, it seems that part of the value of these pattern-welded objects to their owners was their rare and conspicuous beauty. Not only did the men and women in possession of such blades require the services of highly skilled smiths, but they had to have unusually good access to freshly smelted iron-alloy bars. This is because pattern-welded blades could not be made from recycled iron, nor could they be fashioned from a single type of iron alloy. Instead, their cores, their edges and their patterned centers were typically smithed from a variety of bars made from different iron alloys—some low carbon, others carbon-free, some with phosphorus, and still others made with steel. In short, smiths needed multiple bars of at least four different iron alloys in order to produce a pattern-welded blade.[95]

Given the state of iron smelting in early sixth-century England, when swords began to enter the burial record in significant numbers, it is highly unlikely that blade smiths working there would have been able to get hold of the variety of freshly smelted iron-alloy bars they needed from indigenous sources. Instead, they were probably procuring iron from traders, who were bringing it in from the continent, where, as we have seen, quite large-scale smelting concerns still operated.[96] Because so many early swords and iron weaving beaters have been found in Kent, it is not unreasonable to argue that much of the iron used to make Kentish swords, at least initially, was brought in from Francia, alongside the garnets, gold coins, pottery, wine, and high-quality quern stones that were beginning to flow into Kent from Francia as early as c. 500.[97] The discovery in Lyminge, Kent, of a seventh-century iron plow coulter, made from 5.6 kilograms of iron (probably forged from four billets of iron), suggests Frankish connections as well, given that the object itself looks to have been a technological borrowing from Francia.[98] And considering the close proximity of the two places, such trade would hardly be surprising. Impressive amounts of iron, as we have seen, were also being smelted in the Lowlands and in southern Scandinavia. Here archaeologists have uncovered a number of hoards of smallish, standard-sized iron bars, some of them steel, that had been smithed with holes in one end so that they could be tied together into bundles for shipping.[99] We know this material traveled: there is evidence from sixth-century Denmark, for example, that people there were getting hold of higher-carbon iron than they were producing locally, and that it was coming from Norway.[100] And by the early sixth century, there were people from southwestern Norway and Frisia nosing around the northern and eastern coasts of England.[101] Perhaps, like the Franks, one of the things they were doing was trading iron.

In the early sixth century, then, at just the time when a steeply hierarchical society and elites were beginning to emerge, and when individuals and households in England were beginning to compete intensely for social position and resources (something clearly marked in the archaeological record), and in the decades when the possession and burying of pattern-welded blades began to play a central role in this competition, the only people who were going to be able to stay in the game were those with access to imported iron alloys. And in order to get their hands on imported iron, they needed something to trade. Of course, having swords must have helped them command the surplus they needed to get more iron, although admittedly, it seems that what we have here is a classic chicken-and-egg problem: we cannot tell if some households were motivated to get more surplus because they wanted access to important but locally unavailable commodities such as freshly smelted iron-alloy bars, or if they had more surplus because they had managed to get hold of iron. Whatever the case, the point worth emphasizing here is that England's new sword- and iron-weaving-beater-bearing elites were in the ascendant positions they were in not because of ancient warrior pedigrees—social differentiation, after all, is barely visible in the archaeological record of fifth-century lowland Britain—but rather because they had access to transchannel trade networks and traders, as well as control over economic activities at home, which allowed these people to exchange what they had for sought-after imports. Thus, it seems that economic development, trade, a new emphasis on surplus, and the desire for exotic commodities, such as good-quality iron, were driving crucial changes in English social structures in ways that are not reflected in our surviving texts.

From the mid-sixth century on, newly emerging elite families' desire for fresh iron looks to have stimulated smelting at home. Certainly, the archaeology suggests that by the late sixth and early seventh centuries, a number of people within England itself were beginning to put considerable effort into the production of new metal. Chris Loveluck, for example, has argued that the barrow-building, grave-goods-using families establishing themselves in seventh-century Derbyshire may have become the people they were because they had made themselves the masters of lead production.[102] And households in western Britain that were probably in command of tin production were able to trade it for exotic Mediterranean goods.[103] From the late sixth and early seventh centuries on, more iron-smelting furnaces, more smelting slag, and more evidence for long-term iron production are visible in the archaeological record, having now been identified at over three dozen sites. Some of these are quite impressive for the scale of their output and the sophistication of their technological development, particularly smelting operations dating from the late seventh century on.[104] At Worgret, in Dorset, for example, it is possible that a watermill was being used sometime in the late seventh or early eighth century to drive mechanically operated bellows or a heavy hammer at an iron-smelting operation;[105] and by the late eighth or early ninth century ironworkers at Ramsbury, probably by this time an important royal estate, produced something on the order of ten tons of iron over the span of a generation or two.[106] Contemporary with and on a similar scale to the operation at Ramsbury was the iron-production site at Weldon, in Northamptonshire, likely part of another royal estate.[107] Here, remarkably, it seems that smelters were able to produce three different iron alloys: ferretic iron, phosphoric iron, and steel, a feat that points to the existence, by this time, of highly adept smelting practitioners in England.[108] There is also evidence, beginning in the seventh century, for the local production of steel and the making of relatively large quantities of charcoal, a fuel critical for smelting.[109] Indeed, given iron smelting's voracious appetite for charcoal, it is inconceivable that iron production on the scale undertaken at Ramsbury could have taken place without carefully managed woodland resources, because without planned coppicing, smelters would have burned through their fuel supplies quickly.[110] So, this level of production would have been impossible in a period before there were households powerful enough to control extensive woodlands. The few metallurgical comparisons of Roman and Anglo-Saxon slags that have been made, as well as an examination of the furnace technology being used in England in the ninth century, suggest that Roman smelting knowledge in most places had not survived, and that English ironworkers working in these later centuries had adopted techniques used in Scandinavia and northern Germany.[111]

Alongside evidence for the increasing number of smelting sites in England, we find evidence for specialist groups of metalworkers such as the ones active at Bloodmore Hill, Brandon Road, in Thetford; possibly Cottam, in East Yorkshire; and Lyminge, in Kent.[112] At places such as these, workers plying their trade across the seventh century were smithing large numbers of iron implements not only for themselves, but for some broader market; and they clearly had access to increasing supplies of iron—some still coming from scavenging, but some, judging from the off-cuts of fresh billets, now derived from newly smelted iron.[113] The appearance of ironworking groups such as the ones operating in the seventh century coincided with a dramatic standardization of knives in England, which hints at important changes in technology and in the way blacksmiths were organized.[114] Both the knives and the swords produced in England from the seventh century onward were generally of a very high quality and often made from steel.¹¹⁵ These things together argue for the reestablishment of smelting within England over the course of the seventh and eighth centuries, with numerous sites by the ninth century producing enough metal to supply the masters of the large estates of which they were part with sufficient metal for their own needs and even, perhaps, for local markets.

What increasing levels of metal production could do for those who either controlled such sites or had access to the metal they produced is witnessed by evidence provided by a number of collections of iron tools and weapons, placed in the ground in the early medieval period in what look like structured deposits.¹¹⁶ The discovery at a royal hall at Lyminge of an iron plow coulter placed in a structured deposit sometime in the first half of the seventh century, and the central role such plows must have played in the extension of arable land during this period, is suggestive of how crucial a supply of iron was to the households benefiting from the economic transformations taking place during these years.¹¹⁷ Certainly, elite households with smelters and metalworkers not only would have had a commodity worth trading in the region's newly emerging urban markets,¹¹⁸ but they would have been able to provide their own farming operations with high-quality agricultural tools.¹¹⁹ Significant numbers of large lead storage tubs dated from the seventh century on—unlovely but valuable objects, the ownership of which would have been limited to people who had access to trade networks centered on lead—have also been recovered. They enable us to see the ways in which the possession of relatively large supplies of metal might improve the abilities of the period's best-connected households not only to create agricultural surplus, but to store it.¹²⁰

The arguments made in this chapter about the central role of metal production in the reemergence of a steeply hierarchical society in Britain find parallels in Norway during the Roman Iron Age. Kristin Prestvold has argued that the notable increase in iron smelting c. 200 CE was closely linked to the rise of an elite with growing political and economic power and ever more control over landscape and labor. She sees the social changes spurred on by iron smelting linked to increasing warfare in the region, the need by those attempting to benefit from its production to participate in conspicuous display (including new and extravagant forms of weapon burials), and the appearance of high-status settlement sites.¹²¹ All these things can be found in sixth-, seventh-, and eighth-century lowland Britain as well.¹²² Fresh metal production, then, is perhaps both diagnostic for the development of stratified societies and an important engine driving such change.

The collapse of the metal economy in Britain lays bare the extraordinary transformations people lived through as complex systems of production disappeared and as many were left without access to very basic commodities such as freshly smelted metal and nails, things to which most of their great-grandparents would have had easy access. It also underscores the ways in which the collapse of the Roman economy was accompanied by the relatively rapid and dramatic deskilling of Britain's population. Roman society, like modern society, depended on carefully coordinated systems of production, supply, and transportation, but when the economy imploded, when money ceased to have value (as it did in Britain), and when the Roman state withdrew, it was impossible for these systems of production to persevere. With each passing year there would have been fewer people who knew how to do many of the tasks associated with the production of iron, or who could marshal all the necessary resources and know-how to do so. But even in places where a few such individuals survived, it is hard to imagine how the fruits of their activity could have been passed on to "consumers," once towns, markets, and the money economy disappeared. Smelting skills, moreover, were not absolutely necessary, because metal from abandoned Roman sites was widely available. In the new world in which the people of Britain found themselves, it was easier to acquire metal by scavenging than it was to mine, make charcoal, and smelt.[123] One of the more corrosive effects of this general trend was that in the face of small-scale and episodic, but widespread recycling the knowledge used to produce new metal disappeared in many places.[124]

In spite of the economic collapse that accompanied Rome's fall in Britain, by the early sixth century some households had come to have enough surplus to engage in trade with foreigners. It is likely that these people were interested not only in the garnets, gold coins, and wheel-thrown wine bottles we find stuffed in their graves, but in freshly smelted iron-alloy bars, which they could have fashioned into the swords and other sharp-edged implements that were becoming prerequisites for making claims to high social status. Over the course of the sixth and seventh centuries, as social hierarchies solidified and as elite households gained power over both the landscape and the labor of others, a meaningful level of iron and lead production was once again established in lowland Britain. In the long run, not only did the increased availability of freshly smelted metal solidify the economic positions of the people who controlled its production, but it provided many more people with access to better tools, helping to increase surpluses. Thus, the story of the collapse of the metal economy and its gradual return are crucial for understanding what Britain was like in the years between c. 350 and c. 650 and how it evolved from late Roman to early medieval.

CHAPTER 7

Living with Little Corpses

> Where we put [the dead's] remains is generally a conscious and carefully thought-out activity by which the dead are both remembered and forgotten, and through which we reaffirm and construct our attitudes to death and the dead and, through these, to place and identity.
> —M. Parker Pearson, *The Archaeology of Death and Burial*

When one backs into Roman archaeology from the other side of 400 as I have done, it is hard not to be impressed by the number of tiny skeletons one stumbles across at Roman-period sites. Not only were stillborn and infant burials a standard feature of the period's settlements, but they were often well represented in urban cemeteries. The same, however, cannot be said for early medieval sites, where infants rarely make an appearance. The differences in the treatment and visibility of the infant dead in these two periods are disconcerting to say the least. But because of the great chasm dividing Romanists from medievalists, the changing fate of little corpses has gone unnoticed.

In this chapter, we will explore the ways not-very-fancy communities both before and after Rome dealt with their dead babies, and we will think through the meaning of the attitudes and practices surrounding them. Little corpses can help us pinpoint some of the profound transformations in the lived experience and thought worlds of people in Britain, first under and then after Rome. The changing treatment of little corpses hints at broad cultural and cosmological shifts that allow us to sidestep the kinds of discussions that usually dominate historical treatments of the transition between Roman and early medieval in

Britain, discussions that tend to coagulate around questions of high politics and the great movement of peoples. But for scholars who concern themselves with tracking the variety of ways ordinary Britons experienced the aftermath of Rome in Britain, these infants should be of great interest.

Before we look at the evidence in detail, a few of things need to be said about the study of infant burial and about burial practices more generally. In recent years, a number of scholars have challenged two ideas that long dominated the ways historians and archaeologists understood infant burial in the Roman period, and that continue to haunt both write-ups of excavations and stories in the popular press. The first is the notion that infant bodies encountered outside formal cemeteries are evidence of infanticide.[1] The second is that the alleged "casual disposal" of infant corpses, rather than their "proper" burial in cemeteries, reflects either these babies' status as not fully human or their parents' emotional detachment.[2] The most recent assaults on these twin preconceptions are presented in two articles. The first, by Martin Millett and Rebecca Gowland, analyzes the placement and structure of neonate burials at two late Roman rural settlements in East Yorkshire and establishes that the patterns behind their depositions are evidence for something other than the casual discard of murdered babies,[3] although they refrain from saying what it *is* evidence for. Nonetheless, their work and the work of others opens us up to the possibility that families in the Roman period were purposeful in the ways they dealt with the bodies of babies who did not survive infancy. The second article, by Claire Hodson, presents evidence for multiple episodes of disrupted growth and pathological lesions among the neonates buried at the villa site at Piddington, and her work provides clear evidence that many of these stillborn and newborn infants were victims of poor maternal health and poor nutrition, and that these factors help explain their early deaths.[4]

Infant burials also need to be thought about not only by themselves, but in the context of other burials. Work done in the last couple of decades has brought home the fact that the graves found in Britain's organized, late Roman suburban cemeteries, which both dominate the literature and have been the focus of intense archaeological investigation, are not representative of the treatment of most of the period's dead.[5] This fact, however, has not been internalized by historians, whose ideas about late antique burial are based on textual descriptions, primarily preserved in hagiography, of the great inhumation cemeteries ringing every town, which increasingly served as homes to the tombs of the "very special dead."[6] Many people in Britain during the Roman period—not just infants, but agriculturalists who lived on villa estates or in small farming settlements, or low-status workers who resided at the bottom end of roadside settlements—were not buried in organized cemeteries. Indeed, it is now certain that only a minority of people in the period were awarded archaeologically visible burials.[7] Adults buried outside formal cemeteries, unlike infants, are not, of course, usually interpreted as murder victims or individuals who were not considered fully human. This chapter takes as a given that the activities surrounding infant burial outside cemeteries, like those associated with adult burial, were "conscious and carefully thought-out."[8]

In order to build a picture of the material practices surrounding infant burial, we will explore the ways a number of different late Roman communities dealt with dead neonates, that is, stillborn babies and infants who died in the first days, weeks, or months of life.[9] As with so many other categories of evidence from the period, it is impossible to be rigorously systematic in its study. Too many tiny skeletons were brought to light in single-trench commercial excavations, or on sites where bone preservation was terrible or plow damage was severe. And many found before the 1970s are poorly recorded. Take, for example, Philipp Corder's descriptions, written in 1930, of the infants he came across while excavating Malton: "In the floors of these houses were found the huddled bones of newly born infants, sometimes laid in lime and covered by a roofing-tile or stone, but often merely laid in the floor. These burials are too numerous for individual descriptions here, but they number 29 at the time of writing."[10]

Although the complexity and variety of activities hinted at in Corder's description are tantalizing, his account is insufficient for sustained analysis. Indeed, he did not bother to place the infants he encountered on his site plan of Malton. Clearly, the unevenness of our evidence and its at-times slapdash recording mean that it does not lend itself to statistical analysis. What I have done, instead, is work my way through the excavation reports of just over one hundred late Roman sites where infant bodies have been recovered. This has allowed me to identify the broad range of practices from which many late Roman communities chose to construct their particular infant burial rites. From these, I have chosen five, whose treatment of tiny corpses represent the basic contours and standard range of activities engaged in at the death of an infant, selected by each group, no doubt, in light of family traditions, the dictates of cult and regional preferences, social status, and their familiarity, or lack thereof, with practices associated with infant burial in the wider Roman world.

Five Communities, 120 Little Corpses

We begin with a remarkable group of infant burials uncovered at Duroliponte, the Roman antecessor of Cambridge. Duroliponte was a roadside settlement, and typical of this site type, the settlement, by the second century, had a couple of stone buildings.[11] It was also home to a small, locally important, partially subterranean shrine on a site known as Ridgeons Garden.[12] By the fourth century, although Duroliponte's small grid of streets had been encircled by a wall, as a number of late Roman roadside settlements were, almost all its buildings were single-room structures made from timber. A fire had destroyed the shrine, and it had not been rebuilt.[13] Instead, the area where the shrine had once stood had become home to at least thirteen ritual shafts, and they were the focus of intense activity. Most were used to deposit very particular collections of things in a highly choreographed fashion. A layer of potsherds was placed in the shaft. A rush mat was then set on top of the sherds, and a wicker basket was positioned on the mat. Inside the basket was a dead infant, not more than a couple of weeks old,[14] wrapped in textile. Finally, the body of an adult dog was placed to the south of the basket. In a number of shafts, on top of this tableaux was yet another mat, and then a basket, with a dead infant wrapped in textiles, and the body of yet another dog, placed, once again, to the south of the infant.[15] One of the thirteen shafts still had a wooden lid, so it looks as if these pits could be closed between depositional episodes.[16]

There were some variations in these repeated actions. Children's hobnail shoes accompanied five infant burials. One infant lay in a wooden box rather than a basket, and a couple of others were accompanied by whole pots or coins. Most of the shafts also held an assortment of articulated animals besides dogs, as well as collections of animal heads and disarticulated animal bones. There were whole falcons and chickens in these shafts, and the heads of horses, sheep, and cattle. One shaft contained an impressive twenty-eight cattle skulls. Excavators also recovered the disarticulated bones of piglets, pheasants, and pigeons.[17]

Some of the objects given a place alongside these infant corpses are things that—as we have seen—were also included in well deposits. As with the well deposits, it is unlikely that a number of the things present in the Ridgeons Garden shafts would have been considered rubbish when placed in these pits: human remains, whole or nearly whole edible animals,[18] exotic birds, undamaged pots, and coins. This argues that at least some of the events that stood behind these depositions were not mundane, everyday activities.[19] The predictable grammar of these proceedings, the lack of utilitarian explanation for the objects used in them, and their repeated structure suggests that they represent special, indeed ritualized, acts.[20]

The exceptional organic preservation in these shafts allows us to witness some of the complexities of late Roman infant interment that are usually invisible to us. Three things, in particular, stand out. First, the remains of most of the period's babies are present in the archaeological record as tiny skeletons deposited in shallow scoops of earth. Because they are rarely found in organized cemeteries, and because nothing but skeletons survive, theirs are habitually described as "casual" or "informal" burials. But the organic remains associated with the Ridgeons Garden infants argue for the possibility that infant bodies were swaddled or shrouded when they went into the ground, and that many may have rested in baskets or on mats or textiles. We know that this was often the case in late Roman Egypt, where organic preservation is very good,[21] but there are hints beyond the Ridgeon Gardens shafts that this was the case in Britain, at least in a handful of unusually elaborate, high-status infant burials. A sarcophagus found in York, for example, held the body of a woman and an infant covered in plaster, a minority rite in the late Roman period, and the plaster fortuitously formed a cast of the newborn, showing it to have been swaddled (Figure 20).[22]

The Ridgeons Gardens interments also hint that babies might regularly have been buried with other organic materials, something we catch fleeting glimpses of elsewhere in Britain.[23] For example, an infant whose grave was dug through a concrete floor at the villa at Lullingstone was buried not only with six coins and a fragment of a bronze figurine, but with a few grains of wheat.[24] Nightshade and a sprig of box accompanied another coffined infant in the Waveney Valley.[25] Dead infants wrapped in textiles or accompanied by foodstuffs or medicinal plants are impossible to characterize as "rubbish." Instead, their burials look like the product of well-understood and agreed-on acts that had a grammar, a set of gestures, and a meaning all their own.

The second thing that the infant interments of Ridgeons Garden suggests is that conceptually, the disposal of infant bodies in some communities might have been understood as more than burial, something that Millett and Gowland have suggested for the infants buried at Burnbury Lane, Yorkshire; Michael Fulford for those at Silchester's Insula IX; and Barry Cunliffe for the ones he encountered at Portchester.[26] Although the Ridgeons Garden shafts did contain human remains, the constellation of things found within them—hobnail shoes, whole dogs, animal heads, complete pots, the bodies of birds, and coins—are typical of Romano-British structured deposits in deep places, with and without human remains. Such pits, along with decommissioned wells, which as we have seen also acted as sites of ritual deposition, seem to have been associated with the underworld and to have had some kind of chthonic purpose. Indeed, some of the things accompanying infants may have been associated with chthonic

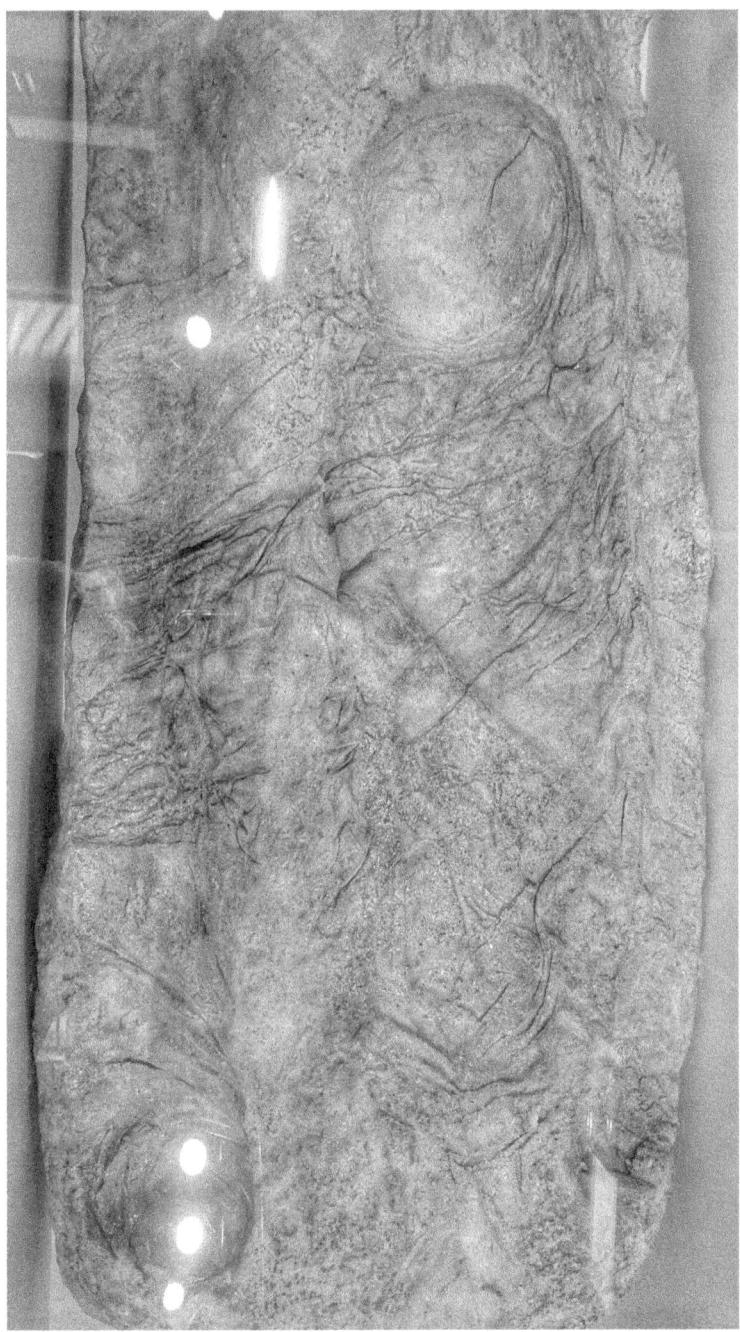

FIGURE 20. A negative impression of a swaddled infant, preserved in a late Roman plaster burial from York. (Yorkshire Museum, York, YORYM: 2007.6126. Photo by author. Used with kind permission of the Yorkshire Museum.)

deities such as Mercury, whose attributes—shoes, dogs, and cockerels—are habitually encountered in pit and well deposits.[27] The people committing the Ridgeons Garden infants to pits may have been participating in acts that they understood less as funerals and more as part of the ritualized activities that punctuated domestic life, which obliged them to place whole dogs, pots, hobnail shoes, and sometimes dead infants into dark places.[28] Although no objects of value accompanied these infants, these deposits betray care, effort, and ritual complexity.

Third and finally, we have little difficulty conjuring up the mourners, rituals, and fraught moments that accompanied adult burials during the Roman period.[29] The finds in the Ridgeons Garden pits provide a window through which we can view the kinds of events that sometimes accompanied infant burial. Each shaft was about 1.5 meters square, big enough for a full-grown adult to get inside the pit and create the elaborate and periodically repeated mise-en-scènes of these burials. Surely the events at Ridgeons Garden involved not just the dead dogs, wicker baskets, and birds we see in the archaeological record, but archaeologically invisible gestures, emotions, and words. These events must have been quite a performance.

Families living in roadside settlements such as Duroliponte were not the only ones who took care when saying farewell to dead infants. Those in small rural settlements also buried their babies purposefully and with care. This was certainly the case for the men and women living in the later fourth and fifth centuries at a small farmstead at Bradley Hill, near Somerton, in Somerset. A couple of households made their homes here in two stone houses.[30] The houses had stone-paved floors and slate roofs as well, and each one had a main room with a hearth and two smaller unheated rooms. But there is no sign at Bradley Hill of underfloor heating, plastered walls, a bathhouse, or any of the other amenities that we associate with grander villa sites.[31] There was a third stone building at Bradley Hill, one that shared a common wall with the westernmost house.[32] Traces of a paved area and stall divisions for three or four animals were uncovered at the western end of this building, along with a drain. Most of the structure, though, had an earthen floor. It was a barn and storehouse.[33]

The site plan also shows a small, likely enclosed cemetery to the south of the barn.[34] The earliest of its burials dates to the fourth century (the two northernmost graves included coins issued between 330 and 348), but some of the skeletons further south have undergone radiocarbon dating, and these belong to the fifth or even sixth century.[35] So, it seems that some of the dead were buried here while our three buildings were in use, but others might have been interred after the settlement was abandoned sometime in the second half of the fifth century.[36]

In many ways, the graves uncovered at the Bradley Hill cemetery are unexceptional. As at other unassuming late Roman rural cemeteries, there were only a small number of graves—twenty-five in all—and most of them, like many late Roman graves, were lined with stones and aligned east-west. Only a couple had surviving grave goods: again, few or no grave goods were often the norm in cemeteries of the period.[37] Finally, like other late Roman cemeteries, in particular the great urban cemeteries outside the walls of important administrative towns such as Dorchester-on-Thames, Winchester, and London, this one did include a few infants and children.[38] Five infants and three children under the age of twelve were recovered from the cemetery.[39] If Bradley Hill's cemetery were the only thing that had been excavated, and not the settlement's buildings, these eight youngsters might have led us to believe that the community burying here always made room in its cemetery for stillborn or very young babies, as well as children. But this impression would be wrong, because it turns out that the formal cemetery contained only a fraction of Bradley Hill's infants. Twenty-six other babies and one child were recovered from under the floors of the site's three buildings.[40]

The site's excavators discovered five under the floors of the two houses. One was placed in the southeast corner of Building One's Room 2, very close to a pit with what looks like a structured deposit, containing a large, whole storage jar, nine coins, and a horned ram's head. Room 2 of Building Two had three underfloor infant burials, and Room 1 had yet another infant under its floor.[41] All the babies here were less than six months old when they died, and all were found tucked up into the corners of rooms or placed tight along a wall. All were also sealed under the houses' well-laid stone floors. At least one of these burials may have taken place during the building's construction and might be viewed not simply as a burial, but as a foundation deposit.[42] Underfloor infant burials are encountered in the corners or along the walls of rooms in urban and rural buildings, not only in Britain, but across the empire;[43] they are regularly found next to pits containing whole animals or animal heads and whole ceramic pots; and they were present in the houses of rich and poor alike.[44]

The remaining twenty-one infants and one child at Bradley Hill lay under the floor of Building Three, the barn/storehouse. The burials here were sealed by a thick deposit layer that formed during the last stages of the building's occupation and after its desertion. None of the fills from any of the barn's graves included material from this layer, which means that the burials predate the final occupation/abandonment layer. Four of the burials, though, were found in the paved area of the building, one cutting through where the stones forming stalls had been, suggesting that this part of the building was no longer being used for housing livestock at the time of these particular burials.[45] But it does look as if most, if not all, of the babies were interred during the period when the barn was still a working barn, and not when it was a deserted ruin. The graves in the barn were well spaced, and not one intercut another. They were all cist burials, that is, stone lined, and had stone-slab coverings, a grave structure that suggests something more than "casual" disposal.[46]

So, here was a community that believed in the efficacy of infant bodies, and which lived in houses knowing that members of their community who had never lived, or who had hardly lived at all, lay beneath their floors, and that those bodies were important components of a house. The people who buried these children thought that sometimes the proper thing to do, if an infant died, was to place its body under the floor of one of its houses.[47] This was also a community of farmers, who went about their daily business in the barn milking cows, shearing and slaughtering sheep, and processing grain with an assembly of dead babies underfoot, in an underfloor zone that grew increasingly crowded with the passing years; but it was a space where the place of each infant was remembered and mapped in some way, so that when yet another baby died, the new infant's carefully constructed cist would not disturb the cists of any of its dead companions. Many rural communities in Roman Britain used agricultural buildings as sites of infant burial.[48] Infant bodies are also regularly encountered in and around pottery kilns, corn driers, and metalworking ovens.[49] This suggests that there was some sort of conceptual link between dead infants and the productive work engaged in by bereaved households. Like the Ridgeons Garden infants, the ones at Bradley Hill were, for the most part, treated differently in death than adults, and like the Ridgeons Garden infants, they were buried not alone, but rather in companionable groups. Their final resting places, like those of the babies placed in the Ridgeons Garden shafts, were not marked by inscribed tombstones bearing their names, the way those of adults sometimes were, so the curation of their memories as individuals does not seem to have been the reason behind preserving knowledge of the location of their graves.[50] Like the Ridgeons Garden babies, a few were also placed in close proximity to structured deposits. And like the Ridgeons Garden infants, they were kept close to the people who buried them and who continued to live and work above their bodies.

Yet another crowd of infants was discovered at a low-status roadside settlement in the Rudstone Dale, in Yorkshire.[51] This site's cluster of houses and paddocks sat a kilometer from what looks to have been a substantial villa at North Newbald.[52] In the late Roman period the settlement, which had been founded in the pre-Roman Iron Age and occupied for centuries, was dramatically reorganized, the way many rural settlements in late Roman Britain were, and its old mix of mostly roundhouses and sub-rectangular structures gave way to a series of new rectangular stone or stone-footed buildings—what we often understand as more "Roman-style" houses. At the same time, the boundary ditches dividing the different plots that made up the settlement were reconfigured, and the trackway along which these people lived was metaled.[53] There was no formal cemetery here, the way there had been at Bradley Hill, and there was no zone of ritual pits, as there had been at Ridgeons Garden. Instead, most of the late Roman adults were found buried on either side of the metaled trackway, although one was found on what looks to have been a boundary line between two enclosures.[54] But, as at Bradley Hill, *very* large numbers of neonates were recovered—fifty-eight in all—most from underneath the settlement's buildings.[55]

All the buildings from the late Roman phase had at least one neonate under their floors or in their foundation trenches, but a couple of buildings sheltered a lot of infants. Structure 6 had three neonates and an animal burial. Structure 11 had ten neonates under its floor and walls, and there were animal burials under the building's floor. And just north of Structure 11's foundation, there were a further five neonates, two of whom were buried with pottery.[56]

Because Rudstone Dale was a multiperiod site, we know that the people living here had laid their infant dead to rest under their floors long before the Roman conquest. One of the pre-Roman Iron Age roundhouses on the site had ten neonates under its floor as well as a whole calf and a whole lamb: here, as elsewhere, baby animals were associated with baby humans. Another of Rudstone Dale's houses, this one likely dated to the early Roman period, had five infant burials and two animal deposits under its floor.[57] In both cases, though, the infant and animal burials seem to have predated the roundhouses, and it looks as if people in the community purposefully constructed these structures over clusters of dead infants after they had already been put in the ground.[58] But in the late Roman period, it was the buildings that came first, and then the infant burials. Not all infants in late Roman Rudstone Dale, though, were buried underneath the floors of buildings. A number were laid to rest, exactly the same way the adults were, in ditches along the metaled road,[59] or along fence lines between enclosures.[60] So passing along the road, which was the settlement's main thoroughfare and a pathway that joined a well-traveled road between Brough-on-Humber and York,[61] would have meant passing by many of the settlement's dead. Burials in ditches such as these are sometimes referred to as "backland burials,"[62] but the ones at Rudstone Dale are quite the opposite, drawing attention to and helping to mark significant boundaries.[63]

The prominence of infants' burial sites at Rudstone Dale reminds us of how important children were for the preservation of rural households, many of which expended the majority of their labor on subsistence, but would nonetheless have had to produce for landlords, the state, and perhaps for the local market as well. Even young children would have engaged in the work of the household. Ethnographic studies of children in Java and Nepal suggest that by the age of nine, what children produce is equal to the cost of keeping them, and by the time they are twelve, their work has essentially repaid the household all the costs of raising them up until this point. In both places, by the age of thirteen, children regularly work as many hours as adults; but even seven-to-nine-year-olds work at least half this amount of time.[64] Statistics such as these are suggestive and hint at the many ways the loss of babies was a blow to their households' future prosperity.

A fourth group of infant burials was discovered at Wattle Syke, in Yorkshire, a place of settlement since the pre-Roman Iron Age, but one, like Rudstone Dale, that had been radically reconfigured in the late Roman period, when it was transformed into an open settlement specializing in cereal production.[65] Twenty-seven sets of remains date to this later phase. Twelve were of adults, two were of children who died between the ages of three and five, and the remaining thirteen were of infants, mostly newborns. For the whole of the Iron Age, infants at Wattle Syke had been buried in or close to domestic structures, and this practice continued into the late Roman period. Dead adults were also buried within the settlement's enclosures during the late Iron Age. In the early Roman period, although infants continued to be buried in close association with buildings, the adults disappeared. Dead adults came to be buried within the settlement, once again, in the late Roman period. So the most dramatic change in burial practice at Wattle Syke in the late Roman period was that dead adults were now buried within the settlement, very near its houses, the way infants had been for centuries.[66] Another quite startling change also dates to the late Roman period. The graves of adults (now found within the settlement) were regularly reopened, and dead infants were given space in already-occupied graves, laid to rest in adult company. Seven babies were buried in this way, and they constitute half of all neonate burials here.[67] This would have required the burial party to confront a decomposing body of what was likely a well-remembered adult.[68] One or two of these burials may represent mothers and babies who had died together in childbirth, but two of the infants were buried with men, and another two with women who were probably beyond their childbearing years.[69] At other late Romano-British cemeteries, neonates have been exclusively found in the graves of men or with older children, so as here, many of those sharing a grave with an infant could not have been their mothers.[70] All the Wattle Sykes dead were buried in and around the settlement's buildings, many of which appear to have been outbuildings associated with corn drying, milling, and metalworking.[71] So here, adults and infants were laid to rest near productive spaces the way infants alone were at Bradley Hill. As in other settlements, there were lots of structured animal deposits on the site, but unlike at Ridgeons Garden, Bradley Hill, and Rudston Dale, none were found in association with the infants.[72] Domestic fowl, however, were placed in many graves.[73]

Our final community buried its dead in a late Roman cemetery at Dunstable, in Bedfordshire, another roadside settlement, this one sited on the intersection of two of Britain's most important Roman roads. A number of households buried their dead within an enclosure there. Enclosed cemeteries such as this were a common feature of late Roman settlements.[74] Fifty-five burials sat within the enclosure. Although infants were not entirely excluded from this space, only three were buried within the cemetery, in their own graves next to those of adult men and women. But the boundary ditches of the cemetery served as an intense focus of burial, and fifty human skeletons were excavated along the cemetery's three surviving ditches, including those of seven neonates.[75]

If the fourth boundary ditch had survived, we might have discovered another dozen or more burials, which would make the ditches of the enclosure a more sought-after burial space than the cemetery they bounded.[76] Adult graves were arranged in these ditches head to head or head to toe, and a few preserved the ghostly remains of postholes, which suggests that wooden posts marked individual graves.[77] The south boundary ditch alone contained the burials of sixteen adults. These burials were similar to those within the enclosure: some were coffined; a number were decapitated postmortem (a minority rite in Britain) or accompanied by small pots, hobnail shoes, or bracelets—again, objects often placed in the ground with the deceased in the fourth century.[78] Three infants were also buried in the southern boundary ditch. There were also four whole horses and a dog buried in the southern boundary ditch. One of the human skeletons buried in this ditch was a corpse that had not completely decomposed when the horse was placed in the ground, so it had had to be scooched up to make room for the animal.[79] Once again, we have evidence for people engaging with decomposing corpses while burying other things.

At Dunstable, then, some families chose to bury adults, babies, and whole animals in graves carefully dug into the boundaries of a relatively empty enclosed cemetery, rather than within the cemetery itself, in spite of the fact that there was plenty of open space within the enclosure.[80] Boundary burial, as we have seen at Rudston Dale, was an important rite for many.[81] People were also associating their dead with animal burials (although these were undertaken at different times than the human burials), and they chose to use both adult and infant bodies in these boundary burials in the same way that people at Rudstone Dale and Wattle Syke had. Although infants are underrepresented at Dunstable (there are only ten infants from a total of fifty burials), we can discern variations on a theme. Babies, like adults, were buried here in boundary ditches; they were associated with animal burials; their graves were marked in some way; and they were laid to rest in the company of others.

Making Sense of Infant Burials

So, what are we to make of late Roman Britain's dead babies? And more importantly, what did the people burying these infants make of them? Before we speculate about the meaning of these infants, it is important to highlight some of the methodological difficulties we face. First, there is a very long history, in Britain, of placing infant corpses in structured deposits within settlement sites, especially within or near the walls of buildings or in boundary ditches. There are many examples from the pre-Roman Iron Age, and a handful from the early medieval period as well.[82] Furthermore, people across the Roman world buried infants under their floors or on boundaries, and some of the things buried with infants in Britain—including dogs and shoes—were also associated with them in low-status, rural, provincial communities far from Britain.[83] The burial of the dead along boundaries and roads during the Roman period was also something that could be found across the Roman world, and such burials seem to have played an important role in guaranteeing and justifying divisions in the landscape in places far from Britain.[84] So it is important to keep Mike Parker Pearson's observation firmly in mind when attempting to understand these burials: "universal generalizations about the meaning of particular rites, spatial relationships, and practices involving the dead are unsupportable."[85] In short, it is impossible to disentangle particularly Roman practices from very old, indigenous ones, or to assign a single meaning to these activities across the whole of the empire for those who practiced them.[86]

Second, one of the ways that scholars have attempted to get at the meaning of dead infants and their burials is to interpret them with the aid of classical literary texts. Cicero, Pliny, and others wrote, on occasion, about newborns, infant burial, and the ritual pollution associated with dead bodies.[87] These authors are habitually invoked by those writing about infant burial, even in provincial contexts in the late Roman period. But if we are committed to listening to what rural people living a long way from Rome are telling us, we cannot allow their lives to be explained by the likes of Cicero.[88] The worldviews, experiences, and actions of low-status, fourth-century peasants and craft workers living in settlements in a peripheral province on the northernmost edge of the Roman world—people who had never read a Latin text and whose lives were completely outside the experience of elite men living on the Italian peninsula—cannot be explained by a set of texts that have nothing to do with them and that were written centuries before they were born. It is like explaining the popularity of cosmetic surgery among New Jersey's teenage girls using the writings of Samuel Johnson. It could certainly be done, but should it?

So, without the intervention of ancient authors, what can we say? First, it seems unlikely that infant burials represent the commemoration of individuals; rather, they look like household or communal acts that played starring roles in the perpetuation of living communities and households—their building of new houses, their ongoing relationships with chthonic deities, and the continued prosperity of their productive spaces. Generations of dead babies took part in the productive and generative work of farmers and craftspeople, and their deaths and interments, and the memory of their graves' locations punctuated the use of houses, barns, corn driers, kilns, and forges, and the lives of the people who labored in or around them.[89] Infant burial also helped inscribe and embody links between families, communities, places, and tasks, and because of the regularity of neonate burial (owing to high infant mortality rates) these events took place more frequently than other interments. As a result, infant bodies were repeatedly called into service in the ongoing process of reinscribing, reaffirming, or reworking links and landscapes.[90] Little corpses actively transformed generic space into place, giving the living a sense of the rightness of the divisions of their landscapes and taskscapes in the same way that in later periods, the annual "beating of the bounds" regularly defined and made place for whole communities.[91]

In short, the most striking thing about these burials is their instrumentality. It is also striking how many of the newborn dead were deployed in projects of pragmatic, collective social memory.[92] Like adults, these babies were sometimes buried in boundary ditches or along fence lines. Memories of their final resting places were maintained, even cultivated, and their bodies were added to generation after generation, serving to mark, define, underscore, or even redefine the boundaries of farmyards, family compounds, or fields,[93] things that in turn were central in the construction of identity in agrarian communities.[94] Little corpses were habitually invoked in acts of spatial ordering, positioned not only to mark "our house" or "our settlement's barn," but to emphasize or rework property boundaries.[95] Much as Simon Esmonde Cleary has argued that "informal" adult burials "were a real part of the conceptual landscape of living Romano-Britons," I would argue that infants helped make place.[96] Thus, the living used the memory of these dead infants and the placement of their graves to refashion or solidify the histories of houses, barns, relationships, and even ritual places.

Another striking feature of these burials is the continued intimacy between dead neonates and their communities. Although babies were not always treated in death the way adults were, they were, nonetheless, kept close to the living.[97] Burials along boundaries are often interpreted as liminal,[98] but I would suggest something more positive—making and remaking boundaries with bodies is altogether different from placing bodies at a distance from the living. The fact of their omnipresence and their underfootedness reminds us how close people in late Roman Britain kept their dead neonates, and how intimate and crucial their relations with them were. So dead babies, far from being relegated to oblivion, continued to engage with and be involved in the lives of their households and communities.[99] When seen in this way, it is hard to fathom how scholars could have ever believed that dead infants were unimportant, forgotten, or rubbish.[100]

Giving Up Old Traditions and Inventing New Ones

We are still, however, left with a puzzle: neonates were everywhere, but where were the children?[101] The Roman period experienced very high rates not just of infant mortality, but of child mortality. In Roman-period Italy and Egypt, between 20 percent and 35 percent of all infants died in the first year of life, and 40 percent to 60 percent of all babies born died before their fifth birthdays.[102] Studies of neonates at Poundbury and Piddington hint that there were probably similar infant mortality rates in Britain. A number of bioarchaeological studies suggest that after the age of five, more children in Britain survived, but most remained undersized and none too healthy, so although the odds for these physically stressed children improved, relatively high numbers would nonetheless not have survived childhood.[103] Although high childhood mortality represents demographic realities, there are relatively few children over the age of six months but under the age of twelve who are archaeologically visible in late Roman Britain outside the large urban extramural cemeteries or in exceptional elite burials.[104] Across Yorkshire, for example, according to Alex Smith, 47 percent of all excavated skeletons dated to the late Roman period belong to adults, and 48 percent belong to infants under the age of one year, but only 5 percent are those of children under the age of sixteen.[105] And his statistics for the East Midlands suggest that less than 8 percent of all excavated burials are those of children who lived past their twelfth month.[106] As we have seen, ordinary people living in roadside and rural communities kept many of their dead newborns close by or underfoot, and they often buried their adult dead in enclosed cemeteries, or along boundary features in and around their settlements. But these statistics suggest that by contrast, they kept very few of their dead children with them.

These practices stand in sharp contrast to practices developing in the first couple of centuries after Rome's withdrawal from Britain.[107] Although children continue in this later period to be underrepresented in the burial record, they are far more in evidence than in the Roman period.[108] In the fifth- and sixth-century cemetery at West Heslerton, in Yorkshire, for example (a place that must have included both indigenous British people and newcomers from the continent),[109] whereas no neonates were found within the cemetery, almost 25 percent of skeletons that could be aged there were those of children who died between the ages of one and ten.[110] At the early medieval cemetery at Berinsfield, in Oxfordshire, with its one hundred excavated graves, there were twenty-six children under the age of ten, but only one neonate.[111] At Beckford B, out of 107 sets of remains, something on the order of nineteen were younger than ten, but none were neonates.[112] Eighteen percent of the aged skeletons found at the cemetery of Eastbourne, in Sussex, died between the ages of one and eleven, but only a single baby less than a year old was recovered.[113] These cemeteries have been labeled "Anglo-Saxon," and they include considerable amounts of the new-style material culture, which is often associated with immigrants from across the sea, and which is often labeled "Anglo-Saxon." But early post-Roman cemeteries in the West of Britain, where continental immigrants had not established themselves, also included comparatively large numbers of children among their dead. In the post-Roman cemetery at Filton, in Gloucestershire, for example, five of the fifty-two excavated individuals were children under the age of ten, and three others were probably older children, but no infants were recovered from the site.[114] Over a quarter of the dead buried in the post-Roman cemetery at Tolpuddle Ball, in Dorset, were young children, but none were neonates.[115] At the cemetery at

Shepherd's Farm, Ulwell, in Dorset, 12 percent of the skeletons excavated were those of children under the age of twelve, but only one infant was found.[116] These examples could be multiplied and serve here simply to highlight the extraordinary shift taking place over the course of the fifth and sixth centuries across Britain as it moved from late Roman to early medieval: dead children become much more visible in the burial record, and they were more often laid to rest in places where adults were buried. But infants in the early medieval period become less visible, not only in cemeteries, but in settlement sites as well, where they cease to be a ubiquitous presence. They were now only very rarely laid to rest under the floors of houses or work buildings, along boundary ditches, or in structured deposits.[117]

Janet Kay has published data on child burials in Britain dated to the long fifth century.[118] Although her age categories conflate neonates and babies under the age of eighteen months, her figures are useful in this discussion.[119] Kay's analysis of 7,424 burials from eighty-seven inhumation cemeteries demonstrates that twice as many prepubescent children were buried in the period's cemeteries than infants.[120] Her datum also shows that the earliest of these cemeteries had on average 11.4 percent of their burial populations under eighteen months, but the latest of her cemeteries contain only 3.1 percent babies in the zero to eighteen-month age range.[121] So those hardworking dead infants, who had been such a notable part of life, ritual, daily practice, and place making in the late Roman period, receded from view in exactly the same generations that dead children started to come out from the shadows.

Because this seems to be a genuine trend, we might be able to use the presence of fewer neonates and relatively larger numbers of children to help date ambiguous cemeteries that may be late Roman, but that could equally be early medieval or include early medieval phases. A case in point is the cemetery at Bradley Hill. We know, thanks in part to grave goods and in part to James Gerrard's radiocarbon work there, that the graves in the north of the cemetery were dug in the fourth century, but those further south date to the fifth or even sixth centuries. Five neonates were buried in the cemetery, and more unusually for a rural Roman-period cemetery, three children were laid to rest there. All the neonates buried in the cemetery were found in the earlier part of the cemetery, but the three children lay in the zone where post-Roman burial took place.[122]

Across the fifth and sixth centuries, then, it seems that communities in Britain came both to bury more children in communal cemeteries and to dispose of dead neonates in novel, although archaeologically invisible ways. New ideas about the proper treatment of infant corpses, which eventually transformed into new traditions, would have taken some generations to develop. In a few early post-Roman cemeteries we can witness novel treatments of dead infants and children, which did not, in the end, win out and become more widely adopted. The post-Roman cemetery outside the walls of the former Roman town of Great Chesterford, in Essex, for example, contained unusually large numbers of infants under one year of age—forty-three in all.[123] Given that 167 sets of remains were recovered, these babies constitute more than a quarter of all excavated burials, a percentage that is never encountered in Britain's cemeteries of the late Roman period, but that aligns with the large numbers of neonates found buried in and around Roman-period settlements.[124] Thirteen children under the age of twelve were also recovered at the Great Chesterford cemetery, representing some 8 percent of the cemetery's dead. It is unlikely that these were the community's only dead children, but their number would not have been out of line in a late Roman extramural cemetery. The Great Chesterford cemetery also contained graves shared by more than one neonate: two were laid to rest in one grave; another grave contained the remains of at least six.[125] Such companionable groups of infants were often found in the Roman period. So it seems that those burying at Great Chesterford in the immediate post-Roman period may have no longer placed neonates under the floors of their houses and barns or along boundary ditches, but that they were bringing them, instead, to the communal cemetery for burial. Another community pioneering new infant and child burial traditions was the one burying at Horcott Quarry, in Gloucestershire. At an enclosed late Roman cemetery there, fifty-nine individuals were buried, three of whom were neonates and one of whom was a child under the age of ten.[126] But in the post-Roman period, people burying in the same enclosure buried twelve individuals. Three were adults, five were under a year old, and the remaining four were children under nine years of age.[127] In the end though, practices such as those pioneered at post-Roman Great Chesterford and Horcott Quarry lost out to what would eventually become more broadly held notions that dead babies belonged neither in settlements nor in inhumation cemeteries.

A few communities also continued to deposit dead neonates under the floors of buildings in the immediate post-Roman period, but they were now placing them in abandoned buildings, something happening on the continent as well.[128] This occurred in the very late phase of Redlands Farm villa, after part of the main domestic building had been demolished by whoever it was who controlled the site. At this time, the villa's abandoned but still-standing west wing became a site of infant burial. Here a number of neonates were buried in the floor tight against the wall, their graves marked with heaps of *tesserae* salvaged from a ripped-up mosaic floor that had once adorned another room in the house.[129] We know that neonates continued to be buried in the building at an even later date, because the later graves, unlike the ones covered with *tesserae*, were dug through rubble that was now covering the floors, and so had to postdate the building's collapse.[130] But the practices attested at Redlands Farm never gained much currency among other fifth-century groups. Clifford Sofield's study of human burials in 142 settlement sites dating from the fifth through the ninth centuries uncovered only seven infants.[131]

The cessation for the most part of the use of infant burials in practices of remembrance and place making, and their disappearance from the archaeological record, paired with the widespread adoption of child burial in communal cemeteries, are surely evidence of major shifts in worldview, cosmology, daily practice, and place making. They mark a sea change in the lifeways of ordinary people living through the period of transition and suggest that the ways an early sixth-century person thought about and practiced rituals of death, inscribed settlement landscapes with boundaries, and connected the present to the past must have been altogether different from those of that person's grandparents or great-grandparents who had lived under Rome. Such profound ruptures in long-standing burial practices argue for a sharp break with the ways of the past.[132] So my argument here is that in the late Roman period the Little Magic of infant bodies was a force in people's lives and in the landscape, and that the memories of the bodies of the infant dead were used to map local worlds and create communal consensus. But I also think that the Little Magic of dead infants collapsed in the early Middle Ages and that these tiny corpses lost their centrality in everyday lifeways.

One final observation: we think of late antiquity as a period in which elite Christian men pioneered new ideas about the efficacy and power of the dead and began using dead bodies in innovative ways, turning settlements inside out and inviting the dead, long banned by Roman law from spaces inhabited by the living, into the very heart of human settlements. The evidence presented in this chapter shows that low-status people in Britain had been doing this for centuries. It is worth wondering if what we understand as new and revolutionary attitudes toward the dead in this period were not on some occasions the adoption by elites and the writers of texts of practices that had been around for centuries in less rarified circles, but were now, for the first time, like so many other practices, being hoisted up from below and made visible to historians for the first time because they came to be described in texts.

CHAPTER 8

Who Was Buried in Early Anglo-Saxon Cemeteries?

> Words gain a terrible power over the concepts they describe.
>
> —Richard Bradley, "A Life Less Ordinary"

Infant burial was not the only category of burial remade in the fifth century: adult burials, in these years, were undergoing a revolution of their own. The dramatic changes in graveside rites, cemetery placement, and grave goods, so clear in the archaeological record, are most often understood—with the aid of early medieval texts—to be the result of an influx of "Anglo-Saxon" immigrants. This is somewhat ironic, given that old-fashioned, culture-historical interpretations— which hold that new styles of material culture and novel burial rites signal the arrival of new peoples—have been out of fashion among British archaeologists for almost half a century.[1] Although it is clear that some places in Britain—in particular East Anglia—were witnessing the settlement of relatively large numbers of immigrants in the fifth century and that these people were bringing new material culture and new material practices with them, it does not necessarily follow that all people burying their dead in new cemeteries, in new ways, and with new-style objects were newcomers to Britain. Nonetheless, the basic narrative of the period has been shaped by the idea that the events and culture change of the period were propelled by ethnic difference.[2]

Before this chapter lays out and grapples with the meaning of material evidence from cemeteries, especially that related to the period's dead women, three methodological points are worth emphasizing. The first is that the words we adopt when we write about the past are crucially important to get right, and that the terminology we are in the habit of using sometimes stands in the way of our seeing what "really happened" in the past. The habitual, sloppy, underinterrogated use of ethnic labels, in particular the word "Anglo-Saxon" by historians and archaeologists—many of whom know how problematic this terminology is but continue to use it—to describe both people and things in fifth-century Britain,[3] makes it difficult to see the material transformations taking place there in its first post-Roman century. Because ethnic adjectives are habitually applied to material culture new to Britain, and because the ethnic things that result are then used to determine the ethnic identities of the people who made and used them, the native population of lowland Britain is erased. This habit forecloses the possibility that Britain's large native population, whose Roman-style material culture was disappearing, had anything at all to do with the creation of the new material world of the early Middle Ages. At the same time, the use of "Anglo-Saxon" to describe the period's newcomers does little justice to the many kinds of people moving into and around Britain in these years. The term gives the impression that these people carried Anglo-Saxon identity with them in the bottoms of their boats alongside a full-blown Anglo-Saxon material culture. This negates any active role they might have had in creating Britain's early medieval material world.[4]

Second, historians, because they depend on texts, write about warbands and conquests and the establishment of petty kingdoms because these are the things that early medieval texts tell us about. But the texts that provide the framework for our basic understanding of the long fifth century are deeply problematic. None were written in fifth-century Britain. A handful of texts were penned elsewhere in the late antique world, but their information on Britain is far from reliable, and some of it is probably not even about Britain.[5] We also have a series of texts that *were* written in what is now England, but mostly only in the later seventh, eighth, and ninth centuries. A detailed, blow-by-blow account of the fifth and sixth centuries, for example, survives in the compilation known as the *Anglo-Saxon Chronicle*, which describes the activities of marauding fifth-century kings and their manly followers. Although historians these days tend to approach the *Chronicle* like a dirty bomb they have been asked to defuse,[6] even the most skeptical of readers have been influenced by the content and tenor of this and other of our retrospective written sources, especially by the fact that for all intents and purposes the only historical actors in them are men, and "Anglo-Saxon" men at that. This has conditioned historians to write narratives focused on weapon-bearing males, and to imagine the Big

Story of the period as a political one, concerned, primarily, with the actions of foreign men "invading," "conquering," and "colonizing."

Historians and archaeologists, taking their cues from these texts, often write implicitly—sometimes explicitly—as though men alone were the earliest incomers to England; or that the majority of people moving into lowland Britain were men; or that the only people who were driving the narrative in this period and doing the important historical and culture-changing work (that is, the change from Roman to medieval) were men.[7] Britain, of course, is not the only place about which these assumptions are made. Bonnie Effros, for example, has observed that much of what has been written about early medieval Gaul, "rather than addressing the population as a whole ... concentrates on the male members of these groups, since it is they who are perceived as actively involved in shaping their communities' identity and future."[8] The results exemplify what the novelist Chimanda Ngozi Adichie has called "the danger of the single story," because this kind of work "show[s] a people as one thing, as only one thing, over and over again, and that is what they become."[9]

A third and final point made in this chapter, one that follows from the second, is that in order to gain an understanding of what was transpiring during Britain's transition from Roman to early medieval, we need to privilege contemporary over later evidence, which in this period means privileging material evidence over texts. We need to take contemporary material evidence where it leads us and study the people it tells us about, even if those people were not of particular interest to writers of early medieval texts. Bringing to the fore life stories of the kinds of people who are not described in our retrospective texts, but who are made visible through excavation, helps combat the tyranny of "the single story."

In spite of changing ideas about gender, ethnicity, and material culture, the rather old-fashioned gendered history just described has received a new lease on life in recent years in the work of geneticists, some of whom argue that a handful of foreign males in this period were able to impose themselves on a large native population, monopolize the women, and swamp the gene pool.[10] The study of ancient populations, however, is in its infancy, and research techniques and understandings are developing so rapidly that work done only ten years ago has already been upended and superseded.[11] Geneticists, moreover, have no training in history or archaeology, so it is not all that surprising to find that some of them have grafted their findings onto outdated historical interpretations.[12] Although some of the new DNA research will be used in this chapter, it will be put into the context of other evidence from the period and thought about with the aid of our most recent understandings of the mechanisms standing behind migration, identity, and culture change.[13]

Women's Grave Goods, Stable Isotopes, and aDNA

Given the male centeredness of our understandings of this period's history, it is salutary to remind ourselves that the majority of our genuinely contemporary evidence—which is material, rather than textual—is associated not with men, but with late-adolescent girls and adult women. Much of it comes from cemetery excavations, in which more women in this early period were buried with grave goods and dress fittings than men were, those buried with objects are found with more of them, and women were buried with a greater variety of objects than men were.[14] And, in spite of all the men running around both our early medieval texts and our modern historical narratives, in actual fact, the basic material culture chronologies that we depend on to date things in this period are largely tethered to the metalwork objects found in the graves of the period's dead women.[15] Because so much of the surviving material culture is associated with women, it behooves us to incorporate it *and them* into whatever narrative we stitch together, not only because they provide us with the bulk of our evidence, but because their evidence's relative abundance hints at the central role women played in whatever it was that was going on in these years. Because they are the people we can see best, they are the ones we should be writing about.

In the pages that follow, we will focus on women who lived in lowland Britain in the fifth and early sixth centuries, although our discussion will occasionally broaden to include men. We will think about these women in relation to mobility and migration on the one hand, and as the consumers, displayers, promoters, and makers of material culture on the other. Before turning to them, though, we will first meet a group of early medieval women living not in Britain, but in what is now Germany, because they very effectively highlight the difficulties and ambiguities of our evidence, and they will help us deploy similar evidence from Britain.

Archaeologists have recovered the skeletons of a number of fifth- and early sixth-century women in Germany whose skulls had been elongated through regimes of head binding during infancy and early childhood.[16] The epicenter of this practice lay far to the east, among Hunnic peoples settled in the Carpathian basin.[17] Their presence in Germany has been used as evidence that women sometimes moved considerable distances and across stunning cultural divides, probably through exogamous, high-status marriages, and that such marriages played a central role in human mobility during the early medieval period.[18] One of the interesting things about the women found in Germany is that they are often alone among all the people in their cemeteries who have a modified skull, or they are found with only a handful of other women who share the same body modification. These same women, however, were usually buried with the same kinds of dress accessories and grave goods buried with other women in the cemeteries in which they lay, women without modified skulls.[19] And because none of the children buried in these cemeteries show signs of having had their heads bound, some of the customs associated with child rearing, which must have been part of these women's own girlhoods, were not carried on in the communities in which they lived as adults.[20] So it does not look as if these women's own natal traditions and material culture made much of an impact on their new communities.

While a number of these women were probably highly mobile, the evidence they present is, as we are about to see, more complicated than it first appears. This is because when scientific analyses of their remains are undertaken, their personal histories begin to look less straightforward. Chemical elements such as oxygen and strontium (which are two important molecules in this cautionary tale) each come in a couple of different forms, or isotopes. All oxygen molecules, for example, have the same number of protons, but different oxygen isotopes have different numbers of neutrons. They are both oxygen, but they are different oxygen isotopes. There are a couple of interesting and useful things to know about these isotopes. As far as oxygen is concerned, there is a general global trend that the ratio of different oxygen isotopes in rainwater changes at a relatively even rate as we move toward the equator, away from coastal zones, and into higher altitudes. Oxygen isotopic ratios are also influenced by levels of aridity and rainfall.[21] The particular ratio of oxygen isotopes found in the rainwater drunk by humans is incorporated into their bodies. What this means is that the oxygen isotopes found in archaeologically excavated human remains can help us determine how far north or south, how far from the coast, or at what altitude that person lived. The ratio of strontium isotopes found in skeletal remains, on the other hand, is determined by the hard geology on which our food is grown. Strontium isotopes move through the food chain and ground water from bedrock, to plants and animals, and into human bodies.[22]

There is one more vital thing to know about these isotopes: oxygen and strontium accumulate not only in bone, but also in tooth enamel. This is important because tooth enamel is laid down very early in life and unlike bones, teeth are not remodeled over time, so the strontium- and oxygen-isotopic ratios found in people's teeth are related to the hard geology and drinking water of the neighborhoods in which they spent their infancies and early childhoods.[23] This allows us to sometimes determine whether a person whose teeth have been examined was born locally, or whether he or she had emigrated from some other region after early childhood.

The use of stable isotopes in the study of human mobility and migration is relatively new and not without methodological and interpretive challenges. Difficulties arise, in part, from the fact that a large swath of northwest Europe shares similar oxygen values in their drinking water and similar surface geology, and therefore similar strontium values.[24] To further complicate matters, diet, climate change, and postburial conditions can sometimes affect stable isotopic ratios in bone, although tooth enamel is relatively impervious to diagenetic alteration.[25] It is also increasingly clear that studies that use large sample sizes and that analyze two or more isotopic systems produce more robust results, but as of yet few such studies have been completed.[26]

With these caveats in mind, let us return to our women in Germany with modified skulls.[27] Isotopic analysis of the tooth enamel of twenty-one women with skull modifications recovered in Thuringian cemeteries suggests that at least nineteen (out of twenty-one) had been born locally.[28] In the same Thuringian cemeteries where the women with "Hunnic" skull modifications have been found, the remains of other women have also been recovered, who because of their grave goods, have been labeled foreigners. One woman for example, who died around the year 500, went into the ground in one of these cemeteries with a suite of grave goods that finds its closest parallel in Denmark, and she has been identified as a "Langobard."[29] But isotopic studies reveal that she, too, was likely a local girl. So, what we need to take away from this is that grave goods and even body modifications should not necessarily be read as evidence for migration or ethnic affiliation.

An analysis of the ancient DNA (aDNA) of a number of women with modified skulls has also been undertaken, and the results have added a further layer of complexity to the mix.[30] We will look, here, at data relating to just four such women from Bavarian cemeteries—two buried at Straubing-Bajuwarenstrasse and two at Altenerding-Klettham—to demonstrate the ways in which the brooches (still presumed by some to be ethnic markers),[31] stable isotopes, and aDNA do not always line up neatly to match our expectations, but instead can be contradictory and confounding in ways that suggest that the fact of mobility on the one hand and the ways individuals marked their immigrant status or natal identities on the other were far from uniform or straightforward.

We have data on strontium isotopes for two women with modified skulls buried at Straubing-Bajuwarenstrasse—G 328 and G 355—as well as for carbon and nitrogen isotopes, which preserve information on diet.[32] Both women, according to their isotopic signatures, were likely raised locally, and their diets, as adults, were much like almost everyone else's in the cemetery. Although one had been buried with "Frankish" and "Alamanic" brooches and although she had an elongated skull, she was genetically similar to many other people in the cemetery, including women without skull modifications and women wearing brooches ascribed to different ethnic groups from the ones she was wearing.[33] The other woman was buried with "Ostrogothic" brooches. Her carbon, nitrogen, and strontium isotopes were also similar to others in the cemetery, suggesting that she, too, had grown up in the area and had shared a local diet. Her aDNA, on the other hand, suggests that her ancestry was quite different from that of most of her neighbors: the population to whom she is most closely related was that of modern-day Anatolia.[34]

An elderly woman (1108) with a modified skull at the cemetery at Altenerding-Klettham was wearing "Thuringian" brooches when buried. A second woman in the same cemetery with a modified skull (125) had no grave goods. We have carbon isotopes for the former, and they suggest that she had eaten food at some point in her life that was quite different from other people in the region in which she died, probably millet, which has a distinctive carbon isotope signature.[35] We do not have carbon isotopes for the second woman, but we do have information on strontium isotopes from both her tooth enamel and her bones, and they, too, are anomalous for the region and suggest that she had been raised elsewhere.[36] There are technical reasons for thinking that both women might have arrived in Bavaria relatively late in life.[37] So, rather than coming to this part of Germany as exogamous brides, they could, instead, have come as attendants to girls who did arrive as brides, or they might have come as captives. Both these women also stood out genetically from other people in their cemetery. The woman with no grave goods was most closely related to modern populations in southeast Europe. The woman with "Thuringian" brooches shared a genetic affinity with modern populations in central Asia.[38]

Although these and other women with modified skulls had the most genetically diverse ancestries in their cemeteries, the majority were related to populations in southeast Europe rather than central Asia or Anatolia. The majority of people with whom they were buried, on the other hand, were most closely related to modern northern or central European populations. There were, however, a handful of people in the two cemeteries without modified skulls who were also significantly different genetically from most of the people they were buried near.

One's aDNA showed her to be related to people living in modern-day Greece, another's to people now living in Turkey.[39]

Women with modified skulls buried in these two cemeteries, then, were not genetically homogeneous. Some may have been raised locally; some came only in middle age; and many could be shown not to have been genetically related to ethnic groups to whom their brooches have long been attributed. At the same time, a few people without modified skulls were also genetic and isotopic outliers, and they are likely to be immigrants as well, but their personal histories of migration were not signaled through body modifications, dress, or grave goods.[40]

This is a salutary tale, one we need to internalize and take to heart as we move to a discussion of material culture in fifth- and early sixth-century lowland Britain. Let us turn to the evidence excavated from the cemetery at West Heslerton, in North Yorkshire. Burial in this cemetery took place between c. 400 and c. 650, and in total archaeologists uncovered three hundred inhumations and a handful of cremations there.[41] Janet Montgomery, Paul Budd, and others have undertaken oxygen and strontium stable isotope analysis on a number of skeletons excavated from the cemetery—we have data for both strontium and oxygen for twenty-seven individuals and for strontium alone for a further five. Here, we will examine the bodies, burials, and grave goods of just seven of the women and children for whom we have isotopic data and use them to help us think about women, migration, and material culture in early medieval Britain.

The teenage girl buried in Grave 117 was not put in the ground with any metalwork dress fittings. She had neither the brooches with close parallels to ones found in Scandinavia, where we think many people were emigrating from, nor wrist clasps, little metal plates with hook-and-eye fastenings attached to the cuffs of women's sleeved undergowns, a Norwegian dress fashion adopted by women in the North and East of Britain beginning in the late fifth century;[42] this in spite of the fact that many women in the cemetery had both.[43] She was, however, buried with a fairly extensive collection of beads, some of which hark back to those worn by women in Britain both in the pre-Roman Iron Age and during the Roman period.[44] She was placed in the ground in a crouched position, a burial posture with a very long history in northeast Britain stretching from the Neolithic all the way through the early Middle Ages.[45] Two other women—the ones found in Graves 133 and 159—lay flat on their backs and were buried with no metalwork dress accessories or grave goods, although the woman in Grave 159 lay in a coffin. Many people in Roman Britain's last century had practiced this stripped-down, no-grave-goods, supine form of burial and coffin burial.[46] Given the large number of women buried in the West Heslerton cemetery with continental-style brooches and wrist clasps, it is tempting to identify these three as native British women—lower-status members of the West Heslerton burial community dominated by "Anglo-Saxon" immigrants from the continent without access to (or perhaps without a taste for) the new-fangled dress fasteners that immigrant women sported, but with hints—their beads, their burial positions, their lack of grave goods—that suggest that some indigenous traditions persisted in the neighborhood in the face of large-scale migration from across the North Sea. The signatures, however, of the oxygen isotopes in their tooth enamel tell a different story. These three women, along with the toddler in Grave 169 (out of twenty-seven sets of early medieval remains for which we have data on oxygen isotopes),[47] had drunk water as children with an isotopic signature found nowhere in Great Britain. Although this information enables us to identify, with some confidence, these women and the child as immigrants, it is more difficult to pinpoint where they had come from. But the general best practice in stable isotope studies (as in so much else in life) is to keep Occam's razor firmly in mind, knowing that the simplest explanation is often the best one. Given the ratios of oxygen isotopes in these four individuals' tooth enamel, the closest place where they might have spent their childhoods is Scandinavia or somewhere in the eastern Baltic.[48]

What about the women and girls at West Heslerton who *were* buried with metalwork that we think of as "Anglo-Saxon" or even Scandinavian? The woman lying in Grave 84 had probably been in her early twenties when she died.[49] She was buried with a mismatched pair of brooches—a cruciform brooch (one of the earliest forms found in the cemetery)[50] and a small long brooch, along with a set of beads strung between the two in typical "Anglo-Saxon" fashion. The woman in Grave 102 shared her final resting place with the body of a child.[51] She was buried with a string of beads suspended between a pair of annular brooches, and mourners placed a lathe-turned, maple bowl beside her corpse. The way her brooches and beads were worn and the use of a wooden bowl as a grave offering are both things we think of as "Anglo-Saxon." Another woman, the one in Grave 89, was wearing wrist clasps, a fashion, as we have seen, that originated in Norway.[52] These three women, in short, were buried with dress fittings and objects that have close parallels to the material culture of peoples on the continent. But both the strontium and the oxygen isotopic signatures of their teeth argue that neither they nor the three men buried in Graves 109, and 145, and 75 (the last of these with weapons)[53] spent their early childhoods in and around West Heslerton; nor did they come from Scandinavia or the Baltic. Their combination of oxygen and strontium values also do not match those found in people from Denmark, Sweden, or Norway. Instead, the closest region that would produce both these oxygen and these strontium isotopic signatures is Britain *west* of the Pennines.[54] That region lay in the British culture zone in the fifth and early sixth centuries—a region, so far as we know, without any continental migration. Thus, these women may have been born in British communities (indigenous, not "Germanic"), and migrated eastward, rather than westward.

The evidence is suggestive and argues that women's individual stories of migration are not reflected in the material culture with which they were buried: some women who may have come from the Baltic or Scandinavia were buried in ways we might expect British women to have been buried, and some women whose origins may have lain on the far side of the Pennines or elsewhere in Britain were dressed in ways that might lead us to identify them as Scandinavian immigrants.

So what we have at West Heslerton is evidence that lots of women and children (and even some infants) were on the move in this period. Indeed, women were as likely to have migrated as men. They seem to have been traveling across the sea, and they were likely moving overland within Britain. The evidence from West Heslerton also underscores the fact that the period's migration was not a single event, because it has produced evidence that immigrant women were present c. 450, and that that they were still coming c. 650.[55] All in all, an impressive minority of the people who died at West Heslerton in the two and a half centuries during which people buried their dead in the cemetery were likely born someplace else.[56] The people of West Heslerton, therefore, were not living in a hermetically sealed, homogeneous, diasporic settlement, but they were residing in a mixed community made up of individuals and families who had arrived at different times and from different places and with quite different cultural baggage.[57] As so many late Roman settlements were abandoned by the first decades of the fifth century,[58] it is not unreasonable to think that people indigenous to the British Isles were on the move, as busy making new settlements and new lives as the newcomers from beyond the sea, alongside whom many were now living.

Isotopic investigations of other of Britain's early medieval cemeteries have similarly uncovered burial communities comprising people born locally, immigrants from other parts of Britain, and immigrants from across the sea. Of the nineteen skeletons analyzed from the cemetery at Eastbourne, in Sussex, ten appear to have been born locally, and two were probably raised in settlements situated a few dozen kilometers away. Of the remaining seven, six either came from more distant parts of Britain or had been born in a variety of places on the continent. But only one—a woman—can be shown with certainty to have come from beyond the sea. So, as at West Heslerton, locally born individuals, people who had come from elsewhere in Britain, and continental immigrants shared a cemetery.[59] Migrants at Eastbourne, like migrants at West Heslerton, hailed from more than one place, and as at West Heslerton, newcomers here had arrived in different generations. Finally, as at West Heslerton, those who spent their childhoods in Britain were much more likely to have grave goods than those who had moved from elsewhere.

The study of another nineteen individuals buried at the early medieval cemetery at Berinsfield, in Oxfordshire, has produced similar results. Fifteen of the individuals examined were probably born locally, and four were isotopic outliers. Three of the outsiders likely came from elsewhere in Britain, although one of these could have also come from central or northern continental Europe. Only one can definitively be said to have come from across the sea. Two of the isotopic outliers were buried without grave goods.[60] The third, a woman, was placed in the ground with a disc brooch on one shoulder and an early, but probably insular-made equal-arm brooch on the other. Both brooches date to the late fifth century and are considered "Anglo-Saxon,"[61] as is the way she was wearing them to fasten a *peplos*-style dress (a tubular gown, over a sleeved undergarment, fastened at each shoulder with a matching brooch). Her isotopes, however, argue that she had spent her early childhood in the west or southwest of Britain. She is, therefore, likely, in spite of her grave goods, to have been of British ancestry.

The disjunction between our habitual (mis)interpretation of grave finds and the quite different reality that sometimes stood behind them fits in with the findings of other studies on stable isotopes, both for the late Roman and for the early medieval periods. Investigations of Romano-British skeletal material, for example, undertaken, for the most part, on those buried in large, late Roman urban cemeteries, have alerted us to the fact that many people in the Roman period were on the move in Britain, and that migration in Britain has a history that long predates the early Middle Ages. They show, for example that important administrative towns such as Gloucester, London, Winchester, and York had very cosmopolitan populations. All included individuals who, based on their strontium and oxygen isotopic ratios, had been born in the Mediterranean basin, and a number included people of African and Middle Eastern descent or individuals who were originally from Pannonia or the Rhineland.[62] Smaller towns, such as Catterick, had populations drawn much more from their hinterlands, but even they were home to a few foreigners.[63] Another of these studies' findings is that many people buried in ways we might think of as typically Romano-British have isotopic ratios suggesting that they were not native to Britain. At the same time, some of those buried with grave goods identified as "Germanic" or "Pannonian" turn out to have been born locally.⁶⁴ Besides people who had moved to Britain's towns from the far reaches of the empire, bioarchaeologists have also identified a fair number of individuals who had likely immigrated from other parts of Britain.⁶⁵

Similar results have been produced in isotopic investigations of post-Roman sites in the West of Britain. Several studies point to sustained and perhaps significant migration within the British Isles and Ireland across much of the early Middle Ages. Impressive numbers of women and men buried in cemeteries in England, in Wales, and on the Isle of Man likely moved from within the British Isles or Ireland between their childhoods and deaths, underscoring internal migration during this period, especially movement from the west to the east.⁶⁶ In a recent article, Janet Kay has identified a dozen fifth-century women out of a sample of twenty-nine for whom isotopic work has been done, moving from modern-day Wales or northwest Britain to England.⁶⁷ The long and the short of all this is that more men, women, and children migrating from within Britain and Ireland have turned up in isotopic investigations of early medieval skeletons than immigrants from the continent.⁶⁸

Isotopic studies have also uncovered long-distance migrants from the seventh and eighth centuries. A couple of people buried in the cemetery at Adwick-le-Street, in South Yorkshire, in the eighth century, may have been born in Scandinavia.⁶⁹ In Arncliffe, in North Yorkshire, a woman was buried with a copper-alloy workbox sometime, according to radiocarbon dating, between 559–653 (at 2 sigma). She turns out to be a "distant" migrant as well, again perhaps from Norway, a surprise given that her workbox is generally understood as an object possessed by high-status women from the South of England.⁷⁰ And at the Bowl Hole cemetery, a burial ground used during the seventh, eighth, and ninth centuries by members of the Northumbrian royal court, half of those buried had been born someplace else. Some were from elsewhere in England or Scotland, but others hailed from Ireland, Scandinavia, or the Mediterranean basin. Among the newcomers were numerous women and children.⁷¹ These findings remind us that women and children were on the move for many centuries, certainly well into the middle Saxon period and beyond.

Although less aDNA work has been undertaken for early medieval Britain than for early medieval Germany, we do have data on four women buried at Oakington, in Cambridgeshire, before the last quarter of the sixth century.⁷² One (Grave 1) was found to bear a close genetic affinity to Britain's Iron Age population, two (Graves 95 and 82) have a closer affinity to modern Dutch or Danish populations, and the fourth (Grave 96) sits in the middle, suggesting that this person was the product of a mixed household. Interestingly, all four were buried in flexed positions, something, as we have seen, once interpreted as a signal of Britishness. One of the two people of continental ancestry had no grave goods, and the one most closely related to Britain's Iron Age population was buried in a *peplos*-style gown, attached at each shoulder with an annular brooch. She was also wearing a belt with metal fittings and a large cruciform brooch, probably on her cloak, and she had a knife and fourteen amber and three glass beads. In short, in spite of her ancestry, she was dressed in death in a style we think of as "Anglo-Saxon."[73] Toby Martin has observed, "It is not far-fetched to imagine some of the inhabitants of post-Roman Britain converting their Roman jewellery and other wares into new material culture forms and in doing so creating the objects we have come to know as Anglo-Saxon. Accordingly, the crucible, or rather those who controlled what went in and came out of it, played no small role in converting the people we call Romans into Anglo-Saxons."[74]

Surely, many women kitted out in new ways were, like this Oakington woman, embracing, making, and participating in the creation of new-style material culture and new-style material practices, because that is what people in Britain were doing in this period of radical material transformation, no matter where their ancestors had been born.

Dressing for a Brave New World

As the evidence of isotopes and aDNA makes clear, women from a variety of home cultures in the long fifth century were experimenting with and pioneered new forms of dress and personal adornment. We should not assume that these women were paper dolls, passively allowing themselves to be dressed by the men in their lives,[75] or that they were required to wear "ethnic" costumes by some all-powerful early medieval Anglo-Saxon Migration Association.[76]

In order to underscore this point, I will first lay out the evidence for women's participation in the creation of the period's dress and then consider the implications of this. The historiographical scene is well set by a quote from a recent excellent article, which gives a sense of how scholars tend to speak about the period's women and their dress: "female costume ... played a key role in communicating messages about identity and ethnicity during much of the early Anglo-Saxon period."[77] Statements such as this are all about the costume and not about the people wearing it. Women themselves in this all-too-typical formulation are reduced to walking billboards, and they are not depicted as historical actors, making choices for themselves, communicating messages that were important to them, or participating in the creation of the identities that they were allegedly proclaiming. There is, moreover, scant acknowledgement that both identities and material expressions of identity are at times extremely unstable,[78] and that both can rapidly morph into something else. It is useful here to think about Diane Hughes's study of the way the wearing of earrings—a mark of Jewishness in early fifteenth-century Italy—was hijacked by Christian women from wealthy merchant families to make altogether different statements about themselves that were completely untethered from the "ethnic" meaning earrings had until recently signified.[79]

Although it is true that there were broad regional differences in women's dress developing by c. 500 CE (although there are also interesting material-culture blurrings and overlaps as well),[80] many archaeologists and a handful of historians have long doubted that fifth- and early sixth-century dress was dictated by biological heritage.[81] As we have seen, this certainly looks like the case at West Heslerton, Eastbourne, Berinsfield, and Oakington. Still, as Susanne Hakenbeck has pointed out, until recently, our understanding of early medieval dressing practices was informed by nineteenth-century ideas of *Tracht*—the notion that costumes worn by local rural groups were timeless and traditional, and above all else were about ethnicity, as that term was understood in the nineteenth century: as a "natural" identity that combined shared blood, history, language, and culture.[82]

In actual fact, it is exceptionally difficult to reconstruct female dress in early medieval Britain, because typically all that remains of women's outfits in the ground are beads and the metal components of dress—mostly in the form of brooches, buckles, and wrist clasps. Evidence for the cloth, on the other hand, which made up the bulk of contemporary dress, is hard to come by, and only tiny bits of mineralized textiles are preserved in graves where cloth came into contact with metal objects.[83] This, of course, means that the costumes of women buried without these items—as was the case for many women—can never be reconstructed.

Scholars, in spite of this dearth of evidence, often write as if female dress during this period was more uniform-like than it actually was. Where textile evidence has survived, no one has done more than Penelope Walton Rogers to uncover the quite remarkable variety in the period's female dress. Some women, so she has shown, were not wearing the standard *peplos*-style dress.[84] One young woman, for example, buried in the fifth century at West Heslerton, was dressed, rather unusually, in an all-linen get-up, rather than the more typical linen undergarment and woolen *peplos* gown. Her undergarment was pinned with a small long brooch on the right shoulder, with the left slide slung under her left arm.

The other linen garment was worn on top of the first one, in mirror image of the undergown, pinned with an annular brooch on the left shoulder.[85] Another woman at West Heslerton may have been wearing a pleated linen garment.[86] A woman buried at Flixton, in Suffolk, looks like she was wearing an old-fashioned, Roman-style *pallium* fastened with a single brooch at the shoulder,[87] and it turns out that quite a few women were wearing their *peploi* attached at only one shoulder.[88] Sometimes the fabrics that went into the making of these garments could give these outfits wildly different looks. A woman buried at Mucking, for example, was wearing a striped cloak,[89] and a girl buried at Flixton was wearing what looks to have been a goat cashmere cloak with a fur collar.[90] Another woman, this one at Wasperton, wore a gray goat-hair cloak.[91]

Women, so Walton Rogers and others have shown, also wore a wide variety of head coverings. The West Heslerton woman in the all-linen outfit was wearing an unusually long, open-weave, semitransparent linen veil.[92] Another woman at West Heslerton wore a shorter dark-red woolen headdress, while one at Scorton, in Yorkshire, sported a net-like, dark-blue head covering.[93] A woman buried in Grave 18 at Butler's Field, Lechlade, on the other hand, seems to have been wearing some sort of beaded ornament in her hair,[94] and a woman at Mill Hill, in Kent, had a fancy brooch pinned at the top of her head to a very long headdress edged with gold braid.[95] Some women also wore unusual, sometimes unique, combinations of brooches.[96] Similarly, women were deploying brooches, beads, even animal pelts on their bodies in quite different ways.[97] So, while broad, regional dressing styles and sets of dressing conventions gradually developed over the course of the later fifth and sixth centuries, there must, in reality, have been noticeable individuality in dress. These examples help bring to life the findings of a much more systematic analysis of fifth- and sixth-century female dress in East Anglia by Genevieve Fisher, which has uncovered not only highly localized costumes there, but alternative dress styles present in the same cemeteries in the same generations, and this, in turn, suggests that although there was a basic grammar of dress, there was nonetheless a good deal of individual expression.[98]

There is also considerable evidence to suggest that the marking of life cycle was central to the period's female dress culture. In fact, it is likely that the deployment of particular dress accessories—especially brooches—was closely linked to menarche, marriage, menopause, and perhaps widowhood.[99] Indeed, there is the very real possibility that demarcations of life cycle were more important to women and their choice of brooches than any desire on their part to declare allegiances to specific kindreds, regions, or "ethnic" groups. In early medieval Britain, indigenous women may have first adopted continental-style brooches as life-cycle markers rather than as statements of ethnicity: their grandmothers had done the same with their jewelry.[100] Or they may have adopted these dress fittings because they looked modern, or because they were available, or because a locally admired woman favored this style of metalwork. All these explanations are more likely than the idea that women dressed as they did because they were the passive bearers of ethnicity. Indeed, most women's exposure to new types of brooches and beads must have been locally mediated, and they likely chose to wear them not because of this metalwork's place of origin, but rather because of the way it was used in their own local contexts. So, it is unlikely that these objects were being adopted in the fifth century because they were thought to symbolize Anglo-Saxon-ness.[101]

There is, then, the very real possibility that women were actively involved in the creation of their own dress, experimenting with different styles of dress fittings, head dresses, and clothing options as they and everyone else in the period were engaged in building a new world on the ruins of the old. Sue Harrington gets it just right when she suggests that "the mixing and matching of female dress fitments, denoting a range of cultural references, may have been another facet of individuals finding their own, new identities in a new place, freed from the constraints of the past."[102]

It is productive to rethink the evidence found in the graves of women and girls, swapping the notion of agency for ethnicity, because when we do, we can more easily see the same mixed signals in the grave goods, dress fasteners, and burial rites of the period's dead women. Take the ten- or twelve-year-old girl found in Grave 29 at the Great Chesterford cemetery, in Essex.[103] Her grave goods hint at cross-cultural interactions, borrowings, and remakings. This child sported an odd collection of beads—some standard "Anglo-Saxon" fare, but others—the ones fabricated from jet and shale—we would expect in late Roman Britain.[104] She was wearing a mismatched pair of iron penannular brooches as well, a brooch type long favored in Britain, and, indeed, one that had started, after a long hiatus, to make a comeback in the late Roman period.[105] Someone had also placed a Roman coin in her left hand, a practice that seems to reference the common Romano-British custom of burying the dead with Charon's obol.[106] But she also wore a pair of wrist clasps, a dress innovation, as we have seen, that hailed from Norway, and this means that she was buried in a style of dress new to lowland Britain. This is a child who lived and died in the first couple of generations after the Roman state's withdrawal, and in the same decades when relatively large numbers of immigrants had begun arriving from across the sea. What exactly is it that her grave goods tell us? The people who supervised the funeral that stood behind her grave could have been early indigenous adopters of bits and pieces of their immigrant neighbors' material culture and mortuary practices or, just as likely, could have been immigrants who took up some of the burial practices of British people among whom they were now living. This grave could even be the handiwork of a mixed household.

We can find evidence for similar material culture remixings at the cemetery at Wasperton, in Warwickshire. This enclosed rural cemetery was first laid out in the late Roman period with three large family plots, but with room to spare for other, future plots. The cemetery's first graves were unexceptional and contained the usual assortment of hobnail boots, bracelets, and postmortem decapitations, although many of the dead, in late Roman fashion, were buried without grave goods. People continued to bury their dead here after 400, most for the first few generations without grave goods. But in the last few decades of the fifth century, people who were wearing new-style dress accessories and who sometimes cremated their dead were now burying in the cemetery. The new graves could be found both in the original family plots and in newly established ones. One, Inhumation 162, dates to the fifth century and was occupied by a child. It was dug in one of the Roman-period family plots and given the same alignment as most of the Roman-period graves, and its digging did not disrupt any of the plot's earlier graves. These things suggest that the child was affiliated in some way with people who had been burying their dead in the plot since the Roman period. But the container used to enclose the child's body was unlike anything seen in Wasperton, or in lowland Britain for that matter, in the Roman period. The body had been placed in a tree-trunk coffin, a burial tradition long practiced both on the far side of the Roman *limes* and in Scotland, Ireland, and Wales,[107] and now found in lowland Britain.[108] So, it looks as if the burial rites of this particular Wasperton funeral had been mediated not only by local tradition, but by ways of doing things from further afield.

In the same cemetery three women and one man (Inhumations 24, 39, 77, 161), each of whom died in a different generation (their deaths stretched from the late fifth to the early seventh centuries), were buried in clothes made from textiles produced using Romano-British weaving techniques,[109] techniques unknown in areas thought to be the homelands of continental immigrants.[110] Two were buried in one of the plots established during the late Roman period; the other two in plots that came into use only after the fall. All three of the women, though, were wearing brooches that we consider "Anglo-Saxon." The man, for his part, wore a single penannular brooch, which both in its style and in the way it was worn could be read as traditional and British. But he also went into the ground with a spear and a small bucket, objects new to Britain's burial repertoire.[111] Similar Roman-style textiles have also been found at two nearby post-Roman cemeteries, so ways of weaving long practiced in the neighborhood (as well, perhaps, as the survival of the Roman two-beam vertical loom) survived for generations among women in some, but not all, households in this part of England.[112] Given that the four people at Wasperton were buried not only with old-school textiles but with new-fangled grave goods and dress fittings, we should see Roman-style weaving techniques as part of "the way we do things" in this corner of Warwickshire, rather than a set of practices limited to a determinedly ethnic-identified or purposefully segregated British enclave, which eschewed new-style material culture.[113] The same Roman-period textile production techniques survived further east as well. They persisted in some Norfolk communities and could also be found at Mucking.[114]

The Wasperton burial community, like the one at West Heslerton, seems (based on oxygen and strontium isotopes) to have included individuals who had spent their childhoods in the West of Britain, both during the Roman period and in the fifth century, as well as people from further afield. So, as at West Heslerton, people long in the neighborhood and various incomers who came from different places at different times developed new material practices together.[115] Wherever their grandparents or great-grandparents had hailed from, they had come to share similar tastes in brooches, and many felt compelled to put objects such as stamped, hand-built pots, spears, and buckets into the graves of their loved ones. The examples just detailed argue against what Steven Ashby has described, in a different context, as "bombastic public displays of ethnic identity,"[116] and what comes through in them is the importance of local difference, individual choice, and the gradual development of a new material culture rather than an imposition of a fully developed foreign one.

Who Did These People Think They Were?

So, who were these women and girls at West Heslerton, Great Chesterford, and Wasperton in the fifth and early sixth centuries? And more importantly, who did they think they were? Our answers to these questions over the last couple of decades have focused on identity: how people were making, remaking, or broadcasting it. This work has been fruitful, but it is better suited to the period after c. 525 than to the period before it, when we can begin to see the formation of larger regional, cultural, and even ethnic identities in lowland Britain. Before this time, I suspect that we might be better off asking an altogether different set of questions of these women, their dress fittings, and their graves—questions such as "How did people in the century after the fall negotiate the extraordinary changes of the period stemming from the collapse of the production of so many basic goods?" or "How did people moving into new areas from within Britain and from outside it, who found themselves living alongside people who had come of age someplace else, respond materially?" These are better questions because what fifth- and early sixth-century women's burials do suggest is the very real possibility that many people in this particular time and place were not at all interested in signaling their genetic origins or natal affinities. What they were interested in, instead, was experimenting with new forms of material culture—out of necessity, to be sure, because this was a period of profound material and population dislocations—but also, perhaps, because they were living in a brave new world where old ways of being were not only unsustainable, but irrelevant. These people—whoever they were and wherever they came from—were occupied, above all else, with building a brand-new material reality.

If one believes, as I do, not just that people make things, but that things make people, and that material culture plays a profound role in making the world seem to its inhabitants "like the way things ought to be," these material transformations are crucial for gauging and understanding the period's Big Story. We can begin to appreciate some of the difficulties of understanding this new material reality when grappling with the mixed origins and mixed signals embodied by the women of West Heslerton, who seem to have been pioneering new forms of personal adornment uncoupled from issues revolving around origins. One way to read the dress accessories we find in women's graves at West Heslerton is as "intrusive." But another way to think about them is how these things were being repurposed or used differently. So, for example, was it native British women living in West Heslerton, who, when encountering wrist clasps, decided to adopt them, but did not think them appropriate for men (who had sometimes worn them on their trouser bottoms in Scandinavia)? Was it local women who thought it best to sew wrist clasps onto garments, rather than rivet them onto clothing, the way it had been done in Norway?[117] To portray the women of West Heslerton as "Anglo-Saxons" dressing like "Anglo-Saxons" makes them nonactors and does not allow us to see the ways in which they were participating in the biggest story of the period—which was the creation of a startlingly different material Britain.

CHAPTER 9

The Great Disentanglement

> People and the things they valued were so complexly intertwined they could not be disentangled.
> —Janet Hoskins, *Biographical Objects: How Things Tell the Stories of People's Lives*

A number of questions are worth asking as we try to make sense of the stark material differences between Britain in c. 325 and c. 425. How were British producers affected by the increasingly unstable conditions of the lower Rhine frontier and by the drip, drip, drip of troop withdrawal from the northwest provinces? What happened when the state withdrew from Britain, and the diocese no longer had a place in the empire's political economy? What happened, in these years, to the myriad networks that had long linked Britain to the rest of the empire? What happened to the large-scale landscapes of production that stood behind so much of late Roman Britain's durable material culture? How did the 15 percent of the population whose livelihoods were most dependent on the state and the imperial economy fare during these years; and what impact did these changes have on the settlements in which they worked and lived? In what ways were the lives of the 85 percent transformed in this same period? Finally, are migration and ethnicity—so often invoked as motivating factors behind Britain's material remaking—sufficient explanations for the totality of the material changes we see?

The Unwinding and Remaking of Late Roman Transchannel Networks

As we have seen, within the later Roman Empire northern Gaul, Britain, and the Rhineland had operated as a single, regional economy; and goods, taxes, currency, people, and ideas routinely moved across this zone. Agricultural production in Britain was organized in part to fulfill the demands of the state within this zone, and basic commodities produced in Britain, such grain, cattle hides, and salt, were likely moved across the channel and consumed in northern Gaul and the Rhineland, shifted there with the aid of imperial administrators, systems of taxation and procurement, transfers of gold and silver currency, and elite landowners, whose continued prosperity and way of life depended on Britain's interconnectivity with other northwestern provinces.[1]

In the first decade of the fifth century, this transchannel regional economy came apart. The year 402–3 was the last that the imperial government supplied Britain with coins. After this date, miniscule numbers of new imperial issues trickled in, but to only a few places.[2] Once the bulk shipment of coins stopped, the large-scale movement of in-kind tax and bulk purchases between Britain and the continent were no longer possible. The end of imperial coin supply likely also marked the moment when administrators and soldiers still in Britain ceased receiving pay in money or in kind from the Roman state, and when imperial officials fresh from postings elsewhere in the empire were no longer sent to Britain.[3]

Within a couple of decades of the cutting off of the coin supply and the cessation of the collection of the *annona*, Britain's villa estates, towns, and military settlements, and the infrastructure associated with large-scale cereal production and transportation—all of which were heavily implicated in and dependent on systems of imperial taxation and the money economy, and all of which had been showing signs of stress since c. 350—were no longer viable, and none survived much past c. 425. Urban and military settlements, moreover, which had acted, in the late Roman period, as nodes in the networks of exchange and communication and which had helped knit the two sides of the channel into a single economic zone, were failing: once they had gone, the large-scale movement of bulk goods and commodities across the region would no longer be possible.[4] In the late fourth and early fifth centuries, northern Gaul was undergoing a severe economic crisis of its own.[5] And because large numbers of troops stationed along the Rhine had been removed by Stilicho in 401–2, military provisioning systems linking Britain to Gaul and the Rhineland would no longer have been as vital to the Roman state as they had once been.[6] It is hardly surprising, in the face of these cascading dislocations, that the economic region came apart.

Although the mechanisms, institutions, and infrastructure standing behind Roman cross-channel exchange ceased to function, historians and archaeologists for many years maintained that trans-channel links persevered in the early fifth century, albeit on a much-diminished scale, thanks to the Franks, a barbarian group who would come to control a successor kingdom, by the late fifth century, centered on Tournai in northern Gaul. It was long held that men in England in the post-Roman period buried with fancy belt sets were Frankish warriors who had formerly fought in Roman armies. Some had come to Britain as "invaders" and "conquerors"; others were hired by the British themselves to settle in lowland Britain in "strategic" locations to protect native settlements from other barbarian war bands.[7] Archaeological evidence was thus used to prove Gildas's claim, penned in the early sixth century, that barbarian *foederati* had been invited into Britain in the early post-Roman period.[8]

The Franks' early presence in lowland Britain helped, in turn, to explain why, by the second quarter of the sixth century, Kent was awash with Frankish material culture and why its women were coming to adopt a distinctive costume, closer to one worn in Francia than sported by women elsewhere in England.[9] A number of scholars used this material to argue that Frankish kings of the Merovingian dynasty came to wield hegemonic power in Kent, and in return, they gave the kingdom of Kent "favored nation status" and granted Kentish kings a monopoly over Frankish goods traded within England.[10] By the second half of the sixth century, Frankish metalwork, glass, and pottery were spreading across much of southern and eastern England thanks to these arrangements.[11] The proof of this interpretation could be found in the more than eight hundred "Merovingian" finds in England dated between 450 and 650.[12] "Anglo-Saxon" brooches and pottery, dating to this same two-hundred-year period, have also been recovered from cemeteries on the Frankish side of the channel, and this material was used to argue that there were official enclaves of "Anglo-Saxon" traders involved in moving goods from Francia into Kent via this monopoly.[13] So a story of Frankish activity in early fifth-century Britain, combined with a narrative of official Frankish political influence in sixth-century Kent, not only explained the precocious development of kingship in Kent in the early Middle Ages and the history of its material culture but inferred that cross-channel exchange networks binding the eastern part of Britain to Gaul had survived Rome's fall, albeit on a much diminished scale.

Although most people working in the field no longer believe that Frankish warriors "invaded" Britain or were settled there as *foederati* in the fifth century, the idea continues to have its supporters.[14] Theories about the hegemonic powers of Merovingian kings over Kent also continue to haunt modern historical narratives of the period.[15] It is important, therefore, to think carefully about post-Roman Britain's belt-set-and-weapon burials and the material culture that made its way from continental Europe to lowland Britain in the first generations after the Roman withdrawal—which sit at the heart of these claims—in order to lay out an alternative interpretation.

It is, of course, possible that some of the people in fifth-century Britain buried with belt sets and weapons were the descendants of warriors who had moved from the far side of the Rhine into Gaul and who had, themselves, fought in Rome's armies: similar burials are also found in northern Gaul.[16] We now understand, however, that contemporaries encountering men dressed or buried in this way in Gaul would have viewed them as late Roman provincials or as members of local elite families rather than as "Franks." Indeed, it is impossible to identify self-consciously "Frankish" burials in Gaul until the very end of the fifth century.[17] It is highly improbable, therefore, that men buried in Britain in the first half of the fifth century with similar belt sets and weapons were signaling Frankish ethnicity. It is much more likely that they were telegraphing the same message as were their contemporaries in northern Gaul: they were presenting themselves as people who were part of a broader, late Roman world. So it is important not to project backward things we know to have been the case in the seventh century into the fifth century.

Increasingly, Britain's belt-set burials—such as that of the "Gloucester Goth," the prone weapon burial found outside of Richborough's defenses,[18] and the "warrior" burial discovered at Dyke Hills in 1874[19]—are considered late Roman rather than "barbarian."[20] Paul Booth, in his analysis of a recently excavated second Dyke Hills belt-set-and-weapon burial, convincingly argues that the man in this grave, in spite of the facts that his belt set and axe were made on the continent and that evidence preserved in his skeletal remains hints that he was born outside of Britain, should be understood as a late Roman official rather than an invading barbarian warrior.[21] Similarly, a careful reevaluation of the fifth-century "Anglo-Saxon" settlement at Mucking also suggests that the individuals buried with belt fittings there was more likely members of a local, indigenous household than "Germanic" hired guns.[22]

But what about the eight hundred "Merovingian" finds in Britain and the "Anglo-Saxon" pottery and metalwork recovered from the continental side of the channel dating to the same period?[23] Surely these are evidence of heartier networks than the ones just portrayed? When we consider the chronology of this material, however, the answer is a resounding "no." Very little of it dates to the fifth century: almost all is sixth century or later.[24] Thus, there seems to have been a genuine rupture in the fifth century in the formerly robust Roman-period, cross-channel networks. Given the fifth-century hiatus, it is likely that the mechanisms standing behind the movement of goods in the sixth century had little to do with those operating in the fourth century.[25]

A few objects found in Britain and that date to the first half of the fifth century witness continued but only very sporadic contact with Gaul and the Rhineland. Like the belt-set-and-weapon burials, this material suggests that the individuals maintaining these connections on the continent should be considered Roman rather than Frankish, and that those in Britain receiving this material either were members of once well-connected native households or were living in communities such as Richborough and Pevensey, which seem to have maintained tenuous connections to Roman officialdom in the first decades of the fifth century, perhaps via the last vestiges of the late Roman Rhineland-to-Britain trade networks.[26] Although this material witnesses the persistence of a few cross-channel connections, its rarity argues that these links were informal, personal, and episodic. So, for example, the Patching Hoard, which includes a handful of mid-fifth-century imperial coins,[27] was found very near a fifth-century cemetery at Highdown, in Sussex. A number of people buried in the cemetery were wearing Quoit-Brooch-style metalwork, and one of the dead there was placed in the ground with an etched fifth-century glass goblet with a Greek inscription.[28] The hoard and the cemetery together hint that there may have been a household in the neighborhood that had maintained some connection to the still-extant Roman world across the channel. But compared with the mountains of material evidence testifying to the links between Britain and Gaul in the fourth century, the rarity of similar material dating to the first half of the fifth century suggests that what we are seeing are the last gasps of the networks that had connected eastern Britain to Gaul and the Rhineland. Indeed, it is not until the middle of the sixth century that luxury items from the Mediterranean, moving up the Rhine, would once again arrive in eastern Britain in any numbers.[29]

If the continuity of late Roman networks linking Britain to Gaul and the Rhineland across the fifth century now seem unlikely, what explains the notable number of objects found in Britain by the sixth century that were either made in Francia or inspired by objects that had been? And how do we account for the arrival of Scandinavian or Scandinavian-inspired dress ornaments in lowland Britain, such as wrist clasps and bracteates? And how do we explain the rise of shared potting and construction techniques across the North Sea coastal zone?

Trade networks extending from eastern Britain across the North Sea into coastal Germany and Scandinavia were almost nonexistent in the Roman period,[30] but from the mid-fifth century on there was an uptick in the movement of people, ideas, and things between the eastern half of Britain and lands to the north and east of the Roman *limes*.[31] By the early sixth century, an important new zone of exchange had been stitched together across the North Sea.[32] During this same period it also appears that links were developing between the terp (or artificial mound) settlements of the coastal and riverine Lowlands and eastern England, with some communities in both regions participating in similar burial customs and making and using similar pottery, brooches, and combs.[33] It seems that coastal communities in a zone that stretched from southern Norway past the mouth of the Rhine and into coastal northern France and along the east and southeast coasts of Britain had come, by the early sixth century, to have considerable contact, and that the people living in this region were connected rather than divided by the sea. We might think of this newly emerging zone as a "fusion corridor," that is, as a maritime and riverine zone along which ideas, cultural practices, and ways of doing and making were spread, adopted, and adapted.[34] The material world of lowland Britain, during this period, increasingly came to follow the same trajectories as those found elsewhere in this zone. Thus, people living in lowland Britain, including people of Romano-British decent, were residing in, affected by, and participating in this new fusion corridor rather than the older fusion corridor that had once linked Britain both to Rome's other northwest provinces and to the Mediterranean world.

There are a number of advantages to rethinking and reorienting our understanding of the collapse of old networks and the beginnings of new ones. First and foremost, it stops us from reading back into the fifth century things we know to have been true in the seventh century. Second, it takes seriously the collapse of the Roman political economy in Britain and forces us to confront its impact on households whose working lives in many ways had been organized to accommodate it. Third, it allows us to see how coastal communities across the new North Sea and transchannel zone in the fifth and sixth centuries, although many were small scale and not particularly high status, were beginning to knit together a fusion corridor in which the region's new early medieval material culture package emerged. Fourth and finally, it helps to defang ideas that changes in material culture in Britain can be explained solely by the *adventus Saxonum* and instead allows for native British families as well as immigrants to be authors of the region's new material world.

The Unraveling of Large-Scale Landscapes of Production, Deskilling, and the Move to Subsistence

The unwinding of the political economy in Britain precipitated a series of dislocations that had a dramatic impact on the material culture of lowland Britain as well as on its makers and users. The large-scale taskscapes and distributive modes of raw-material sourcing, labor, and production, so evident in the early fourth century, were crucial in the creation, mobilization, and distribution of a capacious and varied material culture. Although the 15 percent of the population whose lives were most dependent on the Roman state consumed much of what was produced, by the fourth century many in the bottom 85 percent had come to incorporate things such as mass-produced pots, nails, and coins into their daily lives. In the last decades of the fourth century and the first decades of the fifth, however, lowland Britain's landscapes of production and consumption and the meshworks of relationships and routeways that trussed them together came apart.[35] One of the results was that people whose livings had been dependent on them were no longer able to support themselves in the same way: by c. 425, whole categories of specialist laborers had disappeared. As productive landscapes and meshworks disintegrated, and as specialist skills standing behind everyday categories of Roman-style material culture disappeared, the Roman material culture regime collapsed.

The deskilling of the population and the loss of basic technological knowhow cast very long shadows in Britain. As we have seen, it took centuries for smelting expertise to firmly reestablished itself in Britain, as it did the production of wheel-thrown, kiln-fired pottery and stone-built architecture. But there are many other examples of deskilling. Damien Goodburn's examination of surviving early medieval wood, for example, has revealed that boards produced in England from the fifth to the twelfth century were axe hewn, because woodworking saws, common in the Roman period, were one of many tools lost in Britain after the fall, and they would not be reintroduced for over half a millennium.[36] These kinds of technological losses along with the skills that stood behind them made the creation of basic, everyday objects more difficult and more time-consuming. Deskilling, the loss of technology, and their knock-on effects sat at the heart of many of the dislocations experienced by people living after Rome's withdrawal, and they serve as partial explanations for the material impoverishment endemic in Britain during the period.[37]

Less material, but no less crucial losses stemmed from the extinction of late Roman productive landscapes and skill sets. Systems of social knowledge come to be internalized, understood, and shaped by habitual practices of work.[38] So, as long-standing work practices vanished, not only did technologies disappear, but so, too, did particular worldviews and understandings. The ubiquitous productive structures that had once studded broad swathes of territory, and which were central to people's workaday taskscapes—corn driers, aisled halls, gardens, formal market spaces, industrial zones—had been embedded in their surrounding landscapes by well-trodden paths, roads, droveways, and riverways. These commonplace, interlocking spaces were the kinds of places to which people habitually traveled and in which they labored; and they made possible particular kinds of activities and promoted and perpetuated particular kinds of lives, serving as what Bryan Lawson has called "behavioral settings."[39] It was in such settings that habitual practices of work, so central in the creation of social knowledge, were enacted. As Louise Revell has observed:

> The social practices of production and manufacture provide a . . . means of understanding the social identity of the non-elite. The daily routines of work are involved in the creation and maintenance of the sense of self: these routines form part of a person's knowledge of how to move around their own world and also form the basis for relationships (both equal and unequal) which form a sense of a person's place within the wider society. Certain forms of labour will involve specialisation, leading to the formation of ties between these specialists, but also a knowledge and responsibility which will not be accessible to all, creating a sense of pride and self-definition.[40]

Myriad categories of everyday behavioral settings did not survive the transition from Roman to early medieval, and as they disappeared, so too did the knowledge, identities, and lifeways they had helped create and perpetuate.

As sites of work were abandoned, some of the paths, roads, droveways, and waterways that had stitched together the taskscapes into which they were integrated were abandoned as well.[41] As familiar ways of crossing the landscape disappeared, the cognitive worlds people carried around with them inside their heads must have been reordered in fundamental ways.[42] The loss of ways of getting from one place to another compounded the disappearance of commonplace behavioral settings and brought about fundamental restructurings of individual, household, and communal relationships, because quotidian pathways and everyday behavioral spaces together create and perpetuate social worlds.

In the decades on either side of 400 there was also a shift from intensive, surplus-driven agriculture to subsistence. As we learned in Chapter 1, something on the order of 15 percent of all people living in fourth-century Britain were members of households whose food was mostly raised by other people. Soldiers, state workers high and low, the villa-owning elite, craft workers, people living in towns, and people involved more or less full time in hauling Britain's bounty across Britain and overseas made their livings in ways that depended on the imperial state and the money economy. As a group, this segment of the population might have secured as much as 40 percent of the surplus produced in Britain each year; and the late Roman state, of course, took a share of the surplus as well.[43] In a world in which farming households did not produce all that much to begin with,[44] the hard reality of meeting the demands of the state and the needs of the 15 percent most dependent on it forced the remaining population to produce at least twice subsistence each year, in order that they might feed their families, amass enough seed and breeding stock to farm yet another year, and fulfill the needs of Britain's noncultivators.

In the five decades between 375 and 425, the political economy, which had made the lives of the 15 percent possible, disintegrated. By the second quarter of the fifth century it is difficult to find evidence in lowland Britain for the kinds of people who had traditionally found themselves within this segment of the late Roman population—be they smelters, potters, townspeople, professional carters, or villa owners. The last decades of the fourth and the first decades of the fifth century must have been a period of distressing dislocation for those whose families fell within this group. Most, after a few years of hard adjustment, must have returned to the ranks of rural cultivators.

By the mid-fifth century, some, much, or all the obligations and burdens that had once compelled the bottom 85 percent to support the state and the other 15 percent would have receded, and as they disappeared, the working lives of agriculturalists were transformed. Now that the state, the market, and the money economy had abated, not only did it become harder to store surplus, but it was more difficult to benefit from it. One of the proofs of this is that the once-ubiquitous Roman-period structures associated with large-scale cereal production and storage—barns, granaries, corn-drying ovens, and mills—ceased being built, maintained, or used, and they did not return to lowland Britain in any meaningful way until the late seventh or eighth century.[45] Thus, the networks that stood behind the filling and depleting of what was stored (which had a major impact on how much was stored)[46] changed dramatically in these years. At the same time, archaeobotanical evidence suggests that less land was now under the plow.[47] It also hints that farmers were putting less time and effort into cultivating wheat, a crop beloved by the Roman state, and were instead diversifying their cereal crops, raising more barley, oats, and rye.[48] Farmers participating in subsistence agriculture generally avoid specialization, because the aim of subsistence farming is to minimize risk by raising more than one thing to buffer against crop failure.[49]

Animal management practices during this same period were also undergoing a quiet revolution, with less emphasis on raising and maintaining large plowing and drayage animals and the abandonment of common Roman-period agricultural practices—hay meadows, foddering regimes, and droveways—that had made the armies of hardworking cattle and their movement across the landscape possible.[50] All this suggests that agriculturalists, in the fifth century, were settling into farming practices more suited to their own needs than to the demands of others. The near-invisibility of social differentiation in the archaeology of fifth-century lowland Britain further implies that large numbers of households during this period were practicing subsistence agriculture.

In the postindustrial West, subsistence is something of a dirty word, often associated with hopeless poverty, food shortages, and autarky. But anthropologists have long appreciated that subsistence as a way of life is often both more positive and less dire for cultivators than working within a market system. Anthropologists have shown that subsistence is not so much about scraping by as about "having enough." The definition of "enough" for a fifth-century farm families would have been considerably different than it had been for their fourth-century progenitors. They less often had to consider how much was needed to meet the demands of the state, local elites, and nonagricultural workers. Our fifth-century farmers might, instead, think that "enough" meant enough to allow them to eat well, to have a sufficient amount stored to buffer against bad harvests, and to allow them to be openhanded with their neighbors and kinfolk.[51] Farmers in the fifth century, in short, would have striven to produce what anthropologists call a "normal surplus."[52] In exceptionally bad years, they would be forced to dip into stores set aside for just such catastrophes. But in average years they would have accumulated a modest surplus, and in especially good years, they would have ended up with considerably more than they needed. This, in turn, meant that most households in most years had enough to feast and trade. Indeed, there is some evidence to suggest that people lived longer, healthier lives once the more onerous demands of the state and landlords faded away.[53]

In the post-Roman period, subsistence farmers could be found in the coastal and riverine landscapes across the entire North Sea and cross-channel fusion zone. There is growing evidence to suggest that such people sometimes had dugout canoes or boats, which they used to trade among themselves, not because they were directed to do so from above, but rather to meet the desires of their own households, settlements, and extended kin groups.[54] These networks were not necessarily organized by elite players: many seem to have emerged between the relatively flat-hierarchy, ranked communities found across the emerging zone.[55] So, although the large-scale, transchannel trade networks driven by the needs of the late Roman political economy had gone into abeyance, boat-owning households had begun to form new networks across which goods, ideas, and people could move.

Decentering Ethnicity

Because modes of production for the most visible kinds of Roman material culture disintegrated in Britain in the decades on either side of 400, people in the immediate post-Roman period had less durable material culture in their lives than had their immediate predecessors. At the same time, much of what they were making and using came to look quite different than Roman-period material culture. Because the new-style material culture was developing at the same time as migrants from the continent were beginning to settle in Britain, and because much of it is clearly related to categories of objects found across the channel and the North Sea, it has been used not to think about connections between Britain and continent in the ways they have been thought about by scholars studying the period before 400, but rather as a means of determining the origins, ethnicity, and number of migrants who were moving into Britain in the fifth century and beyond.

There is a very long history of describing peoples living in lowland Britain in the post-Roman period as well as the things they made as "Anglo-Saxon." Standing behind this terminology are a series of nineteenth-century conceptual frameworks, most of which are no longer ascribed to by people working in the field. Nonetheless these ideas continue to dog scholarship of the period, in part because of the language we use to describe both lowland Britain's newcomers and the new-style material culture developing there. Our continued use of the term

"Anglo-Saxon"—including by those of us who know better—to describe people living in Britain in the first generations after 400, and the new forms of material culture developing there, is then adopted by our students and the public more generally, who take the term "Anglo-Saxon" at face value, and not unreasonably come away from our work thinking that the people and things we describe are "Anglo-Saxon."

As the preceding chapters have argued, the arrival of new peoples in Britain is an insufficient explanation for the development of the new, post-Roman material culture package, because it does not take into account the collapse of Roman systems of material production. Groups of people, including people native to Britain in the fifth and early sixth centuries, shared constellations of cultural practices, sensibilities, values, and expectations that individuals acquire and internalize through the activities and experiences of everyday life, which we call *habitus*, and which can be summed up as the way individuals in a society think is "the way things should be." Material culture sits at the heart of *habitus*, because of its central role in social formation and social reproduction.[56] People living in the couple of generations that witnessed the collapse of the money economy, the state, and manufacturing and transportation practices in lowland Britain came of age with a *habitus* that, with the passing of time, became completely unsuitable and unsustainable, given the material dislocations of the period. At the same time, people on the move—both those pulling up stakes within Britain and those crossing the sea—grew up in profoundly different material worlds from the ones in which they eventually found themselves. And, if the mixed communities we looked at in Chapter 8, with their continuous influx of newcomers from a variety of homelands, are anything to go by, many were living alongside people who had come from places where ideas about "the way things should be" were quite different from their own.[57] On top of this, the material dislocations that centered around doing and making, which accompanied the Roman economy's collapse in Britain, meant that many of the things people used to have were no longer available, and they needed to do something about it.

The new material reality and the rapidly evolving and quite different *habitus* of the fifth and early sixth centuries, then, far from being imported wholesale and imposed by war bands, was invented, displayed, repurposed, and experimented with—or so it seems to me—not only by immigrant women and their children, as well as their husbands and fathers, but by a large indigenous British population (some of whom were also newcomers to the neighborhoods in which they were now living), whose supplies of Roman-style, everyday goods had disappeared, and who had had to abandon their grandparents' *habitus* and invent a new one. Much of the hard work of building this new material world, and much of the interesting material culture developing in this period, was domestic—cooking equipment, housing styles, dress accessories—as much the product of women as it was of men. In short, the transformations we see in material culture and lifeways took place in the hall rather than the war band. Its invention was domestic rather than martial, and it was created by all sorts of women and men—indigenous and foreign, local and newcomer, in many places living in the same regions, settlements, and households. So the real work of people living in Britain in the first few generations after Rome's fall, rather than being about one migrating war band duking it out with another the way the *Anglo-Saxon Chronicle* would have us believe, was the creation of a new material reality. Given all this, I would argue not only that labelling people and things "Anglo-Saxon" in this period is anachronistic and misleading, but that it impoverishes our attempts at reimagining the past. Our terminology forecloses the possibility of thinking about these people and their things in the first hundred years after Rome's fall as something other than "Anglo-Saxon," and the new forms of material culture as something other than "intrusive."

The new material world that was coming into being in the fifth and early sixth centuries owed much to new ideas about "how the world should be," which were taking hold across the new North Sea and Cross-channel fusion zone. But in Britain, these ideas were mediated, in crucial ways, by the Roman and even the Iron Age past. This can be illustrated by returning to the maps, discussed in Chapter 3, that plot find spots for various classes of late Roman material culture. All the maps conform, in important ways, to Jeremy Evans's map of pottery use in late Roman Britain.[58] They provide useful approximations of where people, as a matter of course, consumed broad classes of durable Roman-style material culture.[59] The crosshatching on Evans's map (Figure 21) highlights the zone in which Roman material culture was most widely adopted and incorporated into British people's lives during the Roman period. This also happens to be the zone in which English identity began to form and where the earliest English kingdoms coalesced (Figure 22).

But those lands where Roman-style pottery and other categories of Roman-period material culture were never widely adopted are the areas in which Britain's "Celtic" kingdoms emerged. The crosshatched zone on the maps also marks the region, both in the Roman and in the early medieval periods, in which people were enthusiastic adopters of new forms of material culture from the continent.[60] But the white areas mark those places, both under Rome and after it, where communities had a long history of being less enthusiastic about alien material culture.[61] What all this suggests is that underlying habits, lifeways, and material

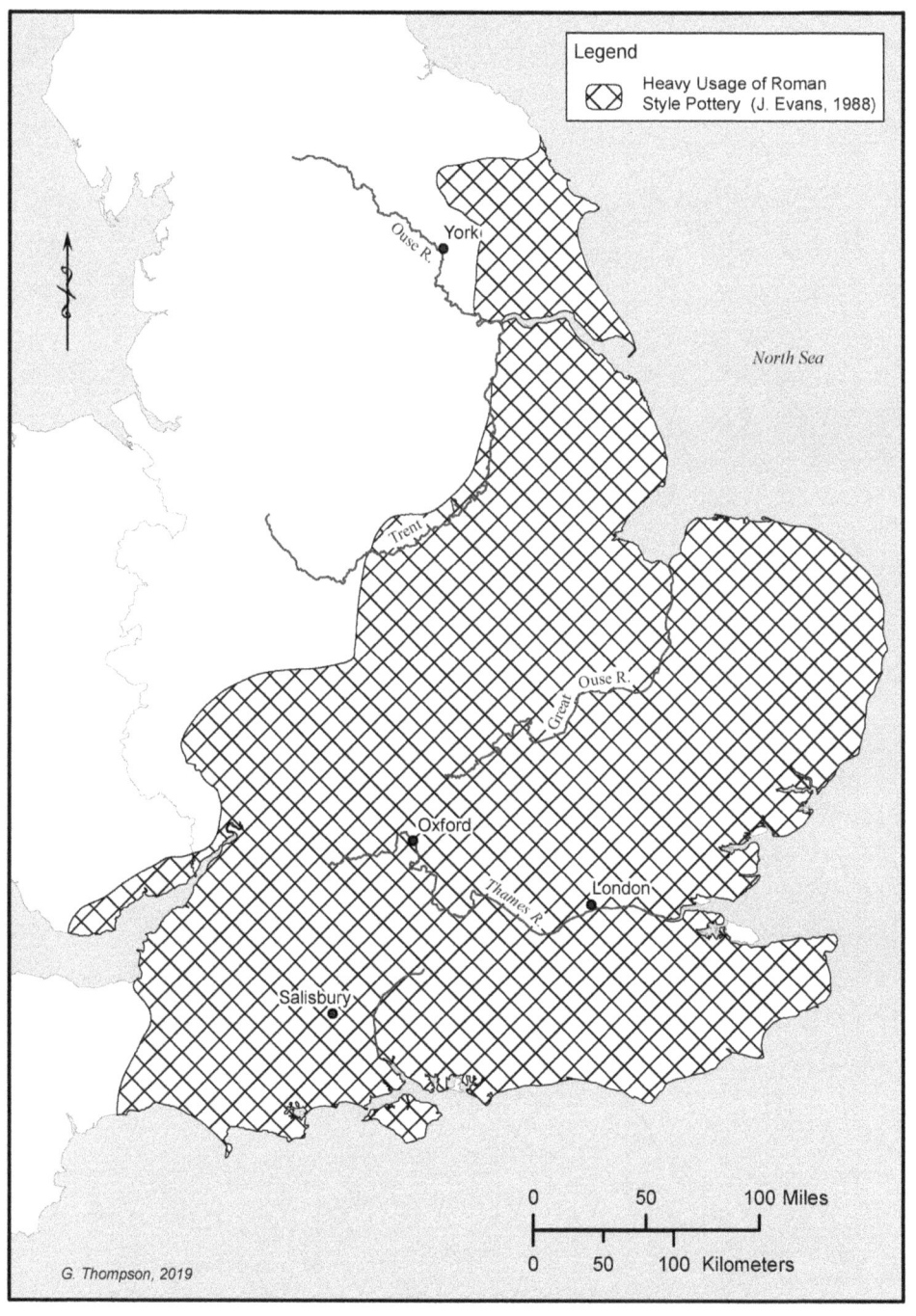

FIGURE 21. A map showing the regions, identified by Jeremy Evans, where Roman-style pottery was heavily used and where it was more rarely used. (Based on a map in "Balancing the Scales: Romano-British Pottery in Early Late Antiquity." Map drawn by Gordon Thompson.)

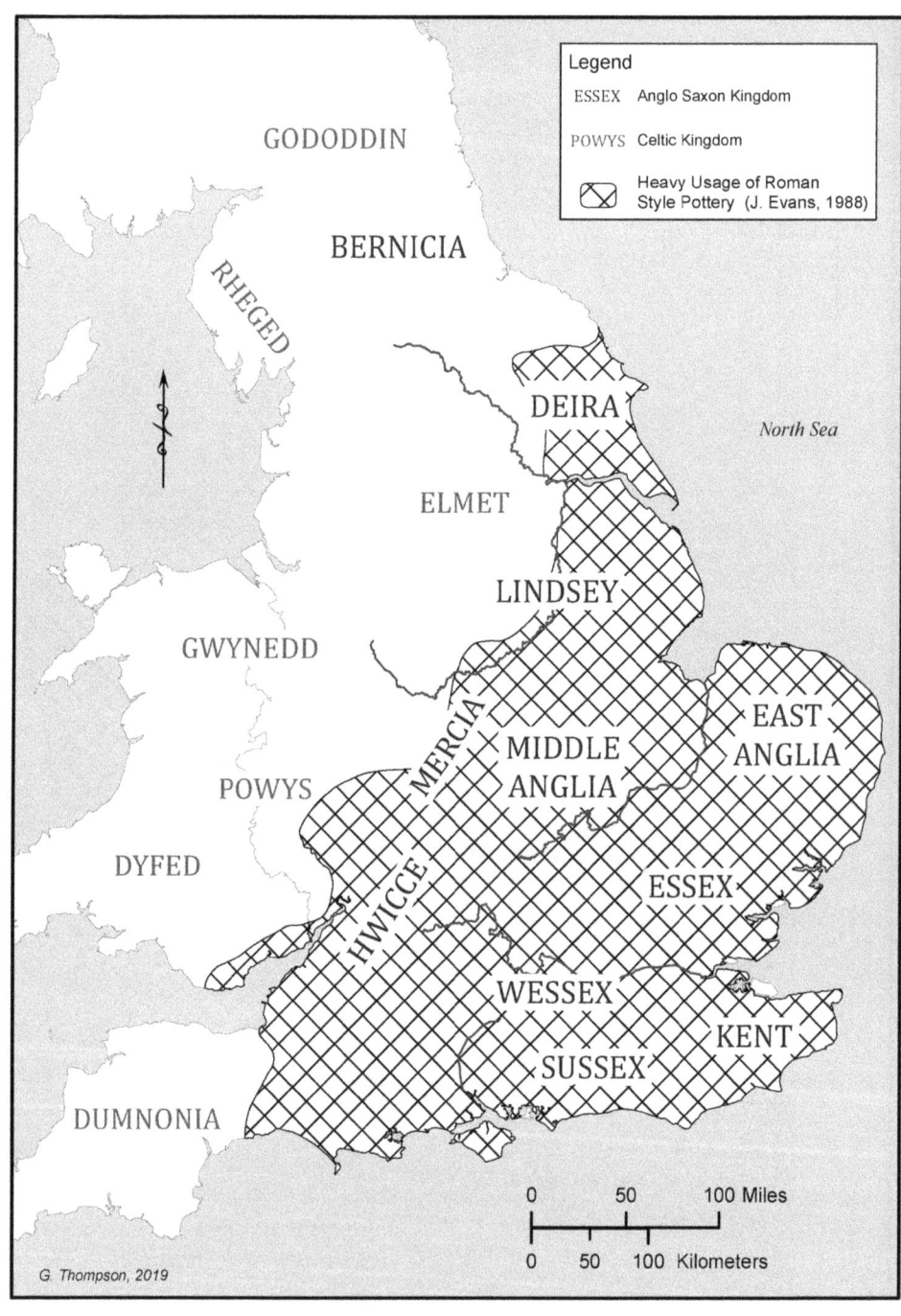

FIGURE 22. Some of Britain's early kingdoms mapped in relation to regions where Roman-style pottery had been regularly used and where it had not much been used. (Map drawn by Gordon Thompson.)

practices found in Britain under Rome (and, indeed, before Rome) continued to shape the ways people thought about and lived in the world in the post-Roman period, and they played a role in the formation of new post-Roman identities in Britain as well.

Over the course of the fifth and sixth centuries, the indigenes and the newcomers together in the crosshatched zones marked on Evans's maps would together build a brand-new material world and forge a new identity; and their descendants, as the writings of Bede make clear, would come to think of themselves as English. But as with most identities, this concoction was rooted in neither birth nor blood, and far from being a timeless, monolithic thing, it was historically constructed, and it was advanced and maintained over the generations by the shared material culture and material practices evolving in the first couple of centuries of the Middle Ages.[62] But the "Anglo-Saxons" and their things were nowhere to be found in the fifth century, because they had not yet invented themselves.

NOTES

Book epigraph: M. Carver, C. Hills, and J. Scheschkewitz, *Wasperton: A Roman, British, and Anglo-Saxon Community in Central England* (Woodbridge: Boydell, 2009), 140.

INTRODUCTION

Epigraph: L. Carroll, *Alice's Adventures in Wonderland* (London: Macmillan and Co., 1865), 10.
1. R. Fleming, *Britain After Rome: The Fall and Rise 400 to 1070* (London: Allen Lane, 2010); and see below, Chapter 9.
2. K. Sisam, "Anglo-Saxon Royal Genealogies," *Proceedings of the British Academy*, 39 (1953), 287–346; D. N. Dumville, "Kingship, Genealogies, and Regnal Lists," in P. Sawyer and I. N. Wood, eds., *Early Medieval Kingship* (Leeds: University of Leeds, 1977), 72–104; P. Sims-Williams, "The Settlement of England in Bede and the Chronicle," *Anglo-Saxon England*, 12 (1983), 1–41; B. Yorke, "Fact or Fiction? The Written Evidence for the Fifth and Sixth Centuries AD," *Anglo-Saxon Studies in Archaeology and History*, 6 (1993), 47–50.
3. Anglo-Saxon Chronicle, *sub anno* 495, 501, 508.
4. For a discussion of this and a bibliography, see Fleming, *Britain After Rome*, 39–59, 374–76.
5. The bulk of the work on the period between 300 and 500 has been done by archaeologists rather than historians. For the basic outlines of their arguments over the last two and a half decades, see H.-W. Böhme, "Das Ende der Römerherrschaft in Britannien und die Angelsächsische Besiedlung Englands im 5. Jahrhundert," *Jahrbuch des Römisch-Germanischen Zentralmuseums Mainz*, 33 (1986), 469–574; S. Bassett, ed., *The Origins of Anglo-Saxon Kingdoms* (London: Leicester University Press, 1989), 469–575; A. S. Esmonde Cleary, *The Ending of Roman Britain* (London: B. T. Batsford, 1989); N. J. Cooper, "Searching for the Blank Generation: Consumer Choice in Roman and Post-Roman Britain," in J. Webster and N. Cooper, eds., *Roman Imperialism: Post-Colonial Perspectives* (Leicester: School of Archaeological Studies, 1996), 85–98; John Hines, ed., *The Anglo-Saxons from the Migration Period to the Eighth Century: An Ethnographic Perspective* (Woodbridge: Boydell, 1997); T. Wilmott and P. Wilson, eds., *The Late Roman Transition in the North*, BAR British Series 299 (Oxford: BAR, 2000); N. Faulkner, *The Decline and Fall of Roman Britain* (Stroud: Tempus, 2000); N. Faulkner with R. Reece, "The Debate About the End: A Review of Evidence and Methods," *Archaeological Journal*, 159 (2002), 59–76; H. Hamerow, *Rural Settlements and Society in Anglo-Saxon England*, (Oxford: Oxford University Press, 2012); C. Hills, *Origins of the English* (London: Duckworth, 2003); R. Collins and J. Gerrard, eds., *Debating Late Antiquity in Britain AD 300–700*, BAR British Series 365 (Oxford: Archaeopress, 2004); B. Ward-Perkins, *The Fall of Rome and the End of Civilization* (Oxford: Oxford University Press, 2005); Ewan Campbell, *Continental and Mediterranean Imports to Atlantic Britain and Ireland, AD 400–800* (York: Council

for British Archaeology, 2007); P. Booth et al., *The Thames Through Time: The Archaeology of Gravel Terraces of the Upper and Middle Thames* (Oxford: Oxford Archaeology, 2007); R. Collins and L. Allason-Jones, eds., *Finds from the Frontier: Material Culture in the 4th–5th Centuries* (York: Council for British Archaeology, 2010); A. Rogers, *Late Roman Towns in Britain: Rethinking Change and Decline* (Cambridge: Cambridge University Press, 2011); S. Esmonde Cleary, "The Ending(s) of Roman Britain," in H. Hamerow, D. A. Hinton, and S. Crawford, eds., *The Oxford Handbook of Anglo-Saxon Archaeology* (Oxford: Oxford University Press, 2011), 13–29; J. Gerrard, *The Ruin of Roman Britain: An Archaeological Perspective* (Cambridge: Cambridge University Press, 2013); S. Esmonde Cleary, *The Roman West, AD 200–500: An Archaeological Study* (Cambridge: Cambridge University Press, 2013); F. K. Haarer, ed., *AD 410: The History and Archaeology of Late and Post-Roman Britain* (London: Society for the Promotion of Roman Studies, 2014).

6. M. Millett, *The Romanization of Britain: An Essay in Archaeological Interpretation* (Cambridge: Cambridge University Press, 1990).

7. Notable exceptions are C. Wickham, *Framing the Early Middle Ages: Europe and the Mediterranean, 400–800* (Oxford: Oxford University Press, 2005), 306–10; G. Halsall, *Worlds of Arthur: Facts and Fictions of the Dark Ages* (Oxford: Oxford University Press, 2013), 87–101.

8. Among the exceptions are John Blair, Caroline Goodson, Wendy Davies, Bonnie Effros, Guy Halsall, Edward James, Michael McCormick, Chris Wickham, and Alex Wolff.

9. For a general discussion of historians' discomfort with scientific evidence and arguments that it is nonetheless important to consider it, see R. Fleming, "Writing Biography at the Edge of History," *American Historical Review*, 114 (109), 606–14; M. McCormick, "History's Changing Climate: Climate Science, Genomics, and the Emerging Consilient Approach to Interdisciplinary History," *Journal of Interdisciplinary History*, 63 (2011), 251–73.

10. The largest cache of gray literature, freely available online, is the *Library of Unpublished Fieldwork Reports*, housed on the Archaeology Data Service site: http://archaeologydataservice.ac.uk/archives/view/greylit/.

11. Roger White discusses some of the structural reasons for this, particularly among archaeologists working in commercial archaeology (R. White, "From the Provinces to the Marches: The West Midlands in the Fifth and Sixth Centuries," in R. White and M. Hodder, eds., *Clash of Cultures? The Romano-British Period in the West Midlands* (Oxford: Oxbow Books, 2018), 207–19, at 208–9.

12. See, for example, P. Stafford, ed., *A Companion to the Early Middle Ages: Britain and Ireland c. 500–1100* (Chichester: Wiley-Blackwell, 2009); B. Yorke, *Kings and Kingdoms of Early Anglo-Saxon England* (London: Seaby, 1990); D. P. Kirby, *The Earliest English Kings* (London: Routledge, 2000).

13. For a discussion of how material culture is useful for understanding the Middle Ages, as well as a bibliography, see R. Fleming and K. French, "Objecthood," in S. Semple and J. Lund, eds., *A Cultural History of Objects* (London: Bloomsbury, in press).

14. Not all archaeologists, however, write in this vein. For a call for archaeologists to write stories about the past and some examples, see C. Holtorf, "Meta-Stories of Archaeology," *World Archaeology*, 42 (2010), 381–93. For a plea to focus on "the agents who created the archaeological record" rather than the objects themselves, see R. Witcher, "Broken Pots and Meaningless Dots? Surveying the Rural Landscapes of Roman Italy," *Papers of the British School at Rome*, 74 (2006), 39–72, at 47–48.

15. The Atlas Group and W. Raad, "My Neck Is Thinner Than a Hair: A History of the Car Bomb in the Lebanese Wars of 1975 to 1991," *Rethinking Marxism*, 15 (2003), 408–9; E. Respini, *Walid Raad* (New York: Museum of Modern Art, 2015), 74–77.

16. S. Esmonde Cleary, "Approaches to the Differences Between Late Romano-British and Early Anglo-Saxon Archaeology," *Anglo-Saxon Studies in Archaeology and History*, 6 (1993), 57–63, at 57; Gerrard, *The Ruin of Roman Britain*, 80.

17. See below, Chapters 3 and 4.

18. See below, Chapter 6.

19. See below, Chapter 5.

20. P. Bourdieu, *Outline of a Theory of Practice* (Cambridge: Cambridge University Press, 1977); A. Appadurai, ed., *The Social Life of Things: Commodities in Cultural Perspective* (Cambridge: Cambridge University Press, 1988); J. Deetz, *In Small Things Forgotten: An Archaeology of Early American Life*, rev. ed. (New York: Anchor Books, 1996); T. Ingold, "Making Culture and Weaving the World," in P. M. Graves-Brown, ed., *Matter, Materiality and Modern Culture* (London: Routledge, 2000), 50–71; C. Gosden, "What Do Objects Want?" *Journal of Archaeological Method and Theory*, 12 (2005), 193–211; D. Miller, *The Comfort of Things* (Cambridge: Polity, UK, 2008); I. Hodder, *Entangled: An Archaeology of the Relationships Between Humans and Things* (Chichester: Wiley-Blackwell, 2012).

CHAPTER 1

Epigraph: A. S. Esmonde Cleary, *The Ending of Roman Britain* (London: B. T. Batsford, 1989), 138.

1. Millett estimates between 3.3 million and 3.66 million (M. Millett, *The Romanization of Britain: An Essay in Archaeological Interpretation* (Cambridge: Cambridge University Press, 1990), 181–86); Hingley's estimate is between 2.5 million and 3.6 million (R. Hingley, "The Roman Landscape of Britain: From Hoskins to Today," in R. Hingley and A. Fleming, *Prehistoric and Roman Landscapes: Landscape History After Hoskins* [Macclesfield: Windgather, 2007], 101–13, at 110); and Mattingly's estimate is 2.5 million (D. J. Mattingly, *Imperialism, Power, and Identity: Experiencing the Roman Empire* [Princeton, N.J.: Princeton University Press, 2011], 219). More recent estimates, based on the work of the Roman Rural Settlement project, suggest that numbers peaked in Britain in the second century, rather than the fourth, and that we may need to scale back our population estimates of the late Roman period to something on the order of 1.75–2.25 million (M. Fulford and M. Allen, "Introduction: Population and the Dynamics of Change in Roman South-Eastern England," in D. Bird, ed., *Agriculture and Industry in South-Eastern Roman Britain* [Oxford: Oxbow Books, 2017], 1–14, at 5–13). For a general discussion of the historiography of these population figures, see M. McCarthy, *The Romano-British Peasant: Towards a Study of People, Landscapes, and Work During the Roman Occupation of Britain* (Oxford: Windgather, 2013), 31–41.

2. C. Grey, *Constructing Communities in the Late-Roman Countryside* (Cambridge: Cambridge University Press, 2011), 30–32.

3. R. Knapp, *Invisible Romans* (Cambridge, Mass.: Harvard University Press, 2011), 97; P. F. Bang, *Roman Bazaar: A Comparative Study of Trade and Markets in a Tributary Empire* (Cambridge: Cambridge University Press, 2008), 119. Dennis Kehoe points out, however, that although a large percentage of the population lived close to subsistence, cumulatively they controlled considerable income (D. Kehoe, "Contract Labor," in W. Scheidel, ed., *The Cambridge Companion to the Roman Economy* [Cambridge: Cambridge University Press, 2012], 114–30, at 114–15).

4. K. Hopkins, "Taxes and Trade in the Roman Empire (200 BC–AD 400)," *Journal of Roman Studies*, 70 (1980), 101–25, at 104.

5. M. Pitts and R. Griffin, "Exploring Health and Social Well-Being in Late-Roman Britain: An Intercemetery Approach," *American Journal of Archaeology*, 116 (2012), 253–76.

6. Grey, *Constructing Communities*; L. Dossey, *Peasants and Empire in Christian North Africa* (Berkeley, Calif.: University of California Press, 2010); McCarthy, *Romano-British Peasant*.

7. J. Taylor, "Encountering Romanitas: Characterising the Role of Agricultural Communities in Roman Britain," *Britannia*, 44 (2013), 171–90.

8. Kehoe, "Contract Labor," 114–21; P. F. Bang, "Predation," in Scheidel, ed., *The Cambridge Companion to the Roman Economy*, 197–217; P. Brown, *Through the Eye of the Needle: Wealth, the Fall of Rome, and the Making of Christianity in the West, 350–500 AD* (Princeton, N.J.: Princeton University Press, 2012), 13.

9. For the general contours of the system, see C. Wickham, *Framing the Early Middle Ages: Europe and the Mediterranean, 400–800* (Oxford: Oxford University Press, 2005), 62–80. For the move from "soft" to "hard" government in late antiquity and the expansion of the imperial bureaucracy during this period, see C. Kelly, *Ruling the Later Roman Empire* (Cambridge, Mass.: Harvard University Press, 2004), 1.

10. Either their landlords collected it from them and then passed it on to the state, or tax collectors collected it from them directly (Theodosius, *The Theodosian Code and Novels, and the Sirmondian Constitutions*, trans. C. Pharr [Princeton, N.J.: Princeton University Press, 1952], 11.1.14; P. Sarris, "The Origins of the Manorial Economy: New Insights from Late Antiquity," *English Historical Review*, 119 [2004], 279–311, at 300; P. Sarris, *Economy and Society in the Age of Justinian* [Cambridge: Cambridge University Press, 2009], 152; D. Rathbone, *Economic Rationalism and Rural Society in Third Century AD Egypt: The Heroninos Archive and the Appianus Estate* [Cambridge: Cambridge University Press, 1991], 404–7). Donatives, however, were funded from a different tax, levied on senators, curatorial families, craftsmen, and merchants, although less of the burden fell on the former two groups than on the latter two (M. F. Hendy, *Studies in Byzantine Monetary Economy, c. 300–1450* [Cambridge: Cambridge University Press, 1985], 175–76).

11. Theodosius, *Theodosian Code*, 7.20.1–7; J. Harries, *Imperial Rome AD 284 to 363: The New Empire* (Edinburgh: Edinburgh University Press, 2012), at 212–13; Kelly, *Ruling the Later Roman Empire*, 188.

12. As identified and characterized by S. Rippon et al., *The Fields of Britannia: Continuity and Change in the Late Roman and Early Medieval Landscape* (Oxford: Oxford University Press, 2015), 48–52.

13. D. Habermehl, *Settling in a Changing World: Villa Development in the Northern Provinces of the Roman Empire* (Amsterdam: Amsterdam University Press, 2013), 121–32. For anthropological literature on these asymmetrical relationships, see J. E. Arnold, "Social Inequality, Marginalization, and Economic Process," in T. D. Price and G. M. Feinman, eds., *Foundations of Social Inequality* (New York: Plenum Press, 1995), 87–103, at 88–89, 98; S. W. Silliman, "Theoretical Perspectives on Labor and Colonialism: Reconsidering the California Missions," *Journal of Anthropological Archaeology*, 20 (2001), 379–407, at 380.

14. M. Given, *The Archaeology of the Colonized* (London: Routledge, 2004), 3.

15. Dossey, *Peasants and Empire*, 62–76, 84–88.

16. Kelly, *Ruling the Later Roman Empire*, 111; Mattingly, *Imperialism, Power, and Identity*, 144; Bang, "Predation," 212.

17. Harries, *Imperial Rome*, 227. For some of the state officials who would have been entitled to *annona* rations, see J. T. Peña, "Mobilization of State Olive Oil in Roman Africa: The Evidence of Late 4th-C. Ostraca from Carthage," in J. T. Peña, ed., *Carthage Papers: The Early Colony's Econ-*

omy, Water Supply, a Public Bath and the Mobilization of State Olive Oil (Portsmouth, R.I.: Journal of Roman Studies, 1998), 116–238, at 153–54.

18. J. Banaji, *Agrarian Change in Late Antiquity: Gold, Labour, and Aristocratic Dominance* (Oxford: Oxford University Press, 2001), 57, 68–69.

19. R. Bland and X. Loriot, *Roman and Early Byzantine Gold Coins Found in Britain and Ireland* (London: Royal Numismatics Society, 2010), 110. Gold *solidi* were also likely given as donatives to important civilians (P. S. W. Guest, "Summary of the Coins," in C. Johns, ed., *The Hoxne Late Roman Treasure: Gold Jewellery and Silver Plate* [London" British Museum, 2010], 195–200, at 196).

20. R. J. Brickstock, "Coins and the Frontier Troops in the 4th Century," in R. Collins and L. Allason-Jones, eds., *Finds from the Frontier: Material Culture in the 4th–5th Centuries* (York: Council for British Archaeology, 2010), 86–91, at 91; R. Collins, *Hadrian's Wall and the End of Empire: The Roman Frontier in the 4th and 5th Centuries* (London: Routledge, 2012), 57; A. D. Lee, "Warfare and the State," in P. Sabin, H. Van Wees, and M. Whitby, eds., *The Cambridge History of Greek and Roman Warfare*, vol. 2, *Rome from the Late Republic to the Late Empire* (Cambridge: Cambridge University Press, 2007), 379–423, at 403; J.-M. Carrié, "L'état à recherche de nouveaux modes de financement des armées (Rome et Byzance, iv^c–viii^c siècles)," in A. Cameron, ed., *The Byzantine and Early Islamic Near East*, vol. 3, *States, Resources and Armies* (Princeton, N.J.: Princeton University Press, 1995), 27–60. For the association of gold coins in Britain with military sites and administrative towns, see Bland and Loriot, *Roman and Early Byzantine Gold Coins*, 53, 72.

21. Brickstock, "Coins and the Frontier Troops," 90.

22. Kelly, *Ruling the Later Roman Empire*, 141.

23. P. S. W. Guest, *The Late Roman Gold and Silver Coins from the Hoxne Treasure* (London: British Museum, 2005), 22–26. For the function of gold and silver in maintaining alliances between the state and its most important members, see P. Guest, "The Hoarding of Roman Metal Objects in Fifth-Century Britain," in F. K. Haarer, ed., *AD 410: The History and Archaeology of Late and Post-Roman Britain* (London: Society for the Promotion of Roman Studies, 2014), 117–29, at 121–22.

24. K. Painter, "Emergency or Votive? Two Groups of Late-Roman Gold and Silver Hoards," in J. Naylor and R. Bland, eds., *Hoarding and the Deposition of Metalwork from the Bronze Age to the 20th Century: A British Perspective*, BAR British Series 615 (Oxford: Archaeopress, 2015), 67–91, at 73–74.

25. Painter, "Emergency or Votive," 81–82.

26. M. A. Guggisberg, "Schlussbetrachtungen," in M. A. Guggisberg, ed., *Der spätrömische Silberschatz von Kaiseraugst: Die neuen Funde; Silber im Spannungsfeld von Geschichte, Politik und Gesellschaft der Spätantike* (Augst: Römerstadt Augusta Raurica, 2003), 285–91. For hoards of the period as "caches of value," see P. Guest, "The Burial, Loss, and Recovery of Roman Coin Hoards in Britain and Beyond: Past, Present, and Future," in Naylor and Bland, *Hoarding and the Deposition of Metalwork*, 101–16, at 111. Gold *solidi* were an especially efficient way to store value. The 584 *solidi* found in the Hoxne treasure would have been equal in value to 42,048 *siliquae* or 1,681,920 *nummi* (Bland and Loriot, *Roman and Early Byzantine Gold Coins*, 110).

27. *Anonymi auctoris De rebus bellicis*, ed. R. Ireland (Leipzig: B. G. Teubner, 1984), 2.1–2.

28. In the eastern half of the empire, we can reconstruct, in some detail, the ways officeholding elites both grew wealthy and became important landholders (Sarris, "Origins of the Manorial Economy," 292; and P. Sarris, "Rehabilitating the Great Estate: Aristocratic Property and Economic Growth in the Late Antique East," in W. Bowden, L. Lavan, and C. Machado, eds., *Recent*

Research in the Late Antique Countryside [Leiden: Brill, 2004], 55–71, at 59; and Sarris, *Economy and Society*, 181–82).

29. L. C. Ruggini, *Economia e società nell' "Italia annonaria": Rapporti fra agricoltura e commercio dal IV al VI secolo d.C.*, 2nd ed. (Bari: Edipuglia, 1995), 25–26.

30. C. Roberto, J. A. Plambeck, and A. M. Small, "The Chronology of the Sites of the Roman Period Around S. Giovanni," in S. Macready and F. H. Thompson, eds., *Archaeological Field Survey in Britain and Abroad* (London: Society of Antiquaries of London, 1985), 136–45.

31. Sarris, "Rehabilitating the Great Estate," 60.

32. Sarris, *Economy and Society*, 181–91.

33. K.-J. Giles, "Neuere Untersuchungen an der Langmauer bei Trier," in F.-R. Herrmann, ed., *Festschrift für Günter Smolla* (Wiesbaden: Landesamt für Denkmalpflege Hessen, 1999), 245–58. Other examples of very large, contiguous estates can be found between Trier and Bitburg, but they may be unique to this region (P. van Ossel and P. Ouzoulias, "Rural Settlement Economy in Northern Gaul in the Late Empire: An Overview and Assessment," *Journal of Roman Archaeology*, 13 [2000], 133–66, at 154, and n. 100).

34. In Roman Egypt, where a wealth of documentary evidence survives, it is possible to chart the development of more direct styles of estate management by the rich during this period, which allowed them to more effectively produce for the market (Sarris, "Rehabilitating the Great Estate," 60–63). Elsewhere, where late Roman estate archives survive, there is also evidence that great landowners were changing the ways they exploited their holdings during this period, moving away from the leasing out of their estates to a more direct management of them (Sarris, "Origins of the Manorial Economy," 289–301; Rathbone, *Economic Rationalism*, 314–18).

35. V. Gaffney and M. Tingle, *The Maddle Farm Project: An Integrated Survey of Prehistoric and Roman Landscapes on the Berkshire Downs*, BAR British Series 200 (Oxford: BAR, 1989), 224–38.

36. J.-G. Gorges, *Les villas hispano-romaines: Inventaire et problématique archéologiques* (Paris: Diffusion E. de Boccard, 1979), 47–49; M. Biró, "Roman Villas in Pannonia," *Acta Archaeologica Academiae Scientiarum Hungaricae*, 26 (1974), 23–57, at 47–49.

37. S. Scott, "Elites, Exhibitionism, and the Society of the Late Roman Villa," in N. Christie, ed., *Landscapes of Change: Rural Evolutions in Late Antiquity and the Early Middle Ages* (Aldershot: Ashgate, 2004), 39–66, at 41; S. Ellis, "Late Antique Housing and the Uses of Residential Buildings: An Overview," in L. Lavan, L. Özgenel, and A. Sarantis, eds., *Housing in Late Antiquity*, vol. 3.2, *From Palaces to Shops* (Leiden: Brill, 2007), 1–22, at 11.

38. K. Bowes, *Houses and Society in the Later Roman Empire* (London: Duckworth, 2010), 87–89; S. Scott, *Art and Society in Fourth-Century Britain: Villa Mosaics in Context* (Oxford: Oxford University School of Archaeology, 2000), 105.

39. J. Gerrard, *The Ruin of Roman Britain: An Archaeological Perspective* (Cambridge: Cambridge University Press, 2013), 133, 142–43; S. Esmonde Cleary, *The Roman West, AD 200–500: An Archaeological Study* (Cambridge: Cambridge University Press, 2013), 215; M. Corney, *The Roman Villa at Box: The Story of the Extensive Romano-British Structures Buried Below the Village of Box in Wiltshire* (Salisbury: Hobnob, 2012), 46.

40. See below, Chapter 5.

41. T. Copeland, *Roman Gloucestershire* (Stroud: History Press, 2011), 115; D. Perring, *The Roman House in Britain* (London: Routledge, 2002), 41–47, 72–79, 122–39.

42. Perring, *Roman House*, 201.

43. S. Esmonde Cleary, "The Ending(s) of Roman Britain," in H. Hamerow, D. A. Hinton, and S. Crawford, eds., *The Oxford Handbook of Anglo-Saxon Archaeology* (Oxford: Oxford Uni-

versity Press, 2011), 13–29, at 17. A similar trend can be discerned in contemporary southwestern Gaul (S. Esmonde Cleary, *Roman West*, 288). The abandonment of relatively elaborate houses in late antiquity, paired with the rise of fewer very rich domestic buildings, also happened in the eastern empire in the sixth century (S. P. Ellis, "The End of the Roman House," *American Journal of Archaeology*, 92 [1988], 565–76, at 573).

44. Rippon et al., *Fields of Britannia*, 48–52 and fig. 2.11; A. Smith et al., *The Rural Settlement of Roman Britain* (London, 2016), figs. 4.1, 5.1, 6.1, 7.1.

45. J. Taylor, "The Idea of the Villa: Reassessing Villa Development in South-East Britain," in N. Roymans and T. Derks, eds., *Villa Landscapes in the Roman North: Economy, Culture and Lifestyle* (Amsterdam: Amsterdam University Press, 2011)," 179–94, at 190; R. Shaffrey, "Intensive Milling Practices in the Romano-British Landscape of Southern England: Using Newly Established Criteria for Distinguishing Millstones from Rotary Querns," *Britannia*, 46 (2015), 55–92, at 72; B. Cunliffe, *The Danebury Environs Roman Programme, a Wessex Landscape During the Roman Era*, vol. 1, *Overview* (Oxford: English Heritage and Oxford University School of Archaeology, 2008), 183; M. G. Allen et al., *The Rural Economy of Roman Britain* (London, 2017), 237–80.

46. S. Esmonde Cleary, *Roman West*, 257.

47. On how this might work, see S. J. B. Barnish, "Pigs, Plebeians and Potentates: Rome's Economic Hinterland, c. 350–600 AD," *Papers of the British School at Rome*, 55 (1987), 157–85, at 167.

48. M. G. Allen et al., *Rural Economy*, 142–77. Rippon et al., *Fields of Britannia*, 81–82, 314–15, and table 3.6.

49. S. Esmonde Cleary, "Britain at the End of Empire," in M. Millett, L. Revell, and A. Moore, eds., *The Oxford Handbook of Roman Britain* (Oxford: Oxford University Press, 2016), 134–49, at 135.

50. S. Heeren, "Military Might for a Depopulated Region? Interpreting the Archaeology of the Lower Rhine Area in the Late Roman Period," in P. Diarte-Blasco and N. Christie, eds., *Interpreting Transformations of People and Landscapes in Late Antiquity and the Early Middle Ages: Archaeological Approaches and Issues* (Oxford: Oxbow Books, 2018), 137–48; D. Wigg-Wolf, "Supplying a Dying Empire? The Mint of Trier in the Late-4th Century AD," in J. Chameroy and P.-M. Guihard, eds., *Produktion und recyceln von Münzen in der Spätantike* (Mainz: Römisch-Germanischen Zantralmuseums, 2016), 217–34.

51. M. Maas and D. Ruths, "Road Connectivity and the Structure of Ancient Empires: A Case Study from Late Antiquity," in S. E. Alcock, J. Bodel, and R. J. A. Talbert, eds., *Highways, Byways, and Road Systems in the Pre-Modern World* (London: Wiley-Blackwell, 2012), 255–64.

52. A. F. Pearson, "Barbarian Piracy and the Saxon Shore: A Reappraisal," *Oxford Journal of Archaeology*, 24 (2005), 73–88, at 82–85.

53. Heeren, "Military Might for a Depopulated Region?"; E. Rizos, "Centres of the Late Roman Military Supply Network in the Balkans: A Survey of *Horrea*," *Jahrbuch des Römisch-Germanischen Zentralmuseums*, 60 (2013), 659–96, at 659–60.

54. Ammianus Marcellinus, *Rerum gestarum libri qui supersunt*, ed. J. C. Rolfe (Cambridge, Mass.: Cambridge University Press, 1935–39), xviii, 2, 3; Zosimus, *Historia Nova*, ed. Ludwig Mendelssohn (Leipzig: B. G. Teubner, 1887), III.5.2; Libanius, *Selected Orations*, vol. 1, ed. and trans. A. F. Norman (Cambridge, Mass.: Harvard University Press, 1969), 18.82–83.

55. M. G. Allen et al., *Rural Economy*, 173.

56. Based on calculations of the least expensive transportation available during the summer months, using *Orbis: The Stanford Geospatial Network Model of the Roman World*, search from *Londinium* to *Lugdunum Canefatium* (http://orbis.stanford.edu/).

57. The calculation, using *Orbis*, from London to Trier using the cheapest method in the summer months is forty-four days (http://orbis.stanford.edu/). The same calculation from Lyon to Trier is 52.4 days. Scheidel notes that maritime transport made Britain, during the good sailing months, a place from which it was relatively easy to transport goods to other parts of the empire (W. Scheidel, "The Shape of the Roman World: Modeling Imperial Connectivity," *Journal of Roman Archaeology*, 27 [2014], 7–32, at 16).

58. G. A. King, "The Alien Presence: Palaeoentomological Approaches to Trade and Migration" (Ph.D. diss., University of York, 2009), 214.

59. King, "Alien Presence," 213–14.

60. M. Fulford, "Pottery and Britain's Foreign Trade in the Later Roman Period," in D. P. S. Peacock, ed., *Pottery and Early Commerce: Characterization and Trade in Roman and Later Ceramics* (London: Academic, 1977), 35–84, at 65–70; J. R. L. Allen and M. G. Fulford, "The Distribution of South-East Dorset Black Burnished Category I Pottery in South-West Britain," *Britannia*, 27 (1996), 223–81, at 267.

61. P. Guest, "Burial, Loss, and Recovery," 110–11; P. J. Walton, *Rethinking Roman Britain: Coinage and Archaeology* (Wetteren: Edition Moneta, 2012); R. Bland, S. Moorhead, and P. Walton, "Finds of Late Roman Silver Coins from Britain: The Contribution of the Portable Antiquities Scheme," in F. Hunter and K. Painter, eds., *Late Roman Silver: The Traprain Treasure in Context* (Edinburgh: Society of Antiquaries of Scotland, 2013), 117–66, at 121; R. Reece, "Silver After 350 and the Lost Generation," in Hunter and Painter, *Late Roman Silver*, 167–74. They are not generally found, however, in Britain's northern military zone, so they must not have been used to pay soldiers (Bland, Morehead, and Walton, "Finds of Late Roman Silver Coins," 121; Reece, "Silver After 350").

62. The dates run from the beginning of the infant Constantine II's reign as Caesar in the West to the end of Julian's reign as emperor (Bland and Loriot, *Roman and Early Byzantine Gold Coins*, 19; P. Walton and S. Moorhead, "Coinage and Collapse? The Contribution of Numismatic Data to Understanding the End of Roman Britain," *Internet Archaeology*, 41 [2016], http://dx.doi.org/10.11141/ia.41.8; P. J. Walton, "Rethinking Romano-British Coins: An Applied Numismatic Analysis of the Roman Coin Data Recorded by the Portable Antiquities Scheme" [Ph.D. diss., University College London, 2011], 197). Stray coin loss between 378 and 388, however, declined markedly, retreating from the rich agricultural heartlands toward Roman roads and urban communities, which may suggest the beginning of the unraveling of the supply systems and markets connecting Romano-British villa owners to the Rhineland (Walton, *Rethinking Romano-British Coins*, 198, 208).

63. T. S. N. Moorhead, "Roman Coin Finds from Wiltshire," in *Roman Wiltshire and After: Papers in Honour of Ken Annable*, ed. P. Ellis (Devizes: Wiltshire Archaeological Society, 2001), 85–105, at 94–95.

64. Wigg-Wolf, "Supplying a Dying Empire?" table 2; Heeren, "Military Might," 144.

65. Fulford, "Pottery and Britain's Foreign Trade," 42. For a discussion of this pottery and an up-to-date bibliography, see R. Fleming, "The Movement of People and Things Between Britain and France in the Late- and Post-Roman Periods," in B. Effros and I. Moreira, eds., *Oxford Handbook of the Merovingian World* (Oxford: Oxford University Press, forthcoming).

66. B. Ward-Perkins, "Specialized Production and Exchange," in A. Cameron, B. Ward-Perkins, and M. Whitby, *The Cambridge Ancient History*, vol. 14, *Late Antiquity: Empire and Successors, AD 425–600* (Cambridge: Cambridge University Press, 2001), 346–91, at 347–48.

67. Fulford, "La céramique et les échanges commerciaux," 102; M. Millett, "Roman Kent," in J. H. Williams, ed., *The Archaeology of Kent to AD 800* (Woodbridge: Boydell, 2007), 135–86, at 142–46.

68. S. Esmonde Cleary, *Roman West*, 320; P. Tyers, *Roman Pottery in Britain* (London: Batsford, 1997), 136.
69. Wickham, *Framing the Early Middle Ages*, 718.
70. E. W. Black, "An Additional Classification of Granaries in Roman Britain," *Britannia*, 12 (1981), 163–65. For a discussion of buildings where grain might have been stored, see A. Smith et al., *Rural Settlement*, 58–60.
71. D. Smith and H. Kenward, "Roman Grain Pests in Britain: Implications for Grain Supply and Agricultural Production," *Britannia*, 42 (2011), 243–62, at 252–54, 257.
72. M. G. Allen et al., *Rural Economy*, 68–71.
73. M. G. Allen et al., *Rural Economy*, 174, 302–3.
74. *CTh* 7.4.15 and 11.1.11. Analysis of grain samples from South Shields, dating to the late third or fourth century, suggests that the spelt stored at the fort was locally grown, given the prevalence of local heath grass seeds among the spelt. The bread wheat found there, however, may have been supplied from southern Britain (M. van der Veen, "Reports on the Biological Remains," in P. T. Bidwell and S. Speak, *Excavations at South Shields Roman Fort*, vol. 1 (New Castle upon Tyne: Society of Antiquaries of Newcastle-upon-Tyne, 1994), 243–58, at 258). Another sign of the increasing dependence on more local provisioning of these soldiers is the fact that some of the pottery from southern Britain, such as BB1, which in earlier generations had played a central role in the transportation of food north to the wall, became scarce in the north in the second half of the fourth century at exactly the same time that local northern pottery production was on the rise (J. R. L. Allen and Fulford, "Distribution of South-East Dorset Black Burnished Category I Pottery").
75. P. Bennett, I. Riddler, and C. Sparey-Green, *The Roman Watermills and Settlement at Ickham Kent* (Canterbury: Canterbury Archaeological Trust, 2010).
76. M. Millett and T. Wilmott, "Rethinking Richborough," in P. Wilson, ed., *The Archaeology of Roman Towns: Studies in Honour of John S. Wacher* (Oxford: Oxbow Books, 2003), 184–94, at 186; Millett, "Roman Kent," 141–46, 182–83; R. Goodburn, M. W. C. Hassall, and R. S. O. Tomlin, "Roman Britain in 1978," *Britannia*, 10 (1979), 267–356, at 350–53.
77. P. Wilkinson, "An Archaeological Investigation of the Roman Aisled Stone Building at Hog Brook, Deerton Street, Faversham, Kent 2004–5" (unpublished report, Kent Archaeological Field School, 2009), https://doi.org/10.5284/1030489.
78. N. Purcell, "The Roman Villa and the Landscape of Production," in T. J. Cornell and K. Lomas, eds., *Urban Society in Roman Italy* (London: Routledge, 1995), 158–84, at 173.
79. For milling facilities, see A. Wilson, "Machines, Power, and the Ancient Economy," *Journal of Roman Studies*, 92 (2002), 1–32, at 11; D. Peacock, "The Problem of Power Mills in Roman Britain and Beyond," in H. Eckhardt and S. Rippon, eds., *Living and Working in the Roman World: Essays in Honour of Michael Fulford on his 65th Birthday* (Portsmouth, R.I.: Journal of Roman Archaeology, 2013), 205–14; Shaffrey, "Intensive Milling Practices." For corn driers, see P. J. Reynolds and J. K. Langley, "Romano-British Corn-Drying Oven: An Experiment," *Archaeological Journal*, 136 (1979), 27–42; J. Proctor and R. Taylor-Wilson, "'Corn-Driers' in Romano-British Archaeology," in P. Boyer, J. Proctor, and R. Taylor-Wilson, eds., *On the Boundaries of Occupation: Excavations at Burringham Road, Scunthorpe and Baldwin Avenue, Bottesford, North Lincoln* (London: Pre-Construct Archaeology, 2009), 28–33. For the large-scale production of beer, see M. van der Veen and T. O'Connor, "The Expansion of Agricultural Production in the Late Iron Age and Roman Britain," in J. Bayley, ed., *Science in Archaeology: An Agenda for the Future* (London: English Heritage, 1998), 127–43, at 134–35. For investments of this kind in general, see Taylor, "Idea of the Villa," 179–94.

80. N. Holbrook, ed., *Cirencester: The Roman Town Defences, Public Buildings, and Shops* (Cirencester: Cotswold Archaeological Trust, 1998), 166–69, 174–75, 383; and N. Holbrook, "Ambiguous Evidence and Obscured Stratigraphy: Interpreting the Archaeology of Late Roman and Early Post-Roman Cirencester," in Eckhardt and Rippon, eds., *Living and Working in the Roman World*, 31–46, at 37–39.

81. Faulkner, "Urban Stratigraphy and Roman History," in Holbrook, ed., *Cirencester*, 371–85, at 383.

82. Holbrook, *Cirencester*, 383. For the long distances some of the animals collected by the Roman state were traveling, see R. Madgwick et al., "On the Hoof: Exploring the Supply of Animals to the Roman Legionary Fortress at Caerleon Using Strontium 87Sr/86Sr Isotope Analysis," *Archaeological and Anthropological Science* (2017), 1–13: doi 10.1007/s12520-017-0539-9.

83. M. Corney, "The Origins and Development of the 'Small Town' of 'Cunetio,' Mildenhall, Wiltshire," *Britannia*, 28 (1997), 337–50, at 349; and M. Corney, "The Romano-British Nucleated Settlements of Wiltshire," in P. Ellis, *Roman Wiltshire and After*, 5–38, at 15–18.

84. B. C. Burnham and J. Wacher, *The Small Towns of Roman Britain* (Berkeley, Calif.: University of California Press, 1990), 149–52.

85. Corney, "Origins and Development," 348–49.

86. Corney, "Origins and Development," 343–45, 348; Gerrard, *Ruin of Roman Britain*, 53–55.

87. E. Hostetter, "The Area Around Cunetio," in E. Hostetter and T. N. Howe, eds., *The Romano-British Villa at Castle Copse, Great Bedwyn* (Bloomington: Indiana University Press, 1997), 38–60, at 48.

88. Corney, "Origins and Development," 349.

89. S. Rippon, "Coastal Trade in Roman Britain: The Investigation of Crandon Bridge, Somerset, a Romano-British Transshipment Port Beside the Severn Estuary," *Britannia*, 39 (2008), 84–144.

90. R. P. J. Jackson and T. W. Potter, *Excavations at Stonea, Cambridgeshire 1980–85* (London: British Museum, 1996), 324 and fig. 100; T. W. Potter, "Roman Fenland," in T. Kirby and S. Oosthuizen, eds., *An Atlas of Cambridgeshire and Huntingdonshire History* (Cambridge: Centre for Regional Studies, 2000), entry 13; T. Malim, *Stonea and the Roman Fens* (Stroud, 2005), 201.

91. J. E. Jones, *The Maritime and Riverine Landscape of the West of Roman Britain: Water Transport on the Atlantic Coasts and Rivers of Britannia*, BAR British Series 493 (Oxford: Archaeopress, 2009).

92. Kelly, *Ruling the Later Roman Empire*, 20.

93. S. Esmonde Cleary, *Roman West*, 58, 83–84; H. E. M. Cool, "A Different Life," in Collins and Allason-Jones, eds., *Finds from the Frontier*, 1–9, at 7; J. Coulston, "Military Equipment of the 'Long' Fourth Century on Hadrian's Wall," in Collins and Allason-Jones, *Finds from the Frontier*, 50–63; D. Janes, "The Golden Clasp of the Late Roman State," *Early Medieval Europe*, 5 (1996), 127–53, at 130–31; E. Swift, *Regionality in Dress Accessories in the Late Roman West* (Montagnac: M. Mergoil, 2000), chapters 5 and 6; V. Van Thienen, "A Symbol of Late Roman Authority Revisited: A Sociohistorical Understanding of the Crossbow Brooch," in N. Roymans, S. Heeren, and W. de Clercq, eds., *Social Dynamics in the Northwest Frontiers of the Late Roman Empire: Beyond Decline or Transformation* (Amsterdam: Amsterdam University Press, 2017), 1–29; S. Esmonde Cleary, "Roman State Involvement in Britain in the Later 4th Century: An Ebbing Tide?" in Roymans, Heeren, and de Clercq, *Social Dynamics in the Northwest Frontiers of the Late Roman Empire*, 179–202. Prick spurs are less common, but there are a number of late Roman ex-

amples from Britain, and like the brooches and belt sets, they are often found in civilian contexts (S. Worrell, "Some New Late-Roman Rivet Spurs," *Lucerna*, 28 [2004], 20–22).

94. E. Swift, *The End of the Western Roman Empire: An Archaeological Investigation* (Stroud: Tempus, 2000), 49–50.

95. For more on the way stable isotopes can be used to investigate mobility, see below, Chapter 8.

96. H. Eckhardt et al., "Oxygen and Strontium Isotope Evidence for Mobility in Roman Winchester," *Journal of Archaeological Science*, 36 (2009), 2816–25; P. Booth, "A Late Roman Military Burial from the Dyke Hills, Dorchester on Thames, Oxfordshire," *Britannia*, 45 (2014), 243–73; H. Eckhardt, G. Müldner, and G. Speed, "The Late Roman Field Army in Northern Britain? Mobility, Material Culture, and Multi-Isotope Analysis at Scorton (N. Yorks)," *Britannia*, 46 (2015), 191–223.

97. G. H. Müldner, C. Chenery, and H. Eckhardt, "The 'Headless Romans': Multi-Isotope Investigations of an Unusual Burial Ground from Roman Britain," *Journal of Archaeological Science*, 38 (2011), 280–90; Eckhardt et al., "Late Roman Field Army."

98. R. Martiniano et al., "Genomic Signals of Migration and Continuity in Britain Before the Anglo-Saxons," *Nature Communications*, 7 (2016), 1–8, at 3.

99. H. Eckhardt, "Foreigners and Locals in *Calleva*," in M. Fulford, ed., *Silchester and the Study of Romano-British Urbanism* (Portsmouth, R.I.: Journal of Roman Archaeology, 2012), 247–56, at 250.

100. S. Leach et al., "A Lady of York: Migration, Ethnicity and Identity in Roman Britain," *Antiquity*, 84 (2010), 131–45; J. Montgomery et al., "'Gleaming White and Deadly': Using Lead to Track Human Exposure and Geographic Origins in the Roman Period in Britain," in H. Eckhardt, ed., *Roman Diasporas: Archaeological Approaches to Mobility and Diversity in the Roman Empire* (Portsmouth, R.I. Journal of Roman Archaeology, 2010), 199–226.

101. M. A. Handley, *Dying on Foreign Shores: Travel and Mobility in the Late-Antique West* (Portsmouth, R.I.: Journal of Roman Archaeology, 2011), 64 and nos. 53, 443, and 456; H. Eckhardt, *Objects and Identities: Roman Britain and the North-Western Provinces* (Oxford: Oxford University Press, 2014), 50–53.

102. E. Swift, "Identifying Migrant Communities: A Contextual Analysis of Grave Assemblages from Continental Late Roman Cemeteries," *Britannia*, 41 (2010), 237–82, at 247–49.

103. Swift, "Identifying Migrant Communities," 250.

104. Swift "Identifying Migrant Communities," 265, 276. The cemetery contains more than four thousand graves, about 640 datable to the fourth century, fifty to the fifth century, and six hundred to the sixth century (J. H. F. Bloemers and J. R. A. M. Thijssen, "Facts and Reflections on the Continuity of Settlement at Nijmegan Between AD 400 and 750," in J. C. Besteman, J. M. Bos, and H. A. Heidinga, eds., *Medieval Archaeology in the Netherlands: Studies Presented to H. H. van Regteren Altena* (Assen: Van Gorcum, 1990), 133–50, at 145.

105. Swift, "Identifying Migrant Communities," 266, 268.

106. Swift, "Identifying Migrant Communities," 270.

107. Swift, "Identifying Migrant Communities," 273. This is the only Hadham-ware vessel that has been found on the continent (R. Brulet, F. Vilvorder, and R. Delage, *La céramique romaine en Gaule du Nord: Dictionnaire des céramiques; La vaisselle à large diffusion* [Turnhout: Brepols, 2010], 266).

108. T. Ivleva, "Britons on the Move: Mobility of British-Born Emigrants in the Roman Empire," in Millett, Revell, and Moore, *Oxford Handbook of Roman Britain*, 245–61, at, 250, 256, and fig. 12.1.

109. N. Hodgson, "A Late Roman Courtyard House at South Shields and Its Parallels," in P. Johnson, ed., *Architecture in Roman Britain* (York: Council for British Archaeology, 1996), 135–51, at 35; Bidwell and Speak, *Excavations at South Shields*, 35–39.

110. Hodgson, "Late Roman Courtyard House," 145; S. Ellis, "Late Antique Housing," 11.

111. For an example, see H. I. Bell, *The Abinnaeus Archive: Papers of a Roman Officer in the Reign of Constantius II* (Oxford: Clarendon, 1962), 7.

112. Hodgson, "Late Roman Courtyard House"; T. Wilmott, "The Late Roman Frontier: A Structural Background," in Collins and Allason-Jones, *Finds from the Frontier*, 10–16, at 12.

113. Bidwell and Speak, *Excavations at South Shields*, 39.

114. I. M. Ferris, *The Beautiful Rooms Are Empty: Excavations at Binchester Roman Fort, County Durham 1976–81 and 1986–1991*, 2 parts (Durham: Durham County Council, 2010), part 2, 551–54. Other commanders stationed in the North may have also lived in courtyard houses. R. Birley, J. Blake, and A. Birley, *Vindolanda 1997 Excavations: Praetorium Site Interim Report* (Greenhead: Roman Army Museum Publications, 1998), 27–48. There was a courtyard-style praetorium at Housesteads, which incorporated the remains of an earlier house of a different form. The dating evidence for this second house is poor, but given the dates of the other peristyle houses in forts, a remodeling of this house in the fourth century would not be surprising. The excavator suggests a considerably earlier date, but he admits that little dating evidence survives (see A. Rushworth, *Housesteads Roman Fort—the Grandest Station*, vol. 1, *Structural Report and Discussion* [London: English Heritage, 2009], 205, 277). See also J. Crow, *Housesteads: A Fort and Garrison on Hadrian's Wall*, 3rd ed. [Stroud: Tempus, 2004], 52–54, 91–92). Piercebridge's courtyard-style praetorium likely dates to the third century (H. E. M. Cool and D. J. P. Mason, *Roman Piercebridge: Excavations by D. W. Harding and Peter Scott 1969–1981* [Durham: Architectural and Archaeological Society of Durham and Northumberland, 2008], 39).

115. Bowes, *Houses and Society*, 17, 87–89; J. N. Dillon, "The Inflation of Rank and Privilege: Regulating Precedence in the Fourth Century AD," in J. Wienand, ed., *Contested Monarchy: Integrating the Roman Empire in the Fourth Century AD* (Oxford: Oxford University Press, 2014), 42–66.

116. Habermehl, *Settling in a Changing World*, 91–131, and below, Chapter 5.

117. Bell, *Abinnaeus Archive*, 7.

118. Bell, *Abinnaeus Archive*, no. 1.

119. See, especially Bell, *Abinnaeus Archive*, nos. 3–5, 26, 35, 37, and 71.

120. Bell, *Abinnaeus Archive*, no. 5.

121. Kelly, *Ruling the Later Roman Empire*, 165.

122. Mattingly, *Imperialism, Power, and Identity*, 204.

123. Bang, "Predation"; A. Gardner, "Thinking About Roman Imperialism: Postcolonialism, Globalisation and Beyond?" *Britannia*, 44 (2013), 1–25, at 12; Mattingly, *Imperialism, Power, and Identity*, 125–45.

124. I. M. Stead, *Rudston Roman Villa* (Leeds, 1980), 102–3, fig. 65, no. 47.

125. See above, n. 93; and Cool, "Different Life," 7.

126. Cool, "Different Life," 6, fig. 1.3

127. Stead, *Rudston*, 102–3, fig. 65.47.

128. K. M. D. Dunbabin, *Mosaics of the Greek and Roman World* (Cambridge: Cambridge University Press, 1999), 99; R. Ferraby et al., *Thwing, Rudston, and the Roman-Period Exploitation of the Yorkshire Wolds* (Leeds: Yorkshire Archaeological and Historical Society, 2017), 260–63.

129. R. J. A. Wilson, "The Rudston Venus Mosaic Revisited: A Spear-Bearing Lion?" *Britannia*, 34 (2003), 288–91, at 289–90; Ferraby et al., *Thwing*, 261.

130. D. J. Smith, *Roman Mosaics at Hull* (Hull: Hull City Museums and Art Galleries, 2005), 9–13; P. Halkon, "Britons and Romans in an East Yorkshire Landscape, UK," *Bollettino di Archeologia on line, Edizione special—Congresso di Archeologia Online Edizione Speciale* (2008), 24–40, at 32–33, http://www.bollettinodiarcheologiaonline.beniculturali.it/bao_es_e_10.php.

131. R. J. A. Wilson, "Aspects of Iconography in Romano-British Mosaics: The Rudston 'Aquatic' Scene and the Brading Astronomer Revisited," *Britannia*, 37 (2006), 295–36, at 302–4; D. J. Smith, *Roman Mosaics at Hull*, 14.

132. D. J. Smith, *Roman Mosaics at Hull*, 21–23; J. H. Humphrey, *Roman Circuses: Arenas for Chariot Racing* (Berkeley, Calif: University of California Press, 1986), 434–35; Ferraby et al., *Thwing*, 264.

133. Halkon, "Britons and Romans," 33.

134. A. S. Esmonde Cleary, *Ending of Roman Britain*, 188–61; Wickham, *Framing the Early Middle Ages*, 79–80, 717.

135. A. S. Esmonde Cleary, *Ending of Roman Britain*, 138–61.

136. S. Esmonde Cleary, "Ending(s) of Roman Britain," 13–29; Gerrard, *Ruin of Roman Britain*, 17–26.

137. Gerrard, *Ruin of Roman Britain*, 19.

138. Gerrard, *Ruin of Roman Britain*, 76–86.

139. H. Härke, "Invisible Britons, Gallo-Romans, and Russians: Perspectives on Culture Change," in N. Higham, *Britons in Anglo-Saxon England* (Woodbridge: Boydell, 2007), 57–67, at 66–67; S. Esmonde Cleary, "Southern Britain in the Fifth Century: A 'Collapsed State'?" in Hunter and Painter, *Late Roman Silver*, 45–53.

CHAPTER 2

Epigraph: A. Appadurai, "Gastro-Politics in Hindu South Asia," *American Ethnologist*, 8 (1981), 494–511, at 494.

1. S. Whatmore, "Materialist Returns: Practicing Cultural Geography in and for a More-Than-Human World," *Cultural Geographies*, 13 (2006), 600–609; N. Sykes, "Worldviews in Transition: The Impact of Exotic Plants and Animals on Iron Age/Romano-British Landscapes," *Landscapes*, 2 (2009), 19–36, at 19–20.

2. T. Ingold, "The Temporality of the Landscape," *World Archaeology*, 25 (1993), 152–74.

3. I. Hodder, *Entangled: An Archaeology of the Relationships Between Humans and Things* (Chichester: Wiley-Blackwell, 2012); M. van der Veen, "The Materiality of Plants: Plant-People Entanglements," *World Archaeology*, 46 (2014), 799–812; Sykes, "Worldviews in Transition," 21; T. Ingold, *What Is an Animal* (London: Unwin Hyman, 1988), 1–17.

4. The most relevant Roman-period texts are Apicius, *De Re Coquinaria*; Cato, *De Agricultura*; Columella, *De re rustica* and *De arboribus*; Dioscorides, *De materia medica*; Pliny, *Naturalis Historiae*, books 20–32; and Varo, *Rerum Rusticarum*.

5. Many of these texts are published in O. Cockayne, ed., *Leechdoms, Wortcunning, and Starcraft of Early England*, Rolls Series, 3 vols. (London: Longman, 1864–66).

6. L. Moffett, "The Archaeology of Medieval Plant Food," in C. M. Woolgar, D. Serjeantson, and T. Waldron, eds., *Food in Medieval England* (Oxford, 2006), 41–55, at 41–43, and L. Moffett, "Food Plants on Archaeological Sites: The Nature of the Archaeobotanical Record," in H. Hamerow, D. A. Hinton, and S. Crawford, eds., *The Oxford Handbook of Anglo-Saxon Archaeology* (Oxford: Oxford University Press, 2011), 346–60, at 347–48; M. van der Veen et al., "New

Plant Foods in Roman Britain—Dispersal and Social Access," *Environmental Archaeology*, 13 (2008), 11–36, at 15–17.

7. Van der Veen et al., "New Plant Foods," 16–17.

8. Van der Veen et al., "New Plant Foods," 11–36; M. van der Veen et al., "The Archaeobotany of Roman Britain," *Britannia*, 38 (2007), 181–210; M. van der Veen et al., "The Archaeobotany of Medieval Britain (c. AD 450–1500): Identifying Research Practices for the 21st Century," *Medieval Archaeology*, 57 (2013), 151–82. These articles came out of the *Seeds of Change—Food Introductions into NW Europe AD 1–1500* project, http://www2.le.ac.uk/departments/archaeology/people/vanderveen/current-research#Seeds of change.

9. Van der Veen et al., "New Plant Foods," 11.

10. For a complete list, including foodstuff that was imported, but not actually grown in Britain, see van der Veen, et al., "New Plant Foods," table 1; M. van der Veen et al., "Archaeobotany of Roman Britain," 181.

11. For a similar exposure to and selective adoption of new food plants during the Roman period in central Europe, see C. Bakels and S. Jacomet, "Access to Luxury Foods in Central Europe During the Roman Period: The Archaeobotanical Evidence," *World Archaeology*, 34 (2003), 542–57. For changes in plants and plant cultivation in this same period along the Mosel and in Thuringia, see A. Kreuz, "Becoming a Roman Farmer: Preliminary Report on the Environmental Evidence from the Romanization Project," in J. Creighton, R. J. A. Wilson, and D. Krausse, eds., *Roman Germany: Studies in Cultural Interaction* (Portsmouth, R.I.: Journal of Roman Archaeology, 1999), 71–98. For diversification of plant foods in Gaul under Roman rule, see J. Wiethold, "How to Trace the 'Romanisation' of Central Gaul by Archaeobotanical Analysis?—Some Considerations on New Archaeobotanical Results from France Centre-Est," in F. Favory and A. Vignot, eds., *Actualité de la recherche en histoire et archéologie agraires: Actes du colloque international AGER V, Septembre 2000* (Besançon: Presses Universitaires Franc-Comtoises, 2003), 269–82, at 278.

12. For the limited adoption of a few exotic plants as foods (most likely imported rather than grown) at high-status sites on the eve of the Roman conquest, see L. Lodwick, "Condiments Before Claudius," *Vegetation History and Archaeobotany*, 23 (2014), 543–49.

13. For the ethnic makeup of imperial colonizers at Colchester in the earliest years after the conquest, see H. E. M. Cool, "Sustenance in a Strange Land," in P. Crummy and P. Ottaway, eds., *A Victory Celebration: Papers on the Archaeology of Colchester and Late Iron Age–Roman Britain Presented to Philip Crummy* (Colchester: Friends of Colchester Archaeological Trust, 2006), 75–82, at 75–76. For an interesting analysis of a first-century centurion's diet, based on an analysis of fecal matter from a latrine at a Roman fort at Alphen aan den Rijn, which included apples, celery, coriander, and fennel, see W. J. Kuijper and H. Turner, "Diet of a Roman Centurion at Alphen," *Review of Palaeobotany and Palynology*, 73 (1992), 187–204. For evidence that many of the exotic foodstuffs imported into Britain in the first century were aimed at the cosmopolitan inhabitants of the city and not at broader markets in Britain, see H. A. Orengo and A. Livarda, "The Seeds of Commerce: A Network Analysis–Based Approach to the Romano-British Transport System," *Journal of Archaeological Science*, 66 (2016), 21–35, at 26. For evidence of imported coriander, celery, and millet at the Roman fort at Alchester as early as 44 BCE, see P. Booth et al., *The Thames Through Time: The Archaeology of the Gravel Terraces of the Upper and Middle Thames; The Early Historical Period AD 1–1000* (Oxford: Oxford Archaeology, 2007), 280–81. For evidence in pre-Boudician London for olives, raisins, almonds, lentils, figs, fennel, coriander, and black cumin, see J. Hill and P. Rowsome, *Roman London and the Walbrook Stream Crossing: Excavations at 1 Poultry and Vicinity, City of London* (London: MoLAS, 2011), 291–92, 532.

14. For the spread of these food plants to rural sites, see M. van der Veen, "Food as Embodied Material Culture: Diversity and Change in Plant Food Consumption in Roman Britain," *Journal of Roman Archaeology*, 21 (2008), 83–109, at 97–98.

15. A. Livarda, "New Temptations? Olive, Cherry, and Mulberry in Roman and Medieval Europe," in *Food and Drink in Archaeology*, 1 (2007), 73–83, at 77–78; H. E. M. Cool, *Eating and Drinking in Roman Britain* (Cambridge: Cambridge University Press, 2006), 120.

16. According to Pliny the Elder, cherry trees were introduced into Italy only in 74 BCE (Pliny the Elder, *Naturalis Historiae*, ed. and trans. H. Rackham [Cambridge, Mass.: Harvard University Press, 1938], 15.102).

17. For the avoidance of native food plants in the Iron Age, see van der Veen, "Food as Embodied Material Culture," 99–101. For the possibility that there were taboos against eating wild animals (and perhaps, by extension, wild plants) in the Iron Age, see N. Sykes, *Beastly Questions: Animal Answers to Archaeological Issues* (London: Bloomsbury, 2015), 64–68.

18. On the selective appropriation and indigenization of foreign food in colonial contexts, see M. Dietler, "Culinary Encounters: Food, Identity, and Colonialism," in K. Twiss, ed., *The Archaeology of Food and Identity* (Carbondale, Ill.: Center for Archaeological Investigations, Southern Illinois University Carbondale, 2007), 218–42, at 223–27.

19. C. Dickson, "Macroscopic Fossils of Garden Plants from British Roman and Medieval Deposits," in D. Moe, J. H. Dickson, and P. M. Jørgensen, eds., *Garden History: Garden Plants, Species, Forms and Varieties from Pompeii to 1800, Symposium Held at the European University Centre for Cultural Heritage, Ravello, June, 1991* (Rixensart: Council of Europe, Division of Scientific Cooperation, 1994), 47–72, at 54; A. Livarda, "Introduction and Dispersal of Exotic Food Plants into Europe During the Roman and Medieval Periods," 2 vols. (Ph.D. diss., University of Leicester, 2008), 125. For a find of cabbage stalks at the Vindolanda fort, see A. R. Hall and J. P. Huntley, "A Review of the Evidence for Macrofossil Plant Remains from Archaeological Deposits in Northern England" (unpublished report, English Heritage, Research Department Report Series 87/2007, 2007), 67.

20. A. Livarda and M. van der Veen, "Social Access and Dispersal of Condiments in North-West Europe from the Roman to the Medieval Period," *Vegetation History and Archaeobotany*, 17 (2008), 201–9, at 206; van der Veen et al., "New Plant Foods," table 5; van der Veen, "Food as Embodied Material Culture," table 2. According to Columella, lettuce was not just grown for the kitchen but was also cultivated alongside potted herbs in *leporaria*, to feed the hares and rabbits raised within them (Columella, *Res Rustica, Books 4–9*, 2 vols., trans. E. S. Forster and E. H. Heffner [Cambridge, Mass.: Harvard University Press, 1954], 9:1).

21. D. Bird, "Croydon, Crocus, and Collyrium," *London Archaeologist*, 13 (2012), 87–90.

22. Van der Veen et al., "New Plant Foods," 18, 21, and fig. 8; van der Veen, "Food as Embodied Material Culture," 91, 97–98; M. Robinson, "The Place of Silchester in Archaeobotany," in M. Fulford, ed., *Silchester and the Study of Romano-British Urbanism [Papers Presented at a One-Day Meeting at the Society of Antiquaries of London in November 2009]* (Portsmouth, R.I.: Journal of Roman Archaeology, 2012), 213–26, at 218; Booth et al., *Thames Through Time*, 292; Dickson, "Macroscopic Fossils," table 1. For the ways the exotic can rapidly indigenize, see D. Miller, "Coca-Cola: A Black Sweet Drink from Trinidad," in D. Miller, ed., *Material Cultures: Why Some Things Matter* (Chicago: University of Chicago Press, 1998), 169–87. For the mechanisms allowing for the spread of exotic foodstuffs from military introductions to widespread use through commercial markets and road networks, see Orengo and Livarda, "Seeds of Commerce."

23. M. van der Veen, "Arable Farming, Horticulture, and Food: Expansion, Innovation, and Diversity in Roman Britain," in M. Millett, L. Revell, and A. Moore, eds., *The Oxford Handbook*

of Roman Britain (Oxford: Oxford University Press, 2016), 807–33, at 819; R. Witcher, "On Rome's Ecological Contribution to British Flora and Fauna: Landscape, Legacy, and Identity," *Landscape History*, 34 (2013), 5–26, at 10.

24. M. Germany, *Excavations at Great Holts Farm, Boreham, Essex 1992–94*, East Anglian Archaeology 105 (Chelmsford: Heritage Conservation, Essex County Council, 2003), 55–56, 203, 211.

25. Germany, *Excavations at Great Holts Farm*, 211, 223.

26. P. Murphy et al., "Production, Imports, and Status: Biological Remains from a Late Roman Farm at Great Holts Farm, Boreham, Essex, UK," *Environmental Archaeology*, 5 (2000), 35–48, at 41–45; Germany, *Excavations at Great Holts Farm*, 200, 223.

27. V. Score, J. Browning, E. Johnson, A. Monckton, and R. Kipling, "A Roman Delicatessen at Castle St, Leicester," *Transactions of the Leicestershire Archaeological and Historical Society*, 84 (2010), 77–94; N. J. Cooper, E. Johnson, and M. J. Sterry, "Eating In and Dining Out in Roman Leicester: Exploring Pottery Consumption Patterns Across the Town and Its Suburbs," *Internet Archaeology*, 50 (2018), https://doi.org/10.11141/ia.50.10.

28. They were also in possession of some of the garden tools introduced after the Roman conquest, including a small hand rake (R. J. Williams, P. J. Hart, and A. T. L. Williams, *Wavendon Gate: A Late Iron Age and Roman Settlement in Milton Keynes* [Aylesbury: Buckinghamshire Archaeological Society, 1995], 87).

29. The term "flavourscape" has been coined by A. Livarda and H. A. Orengo, "Reconstructing the Roman London Flavourscape: New Insights into the Exotic Food Plant Trade Using Network and Spatial Analyses," *Journal of Archaeological Science*, 55 (2015), 244–52.

30. M. G. Allen et al., *The Rural Economy of Roman Britain* (London: Society for the Promotion of Roman Studies, 2017), 82.

31. Here, I use zones defined by S. Rippon, C. Smart, and B. Pears, *The Fields of Britannia: Continuity and Change in the Late Roman and Early Medieval Landscape* (Oxford: Oxford University Press, 2015), 47–56, and fig 2.11.

32. Van der Veen, "Arable Farming"; G. Lambrick "The Development of Late Prehistoric and Roman Farming on the Thames Gravels," in M. Fulford and E. Nichols, eds., *Developing Landscapes of Lowland Britain* (London: Society of Antiquaries of London, 1992), 78–105, at 84–85.

33. M. van der Veen and T. O'Connor, "The Expansion of Agricultural Production in the Late Iron Age and the Roman Period," in J. Bayley, ed., *Science in Archaeology: An Agenda for the Future* (London: English Heritage, 1998), 127–43, at 134–35; A. Douglas, J. Gerrard, and B. Sudds, *Roman Settlement and Bath House at Shadwell: Excavations at Tobacco Dock and Babe Ruth Restaurant, the Highway, London* (London: Pre-Construct Archaeology, 2011), 148; M. van der Veen, "Charred Grain Assemblages from Roman-Period Corn Driers in Britain," *Archaeological Journal*, 146 (1989), 302–19, at 315; J. Taylor, "The Idea of the Villa: Reassessing Villa Development in South-East Britain," in N. Roymans and T. Derks, eds., *Villa Landscapes in the Roman North: Economy, Culture and Lifestyles* (Amsterdam: Amsterdam University Press, 2011), 179–94, at 186–88.

34. C. Martins, *Becoming Consumers: Looking Beyond Wealth as an Explanation of Villa Variability*, BAR British Series 403 (Oxford: Archaeopress, 2005), 24; Taylor, "Idea of the Villa," 186–89; M. Given, *The Archaeology of the Colonized* (London: Routledge, 2004), 30–37.

35. Although wheat production did increase significantly (Rippon et al., *Fields of Britannia*, 81–83, and table 3.6).

36. D. Smith and H. Kenward, "Roman Grain Pests in Britain: Implications for Grain Supply and Agricultural Production," *Britannia*, 42 (2011), 243–62, at 247; G. A. King, "Establishing a Foothold or Six: Insect Tales of Trade and Migration," in P. R. Preston and K. Schörle, eds.,

Mobility, Transition and Change in Prehistory and Classical Antiquity: Proceedings of the Graduate Archaeology Organisation Conference on the Fourth and Fifth of April 2008 at Hertford College, Oxford, UK, BAR International Series 2534 (Oxford: Archaeopress, 2013), 120–30.

37. Smith and Kenward, "Roman Grain Pests," 244; G. A. King et al., "Six-Legged Hitchhikers: An Archaeobiologeographical Account of the Early Dispersal of Grain Beetles," *Journal of the North Atlantic*, 23 (2014), 1–18, at 6–7. Granary weevils have also been found in Roman grain storage facilities along the Rhine and in the eastern desert of Egypt (E. Panagiotakopulus and M. van der Veen, "Synanthropic Insect Faunas from Mons Claudianus, a Roman Quarry Site in the Eastern Desert, Egypt," in A. C. Ashworth et al., eds., *Studies in Quaternary Entomology: An Inordinate Fondness for Insects [a Collection of Papers in Honour of Professor Russell Coope]* [Chichester: John Wiley and Sons, 1997], 199–205, at 201).

38. Smith and Kenward, "Roman Grain Pests," 248–49; D. Smith and H. Kenward, "'Well, Sextus, What Can We Do with This?': The Disposal and Use of Insect-Infested Grain in Roman Britain," *Environmental Archaeology*, 17 (2012), 141–50.

39. King, "Establishing a Foothold," 121.

40. King, "Establishing a Foothold," 120–22. For animals' ability to use human-built environments to their own advantage, see T. O'Connor, "Humans and Animals: Refuting Aquinas," *Archaeological Review from Cambridge*, 28 (2013), 186–94.

41. Smith and Kenward, "Roman Grain Pests," 247, 252. The evidence for the new pests is almost always recovered from infested bulk grain stores (Smith and Kenward, "Well, Sextus," 141). For more on the kinds of buildings in Britain in which grain might have been stored, see above, Chapter 1.

42. P. Armitage et al., "New Evidence of Black Rat in Roman London," *London Archaeologist*, 4 (1984), 375–83; K. Dobney and J. Harwood, "Here to Stay? Archaeological Evidence for the Introduction of Commensal and Economically Important Mammals to the North of England," in N. Benecke, ed., *The Holocene History of the European Vertebrate Fauna: Modern Aspects of Research: Workshop, 6th to 9th April 1998, Berlin* (Rahden: Marie Leidorf, 1999), 373–87, at 375–76; S. Wrathmell and A. Nicholson, *Dalton Parlours: Iron Age Settlement and Roman Villa* (Wakefield: West Yorkshire Archaeological Services, 1990), 256.

43. C. Johnstone, "Commodities or Logistic? The Role of Equids in Roman Supply Networks," in S. Stallibrass and R. Thomas, eds., *Feeding the Roman Army: The Archaeology of Production and Supply in NW Europe* (Oxford: Oxbow Books, 2008), 128–45, at 128–29, 141. There are, however, very few archaeological remains of mules recorded in Britain, in spite of the fact that we know the Roman state heavily depended on these animals. It may be that indigenous ponies made better pack animals in Britain's wet climate than donkeys or mules, or that the people of Britain preferred working with oxen or horses (C. Johnstone, "Donkeys and Mules," in T. O'Connor and N. Sykes, eds., *Extinctions and Invasions: A Social History of British Fauna* [Oxford: Windgather, 2010], 17–25; J. Huntley, "'The World Is a Bundle of Hay': Investigating Land Management for Animal Fodder Around Vindolanda, Based on Plant Remains," in R. Collins and M. Symonds, eds., *Breaking Down Boundaries: Hadrian's Wall in the 21st Century* [Portsmouth, R.I.: Journal of Roman Archaeology, 2013], 33–51). For the most recent list of archaeological evidence for mules and donkeys in Britain, see Allen et al., *Rural Economy of Roman Britain*, table 3.1.

44. Huntley, "World Is a Bundle of Hay," 45.

45. M. MacKinnon, "'Tails' of Romanization: Animals and Inequality in the Roman Mediterranean Context," in B. S. Arbuckle and S. A. McCarty, eds., *Animals and Inequality in the Ancient World* (Boulder, Colo.: University of Colorado Press, 2015), 315–34, at 329–30.

46. U. Albarella, "The End of the Sheep Age: People and Animals in the Late Iron Age," in C. Haselgrove, and T. Moore, eds., *The Late Iron Age in Britain and Beyond* (Oxford: Oxbow Books, 2007), 393–406; U. Albarella et al., "The Development of Animal Husbandry from the Late Iron Age to the End of the Roman Period: A Case Study from South-East Britain," *Journal of Archaeological Science*, 35 (2008), 1828–48; C. Minniti et al., "Widening the Market: Strontium Isotope Analysis on Cattle Teeth from Owslebury (Hampshire, UK) Highlights Changes in Livestock Supply Between the Iron Age and the Roman Period," *Journal of Archaeological Science*, 42 (2014), 305–14.

47. D. W. Yalden, *The History of British Birds* (Oxford: Oxford University Press, 2009), 106–7.

48. K. Poole, "Bird Introductions," in O'Connor and Sykes, *Extinctions and Invasions*, 156–65, at 159–61.

49. Yalden, *History of British Birds*, 106.

50. H. E. M. Cool and J. E. Richardson, "Exploring Ritual Deposits in a Well at Rothwell, Haight, Leeds," *Britannia*, 44 (2013), 191–217, at 210.

51. J. Alexander and J. Pullinger, *Roman Cambridge: Excavations on Castle Hill 1956–1988*, Proceedings of the Cambridge Antiquarian Society 88 (Cambridge: Cambridge Antiquarian Society, 2000), 53–56; Cool and Richardson, "Exploring Ritual Deposits," 210.

52. Varro, *De re rustica*, in W. D. Hooper and H. B. Ash, eds., *Cato and Varro on Agriculture* (Cambridge, Mass.: Harvard University Press, 1934), 1:17, 3:3–11.

53. M. G. Allen and N. Sykes, "New Animals, New Landscapes, and New Worldviews: The Iron Age to Roman Transition at Fishbourne," *Sussex Archaeological Collections*, 149 (2011), 7–24, at 19; N. Sykes and J. Curl, "The Rabbit," in O'Connor and Sykes, *Extinctions and Invasions*, 116–26, at 119–20.

54. R. Madgwick et al., "Fallow Deer (*Dama dama dama*) Management in Roman South-East Britain," *Archaeological and Anthropological Sciences*, 5 (2013), 111–22. Although there is clear evidence that live fallow deer were imported into Britain during the Roman period, there may have also been a trade in fallow deer body parts, in particular antlers, which suggests that the size of live deer populations during the period may have been smaller than previously argued (H. Miller et al., "Dead or Alive? Investigating Long-Distance Transport of Live Fallow Deer and Their Body Parts in Antiquity," *Environmental Archaeology* [2014], 246–59).

55. Cool, *Eating and Drinking in Roman Britain*, 122–23; L. Lodwick, "Identifying Ritual Deposition of Plant Remains: A Case Study of Stone Pine Cones in Roman Britain," *TRAC 2014* (2015), 54–69; C. Palmer and M. van der Veen, "Archaeobotany and the Social Context of Food," *Acta Palaeobotanica*, 42 (2002), 195–202, at 197–98; Livarda, "New Temptations?" 73–74; Dickson, "Macroscopic Fossils," 49; L. A. Lodwick, "Evergreen Plants in Roman Britain and Beyond: Movement, Meaning, and Materiality," *Britannia*, 48 (2017), 135–73.

56. Lodwick, "Evergreen Plants in Roman Britain."

57. S. Applebaum, "Agriculture in Roman Britain," *Agricultural History Review*, 6 (1958), 66–86, at 71; L. Allason-Jones, *Daily Life in Roman Britain* (Oxford: Greenwood, 2008), 109.

58. S. Roskams, "The Urban Poor: Finding the Marginalised," in W. Bowden, A. Gutteridge, and C. Machado, eds., *Social and Political Life in Late Antiquity* (Leiden: Brill, 2006), 487–531, at 526.

59. F. Pigière and D. Henrotay, "Camels in the Northern Provinces of the Roman Empire," *Journal of Archaeological Science*, 39 (2012), 1531–39; R. Hingley, *Londinium: A Biography; Roman London from Its Origins to the Fifth Century* (London: Bloomsbury, 2018), 214.

60. Snails, according to Varro, needed careful attention, because of their proclivity to run away (Varro, *De re rustica*, 3.14). For their presences in Roman Britain, see P. Davies, "Land and

Freshwater Mollusks," in O'Connor and Sykes, eds., *Extinctions and Invasions*, 175–80, at 178. Dormice were likely very rare in Britain. Remains of single individuals have been found at the fort at South Shields and in York, so they may have been limited to military sites (T. P. O'Connor, *Bones from the General Accident Site, Tanner Row*, Archaeology of York, 15/2: *The Animal Bones* [London: Council for British Archaeology, 1988]; D. A. Younger, "The Small Mammals from the Forecourt Granary and the Southwest Fort Ditch," in P. Bidwell and S. Speak, eds., *Excavations at South Shields Roman Fort*, vol. 1 [Newcastle: Society of Antiquaries of Newcastle-upon-Tyne, 1994], 266–68). The one found in York was likely a garden dormouse, a species that may have been used as a substitute for the edible dormouse (*Glis glis*) beloved by Roman cooks (K. Dobney and J. Harwood, "Here to Stay?" 374).

61. Caesar, *The Gallic War*, ed. and trans. H. J. Edwards (Cambridge, Mass.: Harvard University Press, 1917), 5:12. A few, though, have been found in a pre-Roman high-status graves and ritual deposits.

62. M. G. Allen, "Animalscapes and Empire: New Perspectives on the Iron Age/Romano-British Transition" (Ph.D. diss., University of Nottingham, 2011), 342–44. For evidence of the scale of the use of chicken eggs in London, see Hill and Rowsome, *Roman London and the Walbrook Stream Crossing*, 401. For the abundant evidence of chickens in urban communities, see M. Maltby, "Domestic Fowl on Romano-British Sites: Inter-Site Comparisons of Abundance," *International Journal of Osteoarchaeology*, 7 (1997), 402–14.

63. M. Maltby et al., "Counting Roman Chickens: Multidisciplinary Approaches to Human-Chicken Interactions in Roman Britain," *Journal of Archaeological Science: Reports*, 19 (2018), 1003–15.

64. *Vindolanda Tablets Online*, no. 302, http://vindolanda.csad.ox.ac.uk/.

65. M. Parker Pearson, "Eating Money: A Study in the Ethnoarchaeology of Food," *Archaeological Dialogues*, 7 (2000), 217–32, at 222; R. W. Redding, "The Pig and the Chicken in the Middle East: Modeling Human Subsistence Behavior in the Archaeological Record Using Historical and Animal Husbandry Data," *Journal of Archaeological Research*, 23 (2015), 325–68, at 326 and 335–37. For evidence from a slightly later period that chickens were commensal with their humans (and, thus, shared the same food), see Sykes, *Beastly Questions*, 134–35.

66. S. Doherty, "New Perspectives on Urban Cockfighting in Roman Britain," *Archaeological Review from Cambridge*, 28 (2013), 82–95.

67. For the connection with Mithras, see A. Lentacker, A. Ervynck, and W. Van Neer, "Gastronomy or Religion? The Animal Remains from the *Mithreaeum* at Tienen (Belgium)," in S. J. O'Day et al., eds., *Behaviour Behind Bones: The Zooarchaeology of Ritual, Religion, Status, and Identity; Proceedings of the 9th Conference of the International Council of Archaeozoology, Durham, August 2002* (Oxford: Oxbow Books, 2004), 77–94; A. Lentacker et al., "The Symbolic Meaning of the Cock: The Animal Remains from the *Mithraeum* at Tienen (Belgium)," in M. Martens and G. De Boe, eds., *Roman Mithraism: The Evidence of the Small Finds [Papers of the International Conference, Tienen 7–8 November 2001]* (Brussels: Museum Het Toreke, 2004), 57–80; and M. P. Feider, "Chickens in the Archaeological Material Culture of Roman Britain, France, and Belgium" (Ph.D. diss., Bournemouth University, 2017), 320–41, 344–48. For their association with Mercury, see N. Crummy, "Brooches and the Cult of Mercury," *Britannia*, 38 (2007), 225–30.

68. R. Philpott, *Burial Practices in Roman Britain: A Survey of Grave Treatment and Furnishings AD 43–410*, BAR British Series 219 (Oxford: Tempus Reparatum, 1992), 202; N. C. C. White, "Catering for the Cultural Identities of the Deceased in Roman Britain: Interpretive Potential and Problems," *TRAC 2006* (2007), 115–32, at 122–23.

69. D. Brothwell, "Interpreting the Immature Chicken Bones from the Romano-British Ritual Complex on West Hill, Uley," *International Journal of Osteoarchaeology*, 7 (1997), 330–32; A. King, "Animal Remains from Temples in Roman Britain," *Britannia*, 36 (2005), 329–69, at 334; Lentacker et al., "Gastronomy or Religion?" 77–98.

70. In spite of the fact that hares had been present in Britain since the Bronze Age, they are more visible after the Roman conquest. People did not eat them, however, until just before the Roman conquest, and then only occasionally in elite households, which were aligning some of their culinary practices with Roman ways (N. Crummy, "Attitudes to the Hare in Town and Country," in H. Eckhardt and S. Rippon, eds., *Living and Working in the Roman World: Essays in Honour of Michael Fulford on His 65th Birthday* [Portsmouth, R.I.: Journal of Roman Archaeology, 2013], 111–27, at 116–17). At Iron Age sites, whole, articulated hares, like domestic fowl, have also been recovered from ritual deposits. In the Roman period, on the other hand, their bones are regularly found in dumps of food waste (Sykes, *Beastly Questions*, 84–85). Indeed, a number of native species—crane and other wildfowl, red and roe deer—were sometimes eaten on elite sites, which suggests that British elites were gradually adopting Roman attitudes toward the hunt (Allen and Sykes, "New Animals," 7–24).

71. Columella, *Res Rustica*, book 4.

72. Crummy, "Attitudes to the Hare," 113.

73. Crummy, "Attitudes to the Hare," 118–19.

74. Although the methods used in the field to recover faunal material impact the number of species found, so comparing sites that underwent different methods of collection means that the quality of data being compared can be quite different (A. K. Trusler, "The Impact of Recovery Methods on Taxonomic Richness in Roman Faunal Assemblages," *Archaeometry*, 56 [2014], 1075–85).

75. Rippon et al., *Fields of Britannia*, 57–85.

76. Smith and Kenward, "Roman Grain Pests," 249–51; King, "Establishing a Foothold," 122–24.

77. Some argue that although rat populations declined significantly, they did not disappear altogether (Smith and Kenward, "Roman Grain Pests," 253; K. Dobney and J. Harwood, "Here to Stay?" 375–78). But a recent reassessment of rats in early medieval England suggests that they did. This judgement is in part based on the fact that there is no evidence for them in the well-sieved, eighth-century site at Fishergate, or on the early medieval rural sites at West Heslerton and Flixborough. Evidence for rats reappears only in the mid-ninth or early tenth century, when they can be found in England's fast-growing towns, and on the well-connected, high-status sites such as Flixborough (K. Dobney et al., "Evidence for Trade and Contact," in K. Dobney and C. Loveluck, eds., *Farmers, Monks, and Aristocrats: The Environmental Archaeology of Anglo-Saxon Flixborough* [Oxford: Oxbow Books, 2007], 213–16, at 215–16). For more on rats, see M. McCormick, "Rats, Communications, and Plague: Towards an Ecological History," *Journal of Interdisciplinary History*, 34 (2003), 1–25, at 14–16; D. Yalden, *The History of British Mammals* (London: Poyser, 1999), 139.

78. Only eight sites dating between the fifth and seventh centuries have produced either waterlogged or mineralized plant evidence (van der Veen et al., "Archaeobotany of Medieval Britain," table 3).

79. It was found in cess, so even if this represents cabbage rather than mustard, its seeds were likely used in food (Booth et al., *Thames Through Time*, 319); G. Campbell, "Assessment of Charred and Mineral-Replaced Macroscopic Plant Remains from Excavation at Lyminge, Kent, 2008–10" (unpublished report, University of Reading, 2012), http://www.reading.ac.uk/web/files

/archaeology/Campbell2012-palaeobotanical_assessment.pdf; P. Chapman et al., "Anglo-Saxon and Medieval Settlement at the Former Post Office Training Establishment, Wolverton Mill, Milton Keynes," *Records of Bucks*, 55 (2015), 75–115, at 94.

80. W. Carruthers, "The Plant Remains," 64–75, in P. J. Fasham et al., *Archaeology and the M3: The Watching Brief, the Anglo-Saxon Settlement at Abbots Worthy and Retrospective Sections* (Winchester: Hampshire Field Club, 1991), table 19; W. Carruthers, "An Environmental Overview," in the "Stansted Framework Project" (unpublished report, Wessex Archaeology, 2009), https://doi.org/10.5284/1000029.

81. W. Carruthers, "Charred, Mineralized, and Waterlogged Plant Remains," in "Stansted Framework Project."

82. Royal Horticulture Society, "*Papaver somniferum*: Opium Poppy," https://www.rhs.org.uk/Plants/58799/i-Papaver-somniferum-i/Details.

83. W. Carruthers, "The Charred, Mineralised and Waterlogged Plant Remains," in A. Mudd et al., *Iron Age and Middle Saxon Settlements at West Fen Road, Ely, Cambridgeshire: The Consortium Site*, BAR British Series 538 (Oxford: Archaeopress, 2011), 114–16, at 110–16.

84. W. Carruthers, "Mineralised Plant Remains," in V. Birbeck et al., *The Origins of Mid-Saxon Southampton: Excavations at the Friends Provident St Mary's Stadium 1998–2000* (Salisbury: Wessex Archaeology, 2005), 157–73, table 39, although one waterlogged early mid-Saxon pit did have coriander (Carruthers, "Mineralised Plant Remains," 161).

85. R. Cowie et al., *Lundenwic: Excavations in Middle Saxon London, 1987–2000* (London: MoLAS, 2012), CD-ROM, table 8; K. Dobney, A. Hall, and H. Kenward, "The Bioarchaeology of Anglo-Saxon Yorkshire: Present and Future Perspectives," in H. Geake and J. Kenny, eds., *Early Deira: Archaeological Studies of the East Riding in the Fourth to Ninth Centuries AD* (Oxford: Oxbow Books, 2000), 133–40, at 134; Hall and Huntley, "Review of the Evidence for Macrofossil Plant," 98.

86. One of the very latest Roman-period deposits in a well at Silchester, which included coins of the House of Theodosius (388–92), contained evidence for coriander, figs, and walnuts, which suggest that these things were being eaten almost to the bitter end in that town (A. Clarke and M. Fulford, "The Excavation of Insula IX, Silchester: The First Five Years of the 'Town Life' Project, 1997–2001," *Britannia*, 33 [2002], 129–66, at 156).

87. Carruthers, "Mineralised Plant Remains," 162; W. Carruthers, "Charred and Mineralised Plant Remains," in B. M. Ford et al., *Winchester: A City in the Making; Archaeological Excavations Between 2002–2007 on the Sites of Northgate House, Staple Gardens and the Former Winchester Library, Jewry Street* (Oxford: Oxford Archaeology, 2011), 370; Carruthers, "Plant Remains," 73–75.

88. Dickson, "Macroscopic Fossils," 54; Moffett, "Food Plants on Archaeological Sites," 355.

89. There is no sign in Britain, in these centuries, of coriander, fennel, parsley, dill, summer savory, pot marigold, and marjoram, although they survived Rome's fall elsewhere in northwestern Europe (Livarda and van der Veen, "Social Access," 203, 206, 208; A. Livarda, "Spicing up Life in Northwestern Europe: Exotic Food Plant Imports in the Roman and Medieval World," *Vegetation History and Archaeobotany*, 20 [2011], 143–64, at 156–59).

90. Carruthers, "Mineralised Plant Remains," 161–62; K. L. Hunter, "Charred Plant Remains," in Birbeck et al., *Origins of Mid-Saxon Southampton*, 163–73, at 171 and table 38; R. Pelling, "The Deanery, Southampton (62123): The Mineralised and Charred Plant Remains," 4–6 (unpublished report, Wessex Archaeology, 2011), http://archaeologydataservice.ac.uk/archiveDS/archiveDownload?t=arch-1023-1/dissemination/pdf/Environmental/SOU1386_62123_Plant_Remains.pdf; R. Cowie et al., *Lundenwic*, 141, 301, and CD tables 3, 4, 8, and 9; P. Murphy, "Ip-

swich, Suffolk: Part 1. Plant Macrofossils from Middle Saxon and Earlier Contexts at Sites IAS 4201, 4601, 4801, and 5701," Ancient Monuments Laboratory Report 225/87 (unpublished report, English Heritage, 1984), http://services.english-heritage.org.uk/ResearchReportsPdfs/4563.pdf; Dobney, et al., "Bioarchaeology of Anglo-Saxon Yorkshire," 134; H. K. Kenward and A. R. Hall, *Biological Evidence from Anglo-Scandinavian Deposits at 16–22 Coppergate 14/7: The Past Environment of York* (York: Council for British Archaeology, 1995), 757.

91. Campbell, "Assessment," 9; Carruthers, "Charred, Mineralized," 18–19; Carruthers, "Environmental Overview," 29.13.

92. Old Irish texts also suggest that foraged food was an important component of the Irish diet in this period (F. Kelly, *Early Irish Farming: A Study Based Mainly on the Law-Texts of the 7th and 8th Centuries AD* [Dublin: School of Celtic Studies, Dublin Institute for Advanced Studies, 1997], 306–15).

93. Cowie et al., *Lundenwic*, 141.

94. From a couple of extant shopping lists that survive among the Vindolanda tablets, and we know that all kinds of people, even slaves, were buying fruits and vegetables in local food markets as early as the first century CE (*Vindolanda Tablets*, nos. 301–2). The Latin poem *Moretum* describes a very poor farmer, who lavished attention on his little garden, growing herbs and vegetables for the market (H. R. Fairclough, trans., *Aeneid, 7–12: Appendix Vergiliana* [Cambridge, Mass.: Harvard University Press, 2001], 518–22).

95. D. Miller, *Stuff* (Cambridge: Polity, 2010), 94.

96. Van der Veen, "Materiality of Plants," 799–812. For nonhuman agency, see B. Latour, *Reassembling the Social: An Introduction to Actor-Network-Theory* (Oxford: Oxford University Press, 2005); C. Gosden, "What Do Objects Want?" *Journal of Archaeological Method and Theory*, 12 (2005), 193–211.

97. M. Maltby, "Chop and Change: Specialist Cattle Carcass Processing in Roman Britain," *TRAC 2006* (2007), 59–79, at 71; U. Albarella, "End of the Sheep Age"; Albarella et al., "Development of Animal Husbandry"; P. J. Crabtree, "Zooarchaeology and Colonialism in Roman Britain: Evidence from Icklingham," in D. V. Campana et al., eds., *Anthropological Approaches to Zooarchaeology: Colonialism, Complexity, and Animal Transformations* (Oxford: Oxbow Books, 2010), 190–94; R. Hesse "Reconsidering Animal Husbandry and Diet in the Northwest Provinces," *Journal of Roman Archaeology*, 24 (2011), 215–48, at 240; M. Rizzetto et al., "Livestock Changes in the Beginning and End of the Roman Period in Britain: Issues of Acculturation, Adaptation, and 'Improvement,'" *European Journal of Archaeology*, 20 (2017), 535–56. Maltby has data supporting the idea that some portion of the elderly animals being slaughtered were dairy cows past their prime (M. Maltby, *Feeding a Roman Town: Environmental Evidence from Excavations in Winchester, 1972–1985* (Winchester: Winchester Museums, 2010), 146–52. S. Roskams, "Food for Thought: The Potential and Problems of Faunal Evidence for Interpreting Late Antique Society," in L. Lavan and M. Mulryan, eds., *Field Methods and Post-Excavation Techniques in Late Antique Archaeology* (Leiden: Brill, 2015), 513–52, at 530–31.

98. A. Gardner, "Seeking the Material Turn: the Artefactuality of the Roman Empire," *TRAC* (2003), 1–13, at 6.

99. M. Van der Veen, "Arable Farming." For the history of horticulture in antiquity, see L. Cilliers and F. P. Retief, "Horticulture in Antiquity, with Emphasis on the Greco-Roman Era," *Akroterion*, 54 (2009), 1–10. Gardens are difficult to identify in the archaeology. One of the clearest Roman-period examples was excavated in France, at the Le Bois Harlé (Oise, France) site, a large ditched space subdivided with shallow ditches to create small plots. A similar arrangement has been found at Rijswijk, De Bult, in the Netherlands. Both were probably sites where horticul-

ture was practiced. Evidence from the former suggests that cucumbers, bottle gourds, coriander, poppy, and beet were being grown (A. de Hingh, "Bottle Gourd Seeds at Gallo-Roman "Le Bois Harlé" (Oise, France), *Analecta Praehistorica Leidensia*, 26 [1993], 93–97). A number of Roman-period gardens have also tentatively been identified in Britain. The best-known example is the formal garden at Fishbourne, but other gardens have been found. Bedding trenches, some quite extensive, have been uncovered at Frocester Court, Gloucester, and Latimer, Buckinghamshire, and courtyards with pools that likely served as formal garden features have been excavated at Bancroft, Buckinghamshire, and at a first-century, high-status site at Cannon Street, in London (R. J. Zeepvat, "Roman Gardens in Britain," in A. E. Brown, ed., *Garden Archaeology: Papers Presented to a Conference at Knuston Hall, Norhamptonshire, April 1988* [London: Council for British Archaeology, 1991], 53–59). Some of the townhouses in Silchester also had gardens and orchards at their backs (Allason-Jones, *Daily Life in Roman Britain*, 59). Aerial photographs of the villa at Ditchley, Oxfordshire, reveal a four-acre, hedged enclosure that has been interpreted as an orchard (C. A. R. Radford, "The Roman Villa at Ditchley, Oxon," *Oxoniensia*, 1 [1936], 24–69, at 24–25 and plates 3–4). This is the same size as a well-documented thirteenth-century English bishop's garden that supported 129 fruit trees, flax, and vegetables (C. C. Dyer, "Gardens and Garden Produce in the Later Middle Ages," in C. M. Woolgar et al., eds., *Food in Medieval England: Diet and Nutrition* [Oxford: Oxford University Press, 2006], 27–40, at 28). Excavations at Frocester villa, in Gloucester and Bancroft villa, in Buckinghamshire, have uncovered orchards, as well as kitchen and formal gardens (T. W. Potter and C. Johns, *Roman Britain: Exploring the Roman World* [Berkeley, Calif.: University of California Press, 1992], 202). Fifteen parallel horticultural bedding trenches forty-eight meters long and eight meters across have been uncovered at Eye Quarry, in Cambridgeshire (Allen et al., *Rural Economy of Roman Britain*, 73). An area under grape cultivation has been excavated in Northamptonshire (A. G. Brown and I. Meadows, "Roman Vineyards in Britain: Finds from the Nene Valley and New Research," *Antiquity*, 74 [2000], 491–92; A. G. Brown et al., "Roman Vineyards in Britain: Stratigraphic and Palynological Data from Wollaston in the Nene Valley, England," *Antiquity*, 75 [2001], 745–57). A possible complex of late Roman garden plots may have been uncovered in Bishop's Cleeve (A. J. Barber and G. T. Walker, "Home Farm, Bishop's Cleeve: Excavation of a Romano-British Occupation Site 1993–4," *Transactions of the Bristol and Gloucestershire Archaeological Society*, 116 [1998], 117–39, at 123). There is also evidence for soil mounded in rows at what may have been a market garden outside the walls of the town of Colchester (P. Crummy and H. Brooks, *Excavations at Lion Walk, Balkerne Lane, and Middleborough, Colchester, Essex* [Colchester: Colchester Archaeological Trust, 1984], 138–41 and fig. 129). Finally, special-purpose plant propagation pots were being manufactured in Kent, and they may have been traded for the saplings they contained (E. M. Lewis, "The Role of *ollae perforatae* in Understanding Horticulture, Planting Techniques, Garden Design, and Plant Trade in the Roman World," in J. Morel et al., eds., *The Archaeology of Crop Fields and Gardens Archaeology, University of Barcelona, Barcelona, Spain, 1–3 June 2006* [Bari: Edipuglia, 2006], 207–19, at 217).

100. For some of the complexities that arise from gardens' cultivation of multiple species and Roman understandings of these complexities, see J. Henderson, "Columella's Living Hedge: The Roman Gardening Book," *Journal of Roman Studies*, 92 (2002), 110–33.

101. Applebaum, "Agriculture in Roman Britain," 73.

102. S. Willis, "Roman Towns, Roman Landscapes: The Cultural Terrain of Town and Country in the Roman Period," in A. Fleming and R. Hingley, eds., *Prehistoric and Roman Landscapes: Landscape History After Hoskins* (Macclesfield, Cheshire: Windather, 2007), 142–64, at 150.

103. For the importance of women in peasant household economies, especially in horticulture, see A. V. Chayanov, *On the Theory of Peasant Economy*, trans. and ed. D. Thorner et al. (Madison:

University of Wisconsin Press, 1986); E. Boserup, *Women's Role in Economic Development* (London: Allen and Unwin, 1970); R. McC. Netting, *Smallholders, Householders: Farm Families and the Economy of Intensive, Sustainable Agriculture* (Stanford, Calif.: Stanford University Press, 1993).

104. Van der Veen, "Materiality of Plants," 805; Sykes, *Beastly Questions*, 37–40, 43–46.

105. Horticulture, moreover, is very manure dependent, so there may have been a synergy between increasing numbers of cattle, the manure they produced, and the ability to extend horticulture (C. van Driel-Murray, "Those Who Wait at Home: The Effect of Recruitment on Women in the Lower Rhine Area," in U. Brandl, ed., *Frauen und Römisches Militär: Beiträge eines Runden Tisches in Xanten Vom 7. Bis 9. Juli 2005*, BAR International Series 1759 [Oxford: Archaeopress, 2008], 82–91, at 88).

106. For the impact of the awareness of new customs and the necessity of adopting or adapting them because of the demands of empire, see L. Revell, *Roman Imperialism and Local Identities* (Cambridge: Cambridge University Press, 2009). For trade as something that structures colonial relations for the colonized in significant ways, see M. Dietler, *Archaeologies of Colonialism: Consumption, Entanglement, and Violence in Ancient Mediterranean France* (Berkley: University of California Press, 2010), 131–56. For the way colonization can change the kinds of crops grown and the way those crops are processed, and for changes in food preparation and gendered work, see W. Jansen, "French Bread and Algerian Wine: Conflicting Identities in French Algeria," in P. Scholliers, ed., *Food, Drink, and Identity: Cooking, Eating and Drinking in Europe Since the Middle Ages* (Oxford: Berg, 2001), 195–218.

107. D. Miller, *Stuff*, 84. Or, as John Robb has observed about the idea of agency, "the question of who is actually acting—in a social sense, not merely in the purely physical sense—is surprisingly ambiguous. . . . It is really a collectivity which is acting through the individual hand" (J. Robb, "Beyond Agency," *World Archaeology*, 42 [2010], 493–520, at 503).

108. Rippon et al., *Fields of Britannia*, 74–85.

109. Carruthers, "Charred, Mineralized," 18–19, 23; Carruthers, "Mineralised Plant Remains," 161–62; C. Ellis and P. Andrews, "A Mid-Saxon Site at Anderson's Road, Southampton" (unpublished report, Wessex Archaeology, 2005), https://doi.org/10.5284/1018076), 10, 108; Dobney et al., "Bioarchaeology of Anglo-Saxon Yorkshire," 134; Cowie et al., *Lundenwic*, 81, and CD-ROM tables 3, 4, 8, and 9; A. Davis, "The Plant Remains," in G. Malcolm et al., *Middle Saxon London: Excavations at the Royal Opera House 1989–99* (London: MoLAS, 2003), 289–302, at 291.

110. D. Hooke, *Trees in Anglo-Saxon England: Literature, Lore, and Landscape* (Woodbridge: Boydell, 2010), 246–51.

111. G. Hemery and S. Simblet, *The New Sylva: A Discourse of Forest and Orchard Trees for the Twenty-First Century* (London: Bloomsbury, 2014), 139. Both apple trees and pear trees described as "gray," or "great," or "old" appear in later charter boundary clauses, suggesting that trees found in some hedgerows were of great antiquity (Hooke, *Trees in Anglo-Saxon England*, 249–50).

112. Hemery and Simblet, *New Sylvia*, 139, 157.

113. The Old English word for leek, *leac*, was used in compounds to create words for garden and (*lectun*) and gardener (*lec[tun]weard*) (A. Hagen, *Anglo-Saxon Food and Drink: Production, Processing, Distribution and Consumption* [Hockwold cum Wilton, Norfolk: Anglo-Saxon Books, 2006], 35). The Old Irish generic term *lus*, which can mean plant, is also used more specifically for "leek," and leek cultivation is discussed in early Irish legal tracts (Kelly, *Early Irish Farming*, 253–55).

114. Twice as many chickens were being kept at Barton Court Farm in the early Middle Ages as in the Roman period (Booth et al., *Thames Through Time*, 321).

115. L. Sadori and F. Susanna, "Hints of Economic Change During the Late Roman Empire Period in Central Italy: A Study of Charred Plant Remains from 'La Fontanaccia,' near Rome,"

Vegetation History and Archaeobotany, 14 (2005), 386–93; P. Arthur, G. Fiorentino, and A. M. Grasso, "Roads to Recovery: An Investigation of Early Medieval Agrarian Strategies in Byzantine Italy in and Around the Eighth Century," *Antiquity*, 86 (2012), 444–55; L. Peña-Chocarro et al., "Roman and Medieval Crops in the Iberian Peninsula: A First Overview of Seeds and Fruits from Archaeological Sites," *Quaternary International*, 30 (2017), 1–18; C. Brombacher and D. Hecker, "Agriculture, Food, and Environment During Merovingian Times: Plant Remains from Three Early Medieval Sites in Northwestern Switzerland," *Vegetation History and Archaeobotany*, 24 (2015), 331–42, at 333–38; M. Rösch, "New Aspects of Agriculture and Diet of the Early Medieval Period in Central Europe: Waterlogged Plant Material from Sites in South-Western Germany," *Vegetation History and Archaeobotany*, 17 (2008), 225–38; F. Gyulai et al., "Plant Remains from the Early Medieval Lakeshore Settlement Fonyód-Bélatelep (Lake Balaton, Hungary) with Especial Emphasis on the History of Fruit Cultivation in Pannonia," *Vegetation History and Archaeobotany*, 1 (1992), 177–84.

116. Y. Hen, "Food and Drink in Merovingian Gaul," in B. Kasten and D. Hägermann, eds., *Tätigkeitsfelder und Erfahrungshorizonte des ländlichen Menschen in der frühmittelalterlichen Grundherrschaft (bis ca. 1000): Festschrift für Dieter Hägermann zum 65. Geburtstag* (Stuttgart: Steiner, 2006), 99–110.

117. Archaeologists have recovered evidence from early medieval Douai for the cultivation of four different varieties of plums and two types of cherries, as well as apples, peaches, and medlar. Opium poppies, celery, dill, and fennel were also grown and consumed in early medieval Douai (W. van Zeist et al., "Plant Husbandry and Vegetation of Early Medieval Douai, Northern France," *Vegetation History and Archaeobotany*, 3 [1994], 192–218).

118. *Capitulare de villis vel curtis imperii*, printed in A. Boretius, ed., *Capitularia regum Francorum*, I, MGH Leges II (Hanover: Hahn, 1883), no. 32, 82–91, cap 70.

119. *Capitulare de villis vel curtis imperii*, cap. 44, 62. Gardens and orchards are also noted on a number of specific royal estates (occasionally with lists of plants) in the *Brevium exempla* (in Boretius, ed., *Capitularia regum Francorum*, no. 128, 250–56).

120. *Capitulare de villis vel curtis imperii*, cap. 40.

121. For the role of Carolingian aristocratic women in the oversite of the plants and animals within these spaces, and for an astonishing ceramic "watering can" dated to the eighth or ninth century from a female religious community in Hereford see V. L. Garver, *Women and Aristocratic Culture in the Carolingian World* (Ithaca: Cornell University Press, 2009), 204–7 and fig. 3.

122. A.-M. Talbot, "Byzantine Monastic Horticulture: The Textual Evidence," in A. Littlewood et al., eds., *Byzantine Garden Culture [Papers Presented at a Colloquium in November 1996 at Dumbarton Oaks]* (Washington, D.C.: Dumbarton Oaks Research Library and Collection, 2000), 37–67; C. Goodson, "Villamagna in the Early Middle Ages," in E. Fentress et al., eds., *Villa Magna: An Imperial Estate and Its Legacies. Excavations 2006–10* (London: British School at Rome, 2016), 265–72.

123. *Adomnán's Life of Columba*, trans. and ed. A. O. Anderson and M. O. Anderson (Oxford: Clarendon, 1991), 242.

124. M. A. D'Aronco, "Gardens on Vellum: Plants and Herbs in Anglo-Saxon Manuscripts," in P. Dendle and A. Touwaide, eds., *Health and Healing from the Medieval Garden* (Woodbridge: Boydell, 2008), 101–78, at 111; S. Pollington, *Leechcraft: Early English Charms, Plantlore, and Healing* (Hockwold cum Wilton, Norfolk: Anglo-Saxon Books, 2003), 68, 70.

125. M. Tangle, ed., *Epistolae S. Bonifatii et Luli*, MGH *Epistolae Selectae*, vol. 1 (Berlin: Apud Weidmannos, 1892), 247.

126. A. Davis, "Food Production and Consumption," in Cowie et al., *Lundenwic*, 129–32, at 131; A. Davis, "Plant Foods," in Cowie et al., *Lundenwic*, 144–46, at 145, and CD-ROM tables 8–10. Evidence for the cultivation of both verbena and alexanders during the Roman period has been found at Caerwent (Dickson, "Macroscopic Fossils," 51).

127. A. Davies, "Foodstuffs," in Cowie et al., *Lundenwic*, 180. Similar evidence for another later potential garden (again with an emphasis on medicinal plants) has been found in a tenth-century pit on Milk Street in London (A. Vince., ed., *Aspects of Saxo-Norman London*, vol. 2, *Finds and Environmental Evidence* [London: Museum of London and the London and Middlesex Archaeological Society, 1991], 349, 353).

128. Hunter, "Charred Plant Remains," 171; A. J. Chapman, "Waterlogged Plant Remains," in Birbeck et al., *Origins of Mid-Saxon Southampton*, 173–81, at 174; Cowie et al., *Lundenwic*, CD-ROM, table 4; P. Murphy, "Ipswich, Suffolk"; Kenward and Hall, *Biological Evidence*, 754; Cowie et al., *Lundenwic*, CD table 4 and table 192; Hall and Huntley, "Review of the Evidence for Macrofossil Plant Remains," 110, 117, 121.

129. Carruthers, "Charred and Mineralised Plant Remains," 370; Murphy, "Ipswich, Suffolk."

130. H. C. Darby, *Domesday England* (Cambridge: Cambridge University Press, 1977), 135–36.

131. Booth et al., *Thames Through Time*, 294.

132. Wulfstan of Winchester, *Wulfstan of Winchester's Life of St Æthelwold*, ed. and trans. M. Lapidge and M. Winterbottom (Oxford: Oxford University Press, 1991), 17.

133. G. Thomas, *The Later Anglo-Saxon Settlement at Bishopstone: A Downland Manor in the Making* (York: Council for British Archaeology, 2010), 170 and tables 7.10 and 7.11.

134. M. McCormick, "Rats, Communications, and Plague: Towards an Ecological History," *Journal of Interdisciplinary History*, 34 (2003), 1–25.

135. However, until the twelfth century, grain pests are barely visible in Britain's archaeological record (King et al., "Six-Legged Hitchhikers," 7–9).

136. R. Fleming, "The New Wealth, the New Rich, and the New Political Style in Late Anglo-Saxon England," *Anglo-Norman Studies*, 23 (2001), 1–22; N. Sykes, "The Zooarchaeology of the Norman Conquest," *Anglo-Norman Studies*, 27 (2005), 185–97; R. Liddiard, *The Medieval Park: New Perspectives* (Macclesfield: Windgather, 2007); N. Sykes et al., "Wild to Domestic and Back Again: The Dynamics of Fallow Deer Management in Medieval England (c. 11th–16th Century AD)," *Star: Science and Technology of Archaeological Research*, 2 (2016), 113–26.

CHAPTER 3

Epigraph: A. Van Oyen, *How Things Make History: The Roman Empire and its Terra Sigillata Pottery* (Amsterdam: Amsterdam University Press, 2016), 134.

1. P. J. Walton, *Rethinking Roman Britain: Coinage and Archaeology* (Wetteren: Edition Moneta, 2012), 97 and figs. 59–60.

2. R. Bland, S. Moorhead, and P. Walton, "Finds of Late Roman Silver Coins from Britain: The Contribution of the Portable Antiquities Scheme," in F. Hunter and K. Painter, eds., *Late Roman Silver: The Traprain Treasure in Context* (Edinburgh: Society of Antiquaries of Scotland, 2013), 117–66, fig. 10.2–10.3.

3. A. Smith et al., *The Rural Settlement of Roman Britain* (London: Society for the Promotion of Roman Studies, 2016), 397.

4. A. Smith et al., *Rural Settlement*, figs. 2.19, 3.11, and 3.12.

5. For the significance of these objects, see above, Chapter 1 and K. Leahy (with an appendix by B. Ager), "Soldiers and Settlers in Britain, Fourth to Fifth Century—Revisited," in M. Henig and T. Smith, eds., *Collectanea Antiqua: Essays in Memory of Sonia Chadwick Hawkes*, BAR International Series 1673 (Oxford: Archaeopress, 2007), 133–43, fig. 1; S. Esmonde Cleary, "Roman State Involvement in Britain in the Later 4th Century: An Ebbing Tide?" in N. Roymans, S. Heeren, and W. de Clercq, eds., *Social Dynamics in the Northwest Frontiers of the Late Roman Empire: Beyond Decline or Transformation* (Amsterdam: Amsterdam University Press, 2017), 179–202, at 194–95, and fig. 6.

6. J. Evans, "Balancing the Scales: Romano-British Pottery in Early Late Antiquity," in L. Lavan, ed., *Local Economies? Production and Exchange of Inland Regions in Late Antiquity* (Leiden: Brill, 2015), 425–50, at 427–29, and fig. 1.

7. A. Martyn et al., "The Rural Settlement of Roman Britain: An Online Resource," http://archaeologydataservice.ac.uk/archives/view/romangl/map.html.

8. T. Brindle, *The Portable Antiquities Scheme and Roman Britain* (London: British Museum, 2014), 1–9. For the biases in this data, see K. Robbins, "Balancing the Scales: Exploring the Variable Effects of Collection Bias on Data Collected by the Portable Antiquities Scheme," *Landscapes*, 14 (2013), 54–72.

9. R. E. Roth, "Towards a Ceramic Approach to Social Identity in the Roman World: Some Theoretical Considerations," *Digressus Supplement*, 1 (2003), 35–45, at 41.

10. H. E. M. Cool, *Eating and Drinking in Roman Britain* (Cambridge: Cambridge University Press, 2006), 37–46, 53–55, and 223–31.

11. M. Fulford, *New Forest Roman Pottery: Manufacture and Distribution, with a Corpus of Pottery Types*, BAR British Series 17 (Oxford: BAR, 1975); M. A. B. Lyne and R. S. Jefferies, *The Alice Holt/Farnham Roman Pottery Industry* (London: Council for British Archaeology, 1979); M. D. Howe, J. R. Perring, and D. F. Mackreth, *Roman Pottery from the Nene Valley: A Guide* (Peterborough: City Museum and Art Gallery, 1980); J. Evans, "Crambeck: The Development of a Major Northern Pottery Industry," in P. R. Wilson, ed., *The Crambeck Roman Pottery Industry* (Leeds: Roman Antiquities Section, Yorkshire Archaeological Society, 1989), 43–90; M. Millett, *The Romanization of Britain: An Essay in Archaeological Interpretation* (Cambridge: Cambridge University Press, 1990), 164–75; J. R. L. Allen and M. G. Fulford, "The Distribution of South-East Dorset Black Burnished Category 1 Pottery in South-West Britain," *Britannia*, 27 (1996), 223–81; Evans, "Balancing the Scales," 427–29. In a few places, however, more forms were being made in the late Roman period than were being made earlier. Cases in point are the BB1 producers at Bestwall Quarry (L. Ladle, *Excavations at Bestwall Quarry, Wareham 1992–2005*, vol. 2, *The Iron Age and Later Landscape* [Dorchester: Dorset Natural History and Archaeological Society, 2012], 239, 311) and the Crambeck potteries producing parchment ware (P. Bidwell, "The Dating of Crambeck Parchment Ware," *Journal of Roman Pottery Studies*, 12 [2005], 15–21).

12. Allen and Fulford, "Distribution," 253–54.

13. D. P. S. Peacock, *Pottery in the Roman World: An Ethnoarchaeological Approach* (London: Longman, 1982), 52–74.

14. M. Rhodes, "Roman Pottery Lost *en Route* from the Kiln Site to the User—a Gazetteer," *Journal of Roman Pottery Studies*, 2 (1989), 44–58; P. Booth, "Quantifying Status: Some Pottery Data from the Upper Thames Valley," *Journal of Roman Pottery Studies*, 11 (2004), 39–52. For arguments about "market forces" standing behind the distribution of common objects, see M. L. Ratliff, "Globalisation, Consumerism, and the Ancient Roman Economy: A Preliminary Look at Bronze and Iron Production and Consumption," *TRAC 2010* (2011), 32–46, at 37–38.

15. N. J. Cooper, "Pottery, Landscape, and Trade: What Are the Sherds Telling Us?" in P. Bowman and P. Liddle, eds., *Leicestershire Landscapes* (Leicester: Leicestershire Museums Archaeological Fieldwork Group, 2004), 81–94.

16. Booth, "Quantifying Status," 40, 45.

17. Allen and Fulford, "Distribution"; J. Gerrard, "Pots for Cash? A Critique of the Role of the 'Free Market' in the Late Roman Economy," in *TRAC 2001* (2002), 13–23, at 20; and J. Gerrard, "Feeding the Army from Dorset: Pottery, Salt, and the Roman State," in S. Stallibrass and R. Thomas, eds., *Feeding the Roman Army: The Archaeology of Production and Supply in N W Europe* (Oxford: Oxbow Books, 2008), 116–27, at 123–24; P. Reynolds, *Trade in the Western Mediterranean, AD 400–700: The Ceramic Evidence*, BAR International Series 604 (Oxford: Tempus Reparatum, 1995), 126–28.

18. Lyne and Jeffries, *Alice Holt/Farnham Roman Pottery Industry*; Gerrard, "Feeding the Army from Dorset," 121–22.

19. M. G. Allen et al., *The Rural Economy of Roman Britain* (London: Society for the Promotion of Roman Studies, 2017), 357.

20. Evans, "Crambeck," 43, 78; N. J. Cooper, "Searching for the Blank Generation: Consumer Choice in Roman and Post-Roman Britain," in J. Webster and N. Cooper, eds., *Roman Imperialism: Post-Colonial Perspectives* (Leicester: School of Archaeological Studies, 1999), 85–98, at 86–88; S. Roskams, "The Hinterlands of Roman York: Present Patterns and Future Strategies," in P. Crummy and H. Hurst, eds., *The Coloniae of Roman Britain: New Studies and a Review* (Portsmouth, R.I.: Journal of Roman Archaeology, 1999), 45–72; M. Whyman, "Late Roman Britain in Transition, AD 300–500: A Ceramic Perspective from East Yorkshire" (Ph.D. diss., University of York, 2001); Gerrard, "Pots for Cash?" 13–23.

21. M. McCarthy, *The Romano-British Peasant: Towards a Study of People, Landscapes, and Work During the Roman Occupation of Britain* (Oxford: Windgather, 2013), 115; Q. Mould, "Domestic Life," in L. Allason-Jones, ed., *Artefacts in Roman Britain: Their Purpose and Use* (Cambridge: Cambridge University Press, 2011), 154–79, at 164–65; Cooper, "Searching for the Blank Generation," 85, 89; R. Hingley, *Globalizing Roman Culture: Unity, Diversity and Empire* (London: Routledge, 2005), 105–9.

22. S. G. Upex et al., "The Excavation of a Fourth-Century Roman Pottery Production Unit at Stibbington, Cambridge" *Archaeological Journal*, 165 (2008), 265–333.

23. I. Meadows, "The Roman and Early Saxon Periods," in "Nene Valley Archaeological and Environmental Synthesis," ed. Northamptonshire Archaeology, University of Exeter, part 1 (unpublished report, Northamptonshire Archaeology, York, 2009), 89–124, at 110, doi:10.5284/1000170.

24. Meadows, "Roman and Early Saxon Periods," 110. Warry argues that more men would have been involved gathering fuel at ceramic-tile-making operations than preparing or making tegulae (P. Warry, "The Silchester Tile Industry," in M. Fulford, ed., *Silchester and the Study of Romano-British Urbanism* [Portsmouth, R.I.: Journal of Roman Archaeology, 2012], 49–76, at 54 and table 5.2).

25. J. M. Skibo, M. B. Schiffer, and K. C. Reid, "Organic-Tempered Pottery: An Experimental Study," *American Antiquity*, 54 (1989), 122–46, at 134; M. S. Tite, "Pottery Production, Distribution, and Consumption—the Contribution of the Physical Sciences," *Journal of Archaeological Method and Theory*, 6 (1999), 181–233, at 185.

26. Upex et al., "Excavation of a Fourth-Century Roman Pottery Production," 270.

27. For an example, see D. Whittaker and J. Goody, "Rural Manufacturing in the Rouergue from Antiquity to the Present: The Examples of Pottery and Cheese," *Comparative Studies in Society and History*, 43 (2001), 225–45, at 228, 232.

28. Upex et al., "Excavation of a Fourth-Century Roman Pottery Production," 278–80, 316–20. There is considerable evidence from elsewhere in the Roman world for the division of labor when large-scale mass-production was taking place (A. Bowman and A. Wilson, "Quantifying the Roman Economy: Integration, Growth, Decline?" in A. Bowman and A. Wilson, *Quantifying the Roman Economy: Methods and Problems* [Oxford: Oxford University Press, 2009], 3–84, at 32–33.

29. For the importance of the transportation network to Nene Valley potters, as well as other producers such as iron workers, see J. P. Wild, "Roman Settlement in the Lower Nene Valley," *Archaeological Journal*, 131 (1974), 140–70, at 160–67. For ethnographic work on the complex labor arrangements that often stand behind specialist pottery production, see C. L. Costin, "The Use of Ethnoarchaeology for the Archaeological Study of Ceramic Production," *Journal of Archaeological Method and Theory*, 7 (2000), 377–403, at 390–92.

30. C. M. Hearne and R. J. C. Smith, "A Late Iron Age Settlement and Black-Burnished Ware (BB1) Production Site at Worgret, near Wareham, Dorset (1986–7)," *Proceedings of the Dorset Natural History and Archaeological Society*, 113 (1991), 55–105; M. A. B. Lyne, "The Late Iron Age and Romano-British Pottery Production Sites at Redcliff Farm and Stoborough," *Dorset Natural History and Archaeological Society*, 124 (2002), 45–99; Ladle, *Excavations at Bestwall Quarry*.

31. Allen and Fulford, "Distribution," 260; Gerrard, "Feeding the Army from Dorset," 116–27; Ladle, *Excavations at Bestwall Quarry*, 240–42.

32. Lyne, "Late Iron Age and Romano-British Pottery Production Sites at Redcliff," 87, 93, 96, and table 8.

33. Lyne, "Late Iron Age and Romano-British Pottery Production Sites at Redcliff," 86–97.

34. Hearne and Smith, "Late Iron Age Settlement and Black-Burnished Ware (BB1) Production Site at Worgret," 98.

35. Ladle, *Excavations at Bestwall Quarry*, 318.

36. G. Fincham, *Durobrivae: A Roman Town Between Fen and Upland* (Stroud: Tempus, 2004), 122–28.

37. B. Jervis, *Pottery and Social Life in Medieval England: Towards a Relational Approach* (Oxford: Oxbow Books, 2014), 108.

38. Different types of Romano-British pottery often bear the name of the places where the pottery, or kilns where it was made, were first discovered by archaeologists, and thus the names are both overspecific and somewhat arbitrary. For the location of known production sites and distribution of all these wares, and for bibliography, see P. A. Tyers, "Atlas of Roman Pottery," http://potsherd.net/atlas/.

39. Lyne and Jeffries, *Alice Holt/Farnham Roman Pottery*, 3, 59–60; Evans, "Balancing the Scales," 430 and table 1.

40. J. Evans, S. Macaulay, and P. Mills, *The Horningsea Roman Pottery Industry in Context*, East Anglian Archaeology 162 (Bar Hill, Cambridgeshire: Oxford Archaeology East in Conjunction with ALGAO East, 2017), 107, 111, 137.

41. R. Collins, *Hadrian's Wall and the End of Empire* (London: Routledge, 2012), 57–66.

42. Evans, "Balancing the Scales," 441–43; Allen and Fulford, "Distribution," 247–48, 258–59, 267–69; P. Bidwell and A. Croom, "The Supply and Use of Pottery on Hadrian's Wall in the 4th Century AD," in R. Collins and A. Allason-Jones, eds., *Finds from the Frontier: Material Culture in the 4th–5th Centuries* (London: Council for British Archaeology, 2010), 20–36, at 27–28.

43. Evans, "Crambeck," 43–90; Bidwell and Croom, "Supply and Use of Pottery," 29–34.

44. They were also supplying sites in the Nene Valley, the western fen edge, the central fenland, and the Ouse Valley (Evans et al., *Horningsea Roman Pottery Industry*, 100 and fig. 4.4).

45. Evans et al., *Horningsea Roman Pottery Industry*, 106. For the dominance of Harold, Oxfordshire, and Portchester D/Overwey wares in Essex from c. 370 on, as well as the disappearance of locally produced wares, see C. Wallace, "Notes on the Late Dating of Shell-Tempered Ware in Essex," *Journal of Roman Pottery Studies*, 6 (1993), 123–26.

46. Evans et al., *Horningsea Roman Pottery Industry*, 6, 104.

47. The material evidence for these changes may well be the rise of the new prominence of supraregional potteries. Paul Reynolds has posited that "the greater the frequency of contact between major agricultural producers and consumers, the greater the range and quantity of pottery exported" (Reynolds, *Trade in the Western Mediterranean*, 128).

48. Allen et al., *Rural Economy of Roman Britain*, 207.

49. For recent work arguing for the continued production of pottery at a few pottery production centers in the early fifth century, see articles in a themed issue edited by J. Gerrard, "Romano-British Pottery in the Fifth Century," *Internet Archaeology*, 41 (2016), http://intarch.ac.uk/journal/issue41/index.html; and K. J. Fitzpatrick-Matthews and R. Fleming, "The Perils of Periodization: Roman Ceramics in Britain after 400 CE," *Fragments*, 5 (2016), 1–33, http://hdl.handle.net/2027/spo.9772151.0005.001. For other work arguing for the continued production of late Roman wares, see Lyne and Jeffries, *Alice Holt/Farnham Roman Pottery*, 60–61; M. A. B. Lyne, "Late Roman Handmade Wares in South-East Britain," 3 vols. (Ph.D. diss., Reading University, 1994); M. A. B. Lyne, "The Pottery Supply to Roman Sussex," in D. Rudling, ed., *The Archaeology of Sussex to A.D. 2000* (King's Lynn: Heritage Marketing and Publications on Behalf of the Centre for Continuing Education, University of Sussex, 2003), 141–50; P. T. Bidwell and S. Speak, *Excavations at South Shields, Roman Fort*, vol. 1 (Newcastle upon Tyne: Society of Antiquaries of Newcastle upon Tyne, 1994), 225; Whyman, "Late Roman Britain in Transition"; Bidwell and Croom, "Supply and Use of Pottery," 20–36; H. Quinnell, *Trethurgy: Excavations at Trethurgy Round, St Austell; Community and Status in Roman and Post-Roman Cornwall* (Cornwall: Cornwall County Council, 2004), 238; J. Gerrard, "How Late Is Late? Pottery and the Fifth Century in South West Britain," in R. Collins and J. Gerrard, eds., *Debating Late Antiquity in Britain AD 300–700*, BAR British Series 365 (Oxford: Archaeopress, 2004), 65–75; J. Gerrard, "Finding the Fifth Century: A Late Fourth- and Early Fifth-Century Pottery Fabric from South-East Dorset," *Britannia*, 41 (2010), 293–412; J. Gerrard, "Roman Pottery in the Fifth Century: A Review of the Evidence and Its Significance," in F. K. Haarer, ed., *AD 410: The History and Archaeology of Late Roman and Post-Roman Britain* (London: Society for the Promotion of Roman Studies, 2014), 89–98. In places such as Newton Bewley, Hartlepool, and Wellington Row, in York, pots that cannot be distinguished from ones made in the 360s or 370s continued to be used in some quantity in the decades after 400, which may well be evidence for their continued production (A. Platell and R. Johns, "Archaeological Investigations at Newton Bewley, Hartlepool" [unpublished report, Tees Archaeology, 2001], 16–20, 28, 34; Whyman, "Late Roman Britain in Transition," 327, 342).

50. R. J. Brickstock, "Coin Supply in the North in the Late Roman Period," in T. Wilmott and P. Wilson, eds., *The Late Roman Transition in the North*, BAR British Series 299 (Oxford: BAR, 2000), 33–37; S. Moorhead and P. Walton, "Coinage at the End of Roman Britain," in Haarer, ed., *AD 410*, 99–116; Gerrard, "Roman Pottery in the Fifth Century," 91; S. Esmonde Cleary, "Introduction," in Haarer, *AD 410*, 6; Meadows, "Roman and Early Saxon Periods," 89–124, at 112.

51. The ethnographic work of Ben Nelson suggests that those households without potters that do not have access to a lot of cash, and that live in areas where markets are periodic rather than daily or weekly, stockpile pottery (B. A. Nelson, "Ceramic Frequency and Use-Life: A Highland Mayan Case in Cross Cultural Perspective," in W. A. Longacre, ed., *Ceramic Ethnoarchaeology* [Tucson: University of Arizona Press, 1991], 162–81, at 171).

52. M. A. B. Lyne, "The End of Roman Pottery Production in Southern Britain," *Internet Archaeology*, 41 (2016), https://doi.org/10.11141/ia.41.7.

53. Allen and Fulford collected ethnographic evidence on the longevity of pots in twentieth-century ceramic-dependent cultures. They record that bowls tend to survive one to two years and medium-size cooking pots for seven to ten years. Large cooking pots and storage vessels last between fifteen and twenty years (Allen and Fulford, "Distribution," 253). Nelson, however, shows that ceramic use life can vary dramatically from community to community (Nelson, "Ceramic Frequency"). Roger White has observed that once pottery production started to falter, people may have used their pots more carefully, and have gone to greater lengths to repair them, continuing to use them as long as they were complete (R. White, *Britannia Prima: Britain's Last Roman Province* [Stroud: Tempus, 2007], 24).

54. C. Evans, G. Appleby, and S. Lucy, *Lives in Land: Mucking Excavations by Margaret and Tom Jones, 1965–78: Prehistory, Context, and Summary* (Oxford: Oxbow Books, 2016), 492.

55. S. Hirst and D. Clark, *Excavations at Mucking*, vol. 3, *The Anglo-Saxon Cemeteries*, 2 parts (London: MoLAS, 2009), part 2, 763–64; J. Tipper, *The* Grubenhaus *in Anglo-Saxon England: An Analysis and Interpretation of the Evidence form a Most Distinctive Building Type* (Yedingham: Landscape Research Centre, 2004), 52; Evans et al., *Lives in Land*, 436–37.

56. H. Hamerow, *Early Medieval Settlements: The Archaeology of Rural Communities in North-West Europe, 400–900* (Oxford: Oxford University Press, 2002), 48–50; Hirst and Clark, *Excavations at Mucking*, part 2, 689; C. Hills and S. Lucy, *Spong Hill Part IX: Chronology and Synthesis* (Cambridge: McDonald Institute for Archaeological Research, 2013), 314–31.

57. Hirst and Clark, *Excavations at Mucking*, part 2, 486–87, 495, 529–30, 666–68, 706, 708, 766.

58. This happened in both late and just post-Roman communities, who especially favored Samian sherds for this task. Repurposed ceramic spindle whorls were made in some of the communities where immigrants new to Britain were settling in, although these people seem to have favored pot bases taken from late Roman color-coated wares (E. Swift, "Reuse of Glass, Pottery, and Copper-Alloy Objects in the Late to Post Roman Transition Period in Britain," in Haarer, *AD 410*, 130–52, at 143–47.

59. Two well-known examples of this in the East of Britain are West Stow, in Suffolk, and at Heybridge, in Essex (J. Plouviez, "The Late Romano-British Pottery," in S. E. West, *West Stow: The Anglo-Saxon Village*, East Anglian Archaeology 24 [Ipswich: Suffolk County Planning Department, 1985], 82–85; S. Lucy, "Odd Goings-On at Mucking: Interpreting the Latest Romano-British Pottery Horizon," *Internet Archaeology*, 41 [2016], https://doi.org/10.11141/ia.41.6). For examples in post-Roman western Britain, see A. Agate, et al., "Early Medieval Settlement at Mothecombe, Devon: The Interaction of Local, Regional and Long-Distance Dynamics," *Archaeological Journal*, 169 (2012), 343–94, at 381.

60. Lucy, "Odd Goings-On at Mucking," section 2, tables 1 and 6.

61. This is SFB 57. For the contents of this SFB, see H. Hamerow, *Excavations at Mucking*, vol. 2, *The Anglo-Saxon Settlement: Excavations by M. U. Jones and W. T. Jones* (London: English Heritage, 1993), 128–9 and fig. 115. For the redating of the fill of this SFB, see Lucy, "Odd Goings-On at Mucking."

62. Tipper, Grubenhaus *in Anglo-Saxon England*, 148.

63. Hamerow, *Excavations at Mucking*, 2:71, 128; Evans et al., *Lives in Land*, 493.

64. Hirst and Clark, *Excavations at Mucking*, vol. 3, part 2, 529–30, 662–68, 707–8; Evans et al., *Lives in Land*, 492.

65. Hirst and Clark, *Excavations at Mucking*, vol. 3, part 1, 103 and fig. 55.

66. Hirst and Clark, *Excavations at Mucking*, vol. 3, part 1, 167 and fig. 86.

67. Hirst and Clark, *Excavations at Mucking*, vol. 3, part 2, 495.

68. Hirst and Clark, *Excavations at Mucking*, vol. 3, part 2, 662–68; M. Welch, "Relating Anglo-Saxon Chronology to Continental Chronologies of the Fifth Century AD," in U. von Freeden, U. Koch, and A. Wieczorek, eds., *Völker an Nord- und Ostsee und die Franken* (Bonn: Habelt, 1999), 31–38, at 34. See also Chapter 9.

69. Hirst and Clark, *Excavations at Mucking*, vol. 3, part 2, 705–8.

70. A brief summary of the *foederati* theory can be found in D. A. Hinton, *Gold and Gilt, Pots and Pins: Possessions and People in Medieval Britain* (Oxford: Oxford University Press, 2005), 13–15.

71. Lucy, "Odd Goings-On at Mucking," section 3.

72. Evans et al., *Lives in Land*, 350–53, 364–66, 371–73.

73. M. Fulford, "Pottery and Britain's Foreign Trade in the Later Roman Period," in D. P. S. Peacock, ed., *Pottery and Early Commerce: Characterization and Trade in Roman and Later Ceramics* (London: Academic, 1977), 35–84, at 57.

74. Evans et al., *Lives in Land*, 180. A similar assortment of Roman-style ceramics has been recovered from a contemporary post-Roman site nearby, at Aveley. Here, people in the years just after 400 were tending to their cattle at a newly built enclosure. They continued to have access to a little Portchester D/Overwey ware, Oxfordshire color-coated ware, and Hadham shell-tempered ware. Unlike the Mucking community, however, they were also getting a few Alice Holt/Farnham vessels from the Surrey/Hampshire border—another long-lived ware (S. Foreman and D. Maynard, "A Late Iron Age and Romano-British Farmstead at Ship Lane, Aveley: Excavations on the Line of the A13 Wennington to Mar Dyke Road Improvement, 1994–5," *Essex Archaeology and History*, 33 [2002], 123–56, at 135, 144–46). But there were no imported wares here. As at Mucking, none of the Romano-British-style sherds were from locally made wares that had been common in Essex in the first half of the fourth century (Foreman and Maynard, "Late Iron Age and Romano-British Farmstead at Ship Lane, Aveley," 146).

75. E. Biddulph et al., *London Gateway: Iron Age and Roman Salt Making in the Thames Estuary; Excavations at Stanford Wharf Nature Reserve, Essex* (Oxford: Oxford Archaeology, 2012), 105–76.

76. Biddulph et al., *London Gateway*, 150, 159; M. Millett, "The Dating of Farnham (Alice Holt) Pottery," *Britannia*, 10 (1979), 121–37.

77. M. Germany, *Excavations at Great Holts Farm, Boreham, Essex, 1992–94*, East Anglian Archaeology 105 (Chelmsford: Heritage Conservation, Essex County Council, 2003), 126–28, 134–38.

78. J. Drummond-Murray and P. Thompson, with C. Cowan, *Settlement in Roman Southwark: Archaeological Excavations (1991–9) for the London Underground Limited Jubilee Line Extension Project* (London: MoLAS, 2002), 102, 144–45, and fig. 102; L. Rayner and F. Seeley, "The Roman Pottery," in Drummond-Murray and Thompson with Cowan, *Settlement in Roman Southwark*, 162–212; P. R. Symonds and R. S. Tomber, "Late Roman London: An Assessment of the Ceramic Evidence from the City of London," *Transactions of the London and Middlesex Archaeological Society*, 42 (1991), 59–99.

79. C. J. Going, "Economic Long Waves in the Roman Period? A Reconnaissance of the Romano-British Ceramic Evidence," *Oxford Archaeological Journal*, 11 (1992), 93–117, at 101; Germany, *Excavations at Great Holts Farm*, 136–38. Similar patterns of increasing amounts of pottery from important production centers at some distance from the consumption site at the expense of local wares is seen in other places. In Worcester, the important late assemblage of pottery from

1, the Butts, shows the increasing dominance of Oxfordshire table wares and *mortaria*, shell-tempered wares, and BB1 cook pots from Dorset, and a decrease in locally produced ceramics (R. Cuttler, R. Burrows, and C. J. Evans, "14–24 the Butts," in S. Butler and R. Cutler, eds., *Life and Industry in the Suburbs of Roman Worcester*, BAR British Series 533 (Oxford: Archaeopress, 2011), 56–130, at 89–105.

80. Evans et al., *Lives in Land*, 492.

81. Hamerow, *Excavations at Mucking*, 2:42–44, fig. 28. For comparable pottery on the continent, see J. Soulat, A. Bocquet-Liénard, X. Savary, and V. Hincker, "Hand-Made Pottery Along the Channel Coast and Parallels with the Scheldt Valley," in R. Annaert, ed., *The Very Beginning of Europe? Early Cultural and Social Dimensions of Early Medieval Migration and Colonisation (5th–8th Century); Archaeology in Contemporary Europe; Conference Brussels, May 17–19, 2011* (Brussels: Flanders Heritage Agency, 2012), 215–24; A. Nieuwhof, "Anglo-Saxon Immigration or Continuity? Ezinge and the Coastal Area of the Northern Netherlands in the Migration Period," *Journal of Archaeology in the Low Countries*, 5 (2013), 53–83.

82. Tipper, Grubenhaus in *Anglo-Saxon England*, 50.

83. P. M. Barford, *Excavations at Little Oakley, Essex, 1951–78: Roman Villa and Saxon Settlement*, East Anglian Archaeology 98 (Chelmsford: Essex County Council, 2002), 177, 186.

84. Late Roman and organic-tempered wares were also found in two pits on the site (Barford, *Excavations at Little Oakley*, 32, 157–59, 162, 164, 196).

85. Barford, *Excavations at Little Oakley*, 195.

86. Barford, *Excavations at Little Oakley*, 162.

87. S. Lawrence with P. Booth, "The Iron Age Settlement and Roman Villa at Thurnham, Kent" (unpublished report, CTRL Integrated Site Report Series, 2006), 107–8.

88. F. A. Hart, "Excavation of a Saxon Grubenhaus and Roman Ditch at Kent Road, St Mary Cray," *Archaeologia Cantiana*, 101 (1984), 187–216, at 193–95, 201–3.

89. Fitzpatrick-Matthews and Fleming, "Perils of Periodization," 22–23.

90. G. Perry, "Beer, Butter, and Burial: The Pre-Burial Origins of Cremation Urns from the Early Anglo-Saxon Cemetery of Cleatham, North Lincolnshire," *Medieval Ceramics*, 32 (2011), 9–21. This was not so different from Britain's first- and second-century cremation burials, many of which include kitchen wares. For examples see R. J. H. Pearce, "Case Studies in a Contextual Archaeology of Burial Practice in Britain," 2 vols. (Ph.D. diss., Durham University, 1999).

91. See, for example, cremation no. 44, in V. I. Evison, *An Anglo-Saxon Cemetery at Alton, Hampshire* (Gloucester: Hampshire Field Club, 1988), 88 and fig. 42; J. N. L. Myres and B. Green, *The Anglo-Saxon Cemeteries of Caistor-by-Norwich and Markshall Norfolk* (London: Society of Antiquaries of London, 1973), 74–76; cremations 39, 262, 314, and 342; and A. G. Kinsley, *The Anglo-Saxon Cemetery at Millgate, Newark on Trent, Nottinghamshire* (Nottingham: Department of Classics and Archaeological Studies University of Nottingham, 1989), 12 and figs. 24, 62, 74, 79.

92. Hills and Lucy, *Spong Hill Part IX*, 314–20, 328.

93. C. J. Arnold, "The Sancton-Baston Potter," *Scottish Archaeological Review*, 1–2 (1982–83), 17–30. Kevin Leahy's discussion of this pottery upholds the identification of the Sancton/Baston potter for pots from a number of cemeteries but emphasizes that pots in Arnold's Groups B and C are not linked by the use of the same set of stamps, so cannot be said to be the work of the same potter (K. Leahy, *"Interrupting the Pots": The Excavation of Cleatham Anglo-Saxon Cemetery, North Lincolnshire* [York: Council for British Archaeology, 2007], 128).

94. Leahy, *"Interrupting the Pots,"* 128.

95. Leahy, *"Interrupting the Pots,"* 81–82.

96. Hills and Lucy, *Spong Hill Part IX*, 324.

97. Hills and Lucy, *Spong Hill Part IX*, 166–67; Kinsley, *Anglo-Saxon Cemetery at Millgate*, 13–15.

98. G. P. Murdock and C. Provost, "Factors in the Division of Labor by Sex: A Cross-Cultural Analysis," *Ethnology*, 12 (1973), 203–25; C. Kramer, "Ceramic Ethnoarchaeology," *Annual Review of Anthropology*, 14 (1985), 77–102, at 79, 85; J. M. Skibo and M. B. Schiffer, "The Clay Cooking Pot: An Exploration of Women's Technology," in J. M. Skibo, W. H. Walker, and A. E. Nielsen, eds., *Expanding Archaeology* (Salt Lake City: University of Utah Press, 1995), 80–91, at 83–86.

99. C. L. Costin, "Exploring the Relationship Between Gender and Craft in Complex Societies: Methodological and Theoretical Issues of Gender Attribution," in R. P. Wright, ed., *Gender and Archaeology* (Philadelphia: University of Pennsylvania Press, 1996), 111–40, at 113.

100. D. Bolger, "Gender, Labor, and Pottery Production in Prehistory," in D. Bolger, ed., *A Companion to Gender Prehistory* (Hoboken, N.J.: John Wiley and Sons, 2013), 161–79.

101. Skibo and Schiffer, "Clay Cooking Pot," 84; J. Sofaer and S. Budden, "Many Hands Make Light Work: Potting and Embodied Knowledge at the Bronze Age Tell at Százhalombatta, Hungary," in M. L. Stig Sørensen, and K. Rebay-Salisbury, eds., *Embodied Knowledge: Historical Perspectives on Belief and Technology* (Oxford: Oxbow Books, 2013), 117–127.

102. Leahy, *"Interrupting the Pots,"* 81–82; S. West, *West Stow Revisited* (Bury St. Edmunds: West Stow County Park and Anglo-Saxon Village, 2001), 35. For what household production might look like in the archaeological record, see P. M. Rice, "Evolution of Specialized Pottery Production: A Trial Model," *Current Anthropology*, 22 (1981), 219–40, at 222; C. L. Costin, "Craft Specialization: Issues in Defining, Documenting, and Explaining the Organization of Production," *Archaeological Method and Theory*, 3 (1991), 1–56.

103. Kramer, "Ceramic Ethnoarchaeology," 87.

104. E. A. Murphy, "Rethinking Standardisation Through Late Antique Sagalassos Ceramic Production: Tradition, Improvisation, and Fluidity," in A. Van Oyen and M. Pitts, *Materialising Roman Histories* (Oxford: Oxbow Books, 2017), 101–22, at 103.

105. K. P. Fazioli, "Rethinking Ethnicity in Early Medieval Archaeology: Social Identity, Technological Choice, and Communities of Practice," in S. D. Stull, ed., *From West to East: Current Approaches to Medieval Archaeology* (Newcastle upon Tyne: Cambridge Scholars, 2014), 20–39, at 28.

106. T. Ingold, *The Perception of the Environment: Essays in Livelihood, Dwelling, and Skill* (London: Routledge, Taylor and Francis, 2000), 416.

107. P. Crown, "Life Histories of Pots and Potters: Situating the Individual in Archaeology," *American Antiquity*, 72 (2007), 677–90, at 678, 679–80.

108. University of Cambridge Museum of Archaeology and Anthropology, acc. no. 1950.170A, http://www.hideandseekexhibition.org.uk/objects/56. Child-size fingerprints have been found on Roman-period and other early pottery as well, reminding us that potting skills in many contexts are often learned early in life (T. Dzierzykray-Rogalski and C. Gezeszyk, "Les dermatoglyphes: Empreintes des linges papillaires relevés sur les lampes de Kôm el-Dikka (Alexandrie)," *Cahiers de la Céramique Egyptienne*, 2 (1991), 14–21; K. A. Kamp, "Working for a Living: Children in the Prehistoric Southwestern Pueblos," in K. Kamp, ed., *Children in the Prehistoric Puebloan Southwest* (Salt Lake City: University of Utah Press, 2002), 71–89.

109. These are Millgate nos. 254 and 117 and Sancton no. 130 (Kinsley, *Anglo-Saxon Cemetery at Millgate*, figs. 60 and 42; J. N. L. Myres and W. H. Southern, *The Anglo-Saxon Cremation Cemetery at Sancton, East Yorkshire* [Hull: Hull Museums, 1973], fig. 16). A similar combination

of more skilled and less skilled potters has been suggested for pots produced in the Bronze Age (Sofaer and Budden, "Many Hands Make Light Work").

110. See, for example, R. Nugent and H. Williams, "Sighted Surfaces: Ocular Agency in Early Anglo-Saxon Cremation Burials," in I.-M. B. Danielsson, F. Fahlander, and Y. Sjöstrand, eds., *Encountering Imagery: Materialities, Perceptions, Relations* (Stockholm: Department of Archaeology and Classical Studies, Stockholm University, 2012), 187–208 and fig 1. See also, Kinsley, *Anglo-Saxon Cemetery at Millgate*, fig. 34, no. 77.

111. Nugent and Williams, "Sighted Surfaces"; H. Williams, "Material Culture as Memory: Combs and Cremation in Early Medieval Britain," *Early Medieval Europe*, 12 (2003), 89–128.

112. J. D. Richards, *The Significance of Form and Decoration of Anglo-Saxon Cremation Urns*, BAR British Series 166 (Oxford: BAR, 1987); Hills and Lucy, *Spong Hill Part IX*, 167; K. E. Squires, "Piecing Together Identity: A Social Investigation of Early Anglo-Saxon Cremation Practices," *Archaeological Journal*, 170 (2013), 154–200, at 163–68, 189–90.

113. Leahy, *"Interrupting the Pots,"* 85–86.

114. Leahy, *"Interrupting the Pots,"* 83.

115. In late twentieth-century highland Mayan communities, cooking posts have very short lives—from three to six months—and most fail because of thermal shock (Nelson, "Ceramic Frequency," 174.)

116. A. Villing and M. Spataro, "Investigating Ceramics, Cuisine and Culture—Past, Present and Future," in M. Spataro and A. Villing, eds., *Ceramics, Cuisine and Culture: The Archaeology and Science of Kitchen Pottery in the Ancient Mediterranean World* (Oxford: Oxbow Books, 2015), 1–25, at 8. Experimental archaeologists, though, have shown that boiling water in a pot after cooking removes the smell of the previous meals (J. E. Morrison et al., "Cooking Up New Perspectives for Late Minoan IB Domestic Activities: An Experimental Approach to Understanding the Possibilities and Probabilities of Using Ancient Cooking Pots," in Spataro and Villing, eds., *Ceramics, Cuisine, and Culture*, 115–24, at 122).

117. D. P. Braun, "Pots as Tools," in J. A. Moore and A. S. Keene, eds., *Archaeological Hammers and Theories* (New York: Academic, 1983), 107–34, at 108–9, 112; Skibo and Schiffer, "Clay Cooking Pot," 83.

118. A. Hein, N. S. Müller, and V. Kilkoglou, "Heating Efficiency of Archaeological Cooking Vessels: Computer Models and Simulations of Heat Transfer," in Spataro and Villing, *Ceramics, Cuisine and Culture*, 49–54, at 51–53; P. Arthur, "Pots and Boundaries: On Cultural and Economic Areas Between Late Antiquity and the Early Middle Ages," in M. Bonifay and J.-C. Tréglia, eds., *LRCW 2: Late Roman Coarse Wares, Cooking Wares and Amphorae in the Mediterranean: Archaeology and Archaeometry*, BAR International Series 1661, vol. 2 (Oxford: Archaeopress, 2007), 15–28, at 17; Braun, "Pots as Tools."

119. Fitzpatrick and Fleming, "Perils of Periodization."

120. B. Jervis, "Making Do or Making the World? Tempering Choices in Early-Mid Anglo-Saxon Pottery Manufacture," in B. Jervis and A. Kyle, eds., *Make-Do and Mend: Archaeologies of Compromise, Repair and Reuse*, BAR International Series 2408 (Oxford: Archaeopress, 2012), 67–80. At Spong Hill, for example, 48 percent of the pottery recovered within the settlement was organic tempered, and overall, this percentage increased in the sixth century (Hills and Lucy, *Spong Hill Part IX*, 227). And at Mucking, 71 percent of the plain wares were grass tempered (Hirst and Clark, *Excavations at Mucking*, part 2, 604). This was not, however the case with cremation urns, because clay tempered with sand took stamp impressions better than pastes tempered with grass, dung, or chaff.

121. Jervis, "Making Do or Making the World?" 67; H. Hamerow, Y. Hollevoet, and A. Vince, "Migration Period Settlements and 'Anglo-Saxon' Pottery from Flanders," *Medieval Archaeology*, 38 (1994), 1–18; Soulat et al., "Hand-Made Pottery Along the Channel Coast."

122. Skibo et al., "Organic Tempered Pottery," 133.

123. Jervis, "Making Do or Making the World?" 67.

124. Conversely, mineral tempered clays are more difficult to use but are better suited for professional potters who use the potters' wheel and the kiln (B. Jervis, "Making Do or Making the World?" 67; A. Vince, "West Midlands Post-Roman Research Agenda: Ceramics," West Midlands Regional Research Framework for Archaeology, seminar 4 [unpublished paper, 2002–3], http://archaeologydataservice.ac.uk/archiveDS/archiveDownload?t=arch-2285-1/dissemination/pdf/West_Midlands_Regional_Research_Framework_Early_Medieval/AlanVince_Ceramics.pdf, 1–19, at 4; Hamerow, *Excavations at Mucking*, 3:31; Hamerow, Hollevoet, and Vince, "Migration Period Settlements"; B. Sillar and M. S. Tite, "Challenge of 'Technological Choices' for Materials Science Approaches in Archaeology," *Archaeometry*, 42 [2000], 2–20, at 14; Warry, "Silchester Tile Industry," 54).

125. Skibo et al., "Organic-Tempered Pottery," 137; O. S. Rey, "Keeping Your Temper Under Control: Materials and the Manufacture of Papauan Pottery," *Archaeology and Physical Anthropology in Oceania*, 11 (1976), 106–37; S. van der Leeuw, "Giving the Potter a Choice: Conceptual Aspects of Pottery Techniques," in P. Lemonnier, ed., *Technological Choices: Transformations in Material Cultures Since the Neolithic* (New York: Routledge, 1993), 238–88; Skibo and Schiffer, "Clay Cooking Pot," 82–83; J. Evans, "Pottery Function and Finewares in the Roman North," *Journal of Roman Pottery Studies*, 6 (1993), 95–118, at 105. The wheel, workshop production, inorganic tempers, and fulltime specialists go together (Sillar and Tite, "Challenge of 'Technological Choices,'" 3–7).

126. N. S. Müller, V. Kilikoglou, P. M. Day, and G. Vekinis, "Thermal Shock Resistance of Tempered Archaeological Ceramics," in M. Martinón-Torres, ed., *Craft and Science: International Perspectives on Archaeological Ceramics* (Doha: Bloomsbury, Qatar Foundation, 2014), 263–70.

127. B. Jervis, "Making Do or Making the World?" 68; J. Henderson, *The Science and Archaeology of Materials: An Investigation of Inorganic Materials* (London: Routledge, 2000), 147–49; Evans, "Pottery Function," 105–7.

128. Evans, "Pottery Function," 105–6.

129. For evidence of stewing in the northwest Europe during the pre-Roman Iron Age, see B. P. Luley, "Cooking, Class, and Colonial Transformations in Roman Mediterranean France," *American Journal of Archaeology*, 118 (2014), 33–60, at 43–46.

130. M. Maltby, *Feeding a Roman Town: Environmental Evidence from Excavations in Winchester, 1972–1985* (Winchester: Winchester Museums, 2010), 146–52; Cool, *Eating and Drinking*, 85 and nn. 34–35. This type of cuisine was more common under Roman in the lands north of the Alps; but south of the Alps and across the Mediterranean, shallow dishes were often used to cook preparations that were not stew-like and probably required the addition of separately made sauces (C. Schucany, "Cooking Like a Native, Dining Like a Roman: Food Preparation and Consumption in Roman Switzerland," in M. Carroll, D. Hadley, and H. Wilmott, eds., *Consuming Passions: Dining from Antiquity to the Eighteenth Century* (Stroud: Tempus, 2005), 39–48, at 47; Arthur, "Pots and Boundaries," 18).

131. A. T. Croom, "Experiments in Roman Military Cooking Methods," *Arbeia Journal*, 6–7 (2001), 37–47, at 44.

132. L. J. E. Cramp, "Foodways and Identity: Organic Residue Analysis of Roman Mortaria and Other Pottery" (Ph.D. diss., University of Reading, 2008), 208; Cool, *Eating and Drinking*, 39; Evans, "Pottery Function," 105; Arthur, "Pots and Boundaries," 18.

133. Evans et al., *Horningsea Roman Pottery Industry*, 141. This is similar to the use of small, friable cooking pots in the Arctic (L. Frink and K. G. Harry, "The Beauty of 'Ugly' Eskimo Cooking Pots," *American Antiquity*, 73 [2008], 103–20).

134. For the connection between changes in ceramics and changes in foodways, see J. Deetz, *In Small Things Forgotten: An Archaeology of Early American Life*, rev. ed. (New York: Anchor Books, 1996), 73–79.

135. J. Blair, *Building Anglo-Saxon England* (Princeton, N.J.: Princeton University Press, 2018), 67–69.

136. A. J. Donnelly, "Cooking Pots in Ancient and Late Antique Cookbooks," in Spataro and Villing, *Ceramics, Cuisine, and Culture*, 141–47, at 145–46. Helen Cool has marshalled evidence suggesting that many people in Britain in the fourth century were already using a narrower range of pottery types than a century before, and this may hint at a growing disinterest in the kinds of pots used earlier in the Roman period at table, because mealtime practices were already changed (Cool, *Eating and Drinking in Roman Britain*, 225–23).

137. P. Arthur, "Form, Function and Technology in Pottery Production from Late Antiquity to the Early Middle Ages," in L. Lavan, E. Zanini, and A. Sarantis, eds., *Technology in Transition A.D. 300–650* (Leiden: Brill, 2008),159–84, at 182–83.

CHAPTER 4

Epigraph: G. Orwell, *Homage to Catalonia* (Boston: Beacon, 1966), 140.

1. See above, Chapter 3. For the outlines of the establishment of Roman-style pottery in the first and second centuries, see S. Willis, "The Romanization of Pottery Assemblages in the East and North-East of England During the First Century AD: A Comparative Analysis," *Britannia*, 27 (1996), 179–221, at 214, 219; G. de la Bédoyère, *Pottery in Roman Britain* (Princes Risborough: Shire, 2000); P. Tyers, *Roman Pottery in Britain* (London: Batsford, 1996); M. Pitts, "Regional Identities and the Social Use of Ceramics," *TRAC 2004*, 14 (2005), 50–64, at 50–64.

2. N. J. Cooper, "Searching for the Blank Generation: Consumer Choice in Roman and Post-Roman Britain," in J. Webster and N. Cooper, eds., *Roman Imperialism: Post-Colonial Perspectives* (Leicester: School of Archaeological Studies, 1996), 85–98, at 85, 89; R. Hingley, *Globalizing Roman Culture: Unity, Diversity and Empire* (London: Routledge, 2005), 105–9; Q. Mould, "Domestic Life," in L. Allason-Jones, ed., *Artefacts in Roman Britain: Their Purpose and Use* (Cambridge: Cambridge University Press, 2011), 154–79, at 164–65; M. McCarthy, *The Romano-British Peasant: Towards a Study of People, Landscapes, and Work During the Roman Occupation of Britain* (Oxford: Windgather, 2013), 115.

3. G. Woolf, "The Unity and Diversity of Romanisation," *Journal of Roman Archaeology*, 5 (1992), 349–52; R. E. Roth, "Towards a Ceramic Approach to Social Identity in the Roman World: Some Theoretical Considerations," *Digressus Supplement*, 1 (2003), 35–45, at 37–41.

4. H. E. M. Cool, "Glass Vessels of the Fourth and Early Fifth Century in Roman Britain," in D. Foy, ed., *Le verre de l'Antiquité tardive et du Haut Moyen Age: Typologie, chronologie, diffusion* (Guiry-en-Vexin: Musée Archéologique Departmental du Val d'Oise, 1995), 11–23 and H. E. M. Cool, "Local Production and Trade in Glass Vessels in the British Isles in the First to Seventh Centuries AD," in D. Foy and M.-D. Nenna, eds., *Échanges et commerce du verre dans le monde antique* (Montagnac: Éditions Monique Mergoil, 2003), 139–45, at 140; J. Price, "Late Roman Glass Vessels in Britain, from AD 350 to 410 and Beyond," in J. Price, ed., *Glass in Britain and Ireland AD 350–1100* (London: British Museum, 2000), 1–32; J. Price, "Late Roman Glass Vessels in the Hadrian's Wall

Frontier Region," in R. Collins and L. Allason-Jones, eds., *Finds from the Frontier: Material Culture in the 4th–5th Centuries* (London: Council for British Archaeology, 2010), 37–49, at 37–39; H. E. Foster and C. M. Jackson, "Composition of 'Naturally Coloured' Late Roman Vessel Glass from Britain and the Implications for Models of Glass Production and Supply," *Journal of Archaeological Science*, 36 (2009), 189–204, at 189–90, 194–95.

5. C .M. Jackson and J. Price, "Analyses of Late Roman Glass from the Commandant's House of the Fort at South Shields, Tyne and Wear, UK," in D. Ignatiadou and A. Antonaras, eds., *Annales du 18ᵉ congrès de l'Association International pour l'Histoire du Verre* (Thessaloniki: Association Internationale pour l'Histoire du Verre, 2012), 175–82, at 180–81; C. M. Jackson and H. Foster, "The Last Roman Glass in Britain: Recycling at the Periphery of the Empire," in D. Keller, J. Price, and C. Jackson, eds., *Neighbours and Successors of Rome: Traditions of Glass Production and Use in Europe and the Middle East in the Later 1st Millennium AD* (Oxford: Oxbow Books, 2014), 6–14, at 10–12; C. M. Jackson and S. Paynter, "A Great Big Melting Pot: Exploring Patterns of Glass Supply, Consumption, and Recycling in Roman Coppergate, York," *Archaeometry*, 58 (2016), 68–95, at 81–82. Glass recycling, however, was taking place even in the second century (A. Wardle et al., *Glass Working on the Margins of London: Excavations at 35 Basinghall Street, City of London, 2005* [London: MoLAS, 2015], 5).

6. E. M. Stern, "Roman Glass Blowing and Its Cultural Context," *American Journal of Archaeology*, 103 (1999), 441–84, at 456.

7. Stern, "Roman Glass Blowing," 454.

8. Stern, "Roman Glass Blowing," 461.

9. H. E. M. Cool, and M. J. Baxter, "Peeling the Onion: An Approach to Comparing Vessel Glass Assemblages," *Journal of Roman Archaeology*, 12 (1999), 72–100, at 79, 87; Cool, "Local Production and Trade," 143; Price, "Late Roman Glass Vessels in Britain," 1–31; E. M. Stern, "Glass Production," in J. P. Oleson, ed., *Oxford Handbook of Engineering and Technology in the Classical World* (Oxford: Oxford University Press, 2008), 520–47, at 541–42; J. Price, "Romano-British and Early Post-Roman Glass Vessels and Objects," in H. Quinnell, *Trethurgy: Excavations at Trethurgy Round, St Austell; Community and Status in Roman and Post-Roman Cornwall* (Cornwall: Cornwall County Council, 2004), 85–92, at 85–87.

10. M. Grünewald and S. Hartmann, "Glass Workshops in Northern Gaul and the Rhineland in the First Millennium AD as Hints of a Changing Land Use—Including Some Results of the Chemical Analysis of Glass from Mayen," in Keller, Price, and Jackson, *Neighbours and Successors of Rome*, 43–57, at 47; J. Price, "Trade in Glass," in J. du P Taylor and H. Cleere, eds., *Roman Shipping and Trade: Britain and the Rhine Provinces* (London: Council of British Archaeology, 1978), 70–78, at 75.

11. Price, "Late Roman Glass Vessels in Britain," 21; Price, "Late Roman Glass Vessels in the Hadrian's Wall Frontier Region."

12. V. I. Evison, *Catalogue of Anglo-Saxon Glass in the British Museum* (London: British Museum, 2008), 1–20; I. C. Freestone, M. J. Hughes, and C. P. Stapleton, "The Composition and Production of Anglo-Saxon Glass," in Evison, *Catalogue of Anglo-Saxon Glass*, 29–37; Price, "Late Roman Glass Vessels in Britain," 21–23.

13. For this site, see A. Douglas, J. Gerrard, and B. Sudds, *Roman Settlement and Bath House at Shadwell: Excavations at Tobacco Dock and Babe Ruth Restaurant, the Highway, London* (London: Pre-Construct Archaeology, 2011).

14. D. Lakin et al., *The Roman Tower at Shadwell, London: A Reappraisal* (London: MoLAS, 2002).

15. Douglas et al., *Roman Settlement and Bath House at Shadwell*, 13–14, 90–97.

16. Douglas et al., *Roman Settlement and Bath House at Shadwell*, 72.

17. A. Douglas and B. Sudds, "Phased Summary and Assessment Document of the Excavation at 172–176 the Highway, London Borough of Tower Hamlets E1, HGA02" (unpublished report, Pre-Construct Archaeology 2004), 114, https://doi.org/10.5284/1027295; Douglas et al., *Roman Settlement and Bath House at Shadwell*, 57, 160. The pottery from the demolition debris spread over the bathhouse and from a wall-robbing trench included sherds of post-Roman pottery, which may help date the stripping of the building (M. Lyne, "Appendix 2: Assessment of the Roman Pottery," in Douglas and Sudds, "Phased Summary and Assessment Document of the Excavation at 172–176 the Highway," 197–228, at 207).

18. Lakin et al., *Roman Tower at Shadwell*, 24.

19. Douglas et al., *Roman Settlement and Bath House at Shadwell*, 56.

20. Douglas et al., *Roman Settlement and Bath House at Shadwell*, 173. For information on earlier wooden-lined, Roman-period wells in London, see T. Wilmott, "Excavations at Queen Street, City of London, 1953 and 1960, and Roman Timber-Lined Wells in London," *Transactions of the London and Middlesex Archaeological Society*, 33 (1982), 1–78; T. Wilmott, "Water Supply in the Roman City of London," *London Archaeologist*, 4 (1982), 234–42; and T. Wilmott, "Roman Timber Lined Wells in the City of London: Further Examples," *Transactions of the London and Middlesex Archaeological Society*, 35 (1984), 1–10.

21. Lyne, "Appendix 2: Assessment of the Roman Pottery," 181, 199–200; Douglas et al., *Roman Settlement and Bath House at Shadwell*, 62–64, 68–69.

22. S. Esmonde Cleary, *The Roman West, AD 200–500: An Archaeological Study* (Cambridge: Cambridge University Press, 2013), 319–23; T. Brigham and J. Hillam suggest that the settlement at Shadwell was situated where it was because it is where the lower reaches of the River Lea met the Thames (T. Brigham and J. Hillam, "The Late Waterfront in London," *Britannia*, 21 [1990], 99–183, at 160).

23. Lyne, "Appendix 2: Assessment of the Roman Pottery," 181, 199–200; Douglas et al., *Roman Settlement and Bath House at Shadwell*, 68–69; M. Fulford and J. Bird, "Imported Pottery from Germany in Late Roman Britain," *Britannia*, 6 (1975), 171–81.

24. Lyne, "Appendix 2: Assessment of the Roman Pottery," 181; M. Lyne, "Appendix 2," in A. Douglas, "An Archaeological Evaluation at 130–162 the Highway (Tobacco Dock Factory Shops, Phase 11—New Building) London Borough of Tower Hamlets" (unpublished report, Pre-Construct Archaeology, 1997), 4, 8, https://doi.org/10.5284/1027293.

25. Douglas et al., *Roman Settlement and Bath House at Shadwell*, 68, 79.

26. Lyne, "Appendix 2: Assessment of the Roman Pottery," 181; Lyne, "Appendix 2," in Douglas, "Archaeological Evaluation," 1–8.

27. Douglas et al., *Roman Settlement and Bath House at Shadwell*, 57–58, 68, and table 2.

28. We will discuss these deposits further in Chapter 5. For more on the deposit of metal vessels in well closure deposits, see J. Gerrard, "The Drapers' Gardens Hoard: A Preliminary Account," *Britannia*, 40 (2009), 163–83; and J. Gerrard, "Wells and Belief Systems at the End of Roman Britain: A Case Study from London," in L. Lavan and M. Mulryan, ed., *The Archaeology of Late Antique Paganism* (Leiden: Brill, 2011), 551–72, at 558. Similar deposits are also found in purpose-built shafts that never served as wells. For an example, dating sometime after 370, see the large deposit of pots placed in a pit at Smeeth, in Kent. Most were Alice Holt/Farnham and Oxfordshire wares. There were also large numbers of cattle skulls and the bones of sheep, pig, horses, red deer, and domestic fowl. A human skull was also deposited (V. Diez and edited by P. Booth, "The Roman Settlement at Bower Road, Smeeth, Kent" (unpublished report, Oxford Wessex Archaeology Joint Venture, 2006), 21, https://doi.org/10.5284/1009794).

29. M. Napthan, "1 the Butts," in S. Butler and R. Cutler, eds., *Life and Industry in the Suburbs of Roman Worcester*, BAR British Series 533 (Oxford: Archaeopress, 2010), 27–42.

30. K. J. Fitzpatrick-Matthews and G. R. Burleigh, eds., *Excavations at Baldock 1978–1994: Fieldwork by G. R. Burleigh* (Letchworth Garden City: North Hertfordshire District, 2010), 15–16.

31. T. Rook, "The Roman Villa Site at Dicket Mead, Lockleys, Welwyn," *Hertfordshire Archaeology*, 9 (1987), 79–175. This villa was related in some way to another defunct villa, the one at Lockleys, Welwyn (J. B. Ward Perkins, "The Roman Villa at Lockleys, Welwyn," *Antiquaries Journal*, 28 [1938], 339–76, at 351). They may have been owned by a single family (I. Thomas, "Welwyn: Extensive Urban Survey Project Assessment Report" [unpublished report, Hertford County Council, 2000], 4–5).

32. For detailed information on the cemetery, its finds, and a bibliography of publications on the site, see K. J. Fitzpatrick-Matthews, "The Cemeteries of Roman Baldock," *Fragments*, 5 (2016), 34–60, http://hdl.handle.net/2027/spo.9772151.0005.002.

33. T. McDonald and A. Pearson, "Excavations at Welwyn Hall, Welwyn, Hertfordshire Research Archive Report" (unpublished report 4148, Archaeological Solutions, 2012), 14, 28–29, https://doi.org/10.5284/1021930.

34. R. Philpott, *Burial Practices in Roman Britain: A Survey of Grave Treatment and Furnishings AD 43–410*, BAR British Series 219 (Oxford: Tempus Reparatum, 1991); N. Cooke, "The Definition and Interpretation of Late Roman Burial Rites in the Western Empire" (Ph.D. diss., University College London, 1989); G. R. Burleigh, "Some Aspects of Burial Types in the Cemeteries of the Romano-British Settlement at Baldock, Hertfordshire, England" in M. Struck, ed., *Römerzeitliche Gräber als Quellen zu Religion, Bevölkrungsstruktur und Sozialgeschichte* (Mainz: Johannes Gutenberg-Universität Mainz, 1993), 41–49.

35. E.g., G. R. Burleigh and K. J. Fitzpatrick-Matthews, *Draft Catalogue of Burials in the California Late-Roman Cemetery* (unpublished report, North Hertfordshire Museums, last modified 2014), nos. 632, 642; McDonald and Pearson, "Excavations at Welwyn Hall," no. 1026.

36. E.g., Burleigh and Fitzpatrick-Matthews, *Draft Catalogue*, nos. 642, 1005, 1198; McDonald and Pearson, "Excavations at Welwyn Hall," nos. 1089, 1165, 1100.

37. E.g., McDonald and Pearson, "Excavations at Welwyn Hall," 14–30 and nos. 1069, 1152, 1069; Burleigh and Fitzpatrick-Matthews, *Draft Catalogue*, nos. 642, 1005, 1198.

38. See, for example, inhumation 190, an adult male in a nailed coffin. His coffin was reopened after it had begun to decompose. At this time, a small wooden box with a neonate (1088) was placed in the man's grave (Burleigh and Fitzpatrick-Matthews, *Draft Catalogue*, nos. 190 and 1088).

39. A. S. Esmonde Cleary, *The Ending of Roman Britain* (London: B. T. Batsford, 1991), 162–65.

40. On the moral tradition compelling people to bury in the present based on past practices, see K. Rebay-Salisbury, "Inhumation and Cremation: How Burial Practices Are Linked to Beliefs," in M. L. K. Sørensen and K. Rebay-Salisbury, eds., *Embodied Knowledge: Historical Perspectives on Technology and Belief* (Oxford: Oxbow Books, 2013), 15–26.

41. E.g., G. R. Burleigh and M. Sterns, "Baldock Roman Burial and Burial Practice," part 1, "Archive Report" (unpublished report, North Hertfordshire Museums, Museum Resource Centre, Hitchin, 1992), nos. 1318, 1422, and 3632. For more on burial customs in late Roman and post-Roman Britain, see below, Chapters 7 and 8.

42. Burleigh and Fitzpatrick-Matthews, *Draft Catalogue*, nos. 643, 1132, 1141, 1413, 1422; Burleigh and Sterns, "Baldock Roman Burial and Burial Practice," part 1, no. 1318; McDonald and Pearson, "Excavations at Welwyn Hall," nos. 1089, 1110, and 1186. It looks as if old hobnail boots

were curated as well and used in some fifth-century burials (Burleigh and Sterns, "Baldock Roman Burial and Burial Practice," part 1, no. 1413, is a fifth-century grave with a single hobnail shoe, and no. 1132, another fifth-century grave, has a pair of nailed shoes).

43. Burleigh and Fitzpatrick-Matthews, *Draft Catalogue*, no. 3630. The Samian dish is Museums Resource Centre, Hitchin, Hertfordshire, BAL.1, 3630.8871.

44. G. R. Burleigh and K. J. Fitzpatrick-Matthews, *Excavations at Baldock, Hertfordshire, 1978–1994*, vol. 1, *An Iron Age and Romano-British Cemetery at Wallington Road* (Letchworth Garden City: North Hertfordshire District Council Museums Service and North Hertfordshire Archaeological Society, 2010).

45. Museums Resource Centre, Hitchin, Hertfordshire, BAL.1, 3633.8872.

46. For an example of one such beaker, buried in the fourth century at Welwyn Hall, see Mill Green Museum, Hatfield, Hertfordshire, HAT 165.42.190.

47. That the use of pottery in graves is ritualized is taken as a given here, given that almost all human societies, past and present, treat the transition from life to death through ritual practices (R. L. Grimes, *Deeply into the Bone: Re-Inventing Rites of Passage* [Berkeley, Calif.: University of California Press, 2000], 218).

48. Mill Green Museum and Mill, Hatfield, Hertfordshire, HAT 165.1153.70.9. Annette Haug has usefully defined heirlooms as objects that are about the remembrance of the relatively recent past, and are, therefore, objects that cannot be more than three or four generations old (A. Haug, "Constituting the Past—Forming the Present," *Journal of the History of Collections*, 13 [2001], 111–23, at 112).

49. T. McDonald, "Welwyn Hall, Welwyn, Hertfordshire: An Archaeological Excavation" (unpublished report 138, Hertfordshire Archaeological Trust, 1995), no. 510; McDonald and Pearson, "Excavations at Welwyn Hall," 14–30.

50. Museums Resource Centre, Hitchin, Hertfordshire, BAL.1, 1193; Burleigh and Fitzpatrick-Matthews, *Draft Catalogue*, no. 1187.

51. Museums Resource Centre, Hitchin, Hertfordshire, BAL.1, 3632.

52. Mill Green Museum and Mill, Hatfield, Hertfordshire, HAT.165.1153.69, 68, 71, 72.

53. L. Alcock, *Dinas Powys: An Iron Age, Dark Age and Early Medieval Settlement in Glamorgan* (Cardiff: University of Wales Press, 1963); L. Alcock, *Cadbury Castle, Somerset: The Early Medieval Archaeology* (Cardiff: University of Wales Press, 1995); I. C. G. Burrow, "Roman Material from Hillforts," in P. J. Casey, ed., *The End of Roman Britain*, BAR British Series 71 (Oxford: BAR, 1979), 212–29; P. Rahtz et al., *Cadbury Congresbury 1968–73: A Late/Post-Roman Hilltop Settlement in Somerset*, BAR British Series 223 (Oxford: Tempus Reparatum, 1992); E. Wilkes and F. M. Griffith, "Cadbury Castle, Devon, Reconsidered," *Archaeological Journal*, 169 (2012), 237–80.

54. Rahtz et al., *Cadbury Congresbury*, 227–31.

55. M. Corney, "Cadbury Hill Fort: An Analytical Survey; North Somerset HER2011/041" (unpublished report, North Somerset HER, 2011), 15–16; L. Alcock, "Cadbury-Camelot: A Fifteen-Year Perspective," *Proceedings of the British Academy*, 68 (1982), 355–88, at 367. For a general discussion of roundhouses with bibliography, see R. Pope, "Roundhouses: Three Thousand Years of Prehistoric Design," *Current Archaeology*, 222 (2008), 14–21; R. Bradley, *The Idea of Order: The Circular Archetype in Prehistoric Europe* (Oxford: Oxford University Press, 2012), 189–91.

56. Corney, "Cadbury Hill Fort," 16.

57. For the buildings, see Rahtz et al., *Cadbury Congresbury*, 230–37.

58. Rahtz et al., *Cadbury Congresbury*, 231.

59. Rahtz et al., *Cadbury Congresbury*, 147–54, 230.

60. Rahtz et al., *Cadbury Congresbury*, 148–49 and table 10.

61. Rahtz et al., *Cadbury Congresbury*, 131–39.
62. Rahtz et al., *Cadbury Congresbury*, 132–33.
63. Rahtz et al., *Cadbury Congresbury*, 230; Burrow, "Roman Material from Hillforts," 212–29. A more recent taphonomic study of the site supports Rahtz's arguments (E. Campbell, *Continental and Mediterranean Imports to Atlantic Britain and Ireland, AD 400–800* (York: Council for British Archaeology, 2007), 103).
64. Rahtz et al., *Cadbury Congresbury*, 131–39, 228.
65. Rahtz et al., *Cadbury Congresbury*, 132–33, 137, 228.
66. Rahtz et al., *Cadbury Congresbury*, 228, 230; Price, "Late Roman Glass Vessels in Britain," 5–7. For the prevalence of ceramic and glass vessels in cremation cemeteries in Britain and across the Roman provinces of northwestern Europe, see R. J. H. Pearce, "Case Studies in a Contextual Archaeology of Burial Practice," 2 vols. (Ph.D. diss., University of Durham, 1999), 1:149, 156, 162.
67. Rahtz et al., *Cadbury Congresbury*, 147–48.
68. Cooke, "Definition and Interpretation of Late Roman Burial Rites," 228; E. Biddulph, "Last Orders: Choosing Pottery for Funerals in Roman Essex," *Oxford Journal of Archaeology*, 24 (2005), 23–45.
69. L. Watts and P. Leach, *Henley Wood, Temples and Cemetery Excavations 1962–69 by the Late Ernest Greenfield and Others* (York: Council for British Archaeology, 1996), 85–95.
70. Watts and Leach, *Henley Wood*, 46–75, 146–47, and microfiche nos. 772–75.
71. Rahtz et al., *Cadbury Congresbury*, 134, 161–83.
72. Campbell, *Continental and Mediterranean Imports*, 14–26, 128.
73. Rahtz et al., *Cadbury Congresbury*; 134, 139.
74. K. A. Hemer et al., "Evidence of Early Medieval Trade and Migration Between Wales and the Mediterranean Sea Region," *Journal of Archaeological Science*, 40 (2013), 2352–59.
75. Campbell *Continental and Mediterranean Imports*, 122–28, 132. It was long thought that all the people behind this trade were Byzantine merchants from the eastern Mediterranean. Recent work on Mediterranean wares found at Bordeaux and Vigo, however, now suggests that these wares were transported by merchants whose homes were in France and Spain (M. Duggan, "Ceramic Imports to Britain and the Atlantic Seaboard in the Fifth-Century and Beyond," *Internet Archaeology*, 41 [2016], https://doi.org/10.11141/ia.41.3).
76. R. D. Penhallurick, *Tin in Antiquity: Its Mining and Trading Throughout the Ancient World with Particular Reference to Cornwall* (London: Institute of Metals, 1986), 237; C. J. Slater, "Early Tin Extraction in the South-West of England: A Resource for Mediterranean Metalworkers in Late Antiquity?" in M.M. Mango, ed., *Byzantine Trade, 4th–12th Century* (Aldershot: Routledge, 2009), 315–22. Byzantine interest in sources of tin along the Atlantic seaboard is attested by a late sixth-century Byzantine coin found in an early medieval tin mine at Abbaretz in Brittany (L. Fleuriot and P.-R. Giot, "Early Brittany," *Antiquity*, 51 (1977), 106–16, at 114; Campbell, *Continental and Mediterranean Imports*, 76.
77. Evidence from British peat bogs suggests that tin was heavily exploited in the Roman period, but from the early fifth century until the early eighth century there is little evidence for it (A. A. Meharg et al., "First Comprehensive Peat Depositional Records for Tin, Lead and Copper Associated with the Antiquity of Europe's Largest Cassiterite Deposits," *Journal of Archaeological Science*, 39 [2012], 717–27). Silt deposits, however, from the River Erm, which are dated by radiocarbon dating to between the fourth and the seventh centuries, have elevated amounts of tin (V. R. Thorndycraft, D. Pirrie, and A. G. Brown, "Alluvial Records of Medieval and Pre-Historic Tin Mining on Dartmoor, Southwest England," *Geoarchaeology*, 19 [2004], 219–36, at 233).

78. C. D. Morris and Rachel Harry, "Excavations on the Lower Terrace, Site C, Tintagel Island 1990–4," *Antiquaries Journal*, 77 (1997), 1–143, at 82; S. Reed, P. Bidwell, and J. Allan, "Excavation at Bantham, South Devon, and Post-Roman Trade in South West England," *Medieval Archaeology*, 55 (2011), 82–138, at 129–30.

79. Rahtz et al., *Cadbury Congresbury*, 237, 241–42; Campbell, *Continental and Mediterranean Imports*, 103.

80. J. Rossiter, "Convivium and Villa in Late Antiquity," in W. J. Slater, ed., *Dining in Classical Contexts* (Ann Arbor: University of Michigan Press, 1994), 199–214; K. M. D. Dunbabin, "Convivial Spaces: Dining and Entertainment in the Roman Villa," *Journal of Roman Archaeology*, 9 (1996), 66–80; S. P. Ellis, "Late-Antique Dining: Architecture, Furnishing, and Behaviour," in R. Laurence and A. Wallace-Hadrill, eds., *Domestic Space in the Roman World: Pompeii and Beyond* (Portsmouth, R.I.: Journal of Roman Archaeology, 1997), 41–51.

81. Rahtz et al., *Cadbury Congresbury*, 155 and table 11.

82. There are a number of late coins from the site, including one dated 388–402, as well as the kinds of Roman-style pottery that continued to be produced in the first few decades of the fifth century (P. J. Fowler, "The Excavation of a Settlement of the Fourth and Fifth Centuries AD on Overton Down, West Overton, Wiltshire, FWP64," in P. Fowler, "Fyfield and Overton Project, 1959–1998 [Data-Set]" (unpublished report, Archaeological Data Service, 2000), 20, 22, 35–40, 43–44, http://archaeologydataservice.ac.uk/archives/view/fyfod/downloads_64.cfm.

83. P. J. Fowler, *Landscape Plotted and Pieced: Landscape History and Local Archaeology in Fyfield and Overton, Wiltshire* (London: Society of Antiquaries of London, 2000), 106–11.

84. Fowler, *Landscape Plotted and Pieced*, 106–11.

85. Possible villa sites include Fyfield, Barton Down in Preshute, and "Headlands" (E. Hostetter, "Appendix 1: List of Roman Sites and Finds Plotted on Area Maps," in E. Hostetter and T. N. Howe, eds., *The Romano-British Villa at Castle Copse, Great Bedwyn* [Bloomington: Indiana University Press, 1997], 398–401, at 398–99; Fowler, "Excavation of a Settlement," 228).

86. E. Hostetter, "The Area Around Cunetio in the Roman Period," in Hostetter and Howe, *Romano-British Villa at Castle Copse, Great Bedwyn*, 38–58.

87. Hostetter, "Area Around Cunetio," 46; Fowler, *Landscape Plotted and Pieced*, 228.

88. Mark Corney, "The Origins and Development of the 'Small Town' of 'Cunetio,' Mildenhall, Wiltshire," *Britannia*, 28 (1997), 337–50, at 349.

89. B. C. Burnham and J. Wacher, *The Small Towns of Roman Britain* (Berkeley, Calif: University of California Press, 1990), 149–52.

90. Corney, "Origins and Development," 349.

91. Fowler, *Landscape Plotted and Pieced*, 104. The ceramics found in and around building 4A include pottery that is later than pottery elsewhere on the site (P. J. Fowler, "The Romano-British Pottery from OD XII, FWP71," in P. Fowler, "Fyfield and Overton Project, 1959–1998 (Data-Set)" [unpublished report, Archaeological Data Service, 2000], https://doi.org/10.5284/1000336).

92. Fowler, "Excavation of a Settlement," 57–61 and fig. 27.

93. Price, "Romano-British and Early Post-Roman Glass Vessels," 85. The glass found on rural sites in the late Roman period was sometimes brought in as shards, which were modified to make a sharp cutting instrument (E. Swift, "Reuse of Glass, Pottery, and Copper-Alloy Objects in the Late to Post-Roman Transition Period in Britain," in F. K. Haarer, ed., *AD 410: The History and Archaeology of Late and Post-Roman Britain* [London: Society for the Promotion of Roman Studies, 2014], 130–52, at 138–43).

94. Price, "Late Roman Glass Vessels in Britain," 2.

95. J. Price, personal communication.
96. Fowler, "Excavation of a Settlement," 20.
97. J. Price, personal communication.
98. J. G. Rutter and G. Duke, "Excavations at Crossgates near Scarborough 1947–56," *Scarborough and District Archaeological Society*, 1 (1958), 5–67.
99. See above, n. 55.
100. G. R. Pye, "Excavations at Crossgates, near Scarborough in 1957–65," *Transactions of the Scarborough Archaeological and Historical Society*, 19 (1976), 1–22, at 14. P. Leach, "Crossgates: Archaeological Excavations 1989" (unpublished report, Birmingham University Field Archaeological Unit, 1989), 6; N. Mitchelson, "A Late Fourth-Century Occupation Site at Seamer, Near Scarborough," *Yorkshire Archaeological Journal*, 37 (1950), 42–48.
101. Rutter and Duke, "Excavations at Crossgates," 35–36; J. Evans, "Crambeck: The Development of a Major Northern Pottery Industry," in P.R. Wilson, ed., *The Crambeck Roman Pottery Industry* 43–90. (Leeds: Roman Antiquities Section, Yorkshire Archaeological Society, 1989), 43–90, at 43; P. Bidwell and A. Croom, "The Supply and Use of Pottery on Hadrian's Wall in the 4th Century AD," in Collins and Allason-Jones, *Finds from the Frontier*, 20–36, at 26; M. Whyman "Late Roman Britain in Transition, AD 300–500: A Ceramic Perspective from East Yorkshire" (Ph.D. diss., University of York, 2001), 176. Huntcliff-type wares were not likely to have been produced before 360 (Bidwell and Croom, "Supply and Use of Pottery," 30–34). Crambeck ware, produced on a very small scale in the late third century, was not widely distributed until the mid-fourth century (M. McCarthy, "A Post-Roman Sequence at Carlisle Cathedral," *Archaeological Journal*, 171 [2014], 185–257, at 230–31). Crambeck parchment ware was made from 360 on (P. Bidwell, "The Dating of Crambeck Parchment Ware," *Journal of Roman Pottery Studies*, 12 [2005], 15–21, at 18). Whyman, who has studied what remains of the excavated pottery from Crossgates, stored at the Scarborough Museum, estimates that there are five hundred sherds, and that thirty rim EVEs are represented (Whyman, "Late Roman Britain in Transition," 304–5).
102. P. Booth, "Quantifying Status: Some Pottery Data from the Upper Thames Valley," *Journal of Roman Pottery Studies*, 11 (2004), 39–52, at 39, 44; Whyman, "Late Roman Britain in Transition," 176–77. One of the calcite-gritted-ware fabrics (FC 02) found at Crossgates was also present in the latest occupation levels at Wellington Row in York (Whyman, "Late Roman Britain in Transition," 341).
103. Rutter and Duke, "Excavations at Crossgates," 18.
104. Whyman, "Late Roman Britain in Transition," 341.
105. V. G. Swan, "The Roman Pottery of Yorkshire in Its Wider Historical Context," in P. Wilson and J. Price, eds., *Aspects of Industry in Roman Yorkshire and the North* (Oxford: Oxbow Books, 2002), 35–79, at 71.
106. R. Collins, *Hadrian's Wall and the End of Empire: The Roman Frontier in the 4th and 5th Centuries* (London: Routledge, 2012), 64; Evans, "Crambeck," 77–79.
107. R. G. Collingwood, "The Roman Signal Station," in A. Rowntree, ed., *The History of Scarborough* (London: J. M. Dent and Sons, 1931), 42–50; M. R. Hull, "The Pottery from the Roman Signal-Stations on the Yorkshire Coast," *Archaeological Journal*, 89 (1932), 222–53. For a discussion of the date of these signal stations more generally, see P. Ottaway, "Excavations on the Site of the Roman Signal Station at Carr Naze, Filey, 1993–4," *Archaeological Journal*, 157 (2000), 79–199, at 137–31, 186–88; J. G. F. Hind, "The Watchtowers and Fortlets on the North Yorkshire Coast (*Tures et Castra*)," *Yorkshire Archaeological Journal*, 77 (2005), 17–24, at 22.
108. Whyman, "Late Roman Britain in Transition," 340–41.

109. See, for example, Rutter and Duke, "Excavations at Crossgates," 38–40 and fig. 10; Hull, "Pottery from the Roman Signal-Stations on the Yorkshire Coast," 240–43 and plate 2. Filey, the next signal station south of Scarborough, the excavation of which was published more recently, produced a high percentage of jars—88 percent of the ceramics assemblage—and the animal bones suggest that already-butchered meat was being brought to the site and provide evidence for "organized victualing" (Ottaway, "Excavations on the Site of the Roman Signal Station," 144, 164, 177). Generally, in the north during the late Roman period, the range of ceramic shapes narrowed, and coarse-ware jars and cooking pots dominated (Bidwell and Croom, "Supply and Use of Pottery," 35). For the late Roman date and function of these "signal stations," see Hind, "Watchtowers and Fortlets," 22. For the ways these sites were supplied in the late Roman period by local communities, see Collins, *Hadrian's Wall*, 57–66, 96–98.

110. Whyman, "Late Roman Britain in Transition," 136, 357–62.

111. Excavations ahead of development in 1998–2001, on the side of the modern A64 and a parallel railway line, uncovered a Roman limestone-and-timber building, interpreted as part of a Roman villa, likely dating to the later first and second centuries, as well as the remains of a later building, this one with a tile roof in the same vicinity (English Heritage Pastscape, monument no. 1300420; "Crossgates Farm—Phase II and III, Seamer, N. Yorks" [unpublished report, MAP Archaeological Consultancy, 1999], 12 14–17, 30).

112. Whyman, "Late Roman Britain in Transition," 362, 376.

113. Whyman, "Late Roman Britain in Transition," 376.

114. Pye, "Excavations at Crossgates," 2.

115. H. Hamerow, *Rural Settlements and Society in Anglo-Saxon England* (Oxford: Oxford University Press, 2012), 12–16.

116. Pye, "Excavations at Crossgates," 2, 21 and no. 116; Rutter and Duke, "Excavations at Crossgates," 63–65.

117. Pye, "Excavations at Crossgates," 12, 15, 19–21; Rutter and Duke, "Excavations at Crossgates," 52–56. Something similar happened in the excavation report of nearby Wykeham. The remains of a number of structures were labeled "Anglo-Saxon" by site's excavators, but many appear to have been roundhouses rather than SFBs, that is, sunken-featured buildings, and at least one, in good Roman style, had a paved floor. Only sherds of hand-built pots were found in that structure (Pye, "Excavations at Crossgates," 21 and no. 116). Nearby was a building with mostly hand-built wares, including a small, hand-built pedestal pot in an "Anglo-Saxon" fabric. The remains of late Roman pots were also found in this building, including a small Roman "goblet" made in a fabric similar to the Crambeck sherds found there (J. W. Moore, "An Anglo-Saxon Settlement at Wykeham, North Yorkshire," *Yorkshire Archaeological Journal*, 41 [1965], 403–44, at 408–10). Evidence for yet another possible settlement with roundhouses, which gradually transformed into an "Anglian" settlement, was found at Staxton, four kilometers from Crossgates (T. C. M. Brewster, "Excavations at Newham's Pit, Staxton, 1947–48," *Yorkshire Archaeological Journal*, 154 [1957], 193–223.)

118. Whyman, "Late Roman Britain in Transition," 382; Rutter and Duke, "Excavations at Crossgates," fig. 12, nos. 33/1 and 33/2.

119. Rutter and Duke, "Excavations at Crossgates," 52.

120. Whyman, "Late Roman Britain in Transition," 382–83.

121. Rutter and Duke, "Excavations at Crossgates," 21–33; Pye, "Excavations at Crossgates," 9–22; G. R. Pye, "Further Excavations at Crossgates near Scarborough 1966–81," *Transactions of the Scarborough Archaeological and Historical Society*, 25 (1983), 3–12.

122. Rutter and Duke, "Excavations at Crossgates," 21–33. They specifically associate horse eating with "Anglian" practices, but there is evidence for horse butchery in Roman Yorkshire and beyond (S. Roskams, C. Neal, J. Richardson, and R. Leary, "A Late Roman Well at Heslington East, York: Ritual or Routine Practices?" *Internet Archaeology*, 34 [2013], section 5.1, http://intarch.ac.uk/journal/issue34/5/1.html).

123. Rutter and Duke, "Excavations at Crossgates," 21, 23–27.

124. Episodes of large-scale late Roman or immediately post-Roman animal processing at the Roman fort at Binchester (near Bishop's Auckland) have been uncovered in recent excavations and hint at the size of the demands by, and renders made to, the state in the waning days of Roman Britain (D. Petts, "Military and Civilian: Reconfiguring the End of Roman Britain in the North," *European Journal of Archaeology*, 16 [2013], 314–35, at 319–21; "The Binchester International Field School, Interim Report 2011–12" [unpublished report, Archaeological Services Durham University, no. 2910, 2012], 8–11). Large-scale meat processing was also taking place at late Roman Stonea, a site under state control (R. P. J. Jackson and T. W. Potter, *Excavations at Stonea, Cambridgeshire, 1980–85* [London: British Museum, 1996], 605, 690).

125. Similar post-Roman cooking pits and evidence for feasting have been found at Ingleby Barwick very near a defunct late Roman villa building. Although no residual Roman pottery was found in these pits, radiocarbon dates (at 68 percent probability) suggest fifth- and sixth-century dates (S. Willis and P. Carne, eds., *A Roman Villa at the Edge of Empire: Excavations at Ingleby Barwick, Stockton-on-Tees, 2003–4* [York: Council of British Archaeology, 2013], 54–55). A number of "cooking pits" have also been found at West Heslerton (D. Powlesland, "2.6.8. Sampling," in D. Powlesland, ed., "The West Heslerton Assessment," *Internet Archaeology*, 5 [1990]: https://doi.org/10.11141/ia.5.5). Seven others were found at Gravesend, Kent, which have been dated, archaeomagnetically, to 485–510 and 500–530. In these particular pits, cod and pork were being smoked (M. Gaimster and K. O'Connor, "Medieval Britain and Ireland 2004," *Medieval Archaeology*, 49 [2005], 323–474, at 379). Similar cooking pits have also been uncovered at Wykeham, in Yorkshire (Moore, "Anglo-Saxon Settlement at Wykeham, North Yorkshire," 407–8). Pits were also dug, in the post-Roman phase of the Roman villa at West Park, near Fordingbridge, in Hampshire, into the abandoned villa courtyard (A. T. Morley Hewitt, *Roman Villa West Park, Rockbourne, Hants* [Fordingbridge: Morley Hewitt, 1968], 13. For similar cooking pits and evidence for feasting at Wattle Syke in Yorkshire and Barton Seagrave, in Northamptonshire, see A. Chadwick, "Doorways, Ditches, and Dead Dogs—Excavating and Recording Material Manifestations of Practical Magic Amongst Later Prehistoric and Romano-British Communities," in C. Houlbrook and N. Armitage, eds., *The Materiality of Magic: An Artifactual Investigation into Ritual Practices and Popular Beliefs* (Oxford: Oxbow Books, 2015), 37–64. For a brief discussion of the phenomenon, see Hamerow, *Rural Settlements*, 94–95.

126. They collected these wares almost exclusively, rather than the much more ubiquitous Roman coarse wares and large storage jars, which make up the bulk of pottery finds on late Roman sites (P. Booth, "Roman Pottery," in R. Chambers and E. McAdam, eds., *Excavations at Barrow Hills, Radley, Oxfordshire, 1983–5*, vol. 2, *The Romano British Cemetery and Anglo-Saxon Settlement* [Oxford: Oxford Archaeological Unit, 2007], 33–38, at 36–37; R. Tomber and J. Dore, *The National Roman Fabric Reference Collection: A Handbook* [London: MoLAS, 1998], 176 and plate 147). At Cadbury Congresbury a variety of pots—coarse wares, color coats, and *mortaria*—were all targets of scavenging and used on the site (Rahtz et al., *Cadbury Congresbury*, 148–51).

127. Chambers and McAdam, *Excavations at Barrow Hills*, 7.

128. P. Booth and G. Edgeley-Long, "Prehistoric Settlement and Roman Pottery Production at Backbird Leys, Oxford," *Oxoniensia*, 68 (2003), 201–62, at 258–61.

129. P. Booth, A. Boyle, and G. D. Keevill, "A Romano-British Kiln Site at Lower Farm, Nuneham Courtenay, and Other Sites on the Didcot to Oxford and Wootton to Abingdon Water Mains, Oxfordshire," *Oxoniensia*, 58 (1993), 87–217, at 210.

130. Chambers and McAdam, *Excavations at Barrow Hills*, 29–31.

131. Aside from coins, in Oxfordshire the only ubiquitous grave good in late Roman cemeteries is pottery, generally drinking vessels, especially Oxfordshire color-coated beakers (P. Booth, "Late Roman Cemeteries in Oxfordshire: A Review," *Oxoniensia*, 66 [2001], 13–42, at 34).

132. P. M. Booth, J. Evans, and J. Hiller, *Excavations in the Extramural Settlement of Roman Alchester, Oxfordshire, 1991* (Oxford: Oxford Archaeological Unit, 2001), 103, 377, and fig. 7:57.

133. Booth, "Roman Pottery," 37–38.

134. The bases of footed bowls were preferred at Barrow Hills, as well as at other nearby communities, where Roman pot bases were being modified, including Sutton Courtenay and Audlett Drive (J.W. Moore, "Excavations at Oxford Science Park, Littlemore, Oxford," *Oxoniensia*, 66 [2001], 163–219, at 189). At Oxford Science Park, bowls, dishes, *mortaria*, and flagons were being collected (Moore, "Excavations at Oxford Science Park," 186, 188).

135. Chambers and McAdam, *Excavations at Barrow Hills*, 257.

136. Twelve small circular "counters" were, however, made from the walls of early medieval pots at Radley (although Chambers and McAdam, *Excavations at Barrow Hills*, 257 report the number as three). They are Ashmolean Museum, Radley, Barrow Hills, 4666/A/1 (acc. no. 1238); 4598/B/2 (acc. no. 1190); 1/C/3 (acc. no. 1468); 401/C/2 acc. no. 1475); 400 (acc. no. 1474); 600 (acc. no. 1465); 4558/D/1 (acc. no. 1159); 4459/C/1 (acc. no. 1144); 4001/D/4 (acc. no. 1193); 3441/E/3 (acc. no. 1276); 3288/C/1 (acc. no. 1473); and 600 (acc. no. 1653).

137. Reworked, mostly color-coated pot bases have also been found on early medieval sites in Bedfordshire, Buckinghamshire, Cambridgeshire, Essex, Northamptonshire, Norfolk, and Oxfordshire (C. L. Matthews and S. Chadwick Hawkes, "Early Saxon Settlements and Burials on Puddlehill, near Dunstable, Bedfordshire," *Anglo-Saxon Studies in Archaeology and History*, 4 [1985], 59–115, at 67; M. Farley, "Saxon and Medieval Walton, Aylesbury: Excavations 1973–4," *Records of Buckinghamshire*, 20, part 2 [1976], 153–290, at 164–65; P. T. Marney and R. J. Williams, "Roman Pottery from Saxon Contexts at Pennyland," in R. J. Williams, *Pennyland and Hartigans: Two Iron Age and Saxon Sites in Milton Keynes* [Aylesbury: Buckingham Archaeological Society, 1993], 243–45; C. Gibson with J. Murray, "An Anglo-Saxon Settlement at Godmanchester, Cambridgeshire," *Anglo-Saxon Studies in Archaeology and History*, 12 [2003], 137–217, at 156; N. P. Wickenden, D. B. Harden, R. M. Luff, A. Mainman, and R. Reece, "Early Saxon Settlement Within the Romano-British Small Town at Heybridge, Essex," *Medieval Archaeology*, 26 [1982], 1–40, at 22–23; D. F. Mackreth, *Orton Hall Farm: A Roman and Early Anglo-Saxon Farmstead*, East Anglian Archaeology, 76 [Manchester: Nene Valley Archaeological Trust, 1996], 165, 189–90).

138. For a general discussion of these brooches, see T. M. Dickinson, "Early Saxon Saucer Brooches: A Preliminary Overview," *Anglo-Saxon Studies in Archaeology and History*, 6 (1993), 11–44.

139. T. M. Dickinson, "Material Culture as Social Expression: The Case of Saxon Saucer Brooches with Running Spiral Decorations," *Studien zur Sachsenforschung*, 7 (1991), 39–70, at 60.

140. T. M. Dickinson, "Ornament Variation in Pairs of Cast Saucer Brooches: A Case Study from the Upper Thames Region," in L. Webster, ed., *Aspects of Production and Style in Dark Age Metalwork: Selected Papers Given to the British Museum Seminar on Jewellery AD 500–600* (London: British Museum, 1982), 21–50, at 34–35.

141. Dickinson, "Ornament Variation," 23, 30, and table 2. It has previously been suggested that the templates for some, especially those with a convex profile, were made on lathes, and some,

perhaps, from rounds of leather (T. M. Dickinson, "Discussion," in S. Hirst and D. Clark, *Excavations at Mucking*, vol. 3, *The Anglo-Saxon Cemeteries*, 2 parts [London: MoLAS, 2009], part 2, 482–83; T. M. Dickinson, "Translating Animal Art: Style I and Anglo-Saxon Cast Saucer Brooches," *Hikuin*, 29 [2003], 163–86, at 177).

142. For the basic profiles of saucer brooches, see A. MacGregor and E. Bolick, *Summary Catalogue of the Anglo-Saxon Collections* (Oxford: Ashmolean Museum, 1993), 42.

143. Chambers and McAdam, *Excavations at Barrow Hills*, 258–59. The fifty-five saucer brooches in the Ashmolean catalogued by McGregor and Bolick, for example, range from twenty-seven to seventy-three millimeters (MacGregor and Bolick, *Summary Catalogue*, 42). The Upper Thames Valley examples studied by Tanya Dickinson mostly fall between thirty-two and forty millimeters (T. M. Dickinson, "On the Origins and Chronology of the Early Anglo-Saxon Disc Brooch," *Anglo-Saxon Studies in Archaeology and History*, 1 [1979], 39–80, at 41).

144. P. Williams and R. Newman, *Market Lavington Wiltshire: An Anglo-Saxon Cemetery and Settlement: Excavations at Grove Farm, 1986–90* (Salisbury: Wessex Archaeology, 2006), 92 and fig. 50.2.

CHAPTER 5

Epigraph: S. Brand, *How Buildings Learn: What Happens After They're Built* (London: Penguin Books, 2012), 1.

1. There were, however, a few regions within Britain where stone architecture was more widely adopted (D. Perring, *The Roman House in Britain* [London: Routledge, 2002], 106).

2. S. Esmonde Cleary, "The Countryside of Britain in the 4th and 5th Centuries—an Archaeology," in P. Ouzoulias et al., eds., *Les campagnes de la Gaule à la fin de l'Antiquité* (Antibes: Éditions APDCA, 2001), 23–43, at 32–34.

3. Perring, *Roman House*, 83–98.

4. See above, Chapter 1.

5. A. S. Esmonde Cleary, *The Ending of Roman Britain* (London: B. T. Batsford, 1989), 108; M. Millett, *The Romanization of Britain: An Essay in Archaeological Interpretation* (Cambridge: Cambridge University Press, 1990), 186–99; C. Kelly, *Ruling the Late Roman Empire* (Cambridge, Mass.: Harvard University Press, 2004), 152–85; Kim Bowes, *Houses and Society in the Later Roman Empire* (London: Duckworth, 2010), 61–63, 95–99; A. Smith et al., *The Rural Settlement of Roman Britain* (London: Society for the Promotion of Roman Studies, 2016), fig. 211; L. Revell, *Ways of Being Roman: Discourses of Identity in the Roman West* (Oxford: Oxbow Books, 2016), 73–82.

6. For the basic outlines of these practices, see L. Lancaster, "Roman Engineering and Construction," in J. P. Oleson, ed., *The Oxford Handbook of Engineering and Technology in the Classical World* (Oxford: Oxford University Press, 2008), 256–84.

7. T. Ingold, *Making: Anthropology, Archaeology, Art and Architecture* (London: Routledge, 2013), 48.

8. For this list and a discussion of it, see S. G. Bernard, "Workers in the Roman Imperial Building Industry," in K. Verboven and C. Laes, eds., *Work, Labor, and Professions in the Roman World* (Leiden: Brill, 2016), 62–86, at 81.

9. P. Barresi, *Province dell'Asia Minore: Costo dei marmi, architettura pubblica e committenza* (Rome: L'Erma di Bretschneider, 2003), 51–81; M. McCarthy, *The Romano-British Peasant: Towards a Study of People, Landscapes, and Work During the Roman Occupation of Britain* (Oxford:

Windgather, 2013), 101–7; P. Mills, "The Supply and Distribution of Ceramic Building Material in Roman Britain," in L. Lavan, ed., *Local Economies? Production and Exchange of Inland Regions in Late Antiquity* (Leiden: Brill, 2013), 451–69; R. Taylor, "Labor Force and Execution," in R. B. Ulrich and C. K. Quenemoen, eds., *A Companion to Roman Architecture* (Chichester: John Wiley and Sons, 2014), 193–206, at 197–200, 203.

10. The use of stone for country houses begins in earnest in Britain in the Flavian period but becomes ubiquitous only in the second century (J. Taylor, "The Idea of the Villa: Reassessing Villa Development in South-East Britain," in N. Roymans and T. Derks, eds., *Villa Landscapes in the North: Economy, Culture and Lifestyles* [Amsterdam: Amsterdam University Press, 2011], 179–94, at 181).

11. J. DeLaine, "Brick and Mortar: Exploring the Economics of Building Techniques at Rome and Ostia," in D. J. Mattingly and J. Salmon, eds., *Economies Beyond Agriculture in the Classical World* (New York: Routledge, 2001), 230–68; S. J. Baker, "Roman Builders—Pillagers or Salvagers? The Economics of Deconstruction and Reuse," in S. Camporeale, H. Dessales, and A. Pizzo, eds., *Arqueología de la construcción II. Los procesos constuctivos en el mundo romano: Italia y provincias orientales* (Madrid: Anejos de Archivo Español de Arqueologia, 2010), 127–42; S. J. Baker, "Nineteenth-Century Labor Figures for Demolition: A Theoretical Approach to Understanding the Economics of Reuse," *TRAC 2010* (2011), 89–101; S. J. Baker and B. Russell, "Labor Figures for Roman Stone-Working: Pitfalls and Potentials," in S. Camporeale, H. Dessales, and A. Pizzo, eds., *Arqueología de la Construcción III. Los procesos constructivos en el mundo romano: La economía de las obras* (Madrid: Anejos de Archivo Español de Arqueologia, 2012), 83–94; S. J. Baker and Y. A. Marano, "Demolition Laws in an Archaeological Context: Legislation and Architectural Re-Use in the Roman Building Industry," in P. Pensabene, M. Milella, and F. Caprioli, *Decor—Decorazione e architettura nel mondo romano* (Rome: Thiasos Monografie, 2017), 833–50; R. Coates-Stephens, "*Muri dei bassi secoli* in Rome: Observations on the Re-Use of Statuary in Walls Found on the Esquiline and Caelian after 1870," *Journal of Roman Archaeology*, 14 (2001), 217–38; D. Underwood, "Reuse as Archaeology: A Test Case for Late Antique Building Chronologies in Ostia," in L. Lavan and M. Mulryan, eds., *Field Methods and Post-Excavation Techniques in Late Antique Archaeology* (Leiden: Brill, 2013), 383–409.

12. There is evidence for this at the villas at Houghton Down, Fullerton, and Star (B. Cunliffe and C. Poole, *The Danebury Environs Roman Programme, a Wessex Landscape During the Roman Era*, vol. 2, part 1, *Houghton Down, Longstock, Hants, 1997* [Oxford: Oxford University Committee for Archaeology, 2008], 34, 46, and 117; B. Cunliffe and C. Poole, *The Danebury Environs Roman Programme, a Wessex Landscape During the Roman Era*, vol. 2, part 3, *Fullerton, Hants, 2000 and* 2001 [Oxford: English Heritage and Oxford University School of Archaeology, 2008], 71; K. J. Barton, "Star Roman Villa, Shipham, Somerset," *Proceedings of the Somerset Archaeology and Natural History Society*, 108 [1964], 45–93, at 66).

13. T. F. C. Blagg, "The Reuse of Monumental Masonry in Late Roman Defensive Walls," in J. Maloney and B. Hobley, eds., *Roman Urban Defences in the West* (London: Council for British Archaeology, 1983), 130–35, at 130–31; T. F. C. Blagg, "Building Stone in Roman Britain," in D. Parsons, ed., *Stone Quarrying and Building in England, AD 43–1525* (Chichester: Phillimore, 1990), 33–50, at 40; C. Hill, M. Millett, and T. Blagg, *The Roman Riverside Wall and Monumental Arch in London: Excavations at Baynard's Castle, Upper Thames Street, London, 1974–76* (London: London and Middlesex Archaeological Society, 1980), 125–200; G. Parnell, "The Roman and Medieval Defences and the Later Development of the Inmost Ward, Tower of London: Excavations 1955–77," *Transactions of the London and Middlesex Archaeological Society*, 36 (1985), 1–79, at 13, 16, 67–68; J. Maloney, "Recent Work on London's Defences," in Maloney and Hobley, *Roman*

Defences, 96–117, at 105, 108–10, and fig. 103; A. Birley and J. Blake, *Vindolanda Research Report: The Excavations of 2005–6* (Durham: Vindolanda Trust, 2007), fig. 58.

14. I. M. Betts, "Procuratorial Tile Stamps from London," *Britannia*, 26 (1995), 207–29, at 219; I. M. Betts, "The Supply of Tile to Roman London," in D. Bird, ed., *Agriculture and Industry in South-Eastern Roman Britain* (Oxford: Oxbow Books, 2017), 368–83, at 377; T. Williams, *The Archaeology of Roman London III: Public Buildings in the South-West Quarter of Roman London* (London: Council for British Archaeology, 1993), 89–91; R. Bluer, T. Brigham, and R. Nielsen, *Roman and Later Development East of the Forum and Cornhill: Excavations at Lloyd's Register, 71 Fenchurch Street, City of London* (London: MoLAS, 2006), 51.

15. Betts, "Procuratorial Tile Stamps," 220.

16. For examples from wells, see M. Napthan, "1 the Butts," in S. Butler and R. Cutler, eds., *Life and Industry in the Suburbs of Roman Worcester*, BAR British Series 533 (Oxford: Archaeopress, 2011), 27–42, at 30; A. Pickstone and J. Drummond-Murray, "A Late Roman Well or Cistern and Ritual Deposition at Bretton Way, Peterborough," *Proceedings of the Cambridge Antiquarian Society*, 102 (2013), 37–66, at 42–45, 59. For examples from hypocausts, see V. L. Gaffney and R. H. White, *Wroxeter, the Cornovii, and the Urban Process: Final Report on the Wroxeter Hinterland Project 1994–1997*, vol. 1, *Researching the Hinterland* (Portsmouth, R.I.: Journal of Roman Archaeology, 2007), 108–9, and figs. 4.29, 4.3); S. Frere, *Verulamium Excavations*, 2 vols. (London: Society of Antiquaries of London, 1972–84), 2:98, plate XIIa; A. S. Mellor and R. Goodchild, "The Roman Villa at Atworth, Wilts.," *Wiltshire Archaeological and Natural History Magazine*, 49 (1940–42), 46–95, at 57; V. Crosby and L. Muldowney, "Stanwick Quarry, Northamptonshire: Raunds Area Project Phasing the Iron Age and Romano-British Settlements at Stanwick, Northamptonshire (Excavations 1984–1992)," vol. 1 (unpublished report, English Heritage Research Department Report Series no. 54–2011, 2013), 3, 99. For an example from a corn drier, see P. Andrews et al., *Settling the Ebbsfleet Valley: High Speed 1 Excavations at Springhead and Northfleet, Kent; The Late Iron Age, Roman, Saxon, and Medieval Landscape*, vol. 1, *The Sites* (Oxford: Oxford Wessex Archaeology, 2011), 184.

17. S. Willis and P. Carne, eds., *A Roman Villa at the Edge of Empire: Excavations at Ingleby Barwick, Stockton-on-Tees, 2003–4* (York: Council of British Archaeology, 2013), 39, 52, 169.

18. P. Wilkinson, "An Archaeological Investigation of the Roman Aisled Stone Building at Hog Brook, Deerton Street, Faversham, Kent 2004–5" (unpublished report, Kent Archaeological Field School, 2009, 5, 26–28, 35), https://doi.org/10.5284/1030489.

19. Brand, *How Buildings Learn*, 110–31; C. R. Lounsbury, "Architecture and Cultural History," in D. Hicks and M. C. Beaudry, eds., *The Oxford Handbook of Material Culture Studies* (Oxford: Oxford University Press, 2010), 484–501, at 485.

20. G. D. Keevill, "The Reconstruction of the Romano-British Villa at Redlands Farm, Northamptonshire," in P. Johnson and I. Hayes, eds., *Architecture in Roman Britain* (York: Council of British Archaeology, 1996), 44–55.

21. B. Walters and B. Phillips, *Archaeological Excavations in Littlecote Park, Wiltshire 1979 and 80: Second Interim Report* (Littlecote: Littlecote Roman Research Trust, 1981), 6–8; S. R. Cosh and D. S. Neal, *Roman Mosaics of Britain*, vol. 2, *South-West Britain* (London: Society of Antiquaries of London, 2005), 350–56.

22. Crosby and Muldowney, "Stanwick."

23. R. J. Williams and R. J. Zeepvat, *Bancroft: A Late Bronze Age/Iron Ages Settlement, Roman Villa, and Temple-Mausoleum*, 2 vols. (Aylesbury: Buckinghamshire Archaeological Society, 1994), 1:211.

24. G. Webster and L. Smith, "The Excavation of a Romano-British Rural Establishment at Barnsley Park, Gloucestershire, 1961–1979: Part II c. AD 260–400 +," *Transactions of the Bristol and Gloucestershire Archaeological Society*, 100 (1982), 65–189, at 91–93.

25. E. Price, *Frocester: A Romano-British Settlement, Its Antecedents and Successors*, vol. 1, *The Sites* (Stonehouse, Gloucestershire: Gloucester and District Archaeological Research Group, 2000), 98–99, 111.

26. D. J. Smith, L. Hird, and B. Dix, "The Roman Villa at Great Weldon, Northamptonshire," *Northamptonshire Archaeology*, 22 (1988–89), 23–67, at 33, 61, and fig. 3.

27. A. Birley, *The Vindolanda Granary Excavations* (Brampton: Roman Army Museum Publications, 2013), 23–29.

28. D. F. Laefer and J. P. Manke, "Building Reuse Assessment for Sustainable Urban Reconstruction," *Journal of Construction Engineering and Management*, 134 (2008), 217–27.

29. M. Corney, *The Roman Villa at Box: The Story of the Extensive Romano-British Structures Buried Below the Village of Box in Wiltshire* (Salisbury: Hobnob, 2012), 52–53, 57–73.

30. Columella, Lucius Iunius Moderatus. *Res Rustica, Books 4–9*, vol. 2, trans. E. S. Forster and E. H. Heffner (Cambridge, Mass.: Harvard University Press, 1954), 6.1–23.

31. For examples, see Perring, *Roman House*, 44–45; A. Down. *Chichester Excavations 4: The Roman Villas at Chilgrove and Upmarden* (Chichester: Phillimore, 1979), 68; P. Martin and S. Driscoll, "Excavation of a Romano-British Site, Butleigh, Somerset Season One 2009" (unpublished report, Absolute Archaeology, 2009), 16, https://doi.org/10.5284/1029089.

32. For examples, see J. G. P. Erskine and P. Ellis, "Excavations at Atworth Roman Villa, Wiltshire 1970–1975," *Wiltshire Archaeological and Natural History Magazine*, 101 (2008), 51–129, at 65; "Butleigh Roman Villa Investigation 2005–2011" (unpublished report, Absolute Archaeology, no date), http://www.butleigh.org/images/2010%20excavation.pdf.

33. Webster and Smith, "Excavation of a Romano-British Rural Settlement at Barnsley Park: Part II," 93–94; Price, *Frocester*, 1:93, 111.

34. Erskine and Ellis, "Excavations at Atworth," 65; B. Cunliffe, *The Roman Villa at Brading, Isle of Wight: The Excavations of 2008–10* (Oxford: Oxford University Committee for Archaeology, 2013), 105; A. King with C. Grande, "Dinnington and Yarford: Two Roman Villas in South and West Somerset," in M. Henig, G. Soffe, and K. Adcock, eds., *Villas, Sanctuaries and Settlement in the Romano-British Countryside: New Perspectives and Controversies* (Oxford: Oxbow Books, forthcoming).

35. D. Ingham, J. Oetgen, and A. Slowikowski, *Newnham: A Roman Bath House and Estate Centre East of Bedford*, East Anglian Archaeology 158 (Bedford: Albion Archaeology, 2016), 50, 54–55; D. Petts, "Late Roman Military Buildings at Binchester (Co. Durham)," in R. Collins, M. Symonds, and M. Weber, eds., *Roman Military Architecture on the Frontiers: Armies and Their Architecture in Late Antiquity* (Oxford: Oxbow Books, 2015), 32–45, at 43.

36. L. C. Hayward, "The Roman Villa at Lufton, near Yeovil," *Proceedings of the Somerset Archaeology and Natural History Society*, 116 (1972), 59–77, at 61; E. Hostetter and T. N. Howe, *The Romano-British Villa at Castle Copse, Great Bedwyn* (Bloomington: Indiana University Press, 1997), 82; A. C. C. Brodribb, A. R. Hands, and D. R. Walker, *The Roman Villa at Shakenoak Farm, Oxfordshire Excavations, 1960–76*, BAR British Series 395 (Oxford: Archaeopress, 2005), 4.

37. A. Rogers, *Late Roman Towns in Britain: Rethinking Change and Decline* (Cambridge: Cambridge University Press, 2011), 130–40.

38. J. Taylor and M. Flitcroft, "The Roman Period," in M. Tingle, ed., *The Archaeology of Northamptonshire* (Northampton, 2004), 63–77, at 67; "Piddington," *Current Archaeology*, 46

(1996), 61–62; S. Lawrence and P. Booth, "Iron Age Settlement and Roman Villa at Thurnham, Kent" (unpublished report, Oxford Wessex Archaeology Joint Venture, 2006), 102, 104, https://doi.org/10.5284/1008824.

39. G. Ripoll and J. Arce, "The Transformation and End of Roman *Villae* in the West (Fourth–Seventh Centuries): Problems and Perspectives," in G. P. Brogiolo, N. Gauthier, and N. Christie, *Towns and Their Territories Between Late Antiquity and the Early Middle Ages* (Leiden: Brill, 2000), 63–114; T. Lewit, "'Vanishing Villas': What Happened to Élite Rural Habitation in the West in the 5th–6th C?" *Journal of Roman Archaeology*, 16 (2003), 260–74; T. Lewit, "Bones in the Bathhouse: Re-Evaluating the Notion of 'Squatter Occupation' in 5th–7th Century Villas," in G. P. Brogiolo, M. Valenti, and A. Chavarría Arnau, eds., *Dopo la fine delle ville: Le campagne dal VI al IX secolo* (Mantua: Societá Archeologica, 2005), 251–62; A. Chavarría Arnau, "Transformaciones arquitectónicas de los establecimientos rurales en el nordeste de la Tarraconensis durante la antigüedad tardía," *Butlletí de la Reial Acadèmia Catalana de Belles Arts de Sant Jordi*, 10 (1996), 165–202, A. Chavarría Arnau, "Interpreting the Transformation of Late Roman Villas: The Case of Hispania," in N. Christie, ed., *Landscapes of Change: Rural Evolutions in Late Antiquity and the Early Middle Ages* (Aldershot: Ashgate, 2004), 67–102; and A. Chavarría Arnau, "Villas in Hispania during the Fourth and Fifth Centuries," in K. Bowes and M. Kulikowski, eds., *Hispania in Late Antiquity: Current Perspectives* (Leiden: Brill, 2005), 519–52.

40. Chavarría Arnau, "Transformaciones arquitectónicas"; Chavarría Arnau, "Interpreting the Transformation of Late Roman Villas"; Lewit, "Vanishing Villas"; Lewit, "Bones in the Bathhouse"; Rogers, *Late Roman Towns*.

41. For the social use of these spaces before such transformations, see K. M. D. Dunbabin, "Convivial Spaces: Dining and Entertainment in the Roman Villa," *Journal of Roman Archaeology*, 9 (1996), 66–80; S. P. Ellis, "Power, Architecture, and Decor: How the Late Roman Aristocrat Appeared to His Guests," in E. K. Gazda, ed., *Roman Art in the Private Sphere: New Perspectives on the Architecture and Decor of the Domus, Villa, and Insula* (Ann Arbor: University of Michigan Press, 1991), 117–34.

42. For a dramatic example, see Binchester (D. Petts, "Military and Civilian: Reconfiguring the End of Roman Britain in the North," *European Journal of Archaeology*, 16 (2013), 314–35, at 319–22.

43. B. Munro, "Recycling in Late Roman Villas in Southern Italy: Reappraising Hearths and Kilns in Final Occupation Phases," *Mouseion*, 10 (2010), 217–43; B. Munro, "Approaching Architectural Recycling in Roman and Late Roman Villas," *TRAC 2010* (2011), 76–88; B. Munro, "Recycling, Demand for Materials, and Landownership at Villas in Italy and the Western Provinces in Late Antiquity," *Journal of Roman Archaeology*, 25 (2012), 351–70.

44. For a detailed analysis of these late floors and walls, see R. Fleming, "Old Buildings, Building Material, and the Death of Recycling in Post-Roman Britain," in C. Duckworth and A. Wilson, eds., *Ancient Recycling* (Oxford: Oxford University Press, forthcoming).

45. *Opus signinum*, made from crushed tile and mortar, was a kind of cement commonly used in Roman-period construction.

46. For examples, see G. D. Keevill, D. C. A. Shotter, and M. R. McCarthy, "A Solidus of Valentinian II from Scotch Street, Carlisle," *Britannia*, 20 (1989), 254–55, at 254; Birley and Blake, *Vindolanda Research Report*, 49; I. Ferris, *The Beautiful Rooms Are Empty: Excavations at Binchester Roman Fort, County Durham 1976–1981 and 1986–1991*, 2 parts (Durham: Durham County Council, 2010), part 1, 76.

47. For example, at Carlisle, Scotch Street (Keevill, Shotter, and McCarthy, "Solidus of Valentinian," 254–55; R. Collins, *Hadrian's Wall and the End of Empire: The Roman Frontier in the

4th and 5th Centuries [London: Routledge, 2012], 122); and at Chesters villa, in Worcestershire (C. S. Garrett, "Chesters Roman Villa, Woolaston, Gloucestershire," *Archaeologia Cambrensis*, 93 [1938], 93–125).

48. Webster and Smith, "Excavation of a Romano-British Rural Settlement at Barnsley Park: Part II," 65–189, at 93 and plate 1a.

49. For Bath, see B. Cunliffe and P. Davenport, *The Temple of Sulis Minerva at Bath*, vol. 1, *The Site* (Oxford: Oxford University Committee for Archaeology, 1985), 68–72 and plate XXVIIb. For the dating of these events, see J. Gerrard, "The Temple of Sulis Minerva at Bath and the End of Roman Britain," *Antiquaries Journal*, 87 (2007), 148–64. For Maiden Castle, see R. E. M. Wheeler, *Maiden Castle, Dorset* (Oxford: Society of Antiquaries of London, 1943), 75, 133. For Atworth, see Mellor and Goodchild, "Roman Villa at Atworth," 54. For Bucknowle, see T. Light and P. Ellis, *Bucknowle: A Romano-British Villa and Its Antecedents; Excavations 1976–1991* (Dorchester: Dorchester Natural History and Archaeology Society, 2009), 45.

50. R. C. Bosanquet, "Excavations at Housesteads," *Proceedings of the Society of Antiquaries of Newcastle upon Tyne*, 8 (1897–98), 247–54, at 248; A. Rushworth, *Housesteads Roman Fort— the Grandest Station*, vol. 1, *Structural Report and Discussion* (London: English Heritage, 2009), 321–22; J. Crow, *Housesteads: A Fort and Garrison on Hadrian's Wall*, 3rd ed. (Stroud: Tempus, 2004), fig. 59.

51. E. Biddulph, G. D. Keevill, and I. R. Scott, "Redlands Farm, Stanwick, Northamptonshire SP 960705: The Roman Evidence," vol. 1, "Text" (unpublished report, Oxford Archaeology, 2002), 68–89.

52. Wilmott, T., *Birdoswald: Excavations of a Roman Fort on Hadrian's Wall and Its Successor Settlements; 1987–92* (London: English Heritage, 1997), 205, 212, plate 8, and fig. 143

53. For examples, see Fleming, "Old Buildings."

54. Fleming, "Old Buildings."

55. Most stone walls in Britain in the Roman period were built in this fashion (Perring, *Roman House*, 108). Large-scale construction of this type of wall was still being undertaken in the 380s and 390s, as the defensive walls at both London and Cunetio make clear. For London, see Hill, Millett, and Blagg, *Roman Riverside Wall*; Maloney, "Recent Work on London's Defences," 105, 108–10, and fig. 103; Williams, *Archaeology of Roman London III*, 89–91. For the walls at Cunetio and their dating, see M. Corney, "The Origins and Development of the 'Small Town' of 'Cunetio', Mildenhall, Wiltshire," *Britannia* 28 (1997), 337–50, at 348; T. S. N. Moorhead, "A Reappraisal of the Roman Coins Found in J. W. Brooke's Excavation of a Late Roman Well at Cunetio (Mildenhall), 1912," *Wiltshire Archaeological and Natural History Magazine*, 90 (1997), 42–54, at 48; R. S. Smith, "Cunetio Roman Town, Mildenhall, Marlborough, Wiltshire: Archaeological Evaluation and Assessment of Results" (unpublished report, Wessex Archaeology, 2011), 9–10, https://doi.org/10.5284/1039726.

56. Parnell, "Roman and Medieval Defences," 15–16, 67–68.

57. Fleming, "Old Buildings." A particularly good example of such walls is found at Gatcombe Building 13/14 (K. Branigan, *Gatcombe Roman Villa*, BAR British Series 44 [Oxford: BAR, 1977], 23–28, 154–56).

58. B. Cunliffe and C. Poole, *The Danebury Environs Roman Programme, a Wessex Landscape During the Roman Era*, vol. 2, part 3, *Fullerton, Hants, 2000 and 2001* (Oxford: English Heritage and Oxford University School of Archaeology, 2008), 69.

59. Frere, *Verulamium*, 96 and plate Xb. Small-scale industrial features made from odd assortments of recycled material can be found, among other places, at Lufton, Nettelton, Atworth, and Rivenhall (Hayward, "Roman Villa at Lufton," 63; W. J. Wedlake, *The Excavation of the Shrine*

of Apollo at Nettleton, Wiltshire, 1956–1971 [London: Society of Antiquaries of London, 1982], 82; Erskine and Ellis, "Excavations at Atworth," 65; W. J. Rodwell and K. A. Rodwell, *Rivenhall: Investigations of a Roman Villa, Church, and Village, 1950–1977*, 2 vols. [London: Chelmsford Archaeological Trust and the Council for British Archaeology, 1985–93], 1:58–59).

60. Fleming, "Old Buildings."
61. Erskine and Ellis, "Excavations at Atworth," 63.
62. Mellor and Goodchild, "Roman Villa at Atworth," plate IX.
63. Mellor and Goodchild, "Roman Villa at Atworth," 11; Erskine and Ellis, "Excavations at Atworth," 65.
64. Erskine and Ellis, "Excavations at Atworth," 65.
65. Mellor and Goodchild, "Roman Villa at Atworth," 52.
66. Erskine and Ellis, "Excavations at Atworth," 65, 71, 73, 94, 102–3.
67. D. Wilson, A. Bagnall, and B. Taylor, *Report on the Excavation of a Romano-British Site in Wortley, South Gloucestershire*, BAR British Series 591 (Oxford: Archaeopress, 2014), 51 and plate 52.
68. M. Atkinson and S. Preston, "Heybridge, a Late Iron Age and Roman Settlement: Excavations at Elms Farm 1993–5, Volume 2," *Internet Archaeology*, 40 (2015), 2.7, period 6, https://doi.org/10/11141/ia.40.1. Hucclecote villa, in Gloucester, also has a very late tessellated floor. It is dated to after 395 (E. M. Clifford, "The Roman Villa, Hucclecote near Gloucester," *Transactions of the Bristol and Gloucestershire Archaeological Society*, 55 [1933], 323–76, at 329).
69. A. Sargent, "Early Medieval Lichfield: A Reassessment," *Transactions Staffordshire Archaeological and History Society*, 46 (2013), 1–32, at 7–12.
70. For deskilling more generally, see T. Mannoni, "The Transmission of Craft Techniques According to the Principles of Material Culture: Continuity and Rupture," in L. Lavan, E. Zanini, and A. Sarantis, eds., *Technology in Transition AD 300–650* (Leiden: Brill, 2008), xli–lx.
71. Brand, *How Buildings Learn*, 114–15.
72. Fleming, "Old Buildings."
73. Webster and Smith, "Excavation of a Romano-British Rural Settlement at Barnsley Park: Part II," 97; Biddulph, Keevill, and Scott, "Redlands Farm, Stanwick, Northamptonshire," 48; J. Gerrard, "Demolishing Roman Britain," in L. Rakoczy, ed., *The Archaeology of Destruction* (Newcastle: Cambridge Scholars, 2008), 176–94, at 189; Down, *Chichester Excavations 4*, 96; B. Cunliffe and C. Poole, *The Danebury Environs Roman Programme, a Wessex Landscape During the Roman Era*, vol. 2, part 2, *Grateley South, Grateley, Hants, 1998 and 1999* (Oxford: School of Archaeology, 2008), 53; B. Cunliffe, *The Danebury Environs Roman Programme, a Wessex Landscape During the Roman Era*, vol. 1, *Overview* (Oxford: English Heritage and Oxford University School of Archaeology, 2008), 185.
74. S. G. Upex, "Excavations at a Roman and Saxon Site at Haddon, Cambridgeshire, 1992–1993: SMR 8c817801" (unpublished report, 1994); A. Woodward and P. Leach, *The Uley Shrines: Excavation of a Ritual Complex on West Hill, Uley, Gloucestershire; 1977–9* (London: British Museum, 1993), 63.
75. K. Branigan, *Latimer: Belgic, Roman, Dark Age, and Early Modern Farm* (Dorchester: Chess Valley Archaeological and Historical Society, 1971), 94; Hostetter and Howe, *Romano-British Villa at Castle Copse*, 93–94.
76. N. Holbrook, "Ambiguous Evidence and Obscured Stratigraphy: Interpreting the Archaeology of Late Roman and Early Post-Roman Cirencester," in H. Eckhardt and S. Rippon, eds., *Living and Working in the Roman World: Essays in Honour of Michael Fulford on His 65th Birthday* (Portsmouth, R.I.: Journal of Roman Archaeology, 2013), 31–46, at 37–39; Price, *Frocester*, 113.

77. Wilkinson, "Archaeological Investigation of the Roman Aisled Stone Building at Hog Brook," 27–29.

78. This should be compared to the very large-scale campaign of pragmatic recycling of Roman building material in late antique Ravenna (E. Cirelli, "Spolia e riuso di materiali tra la tarda antichità e l'alto medioevo a Ravenna," *Hortus Artium Medievalium*, 17 [2011], 39–48), or in the early mosques of Syria (M. Guidetti, *In the Shadow of the Church: The Building of Mosques in Early Medieval Syria* [Leiden: Brill, 2017], 97–123).

79. J. Haslam et al., "A Middle Saxon Iron Smelting Site at Ramsbury, Wiltshire," *Medieval Archaeology*, 24 (1980), 1–68, at 55; S. E West, *West Stow: The Anglo-Saxon Village*, 2 vols., East Anglian Archaeology 24 (Ipswich: Suffolk County Planning Department, 1985), 1:57–81; R. J. Williams, *Pennyland and Hartigans: Two Iron Age and Saxon Sites in Milton Keynes* (Aylesbury: Buckinghamshire Archaeological Society, 1993), 125; L. Blackmore, D. Bowsher, R. Cowie, and G. Malcolm, "Royal Opera House," *Current Archaeology*, 158 (1998), 60–63, at 62; D. H. Evans and C. Loveluck, eds., *Life and Economy at Early Medieval Flixborough, c. AD 600–1000: The Artefact Evidence* (Oxford: Oxbow Books, 2009), 442; S. Lucy, J. Tipper, and A. Dickens, *The Anglo-Saxon Settlement and Cemetery at Bloodmoor Hill, Carlton Colville, Suffolk*, East Anglian Archaeology 131 (Cambridge: Cambridge Archaeological Unit 2009), 34, 428; S. Anderson, "Ceramic Building Material," in S. Peel, K. Collis, and H. Chapman, *Living with the Flood: Mesolithic to Post-Medieval Archaeological Remains at Mill Lane, Sawston, Cambridgeshire—a Wetland/Dryland Interface* (Oxford: Oxbow Books, 2016), 54.

80. M. U. Jones, "Metallurgical Finds from a Multi-Period Settlement at Mucking, Essex," in W. A. Oddy, ed., *Aspects of Early Metallurgy* (London: British Museum, 1980), 117–20; R. Hall, *The Viking Dig: The Excavations at York* (London: Bodley Head, 1984), 56–57.

81. L. Alcock, *Cadbury Castle, Somerset: The Early Medieval Archaeology* (Cardiff: University of Wales Press, 1995), 140–41.

82. P. M. Barford, *Excavations at Little Oakley, Essex, 1951–78: Roman Villa and Saxon Settlement*, East Anglian Archaeology 98 (Chelmsford: Essex County Council, 2002), 194–97; E. Price, *Frocester*, 93, 111–13.

83. For a detailed look at other of the period's well deposits, see R. Fleming, "The Ritual Recycling of Roman Building Material in Late Fourth- and Early Fifth-Century Britain," *European Journal of Post-Classical Archaeologies*, 6 (2016), 7–31.

84. See below, Chapter 4, "Old Things and Old Ways."

85. Fleming, "Ritual Recycling of Roman Building Material."

86. M. Hammerson, "Excavations Under Southwark Cathedral," *London Archaeologist*, 3 (1978), 206–12, at 209.

87. M. Maltby, "The Animal Bones from a Romano-British Well at Oakridge II, Basingstoke," *Proceedings of the Hampshire Field Club and Archaeology Society*, 49 (1993), 47–76, at 59; J. Lovell, "Excavation of a Romano-British Farmstead at RNAS Yeovilton," *Somerset Archaeology and Natural History*, 149 (2006), 7–70, at 64.

88. K. Branigan, "The Romano-British Villa at Brislington," *Somerset Archaeology and Natural History*, 116 (1972), 78–85, at 84.

89. B. Yule, "A Third Century Well Group, and the Later Roman Settlement in Southwark," *London Archaeologist*, 4 (1982), 243–49, at 248.

90. M. Oliver, "Excavation of an Iron Age and Romano-British Settlement Site at Oakridge, Basingstoke, Hampshire, 1965–6," *Proceedings of the Hampshire Field Club and Archaeological Society*, 48 (1992), 55–94, at 76; Maltby, "Animal Bones from a Romano-British Well," 61–62.

91. J. Richardson, "Rothwell Haigh, Rothwell Leeds West Yorkshire: Excavation Report" (unpublished report, West Yorkshire Archaeological Services, nos. 2170, 2011), 79, https://doi.org/10.5284/1008593); D. Garrow, "Odd Deposits and Average Practice: A Critical History of the Concept of Structured Deposition," *Archaeological Dialogues*, 19 (2012), 85–115; M. Maltby, "Zooarchaeology and the Interpretation of Depositions in Shafts," in J. Morris and M. Maltby, eds., *Integrating Social and Environmental Archaeologies: Reconsidering Deposition*, BAR International Series 2077 (Oxford: Archaeopress, 2010), 24–32. Wells decommissioned earlier in the Roman period were sometimes transformed into pits, which then served as sites of ritual deposition over many generations (J. M. Grimm, "A Dog's Life: Animal Bones from a Romano-British Ritual Shaft at Springhead, Kent (UK)," in N. Benecke, ed., *Beiträge zur Archäozoologie und Prähistorischen Anthropologie*, vol. 6 [Langenweissbach: Beier and Beran, 2007], 54–75).

92. For the basic readings on the subject, see A. Ross, "Shafts, Pits, Wells—Sanctuaries of the Belgic Britons?" in J. M. Coles and D. D. A. Simpson, eds., *Studies in Ancient Europe: Essays Presented to Stuart Piggott* (Leicester: Leicester University Press, 1968), 255–85; M. Millett and D. Graham, *Excavations on the Romano-British Small Town at Neatham, Hampshire 1969–1979* (Gloucester: Hampshire Field Club, 1986), 159; R. Merrifield, *The Archaeology of Ritual and Magic* (New York: New Amsterdam, 1988), 22, 45–50; R. Poulton and E. Scott, "The Hoarding, Deposition, and Use of Pewter in Roman Britain," *Theoretical Roman Archaeology Journal*, 1 (1991), 115–32; S. Clarke, "Abandonment, Rubbish Disposal and 'Special' Deposits at Newstead," *TRAC 1996* (1997), 73–81, at 75; M. Fulford, "Links with the Past: Pervasive 'Ritual' Behaviour in Roman Britain," *Britannia*, 32 (2001), 199–218; E. Black, "Pagan Religion in Rural South-East Britain: Contexts, Deities, and Beliefs," in D. Rudling, ed., *Ritual Landscapes of Roman South-East Britain* (Oxford: Oxbow Books, 2008), 1–25; F. Seeley and A. Wardle, "Ritual Deposits in Wells and Pits," in C. Cowan et al., *Roman Southwark, Settlement and Economy: Excavations in Southwark 1973–1991* (London: MoLAS, 2009), 143–57; J. Gerrard, "Wells and Belief Systems at the End of Roman Britain: A Case Study from Roman London," in L. Lavan and M. Mulryan, eds., *The Archaeology of Late Antique "Paganism"* (Leiden: Brill, 2011), 551–72; N. Collie, "Ritualising Encounters with Subterranean Places: An Investigation of Urban Depositional Practices of Roman Britain" (Ph.D. diss., University of Tasmania, 2013), 39–62, 78–79; S. Roskams et al., "A Late Roman Well at Heslington East, York: Ritual or Routine Practice?" *Internet Archaeology*, 34 (2013), http://dx.doi.org/10.11141/ia.34.5; H. E. M. Cool and J. E. Richardson, "Exploring Ritual Deposits in a Well at Rothwell Haigh, Leeds," *Britannia*, 44 (2013), 191–217, at 192; I. Haynes, "Advancing the Systematic Study of Ritual Deposition in the Greco-Roman World," in A. Schäfer and M. Witteyer, eds., *Rituelle Deponierungen in Heiligtümern der Hellenistisch-Römischen Welt* (Mainz: Generaldirektion Kulturelles Erbe Rheinland-Pfalz, 2013), 7–20.

93. A. B. Powell, *An Iron Age Enclosure and Romano-British Features at High Post, near Salisbury* (Salisbury: Wessex Archaeology, 2011), 31, 61.

94. N. Cooke and A. B. Powell, "Prehistoric Settlement and a Romano-British Pottery Production Site at Groom's Farm, Frithend, Hampshire Ref 59794" (unpublished report, Wessex Archaeology, 2012), 47, http://www.wessexarch.co.uk/system/files/59794_GroomsFarmPublication.pdf.

95. M. Millett, *Shiptonthorpe East Yorkshire: Archaeological Studies of a Romano-British Roadside Settlement* (Leeds: Yorkshire Archaeological Society, 2006), 314–15.

96. S. Lawrence and A. Smith, *Between Villa and Town: Excavations of a Roadside Settlement and Shrine at Higham Ferrers, Northamptonshire* (Oxford: Oxford Archaeology, 2009), 334–35.

97. V. Diez and edited by P. Booth, "The Roman Settlement at Bower Road, Smeeth, Kent" (unpublished report, Oxford Wessex Archaeology Joint Venture, 2006), 212, https://doi.org/10.5284/1009794; H. E. M. Cool and D. J. P. Mason, *Roman Piercebridge: Excavations by D. W.*

Harding and Peter Scott 1969–1981 (Durham: Architectural and Archaeological Society of Durham and Northumberland, 2008), 309–10. It is, however, very difficult to distinguish structured deposits in pits and ditches from deposits resulting from more quotidian activities, such as rubbish disposal (T. S. Martin, "Techniques for Exploring Context, Deposition, and Chronology," in R. Hingley and S. Willis, eds., *Roman Finds: Context and Theory* (Oxford: Oxbow Books, 2007), 86–99; L. G. Broderick, "Ritualisation (or The Four Fully Articulated Ungulates of the Apocalypse)," in A. Pluskowski, ed., *The Ritual Killing and Burial of Animals: European Perspectives* (Oxford: Oxbow Books, 2012), 22–32.

98. See above, Chapter 5, n. 92 for references.

99. P. M. M. Cook, "A Roman Site at Asthall, Oxfordshire," *Oxoniensia*, 20 (1955), 29–39, at 29; Ross, "Shafts, Pits, and Wells," 283; H. Pearman, "Excavation of a Roman Well at Findon in Sussex," *Kent Archaeological Review*, 13 (1968), 16–19; J. Chapman and S. Smith, "Finds from a Roman Well in Staines," *London Archaeologist*, 16 (1988), 3–6; R. Mackey, "The Welton Villa—a View of Social and Economic Change During the Roman Period in East Yorkshire," in P. Halkon, ed., *Further Light on the Parisi: Recent Research in Iron Age and Roman East Yorkshire* (Hull: University of Hull, Department of History, 1999), 21–32, at 24–26; A. Maull, "Bicester Park Phase 4. Archaeological Excavation July–October 2004: Assessment Report and Updated Project Design (unpublished report, Northamptonshire Archaeology, 2005), 15, https://doi.org/10.5284/1028238. For similar depositional practices elsewhere in northwest Europe during and just after the Roman period, albeit without recycled building material, see F. Gerritsen, *Local Identities: Landscape and Community in the Late Prehistoric Meuse-Demer-Scheldt Region* (Amsterdam: Amsterdam University Press, 2003), 95–102; M. Groot, "Searching for Patterns Among Special Animal Deposits in the Dutch River Area During the Roman Period," *Journal of Archaeology in the Low Countries*, 1 (2009), 49–81, at 59–64; M. van Haasteren and M. Groot, "The Biography of Wells: A Functional and Ritual Life History," *Journal of Archaeology in the Low Countries*, 4 (2013), 25–51.

100. C. Bell, *Ritual Theory, Ritual Practice* (Oxford: Oxford University Press, 1992), 74.

101. J. Brück, "Ritual and Rationality: Some Problems of Interpretation in European Archaeology," *European Journal of Archaeology*, 2 (1999), 313–44; J. Pollard, "The Aesthetics of Depositional Practice," *World Archaeology*, 33 (2001), 315–33.

102. Å. Berggren and L. Nilsson Stutz, "From Spectator to Critic and Participant: A New Role for Archaeology in Ritual Studies," *Journal of Social Archaeology*, 10 (2010), 171–97, at 175.

103. We rarely have full inventories of well fills, and detailed accountings of the building material found within them are almost never made. A well at Sewell, in Bedfordshire, for example, included "human bones, Roman tile, pieces of squared sandstone, black flints, red pottery, etc." (A. White, "Remarks on the Antiquities Discovered in the Excavations," *Papers Read at the Royal Institute of British Architects* [London, 1874–75], 96–99, at 99); and a well at Aston, in Northamptonshire, contained a stone column (J. Hadman, "Ashton 1979–82," *Durobrivae: A Review of Nene Valley Archaeology*, 9 [1984], 28–29). The dates of these deposits, however, cannot be established from the publications describing them. It is also sometimes unclear whether or not well deposits contained building materials. Several wells at Baldock, for example, contained human remains and whole deer, but we are not told if building material was included in their fills (I. M. Stead and V. Rigby, *Baldock: The Excavation of a Roman and Pre-Roman Settlement, 1968–72* [London: Society for the Promotion of Roman Studies, 1986], 410).

104. E. Scott, "Aspects of the Roman Villa as a Form of British Settlement," 2 vols. (Ph.D. diss., University of Newcastle upon Tyne, 1988), 1:212.

105. Determining how, exactly, some of these deposits were made is very complex (Maltby, "Animal Bones from a Romano-British Well at Oakridge," 66), and some wells have evidence of

multiple deposit episodes—some quotidian and others less pragmatic looking. Rudston is one such example (E. Scott, "Aspects of the Roman Villa," 1:214–18).

106. E.g., Dalton Parlours (S. Wrathmell and A. Nicholson, ed., *Dalton Parlours: Iron Age Settlement and Roman Villa* [Wakefield: West Yorkshire Archaeological Services, 1990], 195).

107. Merrifield, *Archaeology of Ritual*, 48–50.

108. Van Haasteren and Groot, "Biography of Wells," 32.

109. E.g., Rothwell Haigh (Cool and Richardson, "Exploring Ritual Deposits," 214) and Lower Slaughter (J. Timby, *Excavations at Kingscote and Wycomb, Gloucestershire: A Roman Estate Centre and Small Town in the Cotswolds with Notes on Related Settlements* [Cirencester: Costwold Archaeological Trust, 1998], 387).

110. For example, at Thurnham (Lawrence and Booth, "Iron Age Settlement and Roman Villa at Thurnham," 115–16) and at Silchester (A. Clarke and M. Fulford, "The Excavation of Insula IX, Silchester: The First Five Years of the 'Town Life' Project, 1997–2001," *Britannia*, 33 [2002], 129–66, at 159).

111. I. M. Stead, *Rudston Roman Villa* (Leeds: Yorkshire Archaeological Society, 1980), 26.

112. Stead, *Rudston*, 216.

113. Stead, *Rudston*, 149–51.

114. Stead, *Rudston*, 29; E. Scott, "Aspects of the Roman Villa," 1:216.

115. D. S. Neal, *Excavations on the Roman Villa at Beadlam, Yorkshire* (Leeds: Yorkshire Archaeological Society, 1996), 85.

116. Wrathmell and Nicholson, *Dalton Parlours*, 147, 195–97, 203–6, 244, 272, 289, and fig. 100.

117. Berggren and Nilsson Stutz, "From Spectator to Critic and Participant," 180–83.

118. M. H. Eriksen, "Commemorating Dwelling: The Death and Burial of Houses in Iron and Viking Age Scandinavia," *European Journal of Archaeology*, 19 (2016), 477–96, at 478.

119. Fleming, "Ritual Recycling of Roman Building Material"; R. Hingley, *Londinium: A Biography; Roman London from Its Origins to the Fifth Century* (London: Bloomsbury, 2018), 204–5, 229–32.

120. H. Hamerow, "'Special Deposits' in Anglo-Saxon Settlements," *Medieval Archaeology*, 50 (2006), 1–30.

121. This practice is much more visible in other parts of the post-Roman world. See, for example, D. Krsmanovic and W. Anderson, "Paths of the Dead—Interpreting Funerary Practice at Roman-Period Pessinus, Central Anatolia," *Melbourne Historical Journal*, 40 (2012), 58–87, at 70, 83–84, and figs. 8a and 8b.

122. G. D. Keevill, "Redlands Farm, Stanwick, Northamptonshire, SP 962705" (unpublished report, Oxford Archaeological Unit, 1992), 53–54; Biddulph et al., "Redlands Farm, Stanwick, Northamptonshire," 55, 70–72.

123. J. N. L. Myers and B. Green, *The Anglo-Saxon Cemeteries of Caistor-by-Norwich and Markshall, Norfolk* (London: Society of Antiquaries of London, 1973); 126; F. Haverfield, "Romano-British Northamptonshire," *Victoria County History: Northamptonshire*, vol. 1 (London: Constable, 1902), 157–222, at 182.

124. A. G. Kinsley, *Broughton Lodge: Excavations on the Romano-British Settlement and Anglo-Saxon Cemetery at Broughton Lodge, Willoughby-on-the-Wolds, Nottinghamshire 1964–8* (Nottingham: University of Nottingham, 1993), 70.

125. A. Boyle et al., *The Anglo-Saxon Cemetery at Butler's Field, Lechlade, Gloucestershire*, vol. 2, *The Anglo-Saxon Grave Goods Specialist Reports, Phasing and Discussion* (Oxford: Oxford Archaeology, 2011), 5, 63, 74.

126. M. Carver, C. Hills, and J. Scheschkewitz, *Wasperton: A Roman, British and Anglo-Saxon Community in Central England* (Woodbridge: Boydell, 2009), 292.

127. G. Speed and M. Holst, *A1 Leeming to Barton: Death, Burial and Identity: 3000 Years of Death in the Vale of Mowbray* (Barnard Castle: Northern Archaeological Associates, 2018), https://doi.org/10.5284/1050910, 207.

128. K. Leahy, *"Interrupting the Pots": The Excavation of Cleatham Anglo-Saxon Cemetery, North Lincolnshire* (York: Council for British Archaeology, 2007), 33.

129. A. Maldonado Ramirez, "Christianity and Burial in Late Iron Age Scotland, AD 400–650" (Ph.D. diss., University of Glasgow, 2011), 99–100.

130. Williams and Zeepvat, *Bancroft*, 1:116, 119.

131. For more on the role of stones in post-Roman burials, see A. P. J. Mason, "Listening to the Early Medieval Dead: Religious Practices in Eastern Britain, 400–900 CE" (Ph.D. diss., Boston College, 2012), 146–74.

132. H. Härke, "A Context for the Saxon Barrow," in M. G. Fulford and S. Rippon, "Lowbury Hill, Oxon: A Re-Assessment of the Probably Romano-Celtic Temple and the Anglo-Saxon Barrow," *Archaeological Journal*, 151 (1994), 158–211, at 202–6; H. Williams, "Monuments and the Past in Early Anglo-Saxon England," *World Archaeology*, 30 (1998), 90–108; T. Bell, "Churches on Roman Buildings: Christian Associations and Roman Masonry in Anglo-Saxon England," *Medieval Archaeology*, 42 (1998), 1–18.

133. E.g., Upex, "Excavations at a Roman and Saxon Site at Haddon"; Gaffney and White, *Wroxeter*, 131.

134. P. Bourdieu, *Outline of a Theory of Practice* (Cambridge: Cambridge University Press, 1977), 89–91; A. Rogers, *The Archaeology of Roman Britain: Biography and Identity* (London: Routledge, 2014), 109, 175.

135. R. Hingley, *Globalizing Roman Culture: Unity, Diversity, and Empire* (London: Bloomsbury, 2005), 88.

136. Hingley, *Globalizing Roman Culture*, 104–5. Something similar was true for Swahili stone houses (J. B. Fleisher and A. LaViolette, "The Changing Power of Swahili Houses, Fourteenth to Nineteenth Centuries AD," in R. A. Beck, ed., *The Durable House: House Society Models in Archaeology* [Carbondale, Ill.: Center for Archaeological Investigations, 2007], 175–97).

137. S. Scott, "Elites, Exhibitionism, and the Society of the Late Roman Villa," in Christi, ed., *Landscapes of Change*, 39–65, at 42–44, 47–52; Bowes, *Houses and Society*; E. Swift, *Style and Function in Roman Decoration: Living with Objects and Interiors* (Aldershot: Ashgate, 2009), 29; Revell, *Ways of Being Roman*, 75–80.

138. S. Scott, "Elites, Exhibitionism, and the Society," 53–55; Bowes, *Houses and Society*, 85–99.

139. C. Lévi-Strauss, *Anthropology of Myth: Lectures 1951–82* (Oxford: Blackwell, 1987), 187.

140. This is hinted at in S. Scott, *Art and Society in Fourth-Century Britain: Villa Mosaics in Context* (Oxford: Oxford University School of Archaeology, 2000), 168. See also, M. J. Kolb, "Labor, Mobilization, Ethnohistory, and the Archaeology of Community in Hawai'i," *Journal of Archaeological Method and Theory*, 4 (1997), 265–85, at 268.

141. McCarthy, *Romano-British Peasant*, 101–7; Taylor, "Labor Force and Execution," 197–200, 203.

142. M. Given, *The Archaeology of the Colonized* (London: Routledge, 2004), 105–15.

143. R. Paynter and R. H. McGuire, "The Archaeology of Inequality: Material Culture, Domination, and Resistance," in R. Paynter and R. H. McGuire, eds., *The Archaeology of Inequality* (Oxford: Blackwell, 1991), 1–27; S. W. Silliman, "Theoretical Perspectives on Labor and Colonialism:

Reconsidering the California Missions," *Journal of Anthropological Archaeology*, 20 (2001), 379–407, at 381.

144. R. Bjork, ed. and trans., *Old English Shorter Poems*, vol. 2, *Wisdom and Lyric* (Cambridge, Mass.: Harvard University Press 2014), 118–21.

CHAPTER 6

Epigraph: T. Thwaites, *The Toaster Project: Or a Heroic Attempt to Build a Simple Electric Appliance from Scratch* (New Haven, 2011), 15.

1. For metal production in the Roman Empire, see P. T. Craddock, "Mining and Metallurgy," in J. P. Oleson, ed., *Oxford Handbook of Engineering and Technology in the Classical World* (Oxford: Oxford University Press, 2008), 93–120, at 108; W. V. Harris, "The Late Republic," in W. Scheidel, I. Morris, and R. P. Saller, eds., *The Cambridge Economic History of the Greco-Roman World* (Cambridge: Cambridge University Press, 2007), 1:511–40, at 532; P. Leveau, "The Western Provinces," in Scheidel, Morris, and Saller, *The Cambridge Economic History of the Greco-Roman World*, 1:649–70, at 661; D. J. Mattingly, "Metals and *Metalla*: A Roman Copper-Mining Landscape in the Wadi Faynan, Jordan," in D. J. Mattingly, *Imperialism, Power and Identity: Experiencing the Roman Empire* (Princeton, N.J.: Princeton University Press, 2011), 167–200; J. Lang, "Roman Iron and Steel: A Review," *Materials and Manufacturing Processes*, 32 (2017), 857–66. For metal production in Britain, see H. Cleere and D. Crossley, *The Iron Industry of the Weald*, 2nd ed. (Cardiff: Merton Priory Press, 1995); J. Meredith, *The Iron Industry of the Forest of Dean* (Stroud: Tempus, 2006), 29–56; M. Todd, *Roman Mining in Somerset: Excavations at Charterhouse on Mendip 1993–1995* (Exeter: Mint, 2007); D. Dungworth, "Metals and Metalworking," in M. Millett, L. Revell, and A. Moore, eds., *The Oxford Handbook of Roman Britain* (Oxford: Oxford University Press, 2016), 532–54. For an overview of where mining, smelting, and metalworking were taking place in Britain in the Roman period, and for a discussion of the broad changes in metal production over time, see M. Allen et al., *The Rural Economy of Roman Britain* (London: Society for the Promotion of Roman Studies, 2017), 178–98.

2. For levels of metal production and pollution, see S. Hong et al., "History of Ancient Copper Smelting Pollution During Roman and Medieval Times Recorded in Greenland Ice," *Science*, 272 (1996), 246–49; E. Borsos et al., "Anthropogenic Air Pollution in the Ancient Times," *Acta Climatologica et Chorologica*, 36–37 (2003), 5–15; J. O. Nriagu, "Environmental Pollution and Human Health in Ancient Times," in J. O. Nriagu, ed., *Encyclopedia of Environmental Health*, 2 vols. (Amsterdam: Elsevier, 2011), 2:489–506, at 502–3; D. Sim and I. Ridge, *Iron for Eagles: The Iron Industry of Roman Britain* (Stroud: Tempus, 2002), 23–24. For recent work showing that levels of lead pollution (and metal production) were greater in the first and second centuries of the Common Era than they were in the late Roman period, see J. R. McConnell et al., "Lead Pollution Recorded in Greenland Ice Indicates European Emissions Tracked Plagues, Wars, and Imperial Expansion During Antiquity," *Proceedings of the National Academy of Sciences of the United States of America*, 115 (2018), 5726–31. Within Britain, evidence from peat bogs and speleothems confirm that there was a substantial increase in lead smelting during the Roman period (T. M. Mighall et al., "An Atmospheric Pollution History for Lead-Zinc Mining from the Ystwyth Valley, Dyfed, Mid-Wales, UK as Recorded by an Upland Blanket Peat," *Geochemistry: Exploration, Environment, Analysis*, 2 [2002], 175–84; D. A. McFarlane, J. Lundberg, and H. Neff, "A Speleothem Record of Early British and Roman Mining at Charterhouse, Mendip, England," *Archaeometry*, 56 [2014], 431–43). Evidence from British peat bogs similarly suggests that tin was heavily

exploited in the Roman period, but from the early fifth century until the early eighth century, there is very little evidence for its production (A. A. Meharg et al., "First Comprehensive Peat Depositional Records for Tin, Lead, and Copper Associated with the Antiquity of Europe's Largest Cassiterite Deposits," *Journal of Archaeological Science*, 39 [2012], 717–27).

3. For the recycling of pottery, see J. T. Peña, *Roman Pottery in the Archaeological Record* (Cambridge: Cambridge University Press, 2007). For the recycling of glass, see D. Keller, "Social and Economic Aspects of Glass Recycling," *TRAC 2004* (2005), 65–78; H. Foster and C. Jackson, "The Composition of Late Romano-British Colourless Vessel Glass: Glass Production and Consumption," *Journal of Archaeological Science*, 37 (2010), 3068–80; C. M. Jackson and S. Paynter, "A Great Big Melting Pot: Exploring Patterns of Glass Supply, Consumption, and Recycling in Roman Coppergate, York," *Archaeometry*, 58 (2016), 68–95; S. Paynter and C. Jackson, "Re-Used Roman Rubbish: A Thousand Years of Recycling Glass," *European Journal of Post-Classical Archaeologies*, 6 (2016), 31–52. For the reuse of building materials, see above, Chapter 5.

4. For examples, see S. S. Frere, M. W. C. Hassall, and R. S. O. Tomlin, "Roman Britain in 1988," *Britannia*, 20 (1989), 257–345, at 229; P. Booth and S. Lawrence, "The Iron Age Settlement and Roman Villa at Thurnham, Kent" (unpublished report, Oxford Wessex Archaeology Joint Venture, 2006), 105, https://doi.org/10.5284/1008824; S. Willis and P. Carne, *A Roman Villa at the Edge of Empire: Excavations at Ingleby Barwick, Stockton-on-Tees, 2003–4* (York: Council of British Archaeology, 2013), 102–5; W. H. Manning, "The Roman Army and the Roman Smith: Some Evidence from Britain," in R. Collins and F. McIntosh, eds., *Life in the Limes* (Oxford: Oxbow Books, 2014), 11–17; B. Croxford, "Metal Sculpture from Roman Britain: Scrap but Not Always Scrap," in T. M. Kristensen and L. Stirling, eds., *The Afterlife of Greek and Roman Sculpture: Late-Antique Responses and Practices* (Ann Arbor: University of Michigan Press, 2016), 27–46.

5. For arguments that this was the case in late medieval and early modern Britain, see D. Woodward, "'Swords into Ploughshares': Recycling in Pre-Industrial England," *Economic History Review*, 38 (1985), 175–91, at 186.

6. P. Crew, "The Experimental Production of Prehistoric Bar Iron," *Journal of the Historical Metallurgy Society*, 25 (1991), 21–36, at 35; D. Sim, *Beyond the Bloom: Bloom Refining and Iron Artifact Production in the Roman World*, BAR International Series 725 (Oxford: BAR, 1998), 35. Sim's own experiments have cut down on Crew's time, and rough calculations have led him and Isabel Ridge to suggest that just over 4 percent of the population of Roman Britain was engaged, in some way, in metal production (Sim and Ridge, *Iron for Eagles*, 23–24). Another series of experiments, by Sauder and Williams, further reduced the labor needed from mining ore to producing a kilogram of finished iron bar to twenty-three hours (L. Sauder and S. Williams, "A Practical Treatise on the Smelting and Smithing of Bloomery Iron," *Historical Metallurgy*, 36 [2002], 122–31, at 127–28).

7. L. F. Pitts and J. K. St. Joseph, *Inchtuthil: The Roman Legionary Fortress Excavation 1952–65* (London: Society for the Promotion of Roman Studies, 1985), 109–13, 289–92, 301; C. Mapelli et al., "Nails of the Roman Legionary at Inchtuthil," *Metallurgia Italiana*, 101 (2009), 51–58.

8. For the availability of bronze and iron objects to households of all social classes, see M. L. Ratliff, "Globalisation, Consumerism, and the Ancient Roman Economy: A Preliminary Look at Bronze and Iron Production and Consumption," *TRAC 2010* (2011), 32–46.

9. For a comparison of metal's general availability in Britain before and after the Roman conquest and for the ubiquity of iron tools during the Roman period, see K. Greene, *The Archaeology of the Roman Economy* (Berkeley, Calif.: University of California Press, 1986), 143, 170; L. Bray, "'Horrible, Speculative, Nasty, Dangerous': Assessing the Value of Roman Iron," *Britannia*, 41 (2010), 175–85, at table 3, 183. For metal's use in Britain's Roman-period tools, see L. Allason-Jones,

Daily Life in Roman Britain (Oxford: Greenwood, 2008), 83–87. For iron's centrality to many agricultural and industrial tasks, see W. H. Manning, "Industry," in L. Allason-Jones, ed., *Artefacts in Roman Britain: Their Purpose and Use* (Cambridge: Cambridge University Press, 2011), 68–88; S. Rees, "Agriculture," in Allason-Jones, *Artefacts in Roman Britain*, 89–113; I. Scott, "Ironwork and Its Production," in D. Bird, ed., *Agriculture and Industry in South-Eastern Roman Britain* (Oxford: Oxbow Books, 2017), 301–29, at 304–14.

10. L. S. Bray, "The Archaeology of Iron Production: Romano-British Evidence from the Exmore Region," 2 vols. (Ph.D. diss., University of Exeter, 2006), 2:276, 284, 289.

11. A figure based on experimental work (Sauder and Williams, "Practical Treatise on the Smelting and Smithing of Bloomery Iron," 127–28).

12. For clear descriptions of these processes and the resources and skills needed, see G. McDonnell, "Ore, Slag, Iron, and Steel," in P. Crew and S. Crew, eds., *Iron for Archaeologists* (Plas Tan y Bwlch: Snowdonia National Park Study Centre, 1995), 3–7; Sim, *Beyond the Bloom*, 9; I. Schrüfer-Kolb, *Roman Iron Production in Britain: Technological and Socio-Economic Landscape Development Along the Jurassic Ridge*, BAR British Series 380 (Oxford: Archaeopress, 2004), 7; P. T. Craddock, "Mining and Metallurgy," 101–13. For an ancient description of these processes, see Diodorus of Sicily on metalworking on Elba, *Roman Civilization Sourcebook*, vol. 2, *The Empire*, trans. N. Lewis and M. Reinhold (New York: Harper Torchbooks, 1966), quoted in D. Sim, "Roman Smithing," in F. Hammer, *Industry in North-West Roman Southwark: Excavations 1984–8* (London: MoLAS, 2003), 22–25, at 22. For a helpful diagram that lays out the complex processes required for nonferrous metalworking, see J. Bayley, "Non-Ferrous Metalworking in Roman Yorkshire," in P. Wilson and J. Price, eds., *Aspects of Industry in Roman Yorkshire and the North* (Oxford: Oxbow Books, 2002), 101–8 and fig. 2. For the possibility that different specialist activities, for example smelting and billet making, were sometimes undertaken on different sites by different groups of specialists, see G. Pagès, P. Dillmann, P. Fluzin, and L. Long, "A Study of the Roman Iron Bars of Saintes-Maries-de-la-Mer (Bouches-du-Rhône, France): A Proposal for a Comprehensive Metallographic Approach," *Journal of Archaeological Science*, 38 (2011), 1234–52. At some sites, though, there is evidence that both smelting and billet making were taking place (S. Paynter, "Romano-British Workshops for Iron Smelting and Smithing at Westhawk Farm, Kent," *Historical Metallurgy*, 41 [2007], 15–31).

13. P. T. Craddock, "Cast Iron, Fined Iron, Crucible Steel: Liquid Iron in the Ancient World," in P. T. Craddock and J. Lang, eds., *Mining and Metal Production Through the Ages* (London: British Museum, 2003), 231–57, at 232–34; J. C. Edmondson, "Mining in the Later Roman Empire and Beyond: Continuity or Disruption?" *Journal of Roman Studies*, 79 (1989), 84–102, at 94–97. For fuel requirements, see Sim, "Roman Smithing," 22; R. Pleiner, *Iron in Archaeology: The European Bloomery Smelters* (Prague: Archeologický ústav AVČR, 2000), 118. For a detailed study of the woodland management so necessary for long-term, Roman-period iron smelting in Exmoor, see R. Fyfe et al., "The Environmental Impact of Romano-British Ironworking on Exmoor," in J. Humphris and T. Rehren, eds., *The World of Iron* (London: Archetype, 2013), 462–72.

14. These sites were especially critical for iron production and distribution (Schrüfer-Kolb, *Roman Iron Production*, 115, 52, and table 4; Esmonde Cleary, *The Ending of Roman Britain* [London: B. T. Batsford, 1989], 75, 153–54).

15. R. Jackson, *Ariconium, Herefordshire: An Iron Age Settlement and Romano-British "Small Town"* (Oxford: Oxbow Books, 2012), 195. For the more local systems of supply used in provisioning soldiers living along Hadrian's Wall in the last half of the fourth century, see R. Collins, *Hadrian's Wall and the End of Empire: The Roman Frontier in the 4th and 5th Centuries* (London: Routledge, 2012), 58–60, 97, 101.

16. Sim, "Roman Smithing," 22.

17. For hints of the organization and infrastructure of Roman-period glass recycling, see Foster and Jackson, "Composition of Late Romano-British Colourless Vessel Glass"; Jackson and Paynter, "Great Big Melting Pot," Paynter and Jackson, "Re-Used Roman Rubbish"; J. Bayley et al., "Technological Material from Catterick," in P. R. Wilson, ed., *Cataractonium, Part II: Roman Catterick and Its Hinterland, Excavations and Research, 1958–1997* (York: Council for British Archaeology, 2002), 164–66. For organized, Roman-period building material recycling, see below, Chapter 5. For organized recycling of lead, see M. Boni et al., "Lead Isotopic Evidence for a Mixed Provenance for Roman Water Pipes from Pompeii," *Archaeometry*, 42 (2000), 201–8. For copper-alloy recycling during the Roman period, see J. Bayley et al., "Technological Material," 164–66. For the remarkable find of a sunken Roman merchant ship in Caesarea harbor with a large cargo of scrap metal, see J. Sharvit, "Roman Merchant Ship Cargo of Scrap Metal and Ram Materials in Caeserea Harbour," paper delivered at the "Recycling and Ancient Economy" conference, Oxford, September 2017. Another sunken ship from the second or third century was carrying a barrel of broken glass (A. Silvestri, "The Coloured Glass of Julia Felix," *Journal of Archaeological Science*, 35 [2008], 1489–501). The cargos of both of these shipwrecks illustrate the way recycled material sometimes traveled long distances in the Roman period.

18. B. Munro, "Recycling in Late Roman Villas in Southern Italy: Reappraising Hearths and Kilns in Final Occupation Phases," *Mouseion*, 10 (2010), 217–42; B. Munro, "Approaching Architectural Recycling in Roman and Late Roman Villas," *TRAC 2010* (2011), 76–88; B. Munro, "Recycling, Demand for Materials, and Landownership at Villas in Italy and the Western Provinces in Late Antiquity," *Journal of Roman Archaeology* 25, 351–70.

19. For a summary of the evidence for this from Silchester and Wroxeter, see A. Rogers, *Late Roman Towns in Britain: Rethinking Change and Decline* (Cambridge: Cambridge University Press, 2011), 142.

20. Hammer, *Industry in North-West Roman Southwark*, 166; P. Bennett, I. Riddler, and C. Sparey-Green, *The Roman Watermills and Settlement at Ickham Kent* (Canterbury: Canterbury Archaeological Trust, 2010), 339–40. In earlier periods, although scrap was sometimes used, smiths at these two sites typically used premade billets of freshly smelted metal, which had been manufactured elsewhere (J. Hall, "The Shopkeepers and Craft-Workers of Roman London," in A. Mac Mahon and J. Price, eds., *Roman Working Lives and Urban Living* [Oxford: Oxbow Books, 2005], 125–44, at 131–32; P. M. Booth, *Asthall, Oxfordshire: Excavations in a Roman "Small Town," 1992* [Oxford: Oxford Archaeological Unit, 1997], 94–98).

21. For what this might look like in the twenty-first century, see Thwaites, *Toaster Project*.

22. For the ubiquity of nailed coffins in the Roman period, see D. Petts, "Burial and Gender in Late and Sub-Roman Britain," *TRAC 97* (1998), 112–24, at 115. For hobnail boots, see N. Crummy, "Travel and Transport," in Allason-Jones, ed., *Artefacts in Roman Britain*, 46–67, at 48–50.

23. L. Alcock, "Cadbury-Camelot: A Fifteen Year Perspective," *Proceedings of the British Academy*, 68 (1982), 355–88, at 363–64.

24. C. P. Loveluck, "The Development of the Anglo-Saxon Landscape, Economy, and Society 'on Driffield,' East Yorkshire, 400–750 AD," *Anglo-Saxon Studies in Archaeology and History*, 9 (1996), 25–48, at 27, 35–38. Elsewhere around Driffield, J. R. Mortimer uncovered other early medieval graves with many iron objects (J. R. Mortimer, *Forty Years' Researches in British and Saxon Burial Mounds in East Yorkshire* [London: Brown and Sons, 1905], 271, 279–80, 290–91).

25. B. Adams and D. Jackson, "The Anglo-Saxon Cemetery at Wakerley, Northamptonshire: Excavations by Mr. D. Jackson 1968-9," *Northamptonshire Archaeology*, 22 (1988–89), 69–183;

B. Bellamy, D. Jackson, and G. Johnston, "Early Iron Smelting in the Rockingham Forest Area: A Survey of the Evidence," *Northamptonshire Archaeology*, 29 (2001), 103–28, at 114. Iron smelting also took place in Wakerley in the early Middle Ages, although none of this activity can be dated before the seventh century (D. Fell, "Archaeological Evaluation: Land at Wakerley, Northamptonshire, 698/WKM/1," 2 vols. [unpublished report, Archaeological Services and Consultancy, Milton Keynes, 2006], 2:83, https://doi.org/10.5284/1011997).

26. L. Ladle, *Excavations at Bestwall Quarry, Wareham 1992–2005*, vol. 2, *The Iron Age and Later Landscape* (Dorchester: Dorset Natural History and Archaeological Society, 2012), 94.

27. N. Hall, "Iron Working in Anglo-Saxon England: New Evidence to Show Fresh Iron Smelting of Ironstone Ores from the 6th–10th Centuries CE," *Journal of Archaeological Science: Reports*, 19 (2018), 344–51, at 347.

28. T. Birch, "Living on the Edge: Making and Moving Iron from the 'Outside' in Anglo-Saxon England," *Landscape History*, 32 (2011), 5–23, at 14.

29. Cleere and Crossley, *Iron Industry of the Weald*, 80.

30. R. F. Tylecote, *The Early History of Metallurgy in Europe* (London: Longman, 1987), 65; J. S. Hodgkinson, "Romano-British Iron Production in the Sussex and Kent Weald: A Review of Current Data," *Historical Metallurgy*, 33 (1999), 68–72. At Laxton, in Northamptonshire, for example, slag from the Roman iron-smelting furnaces filled the valley in which they sat, and initially, because there was so much of it, it was thought that it had been produced by the modern ironworks at Corby (D. Jackson, "Roman Ironworking at Laxton," *Northamptonshire Archaeology*, 28 [1998–99], 159). Elsewhere, though, large Roman slag heaps are much reduced because the slag itself was recycled. Iron slag was used in the Roman period for road making in the Weald (J. Bayley, D. Crossley, and M. Ponting, *Metals and Metalworking: A Research Framework for Archaeometallurgy* [London: Historical Metallurgy Society, 2008], 45). Most Roman slag, however, was not exploited until the seventeenth century and beyond. A seventeenth-century entrepreneur, for example, hauled "many thousand tons or loads" of Roman slag away from Worcester so that he could resmelt it in his blast furnace (R. Jackson, "Production: Roman Ironworking," in H. Dalwood and R. Edwards, *Excavations at Deansway, Worcester, 1988–89: Romano-British Small Town to Late Medieval City* (York: Council for British Archaeology, 2004), 100–105, at 101). In Devonshire, slag was used to construct walls and houses (F. Griffith and P. Weddell, "Ironworking in the Blackdown Hills: The Results of Recent Survey," in P. Newman, ed., *The Archaeology of Mining and Metallurgy in South West Britain* [Matlock: Peak District Mines Historical Society, 1996], 27–34, at 31). And much of the slag heap that had engulfed the Roman bathhouse at Beauport Park was used in the nineteenth century for road making, with something on the order of two thousand or three thousand cubic yards of cinder removed each year for a decade (G. Brodribb et al., "The 'Classis Britannica' Bath-House at Beauport Park, East Sussex," *Britannia*, 19 [1988], 217–74, at 217, 239).

31. Cleere and Crossley, *Iron Industry of the Weald*, 80; Jackson, *Ariconium*, 194.

32. F. Condron, "Iron Production in Leicestershire, Rutland, and Northamptonshire in Antiquity," *Transactions of the Leicestershire Archaeological and Historical Society*, 71 (1997), 1–20, at 10–12; Schrüfer-Kolb, *Roman Iron Production*, 101–6.

33. G. Fincham, *Durobrivae: A Roman Town Between Fen and Upland* (Stroud: Tempus, 2004), 118–22.

34. M. G. Fulford and J. R. L. Allen, "Iron-Making at the Chesters Villa, Woolaston, Gloucestershire: Survey and Excavation 1987–91," *Britannia*, 23 (1992), 159–215, at 199–201.

35. M. McCarthy, *The Romano-British Peasant: Towards a Study of People, Landscapes, and Work During the Roman Occupation of Britain* (Oxford: Windgather, 2013), 97–100.

36. Allen et al., *Rural Economy of Roman Britain*, 185; F. Condron, "When Is a Town Not a Town? 'Small Towns' on the Nene and Welland in Their Context," in A. E. Brown, ed., *Roman Small Towns in Eastern England and Beyond* (Oxford: Oxbow Books, 1995), 103–18, at 117.

37. E. Price, *Frocester: A Romano-British Settlement, Its Antecedents and Successors*, 4 vols. (Stonehouse, Gloucestershire: Gloucester and District Archaeological Research Group, 2000–2010), 2:92–94.

38. For example, forty-seven kilograms of metalworking debris, only a tiny fraction of it smelting slag (the bulk was, instead, the by-product of smithing), was recovered at the early medieval settlement at Catholme, in Staffordshire, a place where smelting on a very small scale took place sometime in the early Middle Ages (K. Brown, "Metal Slag," in S. Losco-Bradley and A. G. Kinsley, *Catholme: An Anglo-Saxon Settlement on the Trent Gravels in Staffordshire* [Nottingham: University of Nottingham Press, 2002], 113–15, at 113). More typically only small amounts of smithing slag and no smelting slag are found on early medieval sites. For example, ten kilograms of slag were uncovered at the early medieval settlement at Market Lavington (P. Williams and R. Newman, *Market Lavington, Wiltshire: An Anglo-Saxon Cemetery and Settlement; Excavations at Grove Farm, 1986–90* [Salisbury: Wessex Archaeology, 2006], 83); and at the settlement at Spong Hill, thirteen kilograms of smithing slag were recovered (R. Rickett, *The Anglo-Saxon Cemetery at Spong Hill, North Elmham*, part 7, *The Iron Age, Roman, and Early Saxon Settlement*, East Anglian Archaeology 73 [Dereham: Norfolk Museum Services, 1995], 83).

39. They are published in R. Fleming, "Recycling in Britain After the Fall of Rome's Metal Economy," *Past and Present*, 217 (2012), 3–45, at 37–45.

40. A. J. Welton, "Encounters with Iron: An Archaeometallurgical Reassessment of Early Anglo-Saxon Spearheads and Knives," *Archaeological Journal*, 173 (2016), 206–44, at 231.

41. For iron production and its scale inside the former Roman Empire, see Pleiner, *Iron in Archaeology*, 47–48; L. Eschenlohr and V. Serneels, *Les bas-fourneaux mérovingiens de Boécourt, Les Boulies (JU, Suisse)* (Porrentruy: Office du patrimoine historique, 1991); L. Eschenlohr, "Les ateliers de forgerons de Develier-Courtétételle (Jura, Suisse)," in G. Nicolini and N. Dieudonné-Glad, eds., *Les métaux antiques: Travail et restauration* (Montagnac: M. Mergoil, 1998), 19–22; D. Morin, P. Rosenthal, and M. Fontugne, "Roman-Early Medieval Iron Mining and Smelting at High Altitude in the Alps (Argentera-Mercantour Massif-Alpes-Maritimes, France)," *Antiquity*, project gallery, 81 (2007), https://www.antiquity.ac.uk/projgall/morin313/. For iron production outside the former Roman Empire, see O. Voss, "Snorup: Et jernudvindingsområde i Sydvestjylland," *Nationalmuseets Arbejdsmark* (1993), 97–111; B. J. Groenewoudt and M. van Nie, "Assessing the Scale and Organization of Germanic Iron Production in Heeten, the Netherlands," *Journal of European Archaeology*, 3 (1995), 187–215; I. Joosten, J. B. H. Jansen, and H. Kars, "Geochemistry and the Past: Estimation of the Output of a Germanic Iron Production Site in the Netherlands," *Journal of Geochemical Exploration*, 62 (1998), 129–37; C. Zimmermann, "Zur Entwicklung der Eisenmetallurgie in Skandinavien und Schleswig-Holstein," *Prähistorische Zeitschrift*, 73 (1998), 69–99, at 83–88; H. Jöns, "Zur Eisenverhüttung in Schleswig-Holstein in vor- und frühgeschichtlicher Zeit," *Offa*, 49–50 (1992–93), 41–55; H. Lyngstøm, "Farmers, Smelters, and Smiths," in L. C. Nørbach, ed., *Prehistoric and Medieval Direct Iron Smelting in Scandinavia and Europe: Aspects of Technology and Science* (Aarhus: Aarhus University Press, 2003), 21–25. For an up-to-date bibliography on metal production in late antiquity, see N. Kellens, "Metal Technology in Late Antiquity: A Bibliographic Note," in L. Lavan, E. Zanini, and A. Sarantis, eds., *Technology in Transition AD 300–650* (Leiden: Brill, 2008), 41–51.

42. O. Voss, "Snorup—Iron Producing Settlement in West Jutland, 1st–7th Century AD," in G. Magnusson, ed., *The Importance of Ironmaking: Technical Innovation and Social Change*,

Papers Presented at the Norberg Conference on May 8–13, 1995, vol. 1 (Stockholm: Jernkontorets Berghistoriska Utskott, 1995), 132–39; V. F. Buchwald, *Iron and Steel in Ancient Times* (Copenhagen: Royal Danish Academy of Science and Letters, 2005), 132–39.

43. For more on the small-scale, subsistence agriculture of the fifth century, with only very limited surplus, see P. Booth et al., *Thames Through Time: The Archaeology of the Gravel Terraces of the Upper and Middle Thames; The Early Historic Period AD 1–1000* (Oxford: Oxford Archaeology, 2007), 322.

44. See below, Chapter 9.

45. For the kinds of agricultural and woodworking tools available in the late Roman world, a fifth-century metal hoard from the Roman fort at Osterburken, in Germany, is instructive, particularly its iron plowshares, objects that seem to have disappeared in Britain after the fall of the metal economy (J. Henning, "Zur Datierung von Werkzeug- und Agrargerätefunden im germanischen Landnahmegebiet zwischen Rhein und oberer Donau (Der Hortfund von Osterburken)," *Jahrbuch des Römisch-Germanischen Zentralmuseums Mainz*, 32 [1985], 570–94).

46. See above, Chapter 5.

47. J.-P. Adam, *Roman Building: Materials and Techniques*. Translated by A. Mathews (London: Routledge, 2005), 293–95, 321, and fig. 701; Bayley et al., "Technological Material from Catterick," 164–72; W. H. Manning, *Catalogue of the Romano-British Iron Tools, Fittings, and Weapons in the British Museum* (London: British Museum, 1985), 124–37.

48. B. Cunliffe, *English Heritage Book of Roman Bath* (London: Batsford, 1995), 24.

49. W. H. C. Frend and J. A. Hadman, "A Deposit of Roman Lead from North Lodge Farm, Barnwell, Northants," *Britannia*, 25 (1994), 224–26.

50. S. West with J. Plouvez, "The Romano-British Site at Icklingham," *East Anglian Archaeology Reports*, 3 (1979), 63–126, at 74–79.

51. P. M. Barford, *Excavations at Little Oakley, Essex, 1951–78: Roman Villa and Saxon Settlement*, East Anglian Archaeology 98 (Chelmsford: Essex County Council, 2002), 195–96; A. Douglas, J. Gerrard, and B. Sudds, *A Roman Settlement and Bath House at Shadwell: Excavations at Tobacco Dock and Babe Ruth Restaurant, the Highway, London* (London: Pre-Construct Archaeology, 2011), 57 and 160.

52. J. Gerrard, "The Temple of Sulis Minerva at Bath and the End of Roman Britain," *Antiquaries Journal*, 87 (2007), 148–64.

53. B. Cunliffe and P. Davenport, *The Temple of Sulis Minerva at Bath*, 2 vols. (Oxford: Oxford University Committee for Archaeology, 1985–88), 2:72–73, 185.

54. Cunliffe and Davenport, *Temple of Sulis Minerva*, 1:72–73; Gerrard, "Temple of Sulis Minerva," 158–59.

55. D. L. Bomgardner, *The Story of the Roman Amphitheatre* (London: Routledge, 2000), 30.

56. B. Krusch and W. Levison, eds., *Gregorii episcopi Turonensis, Historiarum libri X, MGH Scriptores rerum Merovingicarum*, vol. 1, part 1 (Hanover: Impensis bibliopholii Hahniani, 1937–51), book 5, cap. 4.

57. D. A. Long, K. Steedman, and L. Vere-Stevens, "The Goodmanham Plane: A Unique Roman Plane, of the Fourth Century AD, Discovered in Yorkshire in AD 2000," *Tools and Trades*, 13 (2002), 9–20, at 13; R. B. Ulrich, *Roman Woodworking* (New Haven, Conn.: Yale University Press, 2007), 43–44; "Ivory Plane from Roman Settlement in the North East," *British Archaeology*, 68 (2002), 43–44. It may, however, be that the plane had been scavenged to use as a tool, rather than as scrap metal, because it is intact.

58. W. H. Manning, "A Hoard of Late Roman Ironwork from Sibson, Huntingdonshire," in J. Bird, ed., *Form and Fabric: Studies in Rome's Material Past in Honour of B. R. Hartley*

(Oxford: Oxbow Books, 1998), 281–95. Although many Roman metalwork hoards are described as votive, some scholars have questioned this assumption. It has been suggested, for example, that the people who buried the late Roman iron hoard discovered at Kilverstone, Norfolk, were responding to political and economic concerns (D. Garrow, S. Lucy, and D. Gibson, *Excavations at Kilverstone, Norfolk: An Episodic Landscape History*, East Anglian Archaeology 113 [Cambridge: Cambridge Archaeological Unit, 2006], 120–29, 169). For a sustained critique, see C. Johns, "The Classification and Interpretation of Romano-British Treasures," *Britannia*, 27 (1996), 1–16.

59. The most common votive offerings at Romano-British ritual sites were jewelry, figurines, miniature weapons, tools, pottery, metal vessels, and coins (T. Malim, "A Romano-British Temple Complex and Anglo-Saxon Burials at Gallows Hill, Swaffham Prior," *Proceedings of the Cambridge Antiquarian Society*, 95 (2006), 91–114, at 112; A. Woodward and P. Leach, *The Uley Shrines: Excavation of a Ritual Complex on West Hill, Uley, Gloucestershire; 1977–9* [London: British Museum, 1993], 327–34, and table 20). For the ubiquity of deposits of metal objects at such shrines, see W. H. Manning, "Ironwork Hoards in Iron Age and Roman Britain," *Britannia*, 3 (1972), 224–50; R. Hingley, "The Deposition of Iron Objects in Britain During the Later Prehistoric and Roman Periods: Contextual Analysis and the Significance of Iron," *Britannia*, 37 (2006), 213–57; J. B. Smith, "Votive Objects and Objects of Votive Significance from Great Walsingham," *Britannia*, 30 (1999), 21–56; D. Petts, "Votive Deposits and Christian Practice in Late Roman Britain," in M. Carver, ed., *The Cross Goes North: Processes of Conversion in Northern Europe, AD 300–1300* (Woodbridge: Boydell, 2003), 109–18.

60. See, below, this chapter, "Metal and the Building of a New Political Order."

61. R. Cowie and L. Blackmore, *Early and Middle Saxon Rural Settlement in the London Region* (London: MoLAS, 2008), 151.

62. For a general discussion of these objects, see R. H. White, *Roman and Celtic Objects from Anglo-Saxon Graves: A Catalogue and Interpretation of Their Use*, BAR British Series 191 (Oxford: BAR, 1988), 136–51; and R. H. White, "Scrap or Substitute: Roman Material in Anglo-Saxon Graves," in E. Southworth, ed., *Anglo-Saxon Cemeteries: A Reappraisal* (Stroud: Alan Sutton, 1990), 125–52. For a discussion of the collecting of Roman coins during this period, see T. S. N. Moorhead, "Roman Bronze Coinage in Sub-Roman and Early Anglo-Saxon England," in B. Cook and G. Williams, eds., *Coinage and History in the North Sea World, c. AD 500–1250: Essays in Honour of Marion Archibald* (Leiden: Brill, 2006), 99–109. For the symbolic meaning of such objects in mortuary contexts, see H. Eckhardt and H. Williams, "Objects Without a Past? The Use of Roman Objects in Early Anglo-Saxon Graves," in H. Williams, ed., *Archaeologies of Remembrance: Death and Memory in Past Societies* (New York: Kluwer Academic/Plenum, 2003), 141–70.

63. S. E. West, *West Stow: The Anglo-Saxon Village*, East Anglian Archaeology 24 (Ipswich: Suffolk County Planning Dept., 1985), 60, 76–85, 122. It has also recently been argued that people in the late Roman period in the North of England carefully husbanded and reused Roman metalwork objects such as belt buckles as is, and this practice, too, may have continued into the fifth century (J. C. N. Coulson, "Military Equipment of the 'Long' Fourth Century on Hadrian's Wall," in R. Collins and L. Allason-Jones, eds., *Finds from the Frontier: Material Culture in the 4th–5th Centuries* [London: Council for British Archaeology, 2010], 50–63, at 59–60).

64. V. I. Evison, *An Anglo-Saxon Cemetery at Alton, Hampshire* (Gloucester: Hampshire Field Club, 1988), 85 and fig. 40. For other scavenged metalwork associated with women's bag collections, see A. L. Meaney, "Women, Witchcraft and Magic in Anglo-Saxon England," in D. G. Scragg, ed., *Superstition and Popular Medicine in Anglo-Saxon England* (Manchester: Manchester Centre for Anglo-Saxon Studies, 1989), 9–40, at 10–12. For an example of a typical bag and its collection of metalwork odds and ends, see F. K. Annable and B. N. Eagles, *The Anglo-Saxon Cemetery*

at Blacknall Field, Pewsey, Wiltshire (Devizes: Wiltshire Archaeological and Natural History Society, 2010), 149–50, 241–42.

65. S. Lucy, J. Tipper, and A. Dickens, *The Anglo-Saxon Settlement and Cemetery at Bloodmore Hill, Carlton Colville, Suffolk*, East Anglian Archaeology 131 (Cambridge: Cambridge Archaeological Unit, 2009), 171. Similarly, at the early medieval settlement at Brixworth, Northamptonshire, evidence for both smithing and scavenging Roman metalwork has been found (S. Ford, "The Excavation of a Saxon Settlement and a Mesolithic Flint Scatter at Northampton Road, Brixworth, Northamptonshire, 1994," *Northamptonshire Archaeology*, 26 [1995], 79–108, at 94–96). The grave goods of a seventh-century smith tell a similar story (D. A. Hinton, *A Smith in Lindsey: The Anglo-Saxon Grave at Tattershall Thorpe, Lincolnshire* [London: Society for Medieval Archaeology, 2000], 5–6, 15, and 67–70).

66. H. Hamerow, *Excavations at Mucking*, vol. 2, *The Anglo-Saxon Settlement* (London: English Heritage, 1993), 70–71; K. J. Barton, "Settlements of the Iron Age and Pagan Saxon Periods at Linford, Essex," *Transactions of the Essex Archaeological Society*, 3rd ser., 1 (1962), 57–104, at 67–68; P. J. Drury et al., "An Early Saxon Settlement Within the Romano-British Small Town at Heybridge, Essex," *Medieval Archaeology*, 26 (1982), 1–40, at 26 and fig. 11.5; J. Murray and T. McDonald, "Excavations at Station Road, Gamlingay, Cambs," *Anglo-Saxon Studies in History and Archaeology*, 13 (2005), 173–330, at 224–25; 232–35; G. D. Keevill, "An Anglo-Saxon Site at Audlett Drive, Abingdon, Oxfordshire," *Oxoniensia*, 57 (1992), 55–79, at 65; L. E. Webster and J. Cherry, "Medieval Britain in 1972," *Medieval Archaeology*, 16 (1973), 133–88, at 145; D. Miles, *Archaeology at Barton Court Farm, Abingdon, Oxon: An Investigation of Neolithic, Iron Age, Romano-British, and Saxon Settlements* (London: Council for British Archaeology, 1986), "The Finds, Part One," microfiche element, 5:A6–7; R. E. M. Wheeler, *London and the Saxons* (London: London Museum, 1935), 136 and fig. 19; Cowie and Blackmore, *Early and Middle Saxon Rural Settlement in the London Region*, 204–6 and table 72; B. Cunliff, *Excavations at Fishbourne 1961–9* (London: Society of Antiquaries of London, 1971), 10–11 and fig. 66; B. Philip et al., *The Roman Villa Site at Keston, Kent: First Report (Excavations 1968–1978)* (Dover Castle: Kent Archaeological Rescue Unit, 1991), 35.

67. Tylecote, *Early History of Metallurgy*, 40. There is also evidence in the West Country for the continued production of lead at Charterhouse-on-Mendip, in Somerset, through c. 600 (McFarlane, Lundberg, and Neff, "Speleothem Record," 438–39).

68. Hamerow, *Excavations at Mucking*, 2:70–71; S. Hirst and D. Clark, *Excavations at Mucking: Excavations by Tom and Margaret Jones*, vol. 3, *The Anglo-Saxon Cemeteries* (London: MoLAS, 2009), 15, 70–71, 477, 559.

69. Tylecote, *Early History of Metallurgy*, 75.

70. Most Roman brooches in Britain, for example, were apparently made from unleaded brass or unleaded bronze (J. Bayley and S. Butcher, *Roman Brooches in Britain: A Technological and Typological Study Based on the Richborough Collection* [London: Society of Antiquaries of London, 2004], 14 and table 6); and locking mechanisms were typically fabricated from a quaternary alloy (D. Dungworth, "Roman Copper Alloys: Analysis of Artefacts from Northern Britain," *Journal of Archaeological Science*, 24 [1997], 901–10, at 906). Although there is evidence that Romano-British copper-alloy workers recycled scrap, filings, and off-cuts, they seem to have sorted this scrap very carefully before they reused it (Bayley et al., "Technological Material from Catterick," 164–66). For more general discussions on this, see J. Bayley, "Non-Ferrous Metalworking: Continuity and Change," in E. A. Slater and J. O. Tate, eds., *Science and Archaeology Glasgow 1987: Proceedings of a Conference on the Application of Scientific Techniques to Archaeology*, BAR British Series 196.1 (Oxford: BAR, 1988), 193–202; Dungworth, "Roman Copper Alloys," 907 and 909;

and D. Dungworth, "Iron Age and Roman Copper Alloys from Northern Britain," *Journal of Internet Archaeology*, 2 (1997), sections 5.4, 7.6, 8.4, 10.2, https://doi.org/10.11141/ia.2.2.

71. C. Mortimer, "Compositional Analysis of Non-Ferrous Metalwork in Wasperton Anglo-Saxon Cemetery," in M. Carver, "Wasperton Anglo-Saxon Cemetery [Data-Set]" (unpublished report, Archaeology Data Service [distributor], 2008), https://doi.org/10.5284/1000052.

72. N. Blades, "Chemical Analysis of the Copper Alloys," in C. Haughton and D. Powlesland, *West Heslerton, the Anglian Cemetery*, 2 vols. (Yedingham: Landscape Research Centre, 1999) vol. 1, 129–37, at 130.

73. Bayley, Crossley, and Pointing, *Metals and Metalworking*, 50–51; I. Meadows, *An Anglian Warrior Burial from Wollaston* (Northampton: Northamptonshire Archaeology, 2004), 36–38.

74. D. A. Hinton, *The Gold, Silver, and Other Non-Ferrous Alloy Objects from Hamwic, and the Non-Ferrous Metalworking Evidence* (Stroud: Alan Sutton, 1996), 6; N. S. H. Rogers, *Anglian and Other Finds from Fishergate: The Small Finds 17/9* (York: Council of British Archaeology for the York Archaeology Trust, 1993), 1357–58.

75. C. Mortimer, "Metallurgy of Brooches and Pendants," in M. Carver, C. Hills, and J. Scheschkewitz, *Wasperton: A Roman, British, and Anglo-Saxon Community in Central England* (Woodbridge: Boydell, 2009), 58–59; P. Wilthew, "Analysis of Non-Ferrous Metal Objects," in S. Chadwick Hawkes and G. Grainger, *The Anglo-Saxon Cemetery at Finglesham, Kent* (Oxford: Oxford School of Archaeology, 2006), 371–79; N. Blades, "Preliminary Report on Analyses of Copper Alloys," in J. R. Timby, *The Anglo-Saxon Cemetery at Empingham II, Rutland* (Oxford: Oxbow Books, 1996), 71–76. One study, however, suggests that matched pairs of saucer brooches were made with metal of different alloy combinations, suggesting that each member of a pair was made from a different melt (C. Caple, "Ancestor Artefacts—Ancestor Materials," *Oxford Journal of Archaeology*, 29 [2010], 305–18, at 311–12).

76. E. S. Blakelock, "The Early Medieval Cutting Edge of Technology: An Archaeometallurgical, Technological, and Social Study of the Manufacture and Use of Anglo-Saxon and Viking Iron Knives, and Their Contribution to the Early Medieval Iron Economy," 2 vols. (Ph.D. diss., University of Bradford, 2012), 1:233–34 and fig. 7.6.

77. G. McDonnell, "Iron and Its Alloys in the Fifth to Eleventh Centuries AD in England," *World Archaeology*, 20 (1989), 373–82.

78. For evidence in the uptick of agricultural surplus, see H. Hamerow, *Early Medieval Settlements: The Archaeology of Rural Communities in North-West Europe 400–900* (Oxford: Oxford University Press, 2002), 120–24, 139, 148–55; M. McKerracher, *Farming Transformed in Anglo-Saxon England: Agriculture in the Long Eighth Century* (Oxford: Windgather, 2018), 118–25. For the reorientation from a ranked to a steeply hierarchical society during the sixth century, see C. Scull, "Social Transactions, Gift Exchange and Power in the Archaeology of the Fifth to Seventh Centuries," in H. Hamerow, D. A. Hinton, and S. Crawford, eds., *The Oxford Handbook of Anglo-Saxon Archaeology* (Oxford: Oxford University Press, 2011), 848–64, at 852–53.

79. McDonnell, "Iron and Its Alloys," 380.

80. K. Wiemer, "Metallurgical Analyses of Iron Knives," in Timby, *Anglo-Saxon Cemetery at Empingham*, 76–86, at 84–85; D. Starley, "The Metallurgical Examination of Ferrous Grave Goods from Wasperton Anglo-Saxon Cemetery MN80–85," in Carver, "Wasperton Anglo-Saxon Cemetery [Data-Set]."

81. Schrüfer-Kolb, *Roman Iron Production*, 34–35, 116.

82. Starley, "Metallurgical Examination," 15, 28–30; B. Gilmour and C. J. Salter, "Ironwork: Technological Examination of the Knives, Spearheads, and Sword/Weaving Batten," in T. Malim and J. Hines, *The Anglo-Saxon Cemetery at Edix Hill (Barrington A), Cambridgeshire* (York:

Council for British Archaeology, 1998), 250–55 and appendix microfiche; V. Fell and D. Starley, *A Technological Study of Ferrous Blades from the Anglo-Saxon Cemeteries at Boss Hall and St Stephen's Lane—Butttermarket, Ipswich, Suffolk*, Ancient Monuments Laboratory Report 18/99 (London: English Heritage, 1999).

83. Welton, "Encounters with Iron," 229–31.

84. D. Starley, "A Technological Study of Knives and Spearheads," in Hirst and Clark, *Excavations at Mucking*, 423–26; Wiemer, "Metallurgical Analyses of Iron Knives," 76–85.

85. Blakelock, "Early Medieval Cutting Edge," 1:231.

86. Starley, "Metallurgical Examination," 5, 22–23, 26; Gilmour and Salter, "Ironwork." For some of the reasons behind this, see Welton, "Encounters with Iron."

87. S. Crawford, "Children, Grave Goods, and Social Status in Early Anglo-Saxon England," in J. Sofaer Derevenski, ed., *Children and Material Culture* (London: Routledge, 2000), 169–79, at 176–77; H. Härke, "'Warrior Graves'? The Background of the Anglo-Saxon Weapon Burial Rite," *Past and Present*, 126 (1990), 22–43, at 25.

88. H. Härke, "Early Saxon Weapon Burials: Frequencies, Distributions, and Weapon Combinations," in S. Chadwick Hawkes, *Weapons and Warfare in Anglo-Saxon England* (Oxford: Oxford University Committee for Archaeology, 1989), 49–59; S. Harrington, *Aspects of Gender Identity and Craft Production in the European Migration Period: Iron Weaving Beaters and Associated Textile Making Tools from England, Norway, and Alamannia*, BAR International Series 1797 (Oxford: Archaeopress, 2008), 96–98.

89. B. Gilmour, "Swords, *Seaxes*, and Saxons: Pattern-Welding and Edged Weapon Technology from Late Roman Britain to Anglo-Saxon England," in M. Henig and T. J. Smith, eds., *Collectanea Antiqua: Essays in Memory of Sonia Chadwick Hawkes*, BAR International Series 1778 (Oxford: Archaeopress, 2007), 91–109, at 101; Harrington, *Aspects of Gender Identity*, 32; S. Fischer, *Les seigneurs des anneaux* (Saint-Germain-en-Laye: Association française d'archéologie mérovingienne, 2008), 22.

90. Gilmour, "Swords, *Seaxes*, and Saxons," 99, 101; Harrington, *Aspects of Gender Identity*, 96–99.

91. J. Lang and B. Ager, "Swords of the Anglo-Saxon and Viking Periods in the British Museum: A Radiographic Study," in Chadwick Hawkes, *Weapons and Warfare*, 85–122, at 107.

92. For swords, see R. F. Tylecote and B. J. J. Gilmour, *The Metallography of Early Ferrous Edge Tools and Edged Weapons*, BAR British Series 155 (Oxford: BAR, 1986), 249. We have no comparable metallographic information for iron weaving beaters.

93. Tylecote and Gilmour, *Metallography of Early Ferrous Edge Tools*, 246; B. Gilmour, "Metallurgical Analysis of the Swords," in J. I. McKinley, "The Early Saxon Cemetery at Park Lane, Croydon," *Surrey Archaeological Collections*, 90 (2003), 1–116, at 97–98; Gilmour, "Swords, *Seaxes*, and Saxons," 104, 107.

94. Harrington, *Aspects of Gender Identity*, 46–49, 52. Sue Harrington has recently argued that weaving swords were actually used as measuring rods, deployed to measure the width of cloth produced in household looms (S. Harrington, "Early Anglo-Saxon Weaving Swords Revisited," in I. Riddler, J. Soulat, and L. Keys, eds., *Le témoignage de la culture matérielle: Mélanges offerts au Professeur Vera Evison/The Evidence of Material Culture: Studies in Honour of Professor Vera Evison* (Autun: Mergoil, 2016), 209–18.

95. Gilmour, "Swords, *Seaxes*, and Saxons," 107.

96. Brian Gilmour, in his discussion of the Croydon swords, comments that the variety of iron bars needed for a pattern-welded sword would have required an iron trade, but he does not speculate as to the origins of this iron (Gilmour, "Metallurgical Analysis," 98).

97. R. Fleming, "Elites, Boats, and Foreigners: Rethinking the Rebirth of English Towns," *Città e campagna prima del mille, Atti delle Settimane di Studio*, 56 (2009), 393–425, at 398–407; Scull, "Social Transactions," 853. During the Viking Age there is also evidence that the metal for high-quality sword blades was being imported from far away: in this case some crucible steel from Persia or India was being brought into Scandinavia for this purpose (A. Williams, "Crucible Steel in Medieval Swords," in S. La Niece, D. Hook, and P. Craddock, eds., *Metals and Mines: Studies in Archaeometallurgy* [London: Archetype, 2007], 233–41).

98. G. Thomas, G. McDonnell, J. Merkel, and P. Marshall, "Technology, Ritual and Anglo-Saxon Agriculture: The Biography of a Plough Coulter from Lyminge, Kent," *Antiquity*, 90 (2016), 742–58, at 746, 748, 752.

99. Buchwald, *Iron and Steel*, 216, 237; Lyngstøm, "Farmers, Smelters, and Smiths," 22; L. E. Narmo, "Iron Production in Medieval Norway," *Ruralia*, 6 (2007), 207–17, at 209–10.

100. Lyngstøm, "Farmers, Smelters, and Smiths," 21–25.

101. J. Hines, *The Scandinavian Character of Anglian England in the Pre-Viking Period*, BAR British Series 124 (Oxford: BAR, 1984), 14; C. Loveluck and D. Tys, "Coastal Societies, Exchange, and Identity Along the Channel and Southern North Sea Shores of Europe, AD 600–1000," *Journal of Maritime Archaeology*, 1 (2006), 140–69.

102. C. P. Loveluck, "Acculturation, Migration, and Exchange: The Formation of Anglo-Saxon Society in the English Peak District, 400–700 AD," in J. Bintliff and H. Hamerow, eds., *Europe Between Late Antiquity and the Middle Ages*, BAR International Series 617 (Oxford: Tempus Reparatum, 1995), 84–98. Certainly, there are indications that elite households had access to freshly processed Derbyshire lead rather than recycled Roman lead by the ninth century (L. M. Wastling, "Evidence for Leadworking," in D. H. Evans and C. Loveluck, *Life and Economy at Early Medieval Flixborough, c. AD 600–1000: The Artefact Evidence* [Oxford: Oxbow Books, 2009], 337–38; P. Ottaway and J. Cowgill, "Woodworking, the Tool Hoard and Its Lead Containers," in Evans and Loveluck, *Life and Economy at Early Medieval Flixborough*, 253–80, at 270, 273). Lead-smelting sites dating to the ninth through eleventh centuries have also been found (for example, in Bollihope Common, County Durham, radiocarbon dated 1050 ± 50 (C. Bronk Ramsey, et al., "Radiocarbon Dates from the Oxford Ams System: Archaeometry Datelist 31," *Archaeometry*, 44 [2002], 1–149, at 49).

103. E. Campbell, *Continental and Mediterranean Imports to Atlantic Britain and Ireland, AD 400–800* (York: Council for British Archaeology, 2007).

104. Fleming, "Recycling in Britain," 37–45.

105. For the site, see M. J. Heaton, "Two Mid-Saxon Grain Driers and Later Medieval Features at Chantry Fields, Gillingham, Dorset," *Proceedings of the Dorset Natural History and Archaeological Society*, 114 (1992), 97–126. For a redating of the site, see D. A. Hinton, "Revised Dating of the Worgret Structure," *Proceedings of the Dorset Natural History and Archaeological Society*, 14 (1992), 258–59.

106. J. Haslam et al., "A Middle Saxon Iron Smelting Site at Ramsbury, Wiltshire," *Medieval Archaeology*, 24 (1980), 1–68.

107. In 1086, Domesday Book tells us specifically that the woodland and ironworking site in Weldon belonged to the king (A. Farley and H. Ellis, *Domesday-Book seu libri censualis, Willelmi Primi Regis Angliae, indices microform: Accessit dissertatio generalis de ratione hujusce libri, printed by command of His Majesty King George III, in pursuance of an address of the House of Commons of Great Britain*, 4 vols. (London: G. Eyre and A. Strahan, 1783–1816), vol. 1., fol. 219v.

108. T. Rayner, "Archaeological Excavation of Land to the Rear of Chapel Road, Weldon, Northamptonshire (WCRE01)" (unpublished report, Archaeological Project Services Report,

2003), 1, 6, 12; J. Cowgill, "Appendix 8: Report on the Slags and Related Debris from the Iron-Smelting Site at Chapel Road, Little Weldon, Northamptonshire (WCRE01)," in Rayner, "Archaeological Excavation of Land to the Rear of Chapel Road, Weldon, Northamptonshire (WCRE01)," 29–30. Smelters working around ninth- or tenth-century Flixborough may have been producing a similar range of different iron alloys (D. Starley, "Physico-Chemical Analysis of Debris," in Evans and Loveluck, *Life and Economy at Early Medieval Flixborough*, 328). Smiths at Wharram Percy in the middle Saxon period had access to iron bars composed of different alloys and originating at a number of different smelting centers (G. McDonnell, E. Blakelock, and S. Rubinson, "The Iron Economy of Wharram Percy—Modelling the Anglo-Saxon Iron Working Landscape," in S. Wrathmell, "Wharram Percy Archives" (unpublished report [data set], Archaeological Data Service, 2012), 5, 16–17, https://doi.org/10.5284/1000415). Another relatively large-scale iron-smelting site, operating within a century of Ramsbury and Weldon, has been excavated at Mersham, in Kent. This site may have been linked to Christ Church, Canterbury. When excavated, the site was found to contain an estimated 3.75 tons of ironworking debris (J. T. Munby and R. Helm, "Medieval Ironworking Evidence at Mersham, Kent" [unpublished report Oxford Wessex Archaeology Joint Venture, Oxford, 2006], https://doi.org/10.5284/1008713).

109. B. Groenwoudt, "Charcoal Burning and Landscape Dynamics in the Early Medieval Netherlands," *Ruralia*, 6 (2007), 327–37; E. Svensson, "Before a World-System? The Peasant-Artisan and the Market," *Ruralia*, 6 (2007), 189–99; J. Bond, "Medieval Charcoal-Burning in England," *Ruralia*, 6 (2007), 277–94, at 286–90.

110. Cowgill, "Appendix 8," 29–30.

111. McDonnell, "Iron and Its Alloys," 374; D. A. Hinton, "Raw Materials: Sources and Demand," in Hamerow, Hinton, and Crawford, eds., *Oxford Handbook of Anglo-Saxon Archaeology*, 423–39, at 424.

112. Lucy et al., *The Anglo-Saxon Settlement and Cemetery at Bloodmore Hill*, 372–81; R. Atkins and A. Connor, *Farmers and Ironsmiths: Prehistoric, Roman, and Anglo-Saxon Settlement Beside Brandon Road, Thetford, Norfolk*, East Anglian Archaeology 134 (Bar Hill: Oxford Archaeology East, 2010), 113–15. At Cottam, larger than usual numbers of knives have been metal-detected, perhaps because knives were being produced there (P. Ottaway, "Cottam Ironwork Recovered by Metal Detector," in J. D. Richards, "Burrow House Farm, Cottam: An Anglian and Anglo-Scandinavian Settlement in East Yorkshire, Archaeological Data Service" [unpublished report (data set), Archaeology Data Service, 2010], https://doi.org/10.5284/1000339).

Large-scale smithing as well as some smelting also seems to have taken place at the edges of the monastic precinct at Lyminge (G. Thomas, "Life Before the Minster: The Social Dynamics of Monastic Foundation at Anglo-Saxon Lyminge, Kent," *Antiquaries Journal*, 93 (2013), 109–45, at 131.

113. Atkins and Connor, *Farmers and Ironsmiths*, 60. Similarly, the smithing of fresh blooms may have been taking place sometime between the seventh and the ninth centuries at a settlement at Church Street, in Maldon, Essex (T. Ennis, "Former Croxley Works Site, Church Street, Maldon: Archaeological Evaluation and Excavation" [unpublished report, Essex County Council Field Archaeology Unit, 2009], 19, https://doi.org/10.5284/1003825).

114. Blakelock, "Early Medieval Cutting Edge," 1:199–203, 237.

115. E. Blakelock and G. McDonnell, "A Review of Metallographic Analyses of Early Medieval Knives," *Historical Metallurgy*, 41 (2007), 40–56, at 48–49, 54; Tylecote and Gilmour, *Metallography of Early Ferrous Edge Tools*, 249; D. Starley, "Metallographic Examination of Knife Blades," in Evans and Loveluck, *Life and Economy at Early Medieval Flixborough*, 229–31.

116. They date from the seventh to the eleventh centuries. K. Leahy, "A Deposit of Early Medieval Iron Objects from Scraptoft, Leicestershire," *Medieval Archaeology*, 57 (2013), 223–37, at 231–32, table 1; Thomas et al., "Technology, Ritual, and Anglo-Saxon Agriculture," 745.

117. Thomas et al., "Technology, Ritual, and Anglo-Saxon Agriculture," 745, 750. For the kinds of transformations and increased agricultural surpluses iron plow coulters could make possible, see S. Oosthuizen, "New Light on the Origins of Open-Field Farming," *Medieval Archaeology*, 49 (2005), 165–93, at 187–91.

118. J. Moreland, "Significance of Production in Eighth-Century England," in C. Wickham and I. Hansen, eds., *The Long Eighth Century* (Leiden: Brill, 2000), 69–98, at 98.

119. P. J. Fowler, *Farming in the First Millennium AD: British Agriculture Between Julius Caesar and William the Conqueror* (Cambridge: Cambridge University Press, 2002), 16.

120. J. Cowgill, "Overview of the Lead Vessels (with Chemical Analysis)," in P. Boyer, J. Proctor, and R. Taylor-Wilson, *On the Boundaries of Occupation: Excavations at Burringham Road, Scunthorpe and Baldwin Avenue, Bottesford, North Lincolnshire* (London: Pre-Construct Archaeology, 2009), 82–83.

121. K. Prestvold, "Iron Production and Society: Power, Ideology, and Social Structure in Inntrøndelag During the Early Iron Age: Stability and Change," *Norwegian Archaeological Review*, 29 (1996) 41–61, at 42, 57.

122. R. Fleming, *Britain After Rome: The Fall and Rise 400 to 1070* (London: Allen Lane, 2010), 65–119.

123. Something very similar has taken place in postcolonial Africa, where iron smelting was ubiquitous until the 1960s, but unlike blacksmithing, is now extinct because of the large amounts of scrap metal available in the rubbish tips and abandoned buildings dating from the colonial period (Sim, *Beyond the Bloom*, 4).

124. On this phenomenon more generally, see T. Mannoni, "The Transmission of Craft Techniques According to the Principles of Material Culture: Continuity and Rupture," in Lavan, Zanini, and Sarantis, eds., *Technology in Transition AD 300–650*, xli–lx.

CHAPTER 7

Epigraph: M. Parker Pearson, *The Archaeology of Death and Burial* (Stroud: Sutton, 1999), 124.

1. For arguments in support of infanticide as an underlying cause, see S. Mays, "Infanticide in Roman Britain," *Antiquity*, 67 (1999), 883–88; S. Mays, "The Archaeology and History of Infanticide, and Its Occurrence in Earlier British Populations," in J. Sofaer Derevenski, ed., *Children and Material Culture* (London: Routledge, 2000), 180–90; S. Mays, "Comment on 'A Bayesian Approach to Ageing Perinatal Skeletal Material from Archaeological Sites: Implications for the Evidence of Infanticide in Roman Britain' by R. L. Gowland and A. T. Chamberlain," *Journal of Archaeological Science*, 30 (2003), 1695–700; S. Mays and J. Eyers, "Perinatal Infant Death at the Roman Villa Site at Hambleden, Buckinghamshire, England," *Journal of Archaeological Science*, 38 (2011), 1931–38; C. Davidson, "Gender Imbalances in Romano-British Cemetery Populations: A Revaluation of the Evidence," in J. Pearce, M. Millet, and M. Struck, eds., *Burial, Society and Context in the Roman World* (Oxford: Oxbow Books, 2000), 231–37; N. Abu-Madil, K. A. Brown, J. Eyers, Terence A. Brown, and S. Mays, "Ancient DNA Study of the Remains of Putative Infanticide Victims from Yewden Roman Villa Site at Hambleden, England," *Journal of Archaeological Science*, 43 (2014), 192–97. For critiques of the infanticide hypothesis, see E. Scott, "A Critical

Review of the Interpretation of Infant Burials, with a Particular Reference to Roman Britain," *Journal of Theoretical Archaeology*, 1 (1990), 30–46; E. Scott, "Unpicking a Myth: The Infanticide of Female and Disabled Infants in Antiquity," *TRAC 2000* (2001), 143–51; R. L. Gowland and A. T. Chamberlain, "A Bayesian Approach to Ageing Perinatal Skeletal Material from Archaeological Sites: Implications for the Evidence for Infanticide in Roman Britain," *Journal of Archaeological Science*, 29 (2002), 677–85; J. H. Schwartz, R. Houghton, F. Macchiarelli, and L. Bandioli, "Skeletal Remains from Punic Carthage Do Not Support Systematic Sacrifice of Infants," *PLoS ONE*, 5 (2010), 2–12; L. Bonsall, "Infanticide in Roman Britain: A Critical Review of the Osteological Evidence," *Childhood in the Past*, 6 (2013), 73–88; R. L. Gowland, A. T. Chamberlain, and R. C. Redfern, "On the Brink of Being: Re-Evaluating Infant Death and Infanticide in Roman Britain," in M. Carroll and E.-J. Graham, eds., *Infant Health and Death in Roman Italy and Beyond* (Portsmouth, R.I.: Journal of Roman Archaeology, 2014), 69–88.

2. P. J. Ucko, "Ethnography and Archaeological Interpretation of Funerary Remains," *World Archaeology*, 1 (1969), 262–80, at 264; M. Golden, "Did the Ancients Care When Their Children Died?" *Greece and Rome*, 35 (1988), 152–63; A. Cannon and K. Cook, "Infant Death and the Archaeology of Grief," *Cambridge Archaeological Journal*, 25 (2015), 399–416, at 403. Similar explanations are sometimes used to talk about the disposal of poorer members of urban communities. For these arguments and a critique of them, see E.-J. Graham, "Discarding the Destitute: Ancient and Modern Attitudes Towards Burial Practices and Memory Preservation Amongst the Lower Classes of Rome," *TRAC 2005* (2006), 57–72.

3. M. Millett and R. Gowland, "Infant and Child Burial Rites in Roman Britain: A Study from East Yorkshire," *Britannia*, 46 (2015), 171–89.

4. C. M. Hodson, "Between Roundhouse and Villa: Assessing Perinatal and Infant Burials from Piddington, Northamptonshire," *Britannia*, 48 (2017), 195–219.

5. For a discussion of the overrepresentation of urban cemeteries in our data, see J. Pearce, "Urban Exits: Commercial Archaeology and the Study of Death Rituals and the Dead in the Towns of Roman Britain," in M. Fulford and N. Holbrook, eds., *The Towns of Roman Britain: The Contribution of Commercial Archaeology Since 1990* (London: Society for the Promotion of Roman Studies, 2015), 138–66; J. Pearce, "Introduction: Death as a Process in Roman Funerary Archaeology," in J. Pearce and J. Weekes, *Death as a Process: The Archaeology of the Roman Funeral* (Oxford: Oxbow Books, 2017), 1–26, at 2.

6. P. R. L. Brown, *The Cult of the Saints: Its Rise and Function in Latin Christianity*, enlarged ed. (Chicago: University of Chicago Press, 2015).

7. J. Pearce, "The Dispersed Dead: Preliminary Observations on Burial and Settlement Space in Rural Roman Britain," *TRAC 98* (1999), 151–62; J. Pearce, "Burial Evidence from Roman Britain: The Un-Numbered Dead," in J. Scheid, ed., *Pour une archéologie du rite: Nouvelles perspectives de l'archéologie funéraire* (Rome: École française de Rome, 2008), 29–42; Davidson, "Gender Imbalances"; S. Esmonde Cleary, "Putting the Dead in Their Place: Burial Location in Roman Britain," in Pearce et al., *Burial, Society and Context*, 127–42, at 127.

8. Pearson, *Archaeology of Death and Burial*, 124; See also above, n. 1.

9. For the age of these neonates, see A. Moore, "Hearth and Home: The Burial of Infants Within Romano-British Domestic Contexts," *Childhood in the Past*, 2 (2009), 33–54, at 38–39; R. Gowland, "Playing Dead: Implications of Mortuary Evidence for the Social Construct of Childhood in Roman Britain," *TRAC 2000* (2001), 152–68, at 157. On child and neonate burials more broadly, see A. T. Chamberlain, "Commentary: Missing Stages of Life—Towards the Perception of Children in Archaeology," in J. Moore and E. Scott, eds., *Invisible People and Processes: Writing Gender and Childhood into European Archaeology* (London: Leicester University Press, 1997),

248–50; R. J. H. Pearce, "Case Studies in a Contextual Archaeology of Burial Practices in Roman Britain," 2 vols. (Ph.D. diss., Durham University, 1999) 1:19–24; Gowland, "Playing Dead," 157. For the ways in which social, chronological, biological, and cultural definitions of childhood map onto one another differently in different times and places, see S. E. Halcrow and N. Tayles, "The Bioarchaeological Investigation of Childhood and Social Age: Problems and Prospects," *Journal of Archaeological Method and Theory*, 15 (2008), 190–215; A. Ingvarsson-Sundström, *Asine III: Supplementary Studies on the Swedish Excavations 1922–1930; Fasc. 2; Children Lost and Found; A Bioarchaeolgical Study of Middle Helladic Children in Asine with a Comparison to Learna* (Stockholm: Svneska institutet i Athen, 2008), especially chapter 1.

10. P. Corder, H. Mattingly, and M. R. Hull, *The Defences of the Roman Fort at Malton* (Oxford: Oxford University Press, 1930), 67.

11. J. Alexander and J. Pullinger, *Roman Cambridge: Excavations on Castle Hill 1956–1988*, Proceedings of the Cambridge Antiquarian Society 88 (Cambridge: Cambridge Antiquarian Society, 2000), 39–40.

12. Alexander and Pullinger, *Roman Cambridge*, 45–46.

13. Alexander and Pullinger, *Roman Cambridge*, 35–47; A. Taylor, "Discussion and Conclusions," in Alexander and Pullinger, *Roman Cambridge*, 75–83, at 82.

14. Alexander and Pullinger, *Roman Cambridge*, 53–57; Taylor, "Discussion and Conclusions," 79.

15. Alexander and Pullinger, *Roman Cambridge*, 53.

16. Alexander and Pullinger, *Roman Cambridge*, 55.

17. Alexander and Pullinger, *Roman Cambridge*, 53–56.

18. S. Clarke, "Abandonment, Rubbish Disposal, and 'Special' Deposits at Newstead," *TRAC 1996* (1997), 73–81, at 75.

19. See above, Chapter 5, n. 92 for references.

20. C. Bell, *Ritual Theory, Ritual Practice* (Oxford: Oxford University Press, 1992), 74.

21. In the fourth-century cemetery at Qasar Ibrim, in Nubia, infants were wrapped in cloth and accompanied by basketry sandals (E. Scott, "Image and Contexts of Infants and Infant Burials: Some Thoughts on Cross Cultural Evidence," *Archaeological Review from Cambridge*, 11 [1992], 77–92, at 89), and the babies buried from the first to the fifth centuries at the cemetery at Kellis, in Egypt, were placed in tightly wrapped linen shrouds, bound with cords or strips of linen cloth (M. Carroll, "The Roman Child Clothed in Death," in M. Carroll and J. P. Wild, eds., *Dressing the Dead in Classical Antiquity* [Stroud: Amberley, 2012], 134–47, at 135).

22. Yorkshire Museum, YORYM: 2007.6026; Carroll, "Roman Child Clothed in Death," 139–40.

23. There are examples from across the Roman world for the inclusion of plant stuffs in burials of both adults and infants. For edible plant remains in preurban Rome's tombs, see H. Helbaek, "Vegetables in the Funeral Meals of Pre-Urban Rome," in E. Gjerstad, ed., *Early Rome*, vol. 2, *The Tombs* (Lund: Skrifter utgivna av Svenska institutet i Rom, 1956), 287–94. For edible plants in graves in Gaul, see L. Bouby and P. Marinval, "Fruits and Seeds from Roman Cremations in Limagne (Massif Central) and the Spatial Variability of Plant Offerings in France," *Journal of Archaeological Science*, 31 (2004), 77–86; S. Preiss, V. Matterne, and F. Laton, "An Approach to Funerary Rituals in the Roman Provinces: Plant Remains from a Gallo-Roman Cemetery at Faulquemont (Moselle, France)," *Vegetation History and Archaeobotany*, 14 (2005), 362–72. For grain and legumes in London cremations, see N. C. C. White, "Catering for the Cultural Identities of the Deceased in Roman Britain: Interpretive Potential and Problems," *TRAC 2006* (2007), 115–32, at 125–27. For other examples with citations, see Pearce, "Introduction: Death as a Process,"

10. For the presence of soft furnishings and luxury textiles in graves, see A. Lefebvre, M. et al., "Premières données sur l'archéologie funéraire de l'Antiquité tardive dans la cité des Médiomatriques: L'example d'Uckange (Moselle)," *Revue archéologique de l'Est*, 62 (2013), 253–81; T. Divièse et al., "First Chemical Evidence of Royal Purple as a Material Used for Funeral Treatment Discovered in a Gallo-Roman Burial (Naintré, France, Third Century AD)," *Analytical and Bioanalytical Chemistry*, 401 (2011), 1739–48.

24. G. W. Meates, *The Roman Villa at Lullingstone, Kent*, vol. 1, *The Site* (Chichester: Kent Archaeological Society, 1979), 88.

25. T. Ashwin and A. Tester, *A Romano-British Settlement in the Waveney Valley: Excavations at Scole, 1993–4*, East Anglian Archaeology 152 (Dereham: Norfolk Historic Environment Service, 2014), 225.

26. Millett and Gowland, "Infant and Child Burial Rites," 183–84; B. Cunliffe, *Excavations at Portchester Castle*, vol. 1, *Roman* (London: Society of Antiquaries of London, 1975), 376–77; M. Fulford, A. Clarke, and H. Eckhardt, *Life and Labour in Late Roman Silchester: Excavations in Insula IX Since 1997* (London: Society for the Promotion of Roman Studies, 2006), 200–205; M. Fulford, "Links with the Past: Pervasive 'Ritual' Behaviour in Roman Britain," *Britannia*, 32 (2001), 199–218, at 211.

27. C. Forcey, "Whatever Happened to Heroes? Ancestral Cults and the Enigma of Romano-Celtic Temples," *TRAC 1997* (1998), 87–98, at 90–91; Esmonde Cleary, "Putting the Dead in Their Place," 138–39.

28. A. Ross, "Shafts, Pits, Wells—Sanctuaries of the Belgic Britons?" in J. M. Coles and D. D. A. Simpson, eds., *Studies in Ancient Europe: Essays Presented to Stuart Piggott* (Leicester: Leicester University Press, 1968), 255–85.

29. For examples, see J. L. Rife and M. M. Morison, "Space, Object, and Process in the Koutsongila Cemetery at Roman Kenchreai, Greece," in Pearce and Weekes, eds., *Death as a Process*, 27–59; J. Aarts and S. Heeren, "Buried Batavians: Mortuary Rituals of a Rural Frontier Community," in Pearce and Weekes, *Death as a Process*, 123–54.

30. For the chronology of the site, see R. Leech, E. M. Besly, R. F. Everton, and E. Fowler, "Excavation of a Romano-British Farmstead and Cemetery on Bradley Hill, Somerton, Somerset," *Britannia*, 12 (1981), 177–252, at 205 and fig. 2; J. Gerrard, "Bradley Hill, Somerton, Somerset and the End of Roman Britain: A Study in Continuity?" *Proceedings of the Somerset Archaeology and Natural History Society*, 148 (2005), 1–10, at 6–7.

31. Leech et al., "Excavation of a Romano-British Farmstead," 182–87.

32. This building was put up after c. 365–80 and was in use into the fifth century (Leech et al., "Excavation of a Romano-British Farmstead," 192).

33. Leech et al., "Excavation of a Romano-British Farmstead," 188–92.

34. Leech et al., "Excavation of a Romano-British Farmstead," 193–95.

35. J. Gerrard, "New Radiocarbon Dates from the Cemetery at Bradley Hill, Somerton," *Proceedings of the Somerset Archaeology and Natural History Society*, 154 (2011) 189–92; Gerrard, "Bradley Hill," 4–5.

36. Indeed, Gerrard suggests that the later burying community could have lived at nearby Dundon, although he prefers the idea that they continued to reside at Bradley Hill (Gerrard, "Bradley Hill," 6–8).

37. R. A. Philpott, *Burial Practice in Roman Britain: A Survey of Grave Treatment and Furnishings AD 43–410*, BAR British Series 219 (Oxford: Tempus Reparatum, 1991).

38. At Poundbury almost 9 percent of those buried were under the age of one, and another 15 percent were between the ages of one and thirteen. At Lankhills there were thirty-four children

under the age of one year and twenty-five between the ages of one and three (R. Gowland, "Playing Dead," 155). At one of Godmanchester's late Roman cemeteries, at total of twelve children between the ages of three and ten were buried, constituting 46 percent of the burial population (A. Jones, ed., *Settlement, Burial and Industry in Roman Godmanchester: Excavations in the Extra-Mural Area; The Parks 1998, London Road 1997–8, and Other Investigations*, BAR British Series 346 [Oxford: Archaeopress, 2003], 29 and table 4). At Newarke Street, Leicester, 27 percent of the burials excavated belonged to infants and children (M. Derrick, "The Excavation of a Roman Cemetery at 21–33 Cemetery Newarke Street, Leicester," *Transactions of the Leicestershire Archaeological and Historical Society*, 83 [2009], 63–102, at 80). At Gloucester's Wootton Cemetery, 15 percent of the burials were of infants or children under the age of ten (P. Ellis and R. King, "Gloucester: The Wootton Cemetery, Excavations, 2002," *Britannia*, 45 [2014], 53–120, at 80). At the Bath Gate Cemetery, something on the order of 19 percent of all aged burials belonged to those who died between birth and the age of ten (L. Viner and R. Leech, "Bath Gate Cemetery, 1969–1976," in A. McWhirr, L. Viner, and C. Wells, *Romano-British Cemeteries at Cirencester* [Cirencester: Cirencester Excavation Committee, 1982], 69–111, at table 33, p. 137). In the extramural cemeteries at Winchester published by Ottaway et al., approximately 14 percent of aged skeletons belonged to individuals between the ages of two and twelve years (P. J. Ottaway, K. E. Qualmann, H. Rees, and G. D. Scobie, *The Roman Cemeteries and Suburbs of Winchester: Excavations 1971–86* [Winchester: Winchester Museums and English Heritage, 2012], 218). At the cemetery at Queenford Farm there were quite a lot of young children, but only one infant under six months (R. A. Chambers, "The Late- and Sub-Roman Cemetery at Queenford Farm, Dorchester-on-Thames, Oxon," *Oxoniensia*, 52 [1987], 35–69, at 46–53). But urban cemeteries were exceptional. Many excavated late Roman rural cemeteries contain few or no infants and children (P. Booth, "Late Roman Cemeteries in Oxfordshire: A Review," *Oxoniensia*, 66 [2002], 13–42, at 30–31).

39. The infants are F123, 124, 130, 132, 150. The children are F137, 140, 152.

40. Although this number may seem large, there are other complexes of Roman buildings with more infant burials than this. Fifty-one, for example, were found under the floors of the buildings of the villa at Bucknowle, Dorset (T. Light and P. Ellis, *Bucknowle: A Romano-British Villa and Its Antecedents; Excavations 1976–1991* [Dorchester: Dorchester Natural History and Archaeology Society, 2009], 156).

41. The infants are F18, F56a, b, and c, F44. Leech et al., "Excavation of a Romano-British Farmstead," 183, 220, 240–41.

42. One burial, however, which Leech et al. argue is a foundation burial, cut through the room's carefully laid subfloor so cannot date to the earliest phase of the building's construction (Leech et al., "Excavation of a Romano-British Farmstead," 183).

43. Placement of infants in corners or along walls of rooms are found in many places in Britain (Moore, "Hearth and Home," 41–43; Pearce, "Case Studies in a Contextual Archaeology of Burial Practice in Roman Britain," 2:113; M. Struck, "Kinderbestattungen in romano-britischen Siedlungen—der Archäologische Befund," in M. Struck, ed., *Römerzeitliche Gräber als Quellen zu Religion, Bevölkerungsstruktur und Sozialgeschichte* (Mainz: Institut für Vor- und Frühgeschichte der Johannes Gutenberg-Universität Mainz, 1993), 313–19; M. Carroll, "'No Part in Earthly Things': The Death, Burial, and Commemoration of Newborn Children and Infants in Roman Italy," in M. Harlow and L. L. Lovén, eds., *Families in the Roman and Late Antique Worlds (50–600 CE)*, (London: Continuum Books, 2012), 41–63, at 45. For the very long history of underfloor infant burials, see D. Borić and S. Stefanović, "Birth and Death: Infant Burials from Vlasac and Lepenski Vir," *Antiquity*, 78 (2004), 526–46, especially 541–42. For more general discussion of the global history of burial in houses as well as a bibliography on the subject, see R. L. Adams

and S. M. King, "Residential Burial in Global Perspective," *Archaeological Papers of the American Anthropological Association*, 20 (2011), 1–16.

44. E. Scott, "Animal and Infant Burials in Romano-British Villas: Revitalization Movement," in P. Garwood et al., eds., *Sacred and Profane: Proceedings of a Conference on Archaeology, Ritual, and Religion, Oxford, 1989* (Oxford: Oxbow Books, 1991), 115–21.

45. Leech et al., "Excavation of a Romano-British Farmstead," 183, 189, 192.

46. Leech et al., "Excavation of a Romano-British Farmstead," 189; Gerrard, "Bradley Hill," 6.

47. At a number of sites, more than one infant was buried in the same room, but in different corners (Moore, "Hearth and Home," 41–42).

48. Infant burials have been found in villa barns. This is the case, for example, at Winterton, where both animal and infant burials (seven in all) were placed in the floor of the barn (I. M. Stead, *Excavations at Winterton Roman Villa and Other Sites in North Lincolnshire 1958–67* [London: H.M. Stationery Office, 1976], 48) and at Water Newton (R. C. Hatton and W. Wall, "A Late-Roman Cemetery at *Durobrivae*, Chesterton," *Proceedings of the Cambridge Antiquarian Society*, 95 [2006], 5–24, at 5). A building used for cereal storage at Alington Avenue, in Dorcester, had the bodies of six infants inserted into its floor (S. M. Davies, P. S. Bellamy, M. J. Heaton, and P. J. Woodward, *Excavations at Alington Avenue, Fordington, Dorchester, Dorset, 1984–87* [Dorchester: Dorset Natural History and Archaeological Society, 2002], 67–70). At an agricultural building at Chalk, near Gravesend, three infants were buried in pits dug into the chalk on which the building stood (D. E. Johnston, J. R. B. Arthur, C. R. Metcalfe, A. Eastham, G. C. Morgan, A. G. Woodhead, R. Reece, and A. W. G. Lowther, "A Roman Building at Chalk, near Gravesend," *Britannia*, 3 [1972], 112–48, at 119). Building 13 at Bucknowle Villa in Dorset, which was probably a work hall, was also the site of infant burial (Light and Ellis, *Bucknowle*, 42, 45, 156). For further examples, see E. Scott, "Aspects of the Roman Villa as a Form of British Settlement," 2 vols. (Ph.D. diss., University of Newcastle upon Tyne, 1988), 11:279–84, and Scott, "Animal and Infant Burials," 115–21.

49. For examples of neonate burials in or near kilns and ovens, see N. Mitchelson, "Roman Malton: The Civilian Settlement; Excavations in Orchard Field, 1949–1952," *Yorkshire Archaeological Journal*, 41 (1964), 209–61, at 229; J. Taylor, "An Assessment Report of Archaeological Investigations at the Former Shippam's Factory and Shippam's Social Club, East Walls, Chichester, West Sussex" (unpublished report, Pre-Construct Archaeology, 2008), 143, https://doi.org/10.5284/1017693); A. Rogers, "Late Roman Towns as Meaningful Places: Reconceptualising Decline in the Towns of Late Roman Britain," in D. Sami and G. Speed, eds., *Debating Urbanism Within and Beyond the Walls AD 300–700* (Leicester: University of Leicester School of Archaeology and Ancient History, 2010), 57–82; Millett and Gowland, "Infant and Child Burial Rites," 185. Both Moore's and Scott's data more generally suggest that infant burials often took place in and around productive buildings (Scott, "Aspects of the Roman Villa," 1:279–84; Moore, "Hearth and Home," 39–40).

50. The epigraphical habit, though, was never strong in Britain. For the ways the dead were remembered as individuals, see M. Carroll, "*Memoria* and *Damnatio Memoriae*: Preserving and Erasing Identities in Roman Funerary Commemoration," in M. Carroll and J. Rempel, eds., *Living Through the Dead: Burial and Commemoration in the Classical World* (Oxford: Oxbow Books, 2011), 65–90. Although there is evidence that the sites of infant burial were remembered, they would not have been remembered in the same way that tomb inscriptions suggest that the burials of adults sometimes were, in that the inscriptions asked that the dead be remembered as named individuals (C. Botturi, "'Landscapes of Life' and 'Landscapes of Death': The Contribution of Funerary Evidence to the Understanding of the Perception and Organisation of Roman Rural Landscapes in Northern Italy," *TRAC 2015* [2016], 43–56, at 46).

51. M. Wood, "Ganstead to Asselby Natural Gas Pipeline: Archaeological Excavations and Watching Brief; Post-Excavation Assessment of Potential for Analysis and Undated Project Design," 2 vols. (unpublished report, Network Archaeology, 2011), 1:48–66, doi:10.5284/1029254. The settlement is named in the report as "Plots 103 and 104."
52. M. Wood, "Ganstead," 1:49.
53. M. Wood, "Ganstead," 1:53–54, 60.
54. M. Wood, "Ganstead," 1:55–57.
55. The body of the text says "fifty-six" (M. Wood, "Ganstead," 1:47), but the human bone assessment lists "fifty-eight" (J. Wood, "Human Bone Assessment," in M. Wood, "Ganstead," appendix 10).
56. M. Wood, "Ganstead," 1:54, 56–57.
57. M. Wood, "Ganstead," 1:51–52
58. M. Wood, "Ganstead," 1:51–52.
59. M. Wood, "Ganstead," 1:55–56.
60. M. Wood, "Ganstead," 1:56.
61. M. Wood, "Ganstead," 1:49.
62. Esmonde Cleary, "Putting the Dead in Their Place," 129. Many other communities similarly perpetuated their boundaries through their placement of burials, sometimes their infant burials (J. Pearce, "Infants, Cemeteries, and Communities in the Roman Provinces," *TRAC 2000* [2001], 125–42). At Rotherley, for example, both adults and infants were found in boundary ditches, but in different ditches (A. H. L. F. Pitt-Rivers, *Excavations in Cranborne Chase, near Rushmore, on the Borders of Dorset and Wilts: 1880–1888* [London: Harrison and Sons, 1888], 69, 190–99, 208). But not all communities deployed infants in this task. At Higham Ferrers, for example, adults were buried head-to-toe along boundary lines, but none of the fourteen neonates recovered from the site were buried in this way. Instead, they were laid to rest under the floors of the settlement's buildings (S. Lawrence and A. Smith, *Between Villa and Town: Excavations of a Roadside Settlement and Shrine at Higham Ferrers, Northamptonshire* [Oxford: Oxford Archaeology, 2009], 277–78, 286).
63. J. Brück, "Rituals and Rationality: Some Problems of Interpretation," *European Journal of Archaeology*, 2 (1999), 313–44, at 331.
64. R. McC. Netting, *Smallholders, Householders: Farm Families and the Ecology of Intensive Sustainable Agriculture* (Stanford, Calif.: Stanford University Press, 1993), 71.
65. L. Martin, J. Richardson, and I. Roberts, *Iron Age and Roman Settlements at Wattle Syke* (Leeds: Archaeological Services WYAS, 2013), 297–300.
66. Martin et al., *Iron Age and Roman Settlements at Wattle Syke*, 102–5.
67. SK1, SK2, SK4, SK5, SK7, SK23, and SK30 are the adults buried with neonates. Two other graves, SK34 and SK35, contain the remains of adults and children between the ages of three and five (Martin et al., *Iron Age and Roman Settlements at Wattle Syke*, 102–8).
68. For what would be confronted in a reopened grave, see H. Duday, F. le Mort, and A. Tillier, "Archaeothanatology and Funeral Archaeology: Application to the Study of Primary Single Burials," *Anthropologie*, 52 (2014), 235–46.
69. The men are SK4 and SK30. The older adult women are SK5 and SK2.
70. For example, at a cemetery at Cirencester all but one adult buried with an infant (most of whom lay at the feet of adults) were deceased males, and the single woman buried with an infant was in her late forties or older and was probably suffering from polio, so it seems unlikely that she was that infant's mother (McWhirr, Viner, and Wells, *Romano-British Cemeteries at Cirencester*, 110–11). At Burnby Lane, Yorkshire, the remains of cremated children were placed in the

same pots as cremated adults. The authors suggest that the remains of children might have been curated until a suitable adult died (Millett and Gowland, "Infant and Child Burial Rites," 78). At Babraham Hall, Cambridgeshire, a number of infants were inserted into earlier adult graves (S. Timberlake, N. Dodwell, and N. Armour, "Roman Cemetery, the Babraham Institute Cambridgeshire: An Archaeological Excavation" [unpublished report, Cambridge Archaeological Unit, 2007], 48, 52, 55, https://doi.org/10.5284/1001160). At the California cemetery at Baldock, an elderly woman was buried with a neonate, and an adult male's grave was reopened, and a neonate placed in a small box was inserted into his grave (G. R. Burleigh and K. J. Fitzpatrick-Matthews, *Draft Catalogue of Burials in the California Late-Roman Cemetery* [unpublished report, North Hertfordshire Museums, last modified 2014], nos. 1196 [1190] with [1502] and 1060 [1088] was found with [1090]). At Navenby, Lincolnshire, a neonate was placed on the chest of a coffined child, who was about seven years of age (M. Allen and C. Palmer-Brown, "Archaeological Watching Brief Report: Land off Chapel Lane, Navenby, Linconshire" [unpublished report, Pre-Construct Archaeology, 2001], 4–7, https://doi.org/10.5284/1015019).

71. Martin et al., *Iron Age and Roman Settlements at Wattle Syke*, 292–94.
72. Martin et al., *Iron Age and Roman Settlements at Wattle Syke*, 297.
73. Martin et al., *Iron Age and Roman Settlements at Wattle Syke*, 102–8.
74. Esmonde Cleary, "Putting the Dead in Their Place."
75. C. L. Matthews, "A Romano-British Inhumation Cemetery at Dunstable," *Bedfordshire Archaeological Journal*, 15 (1981), 1–73, at 3, 18–26.
76. Other late Roman cemeteries betray a similar preference for burial in or near cemetery enclosure ditches, rather than in the space within the enclosure itself, and the result is often an L-shaped pattern of burials along two sides of an enclosure. For examples, see Davies, et al., *Excavations at Alington Avenue*, fig. 55; M. Luke and M. Phillips, "Preliminary Report on the Archaeological Investigation of a Romano-British Cemetery at Burton Latimer, Northamptonshire" [unpublished report, Albion Archaeology, 2011], doi:10.5284/1033894; Derrick, "Excavation of a Roman Cemetery at 21–33 Newarke Street," 73.
77. Matthews, "Romano-British Inhumation Cemetery at Dunstable," 5, 11.
78. Matthews, "Romano-British Inhumation Cemetery at Dunstable," 5–11.
79. Matthews, "Romano-British Inhumation Cemetery at Dunstable," 10.
80. Matthews, "Romano-British Inhumation Cemetery at Dunstable," 4.
81. For other infant burials along boundaries in settlements, see M. Millett, "'By Small Things Revealed': Rural Settlement and Society," in M. Millett, L. Revell, and A. Moore, eds., *The Oxford Handbook of Roman Britain* (Oxford: Oxford University Press, 2016), 699–719, at 715. The burials in the boundary ditch at Dunstable can be contrasted to those found in the ditch of Oram's Arbour enclosure, an Iron Age enclosure in the suburbs of Roman Winchester. This feature was used extensively for many decades in the late Roman period as a site of infant burial. Like the burials in the barn at Bradley Hill, no one grave intercut another. In two excavated segments of the enclosure ditch, forty-two infants were found, along with ten adults and one adolescent. Three of the adults belong to the latest phase of burial, four are buried outside the ditch rather than in it, and two were associated in burial with infants. So, the emphasis here was on infant burial. No burials, however, were made inside the enclosure (Ottaway, et al., *Roman Cemeteries and Suburbs of Winchester*, 137–73, 342–44).
82. B. Tibbetts, "Infant Burials in Iron Age Britain," in K. Bacvarov, ed., *Babies Reborn: Infant/Child Burials in Pre- and Protohistory*, BAR International Series 1832 (Oxford: Archaeopress, 2008), 189–94; and S. Crawford, "Special Burials, Special Buildings? An Anglo-Saxon

Perspective on the Interpretation of Infant Burials in Association with Rural Settlement Structures," in Bacvarov, *Babies Reborn*, 197–204.

83. V. Dasen, "Roman Birth Rites of Passage Revisited," *Journal of Roman Archaeology*, 22 (2009), 199–214, at 209–10; I. Beilke-Voigt, "Burials of Children in Houses and Settlements During the Roman Iron Age and Early Medieval Period in Northern Germany and Denmark," in L. H. Dommasnes and M. Wrigglesworth, eds., *Children, Identity and the Past* (Newcastle: Cambridge Scholars, 2008), 16–35; N. J. Norman, "Death and Burial of Roman Children: The Case of the Yasmina Cemetery at Carthage—Part II. The Archaeological Evidence," *Mortality*, 8 (2003), 36–47; L. M. Stirling, "One Foot in the Grave: Evidence for Footwear in the Graves of Roman North Africa," *Africa Romana*, 17 (2008), 2265–73; Scott, "Image and Context," 88.

84. Botturi, "Landscapes of Life," 45–49.

85. M. Parker Pearson, "The Powerful Dead: Archaeological Relationships Between the Living and the Dead," *Cambridge Archaeological Journal*, 3 (1993), 203–29, at 204.

86. Moore, "Hearth and Home," 41–42; M. Millett, "Interpreting Local and Indigenous Ritual," *Archaeological Dialogues*, 4 (1997), 154–55.

87. Standard texts used to explain Roman attitudes toward infants, infant personhood, and infant death are Plutarch, *Quaest. Rom.* 102, *Numa* 12, and *Moralia*, 612A; Cicero, *Tusculan Disputations* 1.39; Pliny, *Historia Naturalis*, VII, 15.72; and Juvenal, *Satires*, XV, 138–40, along with an antiquarian work of Fabius Planciades Fulgentius (fl. late fifth to early sixth century), *Expositio sermonum antiquorum* VII. For a concise discussion of these texts, see D. Soren and N. Soren, eds., *A Roman Villa and a Late Roman Infant Cemetery: Excavation at Poggio Gramignano Lugnano in Teverina* (Rome: L'Erma di Bretschneider, 1999), 518–20.

88. For arguments against using these texts, see M. Carroll, "Infant Death and Burial in Roman Italy," *Journal of Roman Archaeology*, 24 (2011), 99–120.

89. See above, nn. 48–49.

90. Christopher Tilley long ago laid out the many ways place was made, "constructed in movement, memory, encounter, and association" (C. Tilley, *A Phenomenology of Landscape: Places, Paths, and Monuments* [Oxford: Berg, 1994], 15). Infants were active in place making in all these ways. See also J. Chapman, "From 'Space' to 'Place': A Model of Dispersed Settlement and Neolithic Society," in C. Burgess, P. Topping, and D. Mordant, eds., *Enclosures and Defences in the Neolithic of Western Europe*, BAR International Series 403 (Oxford: Archaeopress, 1988), 21–46.

91. K. Olwig, "Performing on the Landscape Versus Doing Landscape: Preambulatory Practice, Sight, and the Sense of Belonging," in T. Ingold and J. L. Vergunst, eds., *Ways of Walking: Ethnography and Practice on Foot* (Aldershot: Ashgate, 2008), 81–92. For burials as ongoing negotiations, see Pearce, "Dispersed Dead," 154–57.

92. A. Jones, *Memory and Material Culture* (Cambridge: Cambridge University Press, 2007).

93. For short-term memory versus long-term memorialization in another context, see L. Meskell, "Dying Young: The Experience of Death at Deir el Medina," *Archaeological Review from Cambridge*, 13 (1994), 35–45.

94. J. Taylor, "Encountering Romanitas: Characterising the Role of Agricultural Communities in Roman Britain," *Britannia*, 44 (2013), 171–90, at 175.

95. Babies along with some adults were buried alongside or in boundary ditches in the same places structured deposits were placed (M. Beasley, "Roman Boundaries, Roads, and Rituals: Excavating at the Old Sorting Office, Swan Street, Southwark," *Transactions of the London and Middlesex Archaeological Society*, 57 [2006], 23–68, at 62–64).

96. Esmonde Cleary, "Putting the Dead in Their Place," 140.

97. Millett's and Gowland's work suggests that in some communities neonates and slightly older babies were treated differently in death, although their data also suggests that both groups were buried in archaeologically visible ways (Millett and Gowland, "Infant and Child Burial Rites").

98. E. D. Blanning, "Landscape, Settlement and Materiality: Aspects of Rural Life in Kent During the Roman Period," 3 vols. (Ph.D. diss., University of Kent, 2014), 2:336. For an ethnographic example of preterm and just-born babies' close connections with the spirit world, see A. Gottlieb, *The Afterlife Is Where We Come From* (Chicago: University of Chicago Press, 2004).

99. J. Chapman, "The Living, the Dead, and the Ancestors: Time, Life Cycles, and the Mortuary Domain in Later European Prehistory," in J. Davis, ed., *Ritual and Remembrance: Responses to Death in Human Societies* (Sheffield: Sheffield Academic, 1994), 40–85; K. Kostanti, "'Missing Infants': Giving Life to Aspects of Childhood in Mycenaean Greece via Intermural Burials," in E. Murphy and M. Le Roy, eds., *Children, Death, and Burial: Archaeological Discourses* (Oxford: Oxbow Books, 2017), 107–23.

100. Sometimes infant burials are even defined as "deviant" (E. M. Murphy, "Introduction," in E. M. Murphy, ed., *Deviant Burial in the Archaeological Record* (Oxford: Oxbow Books, 2008), xii–xviii.

101. Carroll, "No Part in Earthly Things," 44.

102. N. Pilkington, "Growing Up Roman: Infant Mortality and Reproductive Development," *Journal of Interdisciplinary History*, 44 (2013), 1–36, at 4, 21. Gowland's estimate is similarly 25–35 percent (Gowland, "Playing Dead," 155); A. Chamberlain suggests childhood mortality in premodern societies was at least 50 percent (Chamberlain, "Commentary," 249).

103. P. Stuart-MacAdam, "Anemia in Roman Britain: Poundbury Camp," in H. Bush and M. Zvelebil, eds., *Health in Past Societies: Biocultural Interpretations of Human Skeletal Remains in Archaeological Context*, BAR International Series 567 (Oxford: Tempus, 1991), 101–13; N. A. Arthur, R. L. Gowland, and R. C. Redfern, "Coming of Age in Roman Britain: Osteological Evidence for Pubertal Timing," *American Journal of Physical Anthropology*, 159 (2016), 698–713; Hodson, "Between Roundhouse and Villa." For a general discussion of other signs of ill health among Romano-British children, see R. Gowland, "Ideas of Childhood in Roman Britain: The Bioarchaeological and Material Evidence," in Millett, Revell, and Moore, *Oxford Handbook of Roman Britain*, 303–20, at 307–10.

104. Children are not entirely absent from the burial record. They are most visible in urban cemeteries (see above, n. 38) but they are also well represented in some of the cemeteries associated with roadside settlements (e.g., S. West with J. Plouvez, "The Romano-British Site at Icklingham," *East Anglian Archaeology Reports*, 3 [1979], 63–126, at 103; P. Halkon, M. Millett, and H. Woodhouse, eds., *Hayton, East Yorkshire: Archaeological Studies of the Iron Age and Roman Landscape*, 2 vols. [Leeds: Yorkshire Archaeological Society, 2015], 2:483–92, table 20.1; P. Booth, *Asthall, Oxfordshire: Excavations in a Roman "Small Town," 1992"* [Oxford: Oxford Archaeological Unit, 1997], 136). There are also a number of lavish or ritually complex rural child burials (e.g., A. Taylor, "A Roman Lead Coffin with Pipeclay Figurines from Arrington, Cambridgeshire," *Britannia*, 24 [1993], 191–225; R. C. Brettell, B. Stern, N. Reifarth, and C. Heron, "The 'Semblance of Immortality'? Resinous Materials and Mortuary Rites in Roman Britain," *Archaeometry*, 56 [2014], 444–59; J. P. Wild, "A Roman Silk Damask from Kent," *Archaeologia Cantiana*, 80 [1965], 246–50; G. R. Burleigh, K. J. Fitzpatrick-Matthews, and M. J. Aldhouse-Green, "A Dea Nutrix Figurine from a Romano-British Cemetery at Baldock, Hertfordshire," *Britannia*, 37 [2006], 273–94; Davies et al., *Excavations at Alington Avenue*, 135; L. Brown, "An Unusual Iron Age Enclosure at Fir Hill Bossington, and a Romano-British Cemetery near Brook, Hampshire: The

Broughton to Timsbury Pipeline, Part 2," *Proceedings of the Hampshire Field Club and Archaeological Society*, 64 [2009], 40–80, at 73; S. Lawrence and P. Booth, "The Iron Age Settlement and Roman Villa at Thurnham, Kent" [unpublished report, Oxford Wessex Archaeology Joint Venture, 2006], 108–9, https://doi.org/10.5284/1008824; N. Crummy, "Bears and Coins: The Iconography of Protection in Late Roman Infant Burials," *Britannia*, 41 [2010], 37–93). This suggests that some elite families subscribed to different kinds of infant and child burial practices. There are also a few exceptional rural cemeteries, where children are very well represented, for example those buried in and around some third-century tombs at Keston villa (B. Philip et al., *The Roman Villa Site at Keston, Kent: First Report (Excavations 1968–1978* [Dover Castle: Kent Archaeological Rescue Unit, 1999], 44–56). In spite of these exceptions, overall, children are dramatically underrepresented in the Roman-period burial record.

105. A. Smith, "Burials, Shrines, and Ritual Practices in the Countryside: Initial Observations from Yorkshire," Roman Rural Settlement Project, n.d., http://www.reading.ac.uk/web/FILES/archaeology/Alex_smith_Yorkshire_ritual.pdf.

106. A. Smith, "Romano-British Ritual Practices in the East Midlands," Roman Rural Settlement Project, n.d., https://www.reading.ac.uk/web/FILES/archaeology/E_Midlands_ritual_AlexSmith.pdf.

107. The "missing" neonates and children from early medieval English cemeteries have been the subject of research and debate. The problem was first systematically studied in T. Molleson, "Demographic Implications of Age Structure of Early English Cemetery Samples," *Actes des Journees Anthropologiques*, 5 (1991), 113–21; S. Crawford, "Children, Death and the Afterlife in Anglo-Saxon England," *Anglo-Saxon Studies in Archaeology and History*, 6 (1993), 83–91; and S. Lucy, "Children in Early Medieval Cemeteries," *Archaeological Review from Cambridge*, 13 (1994), 21–34. Crawford and Lucy argue that children are missing as a result of cultural practices. Jo Buckberry, on the other hand, has argued that taphonomic processes (processes that change organisms after death) may account for at least some of our low numbers, although her work shows that under most conditions, infant skeletons survive as well as those of adults (J. Buckberry, "Missing, Presumed Buried? Bone Diagenesis and the Under-Representation of Anglo-Saxon Children," *Assemblage*, 5 [2000], www.assemblage.group.shef.ac.uk/5/buckberr.html). Children in the early medieval period are also underrepresented in cremation cemeteries, although, again, they appear in roughly the same percentages as they do in inhumation cemeteries (K. E. Squires, "Populating the Pots: The Demography of the Early Anglo-Saxon Cemeteries at Elsham and Cleatham, North Lincolnshire," *Archaeological Journal*, 169 [2012], 312–42; and K. E. Squires, "Through the Flames of the Pyre: The Continuing Search for Anglo-Saxon Infants and Children," in D. M. Hadley and K. A. Hemer, eds., *Medieval Childhood: Archaeological Approaches* [Oxford: Oxbow Books, 2014], 114–30).

108. On the dearth of infant burials in this period, see Crawford, "Children, Death and the Afterlife," 84; Lucy, "Children in Early Medieval Cemeteries," 21–34.

109. See below, Chapter 8.

110. C. Haughton and D. Powlesland, *West Heslerton: The Anglian Cemetery*, 2 vols. (Yedingham: Landscape Research Centre, 1999), 1:176–77.

111. A. Boyle et al., *Two Oxfordshire Anglo-Saxon Cemeteries: Berinsfield and Didcot* (Oxford: Oxford Archaeological Unit, 1995), 116.

112. V. I. Evison and P. Hill, *Two Anglo-Saxon Cemeteries at Beckford, Hereford, and Worcester* (York: Council for British Archaeology, 1996), 79–90.

113. A. Doherty and C. Greatorex, *Excavations on St Anne's Hill: A Middle/Late Iron Age and Anglo-Saxon Cemetery at St Anne's Road, Eastbourne, East Sussex* (Portslade: SpoilHeap, 2016), 49, table 3.3 and fig. 3.11.

114. K. Cullen, N. Holbrook, M. Watts, A. Caffell, and M. Holst, "A Post-Roman Cemetery at Hewlett Packard, Filton South Gloucestershire: Excavations in 2005," in M. Watts, *Two Cemeteries from Bristol's Northern Suburbs* (Cirencester: Cotswold Archaeology, 2007), 51–96, at 69–71.

115. C. M. Hearne and V. Birbeck, *A35 Tolpuddle to Puddletown Bypass DBFO, Dorset, 1996–8: Incorporating Excavations at Tolpuddle Ball, 1993* (Salisbury: Trust for Wessex Archaeology, 1999), 58–63, 61–62. During the Roman period, on the other hand, neonate burials were highly visible (Hearne and Birbeck, *A35 Tolpuddle*, 160–61).

116. P. W. Cox, "A Seventh Century Inhumation Cemetery at Shepherd's Farm, Ulwell near Swanage, Dorset," *Dorset Natural History and Archaeological Society*, 110 (1988), 37–47, at 37–39.

117. For the little evidence there is of infant burial in settlement sites in the early Middle Ages, see H. Hamerow, "'Special Deposits' in Anglo-Saxon Settlements," *Medieval Archaeology*, 50 (2006), 1–30; S. Crawford, "Special Burials, Special Buildings? An Anglo-Saxon Perspective on the Interpretation of Infant Burials in Association with Rural Settlement Structures," in Bacvorov, ed., *Babies Reborn*, 197–204; C. M. Sofield, "Living with the Dead: Human Burials in Anglo-Saxon Settlement Contexts," *Archaeological Journal*, 172 (2015), 351–88. At the early medieval settlements of West Heslerton and West Stow, stray infant remains suggest an early phase in which infants might still have been placed in boundary ditches or under the floors of houses, but when boundary ditches and sites were tidied up or reordered, these burials were disturbed (D. Powesland, personal communication). Neonates, however, reappear once again in the seventh and eighth centuries in churchyard burials. Relatively large numbers of them can be found in cemeteries surrounding churches, clustered very close to the walls of churches in what are known as "eaves-drip burials" (E. Craig-Atkins, "Eavesdropping on Short Lives: Eaves-Drip Burials and the Differential Treatment of Children One Year of Age and Under in Early Christian Cemeteries," in D. M. Hadley and K. A. Hemer, eds., *Medieval Childhood: Archaeological Approaches* [Oxford: Oxbow Books, 2014], 95–113).

118. J. E. Kay, "Children's Burials in Fifth-Century Britain and Connections to the Roman Past," *Childhood in the Past*, 9 (2016), 86–108. Another recent study on infant and child burial by Duncan Sayer employs age ranges that make their use here difficult. He divides his populations between infants, whom he ages from one to five, and children, whom he ages from six to twelve. Not only is it unclear where infants under the age of one are in these figures, but it is impossible to separate out babies from older children in his data. Nonetheless, he reports from his sample of 3,412 graves that 21.3 percent of the total were individuals under the age of twelve (D. Sayer, "'Sons of Athelings Given to the Earth': Infant Mortality Within Anglo-Saxon Mortuary Geography," *Medieval Archaeology*, 58 [2014], 78–103). Although his statistics suggest that children continue to be underrepresented in cemeteries, they do show that many more were buried in cemeteries than had been in the late Roman period. Sue Harrington and Martin Welch have also gathered date from early cemeteries in the kingdoms of the South Saxons, Kent, and Wessex, and found that out of a total of 6,219 skeletons that have been aged, 3 percent were under the age of two, 11 percent aged from three to six, and a further 9 percent aged seven to fifteen (S. Harrington and M. Welch, *The Early Anglo-Saxon Kingdoms of Southern Britain AD 450–650: Beneath the Tribal Hidage* [Oxford: Oxbow Books, 2014], 27 and table 12).

119. Data gathered by Rebecca Gowland suggests that stillborn babies and infants under the age of six months were the ones most likely to be selected for the kinds of rites discussed in this chapter (Gowland, "Playing Dead," 157).

120. Kay, "Children's Burials," 90 and table 1. Kay's definition of "infant," is eighteen months or younger, and "juvenile" is from eighteen months to fifteen years of age (Kay, "Children's Burials," 91).

121. Kay, "Children's Burials," table 1.
122. "Excavation of a Romano-British Farmstead," figure 11 and data from table 1; and Gerrard, "New Radiocarbon Dates." Other fifth-century burial groups also include higher percentages of children than earlier cemeteries. See, for example, the post-Roman burials at Bancroft Villa (R. J. Williams and R. J. Zeepvat, *Bancroft: A Late Bronze Age/Iron Age Settlement, Roman Villa, and Temple-Mausoleum* [Aylesbury: Buckinghamshire Archaeological Society, 1994], 2 vols., 108, 550, 558–59; Hearne and Birbeck, *A35 Tolpuddle*, 59, 161–62).
123. V. I. Evison, *An Anglo-Saxon Cemetery at Great Chesterford, Essex* (York: Council for British Archaeology, 1994), 31.
124. The main report states that 171 individuals were found, but this disagrees with the specialist report, which gives the number as 167 (Evison, *Anglo-Saxon Cemetery at Great Chesterford*, 31, 52).
125. Evison, *Anglo-Saxon Cemetery at Great Chesterford*, 31. See also, C. Cave and M. Oxenham, "Out of the Cradle and into the Grave: The Children of Anglo-Saxon Great Chesterford, Essex, England," in Murphy and Le Roy, eds., *Children, Death, and Burial*, 179–96.
126. C. Hayden et al., *Horcott Quarry, Fairford and Arkell's Land, Kempsford: Prehistoric, Roman, and Anglo-Saxon Settlement and Burial in the Upper Thames Valley in Gloucestershire* (Oxford: Oxford Archaeology, 2017), 133 and table 7.2.
127. Hayden et al., *Horcott Quarry*, 247 and table 9.1.
128. In the mid-fifth century, for example, forty-seven neonates were buried in five rooms of a deserted villa at Lugnano, in Umbria (Soren and Soren, eds., *Roman Villa and a Late Roman Infant*, 486–517). Infant burial under floors or near walls of buildings in rural areas happened before the Roman period in Italy, southern Gaul, and the eastern Mediterranean (Carroll, "No Part in Earthly Things," 45; Carroll, "Infant Death," 110).
129. G. D. Keevill, "Redlands Farm, Stanwick, Northamptonshire, SP 962705" (unpublished report, Oxford Archaeological Unit, 1992), 53–54; E. Biddulph, G. D. Keevill, and I. R. Scott, "Redlands Farm, Stanwick, Northamptonshire: The Roman Evidence," vol. 1, "Text" (unpublished report, Oxford Archaeology NGR SP 96–705, 2002), 1:55, 68, 71, 111.
130. Biddulph et al., "Redlands Farm," 1:72.
131. Sofield, "Living with the Dead," 363.
132. For a similar argument about changes in child burial as a mark of important social and ideological changes, see V. Zanoni, "'Youth on Fire': The Role of Sub-Adults and Young Adults in Pre-Roman Italian *Bandopferplätze*," in E. Perego and R. Scopacasa, eds., *Burial and Social Change in First Millennium BC Italy: Approaching Social Agents* (Oxford: Oxbow Books, 2016), 249–72. For discussions of the meaning of shifting burial practices over time, see D. K. Charles and J. E. Buikstra, "Siting, Sighting, and Citing the Dead," *Archaeological Papers of the American Anthropological Association*, 11 (2002), 13–25.

CHAPTER 8

Epigraph: R. Bradley, "A Life Less Ordinary: The Ritualization of the Domestic Sphere in Later Prehistoric Europe," *Cambridge Archaeological Journal*, 13 (2003), 5–23, at 5.
1. B. G. Trigger, *A History of Archaeological Thought* (Cambridge: Cambridge University Press, 1989), 174–86; S. Jones, *The Archaeology of Ethnicity: Constructing Identities in the Past and the Present* (London: Routledge, 1997), 15–39; G. S. Webster, "Culture History: A Culture-Historical Approach," in R. A. Bentley, H. D. G. Maschner, and C. Chippindale, eds., *Handbook*

of Archaeological Theories (Lanham, Md.: AltaMira, 2008), 11–27. For more on the rise of these ideas in treatments of the period, see G. Halsall, "Archaeology and Migration: Rethinking the Debate," in R. Annaert et al., eds., *The Very Beginning of Europe? Cultural and Social Dimensions of Early-Medieval Migration and Colonisation (5th–8th Century): Archaeology in Contemporary Europe; Conference Brussels, May 17–19, 2011* (Brussels: Flanders Heritage Agency, 2012), 29–40.

2. For the history of this intellectual habit in the United Kingdom, see H. Williams, "Forgetting the Britons in Victorian Anglo-Saxon Archaeology," in N. Higham, ed., *Britons in Anglo-Saxon England* (Woodbridge: Boydell, 2007), 27–41. For its history on the continent, see S. Hakenbeck, *Local, Regional and Ethnic Identities in Early Medieval Cemeteries in Bavaria* (Borgo S. Lorenzo: All'Insegna del Giglio, 2011), 11–26; Danijel Dzino and A. Domic-Kunic, "Pannonians: Identity-Perceptions from the Late Iron Age to Later Antiquity," in Branka Migotti, *The Archaeology of Roman Southern Pannonia: The State of Research and Selected Problems in the Croatian Part of the Roman Province of Pannonia*, BAR International Series 2393 (Oxford: Archaeopress, 2012), 93–115.

3. S. Reynolds, "Medieval *origines gentium* and the Community of the Realm," *History*, 68 (1983), 375–90; and S. Reynolds, "What Do We Mean by 'Anglo-Saxon' and 'Anglo-Saxons'?" *Journal of British Studies*, 24 (1985), 395–414.

4. The conditions necessary for the development of coherent ethnic identities—large affinities of people knocking up against one another, or elite groups working hard to mark themselves as different from other elites, or social strivers intent on adopting the identity markers of their betters—are not much in evidence in lowland Britain in the first hundred years after the fall and cannot have been driving historical developments. For the ways early medieval ethnic identity developed and operated, see P. J. Geary, "Ethnic Identity as a Situational Construct in the Early Middle Ages," *Mitteilungen der Anthropologischen Gesellschaft in Wein*, 113 (1983), 15–26; W. Pohl, "Telling the Difference: Signs of Ethnic Identity," in W. Pohl and H. Reimitz, *Strategies of Distinction: The Construction of Ethnic Communities, 300–800* (Leiden: Brill, 1998), 17–69; S. Jones, *Archaeology of Ethnicity*.

5. For one such (rightly) ill-reputed, non-British source—the *Gallic Chronicle*—and arguments surrounding its usefulness as a source for Britain, see M. E. Jones and J. Casey, "The Gallic Chronicle Restored: A Chronology for the Anglo-Saxon Invasions and the End of Roman Britain," *Britannia*, 19 (1988), 367–98; R. W. Burgess, "The Dark Ages Return to Fifth-Century Britain: The 'Restored' Gallic Chronicle Exploded," *Britannia*, 21 (1990), 185–95; M. E. Jones and J. Casey, "The Gallic Chronicle Exploded?" *Britannia*, 22 (1991), 212–15. For snippets of Olympiodorus of Thebes, allegedly preserving information about Britain, see J. F. Matthews, "Olympiodorus of Thebes and the History of the West (AD 470–425)," *Journal of Roman Studies*, 60 (1970), 79–97; P. Bartholomew, "Fifth-Century Facts," *Britannia*, 13 (1982), 261–70; W. Lütkenhaus, "Observations on Zosimus' British 'Cities,'" *Britannia*, 43 (2012), 268–70.

6. For cogent discussions of the *Anglo-Saxon Chronicle* and many of the sources behind it as repositories of origin legends rather than fact, and for bibliography, see B. Yorke, "Anglo-Saxon Origin Legends," in J. Barrow and A. Wareham, eds., *Myth, Rulership, Church, and Charters: Essays in Honour of Nicholas Brooks* (London: Routledge, 2008), 15–30; C. Hills, *Origins of the English* (London: Duckworth, 2003), 21–40.

7. N. Higham, *Rome, Britain and the Anglo-Saxons* (London: Seaby, 1992), 164–78, 228; M. Welch, "The Archaeological Evidence for Federate Settlement in Britain Within the Fifth Century," in F. Vallet and M. Kazanski, eds., *L'Armée romaine et les barbares du IIIe au VIIe siècle* (Rouen: Association française d'archéologie mérovingienne, 1993), 269–78; C. J. Arnold, *From Roman Britain to Saxon England* (London: Croom Helm, 1984). For an overview of the various

models, see H. Härke, "Anglo-Saxon Immigration and Ethnogenesis," *Medieval Archaeology*, 55 (2011), 1–28.

8. B. Effros, "Dressing Conservatively: Women's Brooches as Markers of Ethnic Identity?" in L. Brubaker and J. M. H. Smith, eds., *Gender in the Early Medieval World: Women, Men, and Eunuchs in Late Antiquity and After, 300–900 CE* (Cambridge: Cambridge University Press, 2004), 165–84, at 167.

9. C. N. Adichie, "The Danger of the Single Story," https://www.ted.com/talks/chimamanda _adichie_the_danger_of_a_single_story/transcript.

10. M. E. Weale, D. A. Weiss, R. F. Jager, N. Bradman, and M. G. Thomas, "Y Chromosome Evidence for Anglo-Saxon Mass Migration," *Molecular Biology and Evolution*, 19 (2002), 1008–21; C. Capelli et al., "A Y Chromosome Census of the British Isles," *Current Biology*, 13 (2003), 979–84; M. G. Thomas, M. P. H. Stumpf, and H. Härke, "Evidence for an Apartheid-Like Social Structure in Early Anglo-Saxon England," *Proceedings of the Royal Society, B*, 273 (2006), 2651–57; H. Härke, "Ethnicity, Race, and Migration in Mortuary Archaeology: An Attempt at a Short Answer," *Anglo-Saxon Studies in Archaeology and History*, 14 (2007), 12–18; R. Martiniano et al., "Genomic Signals of Migration and Continuity in Britain Before the Anglo-Saxons," *Nature Communications*, 7 (2016), 1–8, doi: 10.1038/ncomms10326. For cogent critiques see J. E. Pattison, "Is It Necessary to Assume an Apartheid-Like Social Structure in Early Anglo-Saxon England?" *Proceedings of the Royal Society, B*, 275 (2008), 2423–29; C. Hills, "Anglo-Saxon DNA?" in D. Sayers and H. Williams, eds., *Mortuary Practices and Social Identities in the Middle Ages: Essays in Burial Archaeology in Honour of Heinrich Härke* (Exeter: Exeter University Press, 2009), 123–40; J. Moreland, "Going Native, Becoming German: Isotopes and Identities in Late Roman and Early Medieval England," *Postmedieval: A Journal of Medieval Cultural Studies*, 1 (2010), 142–49.

11. D. Reich, *Who We Are and How We Got Here: Ancient DNA and the New Science of the Human Past* (New York: Pantheon Books, 2018), xi–xx.

12. For discussions of the ways geneticists have grafted their results onto outdated or misunderstood historical and archaeological interpretations, see H.-J. Bandelt, V. Macaulay, and M. Richards, "What Molecules Can't Tell Us About the Spread of Languages and the Neolithic," in P. Bellwood and C. Renfrew, eds., *Examining the Farming/Language Dispersal Hypothesis* (Cambridge: McDonald Institute for Archaeological Research, 2003), 99–107; H. Härke, "Die Entstehung der Angelsachsen," in H. Beck, D. Geuenich, and H. Steuer, eds., *Altertumskunde—Altertumswissenschaft—Kulturwissenschaft: Erträge und Perspektiven nach 40 Jahren Reallexikon der Germanischen Altertumskunde* (Berlin: De Gruyter, 2012), 429–58; E. Niklasson, "Shutting the Stable Door After the Horse Has Bolted: Critical Thinking and the Third Science Revolution," *Current Swedish Archaeology*, 22 (2014), 57–63; S. Samida and J. Feuchter, "Why Archaeologists, Historians, and Geneticists Should Work Together—and How," *Medieval Worlds*, 4 (2016), 5–21. For an assessment of what a study of genetics can and cannot tell us about migration, see D. A. Bolnick, "Continuity and Change in Anthropological Perspectives on Migration: Insights from Molecular Anthropology," in G. S. Cabana and J. J. Clark, eds., *Rethinking Anthropological Perspectives on Migration* (Gainesville: University of Florida Press, 2011), 263–77, at 266–67.

13. For the scholarship on early medieval migration and bibliography, see D. W. Anthony, "Migration in Archaeology: The Baby and the Bathwater," *American Anthropologist*, 92 (1990), 895–914; D. W. Anthony, "Prehistoric Migration as Social Process," in J. Chapman and H. Hamerow, eds., *Migrations and Invasions in Archaeological Explanation*, BAR International Series 664 (Oxford: BAR, 1997), 21–32; H. Hamerow, "Migration Theory and the Anglo-Saxon 'Identity Crisis,'" in Chapman and Hamerow, eds., *Migrations and Invasions*, 33–44; H. Härke, "Archaeologists

and Migrations: A Problem of Attitude?" *Current Anthropology*, 39 (1998), 19–46; S. Burmeister, "Archaeology and Migration: Approaches to an Archaeological Proof of Migration," *Current Anthropology*, 41 (2000), 539–67; S. Hakenbeck, "Migration in Archaeology: Are We Nearly There Yet?" *Archaeological Review from Cambridge*, 23 (2008), 9–26; P. Geary, "'Völkerwanderung' as Cross-Cultural Interaction," in M. Borgolte, J. Dücker, M. Müllerburg, P. Predatsch, and B. Schneidmüller, eds., *Europa im Geflecht der Welt: Mittelalterliche Migrationen in globalen Bezügen* (Berlin: de Gruyter, 2012), 45–54; C. Hills, "The Anglo-Saxon Migration: An Archaeological Case Study of Disruption," in B. J. Baker and T. Tsuda, eds., *Migrations and Disruptions: Toward a Unifying Theory of Ancient and Contemporary Migrations* (Gainesville: University of Florida, 2015) 33–51.

14. C. J. Arnold, *An Archaeology of the Early Anglo-Saxon Kingdoms*, 2nd ed. (London: Routledge, 1997), 23; N. Stoodley, *The Spindle and the Spear: A Critical Enquiry into the Construction and Meaning of Gender in the Early Anglo-Saxon Burial Rite*, BAR British Series 288 (Oxford: J. and E. Hedges, 1999).

15. K. Penn and B. Brugmann with K. Høilund Nielsen, *Aspects of Anglo-Saxon Inhumation Burial: Morning Thorpe, Spong Hill, Bergh Apton, and Westgarth Gardens*, East Anglian Archaeology 119 (Dereham: Norfolk Museums Service, 2007); D. Quast, "Communication, Migration, Mobility and Trade: Explanatory Models for Exchange Processes from the Roman Iron Age to the Viking Age," in D. Quast, ed., *Foreigners in Early Medieval Europe: Thirteen International Studies on Early Medieval Mobility* (Mainz: Römisch-Germanischen Zentralmuseums, 2009), 1–26, at 10; S. Hakenbeck, "'Hunnic' Modified Skulls: Physical Appearance, Identity, and the Transformative Nature of Migrations," in Sayer and Williams, eds., *Mortuary Practices and Social Identities*, 64–80, at 79–80.

16. E. Crubézy, "Merovingian Skull Deformations in the Southwest of France," in D. Austin and L. Alcock, eds., *From the Baltic to the Black Sea: Studies in Medieval Archaeology* (London: Unwin Hyman, 1990), 189–208.

17. M. Molnár et al., "Artificially Deformed Crania from the Hun-Germanic Period (5th–6th Century AD) in Northeastern Hungary: Historical and Morphological Analysis," *Journal of Neurosurgery: Neurosurgical Focus*, 36 (2014), 1–9; Hakenbeck, "'Hunnic' Modified Skulls," 65.

18. Hakenback, "'Hunnic' Modified Skulls," 78–79; R. Schafberg and W. Schwarz, "Eine Fremde im Thüringerreich: Eine Frau mit deformiertem Schädel aus Obermöllern," in H. Meller, ed., *Schönheit, Macht und Tod: 120 Funde aus 120 Jahren Landesmuseum für Vorgeschichte Halle* (Halle: Landesmuseum für Vorgeschichte in Halle, 2001), 126–27.

19. Hakenbeck, "'Hunnic' Modified Skulls," 73–75; S. Hakenbeck, "Roman or Barbarian? Shifting Identities in Early Medieval Cemeteries in Bavaria," *Post-Classical Archaeologies*, 1 (2011), 37–66, at 48–49.

20. Hakenbeck, "'Hunnic' Modified Skulls," 73–74, 78.

21. R. Brettell et al., "'Impious Easterners': Can Oxygen and Strontium Isotopes Serve as Indicators of Provenance in Early Medieval European Cemetery Populations?" *European Journal of Archaeology*, 15 (2012), 117–45, at 118.

22. For clear, up-to-date introductions to isotopic research, see R. A. Bentley, "Strontium Isotopes from the Earth to the Archaeological Skeleton: A Review," *Journal of Archaeological Method and Theory*, 13 (2006), 135–87; M. Ben-David and E. A. Flaherty, "Stable Isotopes in Mammalian Research: A Beginner's Guide," *Journal of Mammalogy*, 93 (2012), 312–28; J. D. Bethard, "Isotopes," in E. A. DiGangi and M. K. Moore, eds., *Research Methods in Human Skeletal Biology* (Oxford: Academic, 2013), 425–47.

23. Bentley, "Strontium Isotopes," 162; J. Montgomery, "Passports from the Past: Investigating Human Dispersals Using Strontium Isotope Analysis of Tooth Enamel," *Annals of Human Biology*, 37 (2010), 325–46.

24. Brettell et al., "Impious Easterners," 136.

25. For the problems associated with using strontium alone, see Brettell et al., "Impious Easterners," 132. For the possible impact of disease on isotopic signatures, see M. A. Katzenberg and N. C. Lovell, "Stable Isotope Variation in Pathological Bone," *International Journal of Osteoarchaeology*, 9 (1999), 316–24; N. M. Slovak and A. Paytan, "Applications of Sr Isotopes in Archaeology," in M. Baskaran, ed., *Handbook of Environmental Isotope Geochemistry* (Berlin: Springer, 2011), 743–68. For the possible impact of diet and foodways on isotopic signatures, see R. Brettell, J. Montgomery, and J. Evans, "Brewing and Stewing: The Effect of Culturally Mediated Behaviour on the Oxygen Isotope Composition of Ingested Fluids and the Implications for Human Provenance Studies," *Journal of Analytical Atomic Spectrometry*, 27 (2012), 778–85. On possible diagenetic changes (although tooth enamel is less susceptible than either bone or dentine), see Bentley, "Strontium Isotopes," 163.

26. For the advantages of studying multiple stable isotope systems, see G. Müldner, C. Chenery, and H. Eckhardt, "The 'Headless Romans': Multi-Isotope Investigations of an Unusual Burial Ground from Roman Britain," *Journal of Archaeological Science*, 38 (2011), 280–90; Bentley, "Strontium Isotopes," 136. For the advantages of a large sample size, see T. D. Price et al., "Isotopes and Mobility: Case Studies with Large Samples," in E. Kaiser, J. Burger, and W. Schier, eds., *Population Dynamics in Prehistory: New Approaches Using Stable Isotopes and Genetics* (Berlin: De Gruyter, 2012), 311–21; Brettell et al., "Impious Easterners," 117–45.

27. The relevant data are published in M. M. Schweissing and G. Grupe, "Local or Nonlocal? A Research of Strontium Isotope Ratios of Teeth and Bones on Skeletal Remains with Artificial Deformed Skulls," *Anthropologischer Anzeiger*, 58 (2000), 99–103; S. Hakenbeck et al., "Diet and Mobility in Early Medieval Bavaria: A Study of Carbon and Nitrogen Stable Isotopes," *American Journal of Physical Anthropology*, 143 (2010), 235–49; C. Knipper et al., "Mobility in Thuringia or Mobile Thuringians: A Strontium Isotope Study from Early Medieval Central Germany," in Kaiser, Burger, and Schier, eds., *Population Dynamics in Pre-History*, 287–310; C. Knipper et al., "Dietary Reconstruction in Migration Period Central Germany: A Carbon and Nitrogen Isotope Study," *Archaeological and Anthropological Sciences*, 5 (2013), 17–35.

28. Knipper et al., "Mobility in Thuringia," 290, 302–3; Schweissing and Grupe, "Local or Nonlocal?" 99–103. In any case, the ten women with "Hunnic" skull modifications in the cemetery at Straubing-Bajuwarenstrasse had $∂^{13}C$ values similar to most people buried in this cemetery without modified skulls (Hakenbeck et al., "Diet and Mobility," 245).

29. J. Bemmann, "Mitteldeutschland im 5. und 6. Jahrhundert: Was ist und ab wann gibt es archäologisch betrachtet typisch Thüringisches? Eine kritische Bestandsaufnahme," in H. Castritius, D. Geuenich, and M. Werner, eds., *Die Frühzeit der Thüringer: Archäologie, Sprache, Geschichte* (Berlin: de Gruyter, 2009), 63–81, at 74–75; S. Hakenbeck, "Situational Ethnicity and Nested Identities: New Approaches to an Old Problem," *Anglo-Saxon Studies in Archaeology and History*, 14 (2007), 19–27, at 33; S. Hakenbeck, "Ethnic Tensions in Early Medieval Cemeteries in Bavaria," *Archaeological Review from Cambridge*, 19 (2004), 40–50, at 48–50.

30. K. R. Veeramah et al., "Population Genomic Analysis of Elongated Skulls Reveals Extensive Female-Biased Immigration in Early Medieval Bavaria," *Proceedings of the National Academy of Sciences of the United States of America*, 115 (2018), 3494–99 and supporting information, www.pnas.org/lookup/suppl/doi:10.1073/pnas.1721818115/-/DCSupplemental.

31. For a brief history and historiography of this idea and its downfall, see Hakenbeck, "Situational Ethnicity," 19–22; Hakenbeck, "Ethnic Tensions," 46–47; Effros, "Dressing Conservatively"; F. Theuws, "Grave Goods, Ethnicity, and the Rhetoric of Burial Rites in Late Antique Northern Gaul," in T. Derks and N. Roymans, eds., *Ethnic Constructs in Antiquity: The Role of Power and Tradition* (Amsterdam: Amsterdam University Press, 2009), 283–320; G. Halsall, "Ethnicity and Early Medieval Cemeteries," *Arqueología y Territorio Medieval*, 18 (2011), 15–27. For examples of recent arguments by its proponents, see G. Graenert, "Langobardinnen in Alamannien," *Germania*, 78 (2000), 417–47; V. Bierbrauer, *Ethnos und Mobilität im 5. Jahrhundert aus archäologischer Sicht: Vom Kaukasus bis nach Niederösterreich* (Munich: Bayerischen Akademie der Wissenschaften, 2008).

32. Hakenbeck et al., "Diet and Mobility," table 2.

33. Like most people buried at Straubing-Bajuwarenstrasse, the population she was genetically most closely related to was that of northern and central Europe (Veeramah et al., "Population Genomic Analysis," SI 1, 11–SI13).

34. Veeramah et al., "Population Genomic Analysis," fig. S30.

35. Hakenbeck et al., "Diet and Mobility," table 2.

36. Schweissing and Grupe, "Local or Nonlocal?" 102, table 1; Hakenbeck et al., "Diet and Mobility," 246–47.

37. Hakenbeck et al., "Diet and Mobility," 235–49. One of these women was aged sixty years or older when she died, and the other was forty years or older. The carbon and nitrogen isotopes, however (which are taken by researchers from bone rather than tooth enamel), reflect an individual's diet for the last ten or fifteen years of life because there is a relatively rapid turnover of bone (M. M. Schweissing and G. Grupe, "Stable Strontium Isotopes in Human Teeth and Bone: A Key to Migration Events of the Late Roman Period in Bavaria," *Journal of Archaeological Science*, 30 [2003], 1373–83; A. Fischer et al., "Coast-Inland Mobility and Diet in the Danish Mesolithic and Neolithic: Evidence from Stable Isotope Values of Humans and Dogs," *Journal of Archaeological Science*, 34 [2007], 2125–50; R. E. M. Hedges et al., "Collagen Turnover in the Adult Femoral Mid-Shaft: Modeled from Anthropogenic Radiocarbon Tracer Measurements," *American Journal of Physical Anthropology*, 133 [2007], 808–16). It is thus unlikely that the dietary differences found in older women can be used to argue that they had grown up in a different region, eating differently, before arriving as the result of a long-distance, exogamous marriage. But they might, instead, have come in the last decade or so of their lives, when they were mature women.

38. Veeramah et al., "Population Genomic Analysis," fig. S30.

39. These are Straubing-Bajuwarenstrasse 502 and 300 (Veeramah et al., "Population Genomic Analysis," 3497–98, SI14 and figs. S42a–b).

40. For thoughtful discussions of ways in which genetic data should and should not be interpreted and incorporated into our histories, see Niklasson, "Shutting the Stable Door"; and Feuchter, "Why Archaeologists, Historians, and Geneticists Should Work Together."

41. The data are published in J. Montgomery, "Lead and Strontium Isotope Compositions of Human Dental Tissues as an Indicator of Ancient Exposure and Population Dynamics" (Ph.D. diss., University of Bradford, 2002); P. Budd et al., "Anglo-Saxon Residential Mobility at West Heslerton, North Yorkshire, UK from Combined O- and SR-Isotope Analysis," in G. Holland and S. D. Tanner, eds., *Plasma Source Mass Spectrometry: Applications and Emerging Technologies* (Cambridge: Royal Society of Chemistry, 2003), 195–208; P. Budd et al., "Investigating Population Movement by Stable Isotope Analysis: A Report from Britain," *Antiquity*, 78 (2004), 127–41; J. Montgomery et al., "Continuity or Colonization in Anglo-Saxon England? Isotope Evidence for Mobility, Subsistence Practice, and Status at West Heslerton," *American Journal of Physical*

Anthropology, 126 (2005), 123–38; J. A. Evans, C. A. Chenery, and J. Montgomery, "A Summary of Strontium and Oxygen Isotope Variation in Archaeological Human Tooth Enamel Excavated from Britain," *Journal of Analytical Atomic Spectrometry*, 27 (2012), 754–64, appendix 1.

42. J. Hines, *The Scandinavian Character of Anglian England in the Pre-Viking Period*, BAR British Series 124 (Oxford: BAR, 1984), 109.

43. C. Haughton and D. Powlesland, *West Heslerton: The Anglian Cemetery*, 2 vols. (Yedingham: Landscape Research Centre, 1999), 2:194.

44. Haughton and Powlesland, *West Heslerton*, 1:107–14.

45. M. Faull, "British Survival in Anglo-Saxon Northumbria," in L. Laing, ed., *Studies in Celtic Survival*, BAR British Series 37 (Oxford: BAR, 1977), 1–55 at 5, 9. Crouched burials are very rare in cemeteries in regions on the continent traditionally thought to constitute the "Anglo-Saxon" homelands (S. Crawford, "Britons, Anglo-Saxons and the Germanic Burial Rite," in Chapman and Hamerow, eds., *Migrations and Invasions*, 45–72, at 65).

46. Haughton and Powlesland, *West Heslerton*, 2:227, 281; N. Cooke, "The Definition and Interpretation of Late Roman Burial Rites in the Western Empire" (Ph.D. diss., University College London, 1998), 39–40.

47. Haughton and Powlesland, *West Heslerton*, 2:297.

48. Among these four, only G133 has a strontium signature different from the local signature, but all four had oxygen isotopic signatures that tell a different story. All fall into Budd and colleagues' "population group 1a," which the authors argue are people who spent their childhoods drinking water outside the U.K., most likely in Scandinavia or the Baltic (Budd et al., "Anglo-Saxon Residential Mobility," at 202 and 204.) For the range of strontium and oxygen isotopic variation within Britain, see Evans et al., "Summary of Strontium and Oxygen Isotope Variation," 254–76).

49. Haughton and Powlesland, *West Heslerton*, 2:133–34.

50. Montgomery et al., "Continuity or Colonization," 134.

51. Haughton and Powlesland, *West Heslerton*, 2:164–66. The inhumed child, according to an aDNA analysis, was a boy. Unlike the adult woman with whom he is buried, he has a local Sr isotope signature (Montgomery, "Lead and Strontium," 258).

52. Haughton and Powlesland, *West Heslerton*, 2:144–45.

53. Haughton and Powlesland, *West Heslerton*, 2:116.

54. Oxygen isotopes suggest that all four were nonlocal (Budd et al., "Anglo-Saxon Residential Mobility," 202) as do strontium isotopes (Montgomery et al., "Continuity or Colonization," 132). For the difference in oxygen isotope values between the higher-rainfall region in the West of Britain and the lower-rainfall in the East, see Evans et al., "Summary of Strontium and Oxygen Isotope Variation," 759–60. For a lengthy discussion of why the Sr ratios in these skeletons are more likely to suggest a western British provenance over some putative homeland in Scandinavia or Germany, see Montgomery, "Lead and Strontium," 261–62. For published Sr values from Sweden, Norway, and Denmark, which suggest that this West Heslerton group did not originate from these places, see T. D. Price, "Human Mobility at Uppåkra: A Preliminary Report on Isotopic Proveniencing," in B. Hårdh and L. Larsson, eds., *Studies at Uppåkra, an Iron Age City in Scania, Sweden* (Lund: Institute of Archaeology, 2013), 157–69; C. A. Chenery et al., "A Boat Load of Vikings?" *Journal of the North Atlantic*, 7 (2014), 43–53, at 46; T. D. Price et al., "Who Was in Harold Bluetooth's Army? Strontium Isotope Investigation of the Cemetery at the Viking Age Fortress at Trelleborg, Denmark," *Antiquity*, 85 (2011), 476–89, at 483; S. Voerkelius et al., "Strontium Isotopic Signatures of Natural Mineral Waters: The Reference to a Simple Geographical Map and Its Potential for Authentication of Food," *Food Chemistry*, 118 (2010), 933–40.

55. Montgomery, "Lead and Strontium," 255. The individuals I have just discussed were buried in different phases of the cemetery's life (Haughton and Powlesland, *West Heslerton*, i, 82). There is isotopic evidence for similar slow, small-scale migration of both men and women from more than one region over many generations elsewhere in the former Roman West. See, for example, results from the cemetery at Alegría-Dulantzi in Spain, where most of the burial population, including individuals with "Germanic" grave goods, appear to have been born locally (L. A. Ortega et al., "Strontium Isotopes of Human Remains from the San Martín de Dulantzi Graveyard (Alegría-Dulantzi, Álava) and Population Mobility in the Early Middle Ages," *Quaternary International*, 303 [2013], 54–63).

56. Montgomery, "Lead and Strontium," 257.

57. A similar movement of people into Britain from a number of quite different regions, each with a distinctive material culture, is argued for Kent, Hampshire, and the Isle of Wight during this period (A. Richardson, "The Third Way: Thoughts on Non-Saxon Identity South of the Thames AD 450–600," in S. Brookes, S. Harrington, and A. Reynolds, eds., *Studies in Early Anglo-Saxon Art and Archaeology: Papers in Honour of Martin G. Welch*, BAR British Series 527 [Oxford: Archaeopress, 2011], 72–81, at 79–80); for the first couple of generations of people who practiced cremation at Spong Hill (C. Hills and S. Lucy, *Spong Hill Part IX: Chronology and Synthesis* [Cambridge: McDonald Institute for Archaeological Research, 2013], 329–30); and for people burying at Great Chesterford (M. Medlycott, *The Roman Town of Great Chesterford*, East Anglian Archaeology 137 [Chelmsford: Essex County Council, 2011], 124).

58. A. S. Esmonde Cleary, *The Ending of Roman Britain* (London: B. T. Batsford, 1989), 141–61.

59. S. S. Hughes et al., "Isotopic Analysis of Burials from the Early Anglo-Saxon Cemetery at Eastbourne, Sussex, U.K.," *Journal of Archaeological Science: Reports*, 19 (2018), 513–25; A. Doherty and C. Greatorex, *Excavations on St Anne's Hill: A Middle/Late Iron Age Site and Anglo-Saxon Cemetery at St Anne's Road, Eastbourne, Essex* (Portslade: SpoilHeap, 2016).

60. S. S. Hughes et al., "Anglo-Saxon Origins Investigated by Isotopic Analysis of Burials from Berinsfield, Oxfordshire, UK," *Journal of Archaeological Science*, 42 (2014)," 81–92.

61. A. Boyle et al., *Two Oxfordshire Anglo-Saxon Cemeteries: Berinsfield and Didcot* (Oxford: Oxford Archaeological Unit, 1995), 30–31, 81–82.

62. For Gloucester, see A. Simmonds, N. Marquez-Grant, and L. Loe, *Life and Death in a Roman City: Excavations of a Roman Cemetery with a Mass Grave at 120–122 London Road, Gloucestershire* (Oxford: Oxford Archaeology, 2008), 150–53; C. Chenery et al., "Strontium and Stable Isotope Evidence for Diet and Mobility in Roman Gloucester, UK," *Journal of Archaeological Science*, 37 (2010), 150–63. For London, see K. Eaton et al., "Museum of London Report on the DNA Analyses of Four Roman Individuals," McMaster Ancient DNA Centre, McMaster University, Canada, https://www.museumoflondon.org.uk/application/files/3114/6598/9153/McMaster_Roman_DNA_Report.pdf; R. C. Redfern, "Going South of the River: A Multidisciplinary Analysis of Ancestry, Mobility, and Diet in a Population from Roman Southwark, London," *Journal of Archaeological Science*, 74 (2016), 11–22; H. Shaw et al., "Identifying Migrants in Roman London Using Lead and Strontium Stable Isotopes," *Journal of Archaeological Science*, 66 (2016), 57–68. For Winchester, see J. Evans, N. Stoodley, and C. Chenery, "A Strontium and Oxygen Isotope Assessment of a Possible Fourth Century Immigrant Population in a Hampshire Cemetery, Southern England," *Journal of Archaeological Science*, 33 (2006), 265–72; H. Eckhardt et al., "Oxygen and Strontium Isotope Evidence for Mobility in Roman Winchester," *Journal of Archaeological Science*, 36 (2009), 2816–25; C. Chenery et al., "Oxygen and Strontium Isotope Analysis," in P. Booth et al., *The Late Roman Cemetery at Lankhills, Winchester: Excavations 2000–*

2005 (Oxford: Oxford Archaeology, 2010), 421–28. For York, see G. Müldner and M. P. Richards, "Stable Isotope Evidence for 1500 Years of Human Diet at the City of York, UK," *American Journal of Physical Anthropology*, 133 (2007), 682–97; S. Leach et al., "Migration and Diversity in Roman Britain: A Multidisciplinary Approach to the Identification of Immigrants in Roman York, England," *American Journal of Physical Anthropology*, 140 (2009), 546–61; S. Leach et al., "A Lady of York: Migration, Ethnicity and Identity in Roman Britain," *Antiquity*, 84 (2010), 131–45; J. Montgomery et al., "'Gleaming, White, and Deadly': Using Lead to Track Human Exposure and Geographic Origins in the Roman Period in Britain," *Journal of Roman Archaeology*, supplementary ser., 78 (2010), 199–226, at 216–17; G. Müldner, C. Chenery, and H. Eckhardt, "Headless Romans," 280–90; S. Schiffels and D. Sayer, "Investigating Anglo-Saxon History with Ancient and Modern DNA," in H. H. Meller, F. Daim, J. Krause, and R. Risch, eds., *Migration and Integration from Prehistory to the Middle Ages* (2017, Halle: Landesmuseum für Vorgeschichte), 255–66, at 264.

63. For Catterick, see C. Chenery, H. Eckhardt, and G. Müldner, "Cosmopolitan Catterick? Isotopic Evidence for Population Mobility on Rome's Northern Frontier," *Journal of Archaeological Science*, 38 (2011), 1525–36.

64. Eckhardt et al., "Oxygen and Strontium Isotope Evidence for Mobility in Roman Winchester."

65. C. Chenery, H. Eckhardt, and G. Müldner, "Cosmopolitan Catterick?" 1533; Leach et al., "Migration and Diversity," 555; Eckhardt et al., "Oxygen and Strontium Isotope Evidence for Mobility in Roman Winchester," 2821–22; C. Chenery et al., "Strontium and Stable Isotope Evidence for Diet and Mobility in Roman Gloucester," 156; G. Müldner et al., "Headless Romans," 280–90. Some of the dead identified as foreign born in these studies were high-ranking men buried with crossbow brooches, but other similarly dressed males have isotopic signatures suggesting that they had been born in Britain. And many of the scientifically identified outsiders were women and children. A few had the benefit of elaborate burials, but others did not, which argues that not just military officers and professional administrators traveled with their families in tow, but so too did lesser beings. And, of course, some of the people dying in Britain who had been born in distant lands may have come as human chattel. These findings from Roman Britain echo those from other parts of the Roman world, which uncovered migrating workers, women, and children (H. Eckhardt, ed., *Roman Diasporas: Archaeological Approaches to Mobility and Diversity in the Roman Empire* [Portsmouth, R.I.: Journal of Roman Archaeology, 2010]; K. Kilgrove and J. Montgomery, "All Roads Lead to Rome: Exploring Human Migrations to the Eternal City Through Biochemistry of Skeletons from Two Imperial-Era Cemeteries (1st–3rd C AD)," *PLoS ONE*, 11 [2016], 1–30, https://doi.org/10.1371/journal.pone.0147585).

66. For examples, see S. S. Hughes et al., "Anglo-Saxon Origins Investigated by Isotopic Analysis of Burials from Berinsfield, Oxfordshire"; J. Montgomery, J. Evans, C. Chenery, and G. Müldner, "Stable Isotope Analysis of Bone," in M. Carver, C. Hills, and J. Scheschkewitz, *Wasperton: A Roman, British and Anglo-Saxon Community in Central England* (Woodbridge: Boydell, 2009), 48–49; K. A. Hemer et al., "Evidence of Early Medieval Trade and Migration Between Wales and the Mediterranean Sea Region," *Journal of Archaeological Science*, 40 (2013), 2352–59; K. A. Hemer, "A Bioarchaeological Study of the Human Remains from the Early Medieval Cemetery of Cronk Keeillane," *Proceedings of the Isle of Man Natural History and Antiquarian Society*, 12 (2012), 469–86, at 475–79; K. A. Hemer et al., "No Man Is an Island: Evidence of Pre-Viking Age Migration to the Isle of Man," *Journal of Archaeological Science*, 52 (2014), 242–29, at 246; P. Groom et al., "Two Early Medieval Cemeteries in Pembrokeshire: Brownslade Barrow and West Angle Bay," *Archaeologia Cambrensis*, 160 (2012), 133–203, at 183–87; S. E. Groves et al., "Mobility

Histories of 7th–9th Century AD: People Buried at Early Medieval Bamburgh, Northumberland, England," *American Journal of Physical Anthropology*, 151 (2013), 462–76. The cemetery associated with the terp settlement at Oosterbeintum, in Friesland, the Netherlands, has also produced a few nonlocal individuals, including one whose childhood may have been spent in the South or West of Britain, suggesting, once again, that people may have been moving in this period not only east to west, but west to east (E. McManus et al., "'To the Land or to the Sea': Diet and Mobility in Early Medieval Frisia," *Journal of Island and Coastal Archaeology*, 8 [2013], 255–77).

67. J. Kay, "Moving from Wales and the West in the Fifth Century: Isotope Evidence for Eastward Migration in Britain," in P. Skinner, ed., *The Welsh and the Medieval World: Travel, Migration, and Exile* (Cardiff: University of Wales Press, 2018).

68. Because the interpretation of this evidence is often fit within the paradigm presented to us in our flawed early medieval texts, researchers sometimes assume that the movement from east to west, although an explanation that best fits the evidence, "is at odds with historically documented patterns of migration" (Evans et al., "Summary of Strontium and Oxygen Isotope Variation," 760).

69. J. I. McKinley, "A Conversion-Period Cemetery at Woodlands, Aldwick-le-Street, South Yorkshire," *Yorkshire Archaeological Journal*, 88 (2016), 77–120, at 101–4, 110.

70. J. Lunnon and R. Martlew, "An Anglo-Saxon Amulet Canister from Arncliffe, North Yorkshire," *Yorkshire Archaeological Journal*, 88 (2016), 235–37.

71. Groves et al., "Mobility Histories of 7th–9th Century AD People Buried at Early Medieval Bamburgh," 467–76.

72. The cemetery has not yet been fully published. Twenty-six burials uncovered in 1994 have been published in A. Taylor, C. Duhig, and J. Hines, "An Anglo-Saxon Cemetery at Oakington, Cambridgeshire," *Proceedings of the Cambridge Antiquarian Society*, 86 (1997), 57–90. A brief description of burials found between 2006 and 2011 appears in D. Sayer, R. Mortimer, and F. Simpson, "Anglo-Saxon Oakington: Life and Death in the East Anglian Fens," *Current Archaeology*, 261 (2011), 20–27, and a longer report in R. Mortimer, D. Sayer, and R. Wiseman, "Anglo-Saxon Oakington: A Central Place on the Edge of the Cambridgeshire Fen," in S. Semple, C. Orsini, and S. Mui, *Life on the Edge: Social, Political and Religious Frontiers in Early Medieval Europe* (Wendeburg: Braunschweigisches Landesmuseum, 2017), 305–16. The dates of the four Oakington individuals are based on radiocarbon dates (S. Schiffels et al., "Iron Age and Anglo-Saxon Genomes from Eastern England Reveal British Migration History," *Nature Communications* 7 [2016], 1–9, and supplementary information, https://media.nature.com/original/nature-assets/ncomms/2016/160119/ncomms10408/extref/ncomms10408-s1.pdf, supplementary information, table 2). I am grateful to Duncan Sayer for providing me with further, unpublished material on this cemetery.

73. Schiffels et al., "Iron Age and Anglo-Saxon Genomes from Eastern England Reveal British Migration History," 1–9, and supplementary information, note 1; Schiffels and Sayer, "Investigating Anglo-Saxon History with Ancient and Modern DNA," 255–66. Elsewhere in the former Roman world there is evidence for mixed burial communities, and incomers and older established populations living together, burying together, and changing one another's basic subsistence strategies. See, for example, S. E. Hakenbeck et al., "Practicing Pastoralism in an Agricultural Environment: An Isotopic Analysis of the Impact of the Hunnic Incursions on Pannonian Populations," *PLoS ONE*, 12 (2017), doi:10.1371/journal.pone.0173079.

74. T. F. Martin, *The Cruciform Brooch in Anglo-Saxon England* (Woodbridge: Boydell, 2015), 142.

75. For the ways women "dressed for themselves" in the Roman period, see M. Harlow, "Dressing to Please Themselves: Clothing Choices for Roman Women," in M. Harlow, ed., *Dress and Identity*, BAR International Series 2356 (Oxford: Archaeopress, 2012), 37–46.

76. B. Magnus, "Brooches on the Move in Migration Period Europe," *Fornvännen*, 99 (2004), 273–83, at 280; P. von Rummel, "Gotisch, barbarisch, oder römisch? Methodologische Überlieferungen zur ethnischen Interpretation von Kleidung," in W. Pohl and M. Mehoffer, eds., *Archaeology of Identity/Archäologie der Identität* (Vienna: Österreichischen Akademie der Wissenschaften, 2010), 51–77; Moreland, "Going Native," 142–49; Halsall, "Ethnicity and Early Medieval Cemeteries," 15–27; Hakenbeck, "Roman or Barbarian?" 38–39.

77. Richardson, "Third Way," 79.

78. S. Brather, "New Questions Instead of Old Answers: Archaeological Expectations of aDNA Analysis," *Medieval Worlds*, 4 (2016), 22–41, at 29.

79. D. O. Hughes, "Distinguishing Signs: Ear-Rings, Jews, and Franciscan Rhetoric in the Italian Renaissance City," *Past and Present*, 112 (1986), 3–59, at 40–44.

80. S. Hirst and D. Clark, *Excavations at Mucking: Excavations by Tom and Margaret Jones*, vol. 3, *The Anglo-Saxon Cemeteries* (London: MoLAS, 2009), part 2, 767–70; Hills and Lucy, *Spong Hill Part IX*, 300–31.

81. Richardson, "Third Way," 75.

82. Hakenbeck, "Roman or Barbarian?" 38; S. Brather, *Ethnische Interpretationen in der frühgeschichtlichen Archäologie: Geschichte, Grundlagen, und Alternativen* (Berlin: de Gruyter, 2004), 169.

83. For useful lists of textile survivals, see P. Walton Rogers, *Cloth and Clothing in Early Anglo-Saxon England, AD 450–700* (York: Council for British Archaeology 2007), 52–57; T. F. Martin, "Identity and the Cruciform Brooch in Early Anglo-Saxon England: An Investigation of Style, Mortuary Context, and Use," 4 vols. (Ph.D. diss., University of Sheffield, 2011), iv, 7–28.

84. Walton Rogers, *Cloth and Clothing*, 144.

85. Grave 78. Haughton and Powlesland, *West Heslerton*, 2:122–24; P. Walton Rogers, "The Textiles," in Haughton and Powlesland, *West Heslerton*, 1:155. For references for other single-shoulder peplos gowns found in the cemeteries of Barrington A, Easington, Empringham II, Norton, Oakington, and Spong Hill, see Martin, "Identity and the Cruciform Brooch," 4:422–23, 425.

86. Walton Rogers, "Textiles," 155; G. Edwards, "Costume," in Hirst et al., *Excavations at Mucking*, vol. 3, part 2, 575–84, at 580.

87. P. Walton Rogers, "Reconstructing the Flixton Women," in S. Boulter and P. Walton Rogers, *Circles and Cemeteries: Excavations at Flixton*, vol. 1, East Anglian Archaeology 147 (Bury St. Edmunds: Suffolk County Council Archaeological Service, 2012) 158–77, at 162.

88. Walton Rogers, *Cloth and Clothing*, 152–55; Martin, *Cruciform Brooch and Anglo-Saxon England*, 202–4.

89. Walton Rogers, *Cloth and Clothing*, 74.

90. Walton Rogers, "Reconstructing the Flixton Women," 162; P. Walton Rogers, *Tyttel's Halh: The Anglo-Saxon Cemetery at Tittleshall, Norfolk*, East Anglian Archaeology 150 (Lincoln: Lincoln Network Archaeology, 2013), 68; P. Walton Rogers, "Continuity Within Change: Two Sites in the Borders of the Former Iceni Territory in East Anglia," in Annaert et al., eds., *The Very Beginning of Europe?*, 109–22, at 115.

91. P. Walton Rogers, "Wider Cultural Affiliations of the Textiles," in Carver et al., *Wasperton*, 83–85, at 84.

92. Walton Rogers, "Textiles," 147, 155–56.

93. O. Magoula, "Usage and Meaning of Early Medieval Textiles: A Structural Analysis of Vestimentary Systems in Francia and Anglo-Saxon England," 2 vols. (Ph.D. diss., University of Birmingham, 2008), 1:99.

94. G. Owen-Crocker, *Dress in Anglo-Saxon England*, 2nd ed. (Woodbridge: Boydell, 2004), 80.

95. K. Parfitt and B. Brugmann, *The Anglo-Saxon Cemetery on Mill Hill, Deal, Kent* (London: Society for Medieval Archaeology, 1997), 32.

96. G. Fisher, "Faces in a Crowd or a Crowd of Faces? Archaeological Evidence for Individual and Group Identity in Early Anglo-Saxon England," in J. R. Mathieu and R. E. Scott, eds., *Exploring the Role of Analytical Scale in Archaeological Interpretation*, BAR International Series 1261 (Oxford: Archaeopress, 2004), 49–58, at 51.

97. For women wearing modified brooches, see T. Martin, "Riveting Biographies: The Theoretical Implications of Early Anglo-Saxon Brooch Repair, Customisation and Use-Adaptation," in B. Jervis and A. Kyle, eds., *Make-Do and Mend: Archaeologies of Compromise, Repair and Reuse*, BAR International Series 2408 (Oxford: Archaeopress, 2012), 53–65, at 58. For their wearing short, animal-pelt capes and sheepskin garments, see Walton Rogers, *Cloth and Clothing*, 172; Owen-Crocker, *Dress in Anglo-Saxon England*, 76.

98. Fisher, "Faces in a Crowd." See also, Rogers Walton, "Reconstructing the Flixton Women," 159.

99. Stoodley, *Spindle and the Spear*, 108, 465; R. Gowland, "Aging the Past: Examining Age Identity from Funerary Evidence," in R. Gowland and C. Knüsel, eds., *Social Archaeology and Funerary Remains* (Oxford: Oxbow Books, 2006), 143–54; Hirst et al., *Excavations at Mucking*, vol. 3, part 2, 743–52, 692–94; Martin, *Cruciform Brooch in Anglo-Saxon England*, 215–22.

100. R. Gowland, "Beyond Ethnicity: Symbols of Identity in Fourth to Sixth Century AD England," *Anglo-Saxon Studies in Archaeology and History*, 14 (2007), 56–65, at 61–63.

101. For a discussion of the local mediation of new material culture, see M. Grahame, "Material Culture and Roman Identity: The Spatial Layout of Pompeian Houses and the Problem of Ethnicity," in R. Laurence and J. Berry, eds., *Cultural Identity in the Roman Empire* (London: Routledge, 1998), 156–78, at 176.

102. S. Harrington, "Beyond Exogamy: Marriage Strategies in Early Anglo-Saxon England," in Brookes and Reynolds, *Studies in Early Anglo-Saxon Art and Archaeology*," 88–97, at 96.

103. V. Evison, *An Anglo-Saxon Cemetery at Great Chesterford, Essex* (York: Council for British Archaeology, 1994), 96.

104. E. Swift, "Late Roman Bead Necklaces and Bracelets," *Journal of Roman Archaeology*, 16 (2003), 336–49.

105. P. Booth et al., *Late Roman Cemetery at Lankhills*, 285.

106. J.-M. Doyen, "'Charon's Obol': Some Methodological Reflexions," *Journal of Archaeological Numismatics*, 2 (2012), i–xviii.

107. M. Carver et al., *Wasperton*, inhumation 302; Adrián D. Maldonado Ramírez, "Christianity and Burial in Late Iron Age Scotland, AD 400–650" (Ph.D. diss., University of Glasgow 2011), 104.

108. As, for example, at Mucking. Hirst et al., *Excavations at Mucking*, vol. 3, part 2, 468, 642.

109. Walton Rogers, "Wider Cultural Affiliations of the Textiles."

110. G. R. Owen-Crocker, "British Wives and Slaves? Possible Romano-British Techniques in 'Women's Work,'" in Higham, ed., *Britons in Anglo-Saxon England*, 80–90, at 83–84.

111. Carver et al., *Wasperton*, 170–72, 182–83, 224–27, 299–301; B. Solberg, "Turned and Coopered Vessels of Wood in Late Roman and Migration Period Graves in Norway," *Studien zur*

Sachsenforschung, 15 (2005), 421–36; A. Mason, "Buried Buckets: Rethinking Ritual Behavior Before England's Conversion," *Haskins Society Journal*, 20 (2008), 3–18.

112. W. J. Ford, "Anglo-Saxon Cemeteries Along the Avon Valley," *Transactions of Birmingham and Warwickshire Archaeological Society*, 100 (1995), 59–98, at 66–68; Walton Rogers, *Cloth and Clothing*, 229–32.

113. Carver et al., *Wasperton*, 85, 88.

114. P. Walton Rogers, "Continuity Within Change," 111–13.

115. Carver et al., *Wasperton*, 86.

116. S. P. Ashby, "Technologies of Appearance: Hair Behaviour in Early Medieval Europe," *Archaeological Journal*, 171 (2014), 151–84, 154.

117. Owen-Crocker, *Dress in Anglo-Saxon England*, 56–57.

CHAPTER 9

Epigraph: J. Hoskins, *Biographical Objects: How Things Tell the Stories of People's Lives* (London, 1998), 2.

1. See above, Chapter 1; S. Esmonde Cleary, *The Ending of Roman Britain* (London: B. T. Batsford, 1989), 131–61; S. Esmonde Cleary, *The Roman West AD 200–500: An Archaeological Study* (Cambridge: Cambridge University Press, 2013), 257; G. Halsall, *Worlds of Arthur: Facts and Fictions of the Dark Ages* (Oxford: Oxford University Press, 2013), 93–96.

2. S. White et al., "A Mid-Fifth Century Hoard of Roman and Pseudo-Roman Material from Patching, West Sussex," *Britannia*, 30 (1999), 301–15; R. Abdy and G. Williams, "A Catalogue of Hoards and Single Finds from the British Isles c. AD 410–675," in B. Cook and G. Williams, eds., *Coinage and History in the North Sea World, c. AD 500–1250: Essays in Honour of Marion Archibald* (Leiden: Brill, 2006), 11–73; R. Collins, "The Latest Roman Coin from Hadrian's Wall: A Small Fifth-Century Purse Group," *Britannia*, 39 (2008), 256–61; P. J. Walton, *Rethinking Roman Britain: Coinage and Archaeology* (Wetteren: Edition Moneta, 2012), 113 and tables 35–38; P. Walton and S. Moorhead, "Coinage and Collapse? The Contribution of Numismatic Data to Understanding the End of Roman Britain," *Internet Archaeology* 41 (2016), http://dx.doi.org/10.11141/ia.41.8.

3. S. T. Loseby, "Post-Roman Economies," in W. Scheidel, ed., *The Cambridge Companion to the Roman Economy* (Cambridge: Cambridge University Press, 2012), 334–60, at 339. Troops had been withdrawn from Britain on a number of occasions in the late Roman period, most famously under Constantine III (R. Collins and D. Breeze, "*Limitanei* and *Comitatenses*: Military Failure at the End of Roman Britain?" in F. K. Haarer, ed., *AD 410: The History and Archaeology of Late and Post-Roman Britain* [London: Society for the Promotion of Roman Studies, 2014], 61–72, at 65–66, 70).

4. M. McCormick, *Origins of the European Economy: Communications and Commerce AD 300–900* (Cambridge: Cambridge University Press, 2002), 64–67.

5. P. van Ossel and P. Ouzoulias, "Rural Settlement Economy in Northern Gaul in the Late Empire: An Overview and Assessment," *Journal of Roman Archaeology*, 13 (2000), 133–66; G. Halsall, *Barbarian Migrations and the Roman West, 376–568* (Cambridge: Cambridge University Press, 2007), 383–87; S. Esmonde Cleary, "The Ending(s) of Roman Britain," in H. Hamerow, D. A. Hinton, and S. Crawford, eds., *The Oxford Handbook of Anglo-Saxon Archaeology* (Oxford: Oxford University Press, 2011), 13–29.

6. J. Oldenstein, "De Valentinien Ier à la fin de l'Empire romain occidental," in M. Reddé, R. Brulet, R. Fellmann, J.-K. Haalebos, and S. Von Schnurbein, eds., *L'architecture de la Gaule*

romaine: Les fortifications militaires (Paris: Éditions de la Maison des sciences de l'homme, 2006), 47–50.

7. S. C. Hawkes, "Soldiers and Settlers in Britain, Fourth and Fifth Century," *Medieval Archaeology*, 5 (1961), 1–70; V. Evison, *The Fifth-Century Invasions South of the Thames* (London: Athlone, 1965); J. R. Kirk and E. T. Leeds, "Three Early Saxon Graves from Dorchester, Oxon," *Oxoniensia*, 17–18 (1954), 63–76.

8. Gildas, *The Ruin of Britain and Other Works*, ed. and trans. M. Winterbottom (Chichester: Phillimore, 1978), cap. 23.5.

9. For women's dress in Kent, see P. Walton Rogers, *Cloth and Clothing in Early Anglo-Saxon England: AD 450–700* (York: Council for British Archaeology, 2007), 190–93; L. Bender Jørgensen, "The Textile of the Saxons, Anglo-Saxons, and Franks," *Studien zur Sachsenforschung*, 7 (1991), 11–23, at 14–15, 17; G. R. Owen-Crocker, *Dress in Anglo-Saxon England*, 2nd ed. (Woodbridge: Boydell, 2004), 90–102.

10. S. Chadwick Hawkes, "Early Anglo-Saxon Kent," *Archaeological Journal*, 126 (1970), 186–92; I. Wood, *The Merovingian North Sea* (Alingsås: Viktoria bokförlag, 1983), 16–17; I. Wood, "Frankish Hegemony in England," in M. Carver, ed., *The Age of Sutton Hoo* (Woodbridge: Boydell, 1992), 235–41; J. W. Huggett, "Imported Grave Goods and the Early Anglo-Saxon Economy," *Medieval Archaeology*, 32 (1988), 63–96; C. Behr, "The Origins of Kingship in Early Medieval Kent," *Early Medieval Europe*, 9 (2000), 25–52, at 46–47; M. Welch, "Cross-Channel Contacts Between Anglo-Saxon England and Merovingian Francia," in S. Lucy and A. Reynolds, eds., *Burial in Early Medieval England and Wales* (London: Society for Medieval Archaeology, 2002), 122–31; and M. Welch, "Anglo-Saxon Kent," in J. H. Williams, ed., *The Archaeology of Kent to AD 800* (Woodbridge: Boydell, 2007), 187–248, at 191–92.

11. M. Parker Pearson, R. Van De Noort, and A. Woolf, "Three Men and a Boat: Sutton Hoo and the East Saxon Kingdom," *Anglo-Saxon England*, 22 (1993), 27–50, at 31–32; S. Harrington and M. Welch, *The Early Anglo-Saxon Kingdoms of South Britain AD 450–650: Beneath the Tribal Hidage* (Oxford: Oxbow Books, 2014), 174–210.

12. J. Soulat, "Des Mérovingiens en Angleterre," *Histoire et image médiévales*, 34 (2010), 49–55, at 50.

13. M. Welch, "Contacts Across the Channel Between the Fifth and the Seventh Centuries: A Review of the Archaeological Evidence," *Studien zur Sachsenforschung*, 7 (1991), 261–69; J. Soulat, *Le matériel archéologique de type Saxon et Anglo-Saxon en Gaule mérovingienne* (Saint-Germain-en-Laye: Association française d'archéologie mérovinginne, 2009).

14. M. Welch, "The Archaeological Evidence for Federate Settlement in Britain Within the Fifth Century," in F. Vallet and M. Kazanski, eds., *L'Armée romaine et les barbares du IIIe au VIIe siècle* (Rouen: Association française d'archéologie mérovingienne), 268–78; Welch, "Cross-Channel Contacts"; Welch, "Anglo-Saxon Kent," 199–200; Soulat, *Le materiel archéologique*; Harrington and Welch, *Early Anglo-Saxon Kingdoms*, 180; J. Soulat, "Between Frankish and Merovingian Influences in Early Anglo-Saxon Sussex (Fifth–Seventh Centuries)," in S. Brookes, S. Harrington, and A. Reynolds, eds., *Studies in Early Anglo-Saxon Art and Archaeology: Papers in Honour of Martin G. Welch*, BAR British Series 527 (Oxford: Archaeopress, 2011), 62–71, at 63–65.

15. For some examples and a critique, see R. Collins and J. McClure, "Canterbury and Wearmouth-Jarrow: Three Viewpoints on Augustine's Mission," in S. Barton and P. Linehan, eds., *Cross, Crescent, and Conversion: Studies on Medieval Spain and Christendom in Memory of Richard Fletcher* (Leiden: Brill, 2008), 17–42; R. Fleming, "Elites, Boats and Foreigners: Rethinking the Rebirth of English Towns," *Città e campagna prima del mille, Atti delle Settimane di Studio*, 56 (2009), 393–425.

16. C. M. Hills and H. R. Hurst, "A Goth at Gloucester?" *Antiquaries Journal*, 69 (1989), 154–58; F. Theuws, "Grave Goods, Ethnicity and the Rhetoric of Burial Rites in Late Antique Northern Gaul," in T. Derks and N. Roymans, eds., *Ethnic Constructs in Antiquity: The Role of Power and Tradition* (Amsterdam: Amsterdam University Press, 2009), 283–320; Esmonde Cleary, *Roman West*, 82–90.

17. G. Halsall, "Archaeology and the Late Roman Frontier in Northern Gaul: The So-Called Föderatengräber Reconsidered," in W. Pohl and H. Reimitz, eds., *Grenze und Differenz im frühen Mittelalter* (Vienna: Österreichische Akademie der Wissenschaften, 2000), 167–80; B. Effros, *Merovingian Mortuary Archaeology and the Making of the Early Middle Ages* (Berkeley: University of California Press, 2003); H. W. Böhme, "Migrants' Fortunes: The Integration of Germanic Peoples in Late Antique Gaul," in D. Quast, ed., *Foreigners in Early Medieval Europe* (Mainz: Verlag des Römisch-Germanischen Zentralmuseums, 2009), 131–47; Theuws, "Grave Goods, Ethnicity and the Rhetoric of Burial Rites."

18. Hills and Hurst, "Goth at Gloucester?"; J. P. Bushe-Fox, *Fourth Report on the Excavations of the Roman Fort at Richborough, Kent* (London: Society of Antiquaries of London, 1949), 80 and plate 63.

19. Hawkes, "Soldiers and Settlers in Britain."

20. Esmonde Cleary, *Roman West*, 79–90; P. Booth, "A Late Roman Military Burial from the Dyke Hills, Dorchester on Thames, Oxfordshire," *Britannia*, 45 (2014), 243–73, at 268–69; R. Collins, "Soldiers in Life and Death: Material Culture, the Military, and Mortality," in A. Van Oyen and M. Pitts, eds., *Materialising Roman Histories* (Oxford: Oxbow Books, 2017), 31–45.

21. Booth, "Late Roman Military Burial." A distinctive decorative style used to embellish some early fifth-century brooches, bracelets, and belt sets, known as the Quoit Brooch style, were being manufactured and worn by and buried with high-status individuals on both sides of the channel in the fifth century. This, too, suggests episodic contact between the sorts of people in Britain and Roman Gaul in the fifth century who favored similar styles of personal adornment and self-presentation (P. Inker, "Technology as Active Material Culture: The Quoit-Brooch Style," *Medieval Archaeology*, 44 [2000], 25–52).

22. S. Lucy, "Odd Goings-On at Mucking: Interpreting the Latest Romano-British Pottery Horizon," *Internet Archaeology*, 41 (2016), http://dx.doi.org/10.11141/ia/41/6; S. Hirst and D. Clark, *Excavations at Mucking by Tom and Margaret Jones*, vol. 3, *The Anglo-Saxon Cemeteries. Part II: Analysis and Discussion* (London: MoLAS, 2009), 662–68. For a complete list of burials with belt sets and weapons of men who were likely born outside of Britain, and who probably came to Britain as imperial civilian or military officials, see Collins, "Soldiers in Life and Death," 42.

23. Soulat, *Le matériel archéologique*, 133–36; J. Soulat et al., "Hand-Made Pottery Along the Channel Coast and Parallels with the Scheldt Valley," in R. Annaert et al., eds., *The Very Beginning of Europe? Cultural and Social Dimensions of Early-Medieval Migration and Colonisation (5th–8th Century): Archaeology in Contemporary Europe; Conference Brussels, May 17–19 2011* (Brussels: Flanders Heritage Agency, 2012), 215–24; Harrington and Welch, *Early Anglo-Saxon Kingdoms*, 183–205.

24. Esmonde Cleary, *Roman West*, 282–85; M. Dijkstra, "Between Britannia and Francia: The Nature of External Socio-Economic Exchange at the Rhine and Meuse Estuaries in the Early Middle Ages," *Bodendenkmalpflege in Mecklenburg-Vorpommern: Jahrbuch*, 51 (2003), 397–408; M. Dijkstra and J. de Koning, "'All Quiet on the Western Front'? The Western Netherlands and the 'North Sea Culture' in the Migration Period," in J. Hines and N. Ijssennagger, eds., *Frisians and Their North Sea Neighbours: From the Fifth Century to the Viking Age* (Woodbridge: Boydell, 2017), 53–73, at 62–66.

25. R. Fleming, "The Movement of People and Things Between Britain and France in the Late- and Post-Roman Periods," in B. Effros and I. Moreira, eds., *Oxford Handbook of the Merovingian World* (Oxford: Oxford University Press, in press).

26. M. Fulford and S. Rippon, *Pevensey Castle, Sussex: Excavations in the Roman Fort and Medieval Keep, 1993–95* (Salisbury: Wessex Archaeology and University of Reading, 2011), 125.

27. White et al., "Mid-Fifth Century Hoard"; R. Abdy, "The Patching Hoard," in F. Hunter and K. Painter, eds., *Late Roman Silver and the End of Empire: The Traprain Treasure in Context* (Edinburgh: Society of Antiquaries of Scotland, 2013), 107–15.

28. D. B. Harden, "The Highdown Hill Glass Goblet with Greek Inscription," *Sussex Archaeological Collections*, 97 (1959), 3–20.

29. A. Harris, *Byzantium, Britain, and the West: The Archaeology of Cultural Identity AD 400–650* (Stroud: Tempus, 2003), 161–88.

30. F. M. Morris, "Cross–North Sea Contacts in the Roman Period," *Oxford Journal of Archaeology*, 34 (2015), 415–38, at 424–27.

31. J. Hines, "The Origins of East Anglia in a North Sea Zone," in D. Bates and R. Liddiard, eds., *East Anglia and Its North Sea World in the Middle Ages* (Woodbridge: Boydell, 2013), 16–43; Dijkstra and de Koning, "All Quiet on the Western Front?"; J. Nicolay, "Power and Identity in the Southern North Sea Area: The Migration and Merovingian Periods," in Hines and Ijssennagger, eds., *Frisians and Their North Sea Neighbours*, 75–92, at 76–80.

32. Hines, "Origins of East Anglia"; P. Deckers and D. Tys, "Early Medieval Communities Around the North Sea: A 'Maritime Culture'?" in Annaert et al., *Very Beginning of Europe?* 81–88.

33. H. Hamerow, Y. Hollevoet, and A. Vince, "Migration Period Settlements and 'Anglo-Saxon' Pottery from Flanders," *Medieval Archaeology*, 38 (1994), 1–18; E. Knol, "Anglo-Saxon Migration Reflected in Cemeteries in the Northern Netherlands," in Quast, *Foreigners in Early Medieval Europe*, 112–29; B. Jervis et al., "Early Anglo-Saxon Pottery in South-East England: Recent Work and a Research Framework for the Future," *Medieval Ceramics*, 36 (2016), 17–29; B. Jervis, "Trade, Cultural Exchange and Coastal Identities in Early Anglo-Saxon Kent: A Ceramic Perspective," in A. Willemsen and H. Kik, eds., *Golden Middle Ages in Europe: New Research into Early-Medieval Communities and Identities; Proceedings of the Second 'Dorstad Congress' Held at the National Museum of Antiquities, Leiden, the Netherlands 2–5 July, 2014* (Turnhout: Brepols, 2016), 57–63; Deckers and Tys, "Early Medieval Communities"; Soulat et al., "Hand-Made Pottery"; T. N. Krol, K. Struckmeyer, and A. Nieuwhof, "Anglo-Saxon Style Pottery from the Northern Netherlands and North-Western Germany: Fabrics and Finish, Regional and Chronological Patterns, and Their Implications," *Archaeometry*, 60 (2018), 713–30.

34. The phrase is borrowed from S. Needham, "Transforming Beaker Culture in North-West Europe: Processes of Fusion and Fission," *Proceedings of the Prehistoric Society*, 71 (2005), 171–217, especially 176–82.

35. On the ways late Roman landscapes and infrastructure were organized in ways that made the mobilization, processing, storage, and movement of its agricultural production, see J. Taylor, "Encountering Romanitas: Characterising the Role of Agricultural Communities in Roman Britain," *Britannia*, 44 (2013), 171–90.

36. D. M. Goodburn, "Woods and Woodland: Carpenters and Carpentry," in G. Milne, ed., *Timber Building Techniques in London c. 900–1400: An Archaeological Study of Waterfront Installations and Related Material* (London: London and Middlesex Archaeology Society, 1992), 112–14; G. Milne, "Medieval Circular Saws for Shipbuildings?" *International Journal of Nautical*

Archaeology, 22 (1993), 291–92, at 291; J. Hill and A. Woodger, *Excavations at 72–75 Cheapside/83–93 Queen Street City of London* (London: MoLAS, 1999), 27–37.

37. On the knock-on effects of deskilling more generally, see B. Ward-Perkins, "Specialized Production and Exchange," in A. Cameron, B. Ward-Perkins, and M. Whitby, *The Cambridge Ancient History*, vol. 14, *Late Antiquity: Empire and Successors, AD 425–600* (Cambridge: Cambridge University Press, 2001), 346–91, at 381–83.

38. S. Kohring, "Conceptual Knowledge as Technologically Materialised: A Case Study of Pottery Production, Consumption, and Community Practice," in M. L. Stig Sørensen and K. Rebay-Salisbury, eds., *Embodied Knowledge: Historical Perspectives on Belief and Technology* (Oxford: Oxbow Books, 2013), 106–16.

39. B. Lawson, *The Language of Space* (Oxford: Elsevier, 2001), 23–25.

40. Louise Revell, *Ways of Being Roman: Discourses of Identity in the Roman West* (Oxford: Oxbow Books, 2016), 90.

41. On the impact this can have, see H. M. L. Miller, "Comparing Landscapes of Transportation: Riverine-Oriented and Land-Oriented in the Indus Civilization and the Mughal Empire," in E. C. Roberts et al., *Space and Spatial Analysis in Archaeology* (Calgary: University of Calgary Press, 2006), 281–91; T. Ingold, "The Temporality of the Landscape," *World Archaeology*, 25 (1993), 167. On the laying out, maintaining, and then abandonment of droveways in the post-Roman period, see A. M. Chadwick, "Foot-Fall and Hoof-Hit: Agencies, Movements, Materialities, and Identities; And Later Prehistoric and Romano-British Trackways," *Cambridge Archaeological Journal*, 26 (2016), 93–120, at 112.

42. C. Grey et al., "Familiarity, Repetition, and Quotidian Movement in Roman Tuscany," *Journal of Mediterranean Archaeology*, 28 (2015), 195–219; Chadwick, "Foot-Fall and Hoof-Hit"; Ingold, "Temporality of the Landscape," 156.

43. H. Ziche, "Making Late Roman Taxpayers Pay: Imperial Government Strategies and Practice," in H. A. Drake, ed., *Violence in Late Antiquity: Perceptions and Practices* (Aldershot: Ashgate, 2006), 125–34; W. Scheidel and S. J. Friesen, "The Size of the Economy and the Distribution of Income in the Roman Empire," *Journal of Roman Studies*, 99 (2009), 61–91; D. J. Mattingly, *Imperialism, Power, and Identity: Experiencing the Roman Empire* (Princeton: Princeton University Press, N.J., 2011), 125–45; P. F. Bang, "Predation," in Scheidel, *Cambridge Companion to the Roman Economy*, 197–217, at 200–203.

44. R. Knapp, *Invisible Romans* (Cambridge, Mass: Harvard University Press, 2011), 103.

45. M. McKerracher, *Farming Transformed in Anglo-Saxon England: Agriculture in the Long Eighth Century* (Oxford: Windgather, 2018), 70–72, 76–79.

46. C. A. Hastorf and L. Foxhall, "The Social and Political Aspects of Food Surplus," *World Archaeology*, 49 (2017), 26–39, at 28.

47. S. Rippon et al., *The Fields of Britannia: Continuity and Change in the Late Roman and Early Medieval Landscape* (Oxford: Oxford University Press, 2015), 94–95.

48. Rippon et al., *Fields of Britannia*, 83.

49. M. van der Veen and T. O'Connor, "The Expansion of Agricultural Production in Late Iron Age and Roman Britain," in J. Bayley, ed., *Science in Archaeology: An Agenda for the Future* (London: English Heritage, 1998), 127–43, at 129–30; Hamish Forbes, "Surplus, Storage, and Status in a Rural Greek Community," *World Archaeology*, 49 (2017), 8–25.

50. Rippon et al., *Fields of Britannia*, 80; McKerracher, *Farming Transformed*, 30, 41; Chadwick, "Foot-Fall and Hoof-Hit," 112.

51. Hastorf and Foxhall, "Social and Political Aspects of Food Surplus."

52. P. Halstead, "The Economy Has a Normal Surplus: Economic Stability and Social Change Among Early Farming Communities of Thessaly, Greece," in P. Halstead and J. M. O'Shea, eds., *Bad Year Economics: Cultural Responses to Risk and Uncertainty* (Cambridge: Cambridge University Press, 1989), 68–80.

53. C. Roberts and M. Cox, *Health and Disease in Britain: From Prehistory to the Present Day* (Stroud: Sutton, 2003), 134–42; R. Fleming, "Bones for Historians: Putting the Body Back into Biography," in D. Bates, J. Crick, and S. Hamilton, eds., *Writing Medieval Biography: Essays in Honour of Frank Barlow* (Woodbridge: Boydell, 2006), 29–48, at 45–46; J. J. Peck, "The Biological Impact of Culture Contact: A Bioarchaeological Study of Roman Colonialism in Britain" (Ph.D. diss., Ohio State University, 2009); R. Griffin et al., "Inequality at Late Roman Baldock, UK: The Impact of Social Factors on Health and Diet," *Journal of Anthropological Research*, 67 (2011), 533–56, at 544–45; W. Scheidel, "Physical Well-Being," in Sheidel, *Cambridge Companion to the Roman Economy*, 321–33.

54. Fleming, "Elites, Boats, and Foreigners," 398–407.

55. D. Tys, "Maritime and River-Traders, Landing-Places and Emporia Ports in the Merovingian Period in and Around the Low Countries," in Effros and Moreira, *Oxford Handbook of the Merovingian World*.

56. P. Bourdieu, *Outline of a Theory of Practice* (Cambridge: Cambridge University Press, 1977), 94; *Habitus* is both enduring and transferable from one context to another, but it is neither fixed nor permanent (Z. Navarro, "In Search of Cultural Interpretations of Power," *IDS [Institute of Developmental Sciences] Bulletin*, 37 [2006], 11–22, at 11).

57. K. A. Yelvington, "Ethnicity as Practice? A Comment on Bentley," *Comparative Studies in Society and History*, 31 (1991), 158–68, at 168.

58. J. Evans, "Balancing the Scales: Romano-British Pottery in Early Late Antiquity," in L. Lavan, ed., *Local Economies? Production and Exchange of Inland Regions in Late Antiquity* (Leiden: Brill, 2013), 425–50, at 427–29, and fig. 1.

59. T. Brindle, *The Portable Antiquities Scheme and Roman Britain* (London: British Museum, 2014), 1–9. For the biases in this data, see K. Robbins, "Balancing the Scales: Exploring the Variable Effects of Collection Bias on Data Collected by the Portable Antiquities Scheme," *Landscapes*, 14 (2013), 54–72.

60. For this divide in the Roman period, see A. Sargent, "The North-South Divide Revisited: Thoughts on the Character of Roman Britain," *Britannia*, 33 (2002), 219–26.

61. Evans, "Balancing the Scales," 427–29, 446.

62. S. Jones, *The Archaeology of Ethnicity: Constructing Identities in the Past and Present* (London: Routledge, 1997).

INDEX

Abbots Worthy, Hants., 42
Abinnaeus, 29
adult burial: with beads, 164–65; with belt sets, 25–27, 62, 178–80; clothing used in, 169–74; in early medieval Germany, 160–64; as evidence of migration, 166–69; high-status, 62; with metalwork, 165–66; scholarly reassessment of, 157–60; use of Roman-period building material in, 114; use of Roman-style ceramics in, 81–82
Adwick-le-Street, S. Yorks., 168
Alchester, Oxon., 24, 65, 206n13
Alice Holt/Farnham. *See* pottery
Altenerding-Klettham, 162–63
Alton, Hants., 129
Alzy, 24
Ammianus Marcellinus, 19
Anatolia, 163
"Anglo-Saxon" as a problematic term, 5, 62–63, 65–66, 158–59, 167, 175, 179–80, 186–91
Anglo-Saxon Chronicle, 2, 158, 188, 278n6
animals: disappearance of new animals, 41–42; introduction of new animals, 34–35, 38–41; labor practices, 46–47; relationship to plants, 44–45; survival and return of new animals, 47–50; synanthropic animals, 39
annona. *See* Roman tax system
Antioch, 29
Ariconium, Here., 122, 124
Arncliffe, N. Yorks., 168

Bad Kreuznach, 24
Bainesse, N. Yorks., 114
Baldock, Herts., 78–82, 249n103, 272n70
Bardown, E. Sx., 124
Barrow Hills, Oxon., 90–93

Bath, Som., 24, 101, 127; temple of Sulis Minerva, 101, 127–28
baths and bathhouses, 13, 28, 30, 37, 76, 97–99, 106, 111–12, 114, 116–18, 124, 127, 144
Bavaria, 162–63
BB1 (black burnished ware). *See* pottery
Beauport Park, E. Sx., 124, 256n30
Beckford, Worcs., 153
Bede, 2, 191
Bedfordshire, 58, 60, 149, 239n137, 249n103
Belgium, 27, 75
Berinsfield, Oxon., 153, 167, 170
Berkshire Downs, 17
Bestwall Quarry, Dor., 56, 124
Billingford, Norf., 65
Binchester, Co. Dur., 28–29
Birdoswald, Cumb., 101
Blackfield, Wilts. *See* Cunetio, Wilts.
blacksmiths. *See* smiths
Bloodmore Hill, Suff., 129, 135
Boss Hall, Suff., 131
Boulogne, 22–23, 28
Bowl Hole, Northumb., 168
Bradley Hill, Som., 144–47, 149, 154, 268n36, 272n81
Brandon Road, Norf., 135
Brandon, Suff., 43
Broadfields, W. Sx., 124
brooches: in burials, 162–65, 167, 169–74, 178; crossbow brooches, 14, 25–28, 30, 53; as evidence of metal production, 13, 124, 129–31; as evidence of trade networks, 181; penannular brooches, 62, 172–73; Quoit Brooch-style, 62, 180, 291n21; women's brooches, 91–93
Brough-on-Humber, E. Yorks., 147
Broughton Lodge, Notts., 114
Buckinghamshire, 38, 42, 65, 98, 114, 215n99

Burgess Hill, W. Sx., 65
burial. *See* adult burial; infant burial
Burnbury Lane, E. Yorks., 142
Butler's Field, Gloucs., 114, 171

Cadbury Castle, Som., 124
Cadbury Congresbury, Som., 82–87, 92–94
Caesarea, 255n17
Caistor-by-Norwich, Norf., 114
California cemetery. *See* Baldock, Herts.
Cambridge, 140–49; Ridgeons Garden, 141–47, 149
Cambridgeshire, 55, 58, 60, 168
Capitulare de villis vel curtis imperii, 48
Castrum Rauracense. *See* Kaiseraugst
Catterick, N. Yorks., 26, 167
ceramics. *See* pottery
Chilperic, 128
Cicero, 151
Cirencester, Gloucs., 23–24, 30, 108, 271n70
Cleatham, Lincs., 67, 69, 114
clothing. *See* adult burial
coins: as everyday objects 6, 13, 182; as evidence for dating, 24, 28, 62, 106; as evidence of movement of goods and people, 21, 25, 133; in graves, 137, 141–42, 144–45, 172; in hoards, 16, 180; *nummi*, 13–14; as objects of standard assemblage, 110, 112, 129; as recycled objects, 130; *siliqua*, 14, 21, 51; *solidi*, 14, 197n19, 197n26; usage and circulation, 15, 51–54, 60, 88, 177
Colchester, Essex, 22, 46, 206n13, 215n99
Constantine, 12
construction practices: timber, 22, 38, 64, 83, 88, 95, 104, 107–9, 112, 115, 141; stone, 95–109
Cornwall, 131
Cottam, E. Yorks., 135, 264n112
Crambeck, N. Yorks., 54, 58–59, 71, 88, 112, 236n101, 237n117
Crandon Bridge, Som., 25
Crossgates, N. Yorks., 65, 87–89, 93
Cunetio, Wilts., 22, 24, 86–87

Danube, 26, 48
De rebus bellicis, 16
Deerton, Kent, 23, 98, 108
Denmark, 126, 133, 162, 165
Derbyshire, 134
Diocletian, 12, 74, 97
Domesday Book, 49, 263n107

Dorchester, Oxon., 26, 145
Dorset, 56–58, 101, 124, 135, 153–54
Driffield Terrace, York, 27, 255n24
Dunstable, Beds., 149–50, 272n81
Duroliponte. *See* Cambridge
Dyke Hills, Oxon., 179

East Anglia, 66, 157, 171
Eastbourne, E. Sx., 153, 166–67, 170
Eastington, Gloucs., 65
economy: collapse and remaking of networks, 32–33, 48–49, 61, 65–66, 133–34, 136, 176–82, 184–86; de-skilling, 53–54, 60, 65–66, 72, 80–82, 100–108, 123, 126, 136–37, 182–84; integration into larger networks, 19–25, 32, 58, 63–65, 77, 84–85, 177–82; subsistence, 47, 67–68, 119, 184–86
Edix Hill, Cambs., 131
Egypt, 29, 142, 152, 198n34, 209n37
Elbe, 61, 66
Elmswell, Suff., 124
Ely, Cambs. *See* West Fen Road, Cambs.
Empingham, Rut., 131
Essex, 37, 42, 61, 63–65, 76, 107, 109, 127, 130, 155, 172
ethnicity, 5, 159, 169–70, 172, 176, 179, 186–91

Faversham, Kent. *See* villas, Hog Brook
Fenlands, 25
Filton, Gloucs., 153
Fishergate, York, 43, 212n77
Flanders, 70
Flixton, Suff., 171
foederati theory, 62, 178–79
foodways, 7, 12, 34–38, 40–44, 46, 48–49, 53, 69–72, 78, 85–88, 92–94, 185, 238n125
Francia, 48, 72, 128, 133, 178, 180
Frisia, 133
fuel, 56, 67, 76, 120–22, 125, 135–36

gardens, 33, 37–50, 117, 183
Gaul, 19, 21–22, 25, 27, 37, 48, 56, 99, 123, 159, 177–80
Germany, 135, 160–63, 168, 181
Gildas, 178
glassware: at Cadbury Congresbury, 82–85, 92; late Roman production and use of, 74–76; at OD XII, 87, 92–93
Gloucester, 26, 102, 109, 215n99, 246n68
"Gloucester Goth," 179

Gloucestershire, 58, 65, 98, 101–2, 107, 125, 153, 155, 167
Goodmanham, E. Yorks., 128
grain pests, 21–22, 39, 42, 49, 218n135
Great Chesterford, Essex, 155, 172, 174
Greece, 164
Gregory of Tours, 128
Gwithian, Corn., 131

Hadham, Herts., 27, 58–59, 62, 64, 76, 80, 82, 224n74
Hadrian's Wall, 7, 28, 39, 56, 58, 87, 98, 122
Hampshire, 58, 129
Hamwic, Hants., 43, 49
Harold, Beds., 58, 222n45
Henley Wood, Som., 84
Herefordshire, 122
Hertfordshire, 27, 58, 64, 78–82, 86, 88–90, 92
Heybridge, Essex, 107, 223n59
High Post, Wilts., 65
Highdown, W. Sx., 180
hillforts, 82–85, 94, 109, 124
hobnail shoes, 6, 32, 78, 123, 141–42, 144, 149, 173, 232n42
Horcott Quarry, Gloucs., 154
Horningsea, Cambs., 58, 60
horticulture. *See* gardens

Ickham, Kent, 23, 123
Icklingham, Essex, 127
Inchtuthil, 120
infant burial: changes in practice of, 148–49, 154–56; compared to children's burial, 152–56; in enclosed cemeteries, 149–50; items buried with, 141–44; prominence of, 148; scholarly reassessment of, 139–40, 150–52, 156; under house floors, 145–47. *See also* Bradley Hill, Som.; Dunstable, Beds.; Cambridge, Ridgeons Garden; Rudstone Dale, E. Yorks.; Wattle Syke, W. Yorks.
Ingleby Barwick, N. Yorks., 98, 238n125
Ipswich, Suff., 43
Iraq, 28
Ireland, 168, 173
ironsmiths. *See* smiths
Isle of Man, 168
Italy, 28, 31, 35, 37, 41, 48, 72, 99, 123, 125, 152, 170

Julius Caesar, 40

Kaiseraugst, 16
Kelleythorpe, E. Yorks., 124
Kent, 23, 40, 42, 58, 61, 65, 98, 123, 132–33, 135, 171, 178–79
knives, 131–32, 169
Krefeld-Gellep, 27

landscapes and networks of production: in Roman period, 18–19, 23–24, 34–35, 54–58, 63, 72, 104, 107, 121–23, 176, 182–84; post-Roman collapse and remaking of, 33, 66–68, 100, 135–36, 182–84
Lechlade, Gloucs. *See* Butler's Field, Gloucs.
Leicester, 37
Lévi-Strauss, Claude, 116
Libanius, 19, 29
Lincoln, 39, 97
Lincolnshire, 66–67, 124, 272n70
Lodge Field, Norf., 65
London, 22–23, 27, 37, 40, 46, 56, 63, 74, 76–77, 92, 97–98, 103, 127, 145, 167; Huggin Hill, 98; Lundenwic, 43, 49
Lower Farm, Oxon., 90
Lyminge, Kent, 42, 133, 135–36, 264n112

Maiden Castle, Dor., 101
Malton, N. Yorks., 140
Market Lavington, Wilts., 92, 257n38
masonry construction: deskilling of crafts, 100–108; under Rome, 97–100
material culture: adoption by different social groups, 6–7, 12–13, 25–26, 37–38, 40, 49–50, 53, 55, 74–75, 92–94, 116–18, 134, 137, 182; collapse of Roman-period production, 6–9, 32–33, 41–42, 46–47, 50, 53–54, 57–69, 72–75, 78, 96–97, 122–25, 182–85; regions that heavily adopted Roman-style, 6–7, 38, 51–54, 188–91; Roman-period production, 6–7, 13, 32–33, 53–57, 72, 74, 97–109, 120–22
metal economy: fall of Roman, 122–26; post-Roman, 131–37; under Rome, 120–22
metalsmiths. *See* smiths
Midlands, 51, 58, 153, 194n11
Mildenhall, Wilts. *See* Cunetio, Wilts.
Mill Hill, Kent, 171
Millgate, Notts., 67–68
mortaria, 55, 83, 225n79, 238n126
Much Hadham, Herts. *See* Hadham, Herts.
Mucking, Essex, 61–64, 130–31, 172, 174, 179

Nene Valley, 54–55, 57–58, 60, 62–64, 76, 79–81, 221n44
Netherlands, 64, 125
Norfolk, 65, 67, 174
Northamptonshire, 65, 98, 113–14, 127, 135, 215n99, 239n137, 256n30, 260n65
Norway, 133, 136, 165, 168, 172, 175, 181
Notita dignitatum, 15, 28
Nottinghamshire, 68, 114
Nuneham Courtenay, Oxon. *See* Lower Farm, Oxon.

Oakington, Cambs., 168–70, 286n72
OD XII, 86–87, 92–93
Orpington, Kent, 65
Oudenburg, 27
Overton Down, Wilts. *See* OD XII
Oxfordshire, 22, 42, 54–55, 57, 62–65, 76–77, 83–84, 90, 92, 153, 167

Pannonia, 27, 167
Patching Hoard, 180
Petronius, 85
Pevensey, E. Sx., 65, 180
plants: cereal crops, 21–22, 35, 38–39, 42, 44, 46, 51, 53, 56, 77, 86, 148, 177, 184–85, 270n48; disappearance of new plants, 41–43, 70; introduction of new plants, 34–38; labor practices, 46–47; survival and return of new plants, 47–50; wild plants, 43–44. *See also* gardens
Pliny, 151, 207n16
Poole Harbor, Dor., 54, 59
population mobility, 25–32, 160–69
Portchester D/ Overwey. *See* pottery
pottery: Alice Holt/Farnham, 54, 58–59, 63, 65, 76–77, 224n74, 231n28; BB1 (black burnished ware), 56, 58, 71, 77, 201n74, 225n79; *céramique à l'éponge*, 63; Dales-ware, 27; decline of Roman pottery regime, 57–60; hand-built, 56, 61, 64–72, 77, 80–82, 85, 88–90, 94; Huntcliff-ware, 58, 88–89, 112; in closure deposits, 110–12; late Roman production and use of, 54–57; Mayen-ware, 63, 77; Mediterranean amphorae, 40, 77, 84; Portchester D/ Overwey, 58, 62–63, 65, 76, 142, 224n74; post-Roman use of, 71–72; Samian, 78–80, 94; Sancton/Baston potter, 67–68; "small-scale family production" of, 67–68; transshipment of, 21–22; use in burial, 53,

66–67, 69, 78–81, 147; use of during and after Roman withdrawal, 60–66. *See also* foodways
Poundbury, Dor., 152, 268n38
praetorium, 28, 204n114

Quarrington, Lincs., 124
Quarry Farm, N. Yorks. *See* Ingleby Barwick, N. Yorks.
Quoit Brooch-style, 62, 180, 291n21

Radley, Oxon. *See* Barrow Hills, Oxon.
Ramsbury, Wilts., 25, 135, 264n108
recycling: building material, 95, 97–111, 113–15; glass, 73–76, 82–84, 86–87, 92–94, 100, 122–23; metal, 120–24, 128–32, 137; pottery, 60–61, 76–94; wood, 76, 108
Redcliff Farm, Dor., 56–57
Rhine, 14, 19, 21, 25, 27, 38, 63, 176, 178–81
Rhineland. *See* Rhine
Richborough, Kent, 21–23, 28, 180
Ridgeons Garden. *See* Cambridge
River Cam, 58
River Frome, 56–57
River Kennet, 25
River Lea, 77, 231n22
River Severn, 37, 58
River Thames, 22, 58, 61, 63–65, 76, 90–91, 132
Rochester, Kent, 97
Rockingham Forrest. *See* Wakerley, Northants.
Roman monetary system, 13–17. *See also* coins
Roman tax system, 12–13; *annona*, 19, 21–24, 29, 38, 43–44, 46, 51, 58, 77, 86, 88–89, 177; *coemptiones*, 19, 58
Roman withdrawal from Britain, 1, 10, 32–33, 35, 47, 50, 65, 70, 75, 95–96, 126, 132, 153, 172, 176–79, 183
"Romanization" as a contested term, 4
Romney Creek, 64
roundhouses, 38, 83, 87, 89, 147, 237n117
Rudstone Dale, E. Yorks., 146–48, 150
Ruin, The, 117–18

S. Giovanni di Ruoti, 17
Salisbury, Wilts., 65
Saxon Shore forts, 19, 77
Scandinavia, 113, 125, 133, 135, 164–66, 168, 175, 181, 263n97, 283n48, 283n54
Scarborough, N. Yorks., 87–88
Schleswig-Holstein, 61, 66, 125

Scorton, N. Yorks., 26, 171
Scotland, 114, 120, 168, 173
SFB (sunken-featured building), 61–65, 237n117
Shadwell, London, 76–78, 86, 92, 110, 127, 231n22
Shakenoak, Oxon., 65
Shepherd's Farm, Dor., 154
Sibson, Hunts., 128
Silchester, Hants., 24, 142, 213n86, 215n99
Silistra, 26
smelting: iron, 120–26, 134–36; lead, 120, 122
smiths, 92, 97, 120–23, 128–35, 255n20, 264n108
Snorup, 126
social stratification, 7, 10–18, 37–38, 50, 82–86, 116–19, 131–37, 184–85
Somerset, 25, 82–83, 124, 144
Somerton. *See* Bradley Hill, Som.
South Shields, Twr., 28–29, 201n74, 211n60
Southampton, Hants., 131
Southwark, London, 63, 76, 123
Spain, 31, 37, 40, 48, 84, 234n75, 284n55
Spong Hill, Norf., 67, 69, 227n120, 257n38
St. Albans, Herts., 78
St. Mary Cray, Kent, 65
Stanford Wharf Nature Reserve, 63
Stansted, Essex, 42
Stibbington, Cambs., 55–56
Stonea, Cambs., 25, 238n124
Straubing-Bajuwarenstrasse, 162–63, 281n28, 282n33, 282n39
structured deposits, 40, 77–78, 109–15, 136, 142, 146, 150, 154, 249n97, 273n95
Suffolk, 43, 68–69, 129
Surrey, 58, 65, 224n74
Sussex, 65, 124, 153, 166, 180,
Sutton Courtenay, Oxon., 42, 239n134
Sweden, 165
Switzerland, 16, 125
swords, 132–35, 137
Syria, 29, 247n78

Theodosius, 106, 213n86
Thuringia, 162–63
Tolpuddle Ball, Dor., 153
Tournai, 178
trade and trade networks, 23, 42, 49, 57, 78, 84–85, 130, 133–37, 178, 180–81, 185–86, 210n54, 215n99, 234n75; transchannel networks, 177–82
Trier, 17, 19, 21–22, 31, 198n33, 200n57

Uley, Gloucs., 65, 108
Ulwell, Dor. *See* Shepherd's Farm, Dor.
urns, 66–69, 130

Vale of Pickering, 51
Verulamium, Herts., 104–5
villas: Atworth, Wilts., 101, 104–6, 245n59; Bancroft, Bucks., 65, 98, 114–15, 215n99; Barnsley Park, Gloucs., 98, 101–2; Barton Court Farm, 216n114; Beadlam, N. Yorks., 112; Beddington, Sy., 65; Box, Wilts., 99; Bucknowle, Dor., 101, 269n40, 270n48; Castle Copse, Wilts., 108; Chesters, Gloucs., 125; Dalton Parlours, W. Yorks., 112; Dicket Mead, Herts., 78, 232n31; elite residences, 17–18, 28–32, 37–38, 40, 95–99, 115–19; final phases of, 64–65, 78, 86–87, 92, 99–108, 122–23, 177; Frocester, Gloucs., 65, 98, 108–9, 125, 215n99; Great Holt's Farm, Essex, 37, 63; Great Weldon, Northants., 98; grounds, parklands, outbuildings, and industrial features, 17–19, 23, 25, 39–40, 53, 97, 125; Haddon, Cambs., 108; Hog Brook, Kent, 23, 98; Langmauer, 17; Latimer, Bucks., 108, 215n99; Littlecote, Wilts., 25, 98; Little Oakley, Essex, 64, 109, 127; Lullingstone, Kent, 142; Maddle Farm, Berks., 17, 19; Mount Pleasant, Lincs., 114; North Newbald, E. Yorks., 147; Piddington, Northants., 99, 139, 152; Redlands Farm, Northants., 65, 98, 101, 113, 155–56; repurposing of, 99–100; ritual acts marking abandonment of, 109–13; in Roman forts, 28–30; Romana del Casale, 37; Roughground Farm, Gloucs., 114; Rudston, E. Yorks., 30–32, 111–12; Stanwick, Northants., 98; Thurnham, Kent, 65, 99; Wortley, Gloucs., 107
Vindolanda, Northumb., 41, 97

Wakerley, Northants., 124, 256n25
Wales, 23, 51, 75, 168, 173
Warwickshire, 114, 173–74
Wasperton, Warw., 114, 131, 171–74
Wattle Syke, W. Yorks., 148–50, 238n125
Wavenden Gate, Bucks., 38
Waveney Valley, 142
weaving beaters. *See* swords
weaving swords. *See* swords
well deposits. *See* structured deposits

Welwyn Hall, Herts., 78–80
Weser, 61, 66
Wessex, 276n118
West Fen Road, Cambs., 43
West Heslerton, N. Yorks., 153, 164–67, 170–71, 174–75, 212n77, 238n125, 276n117, 283n54
West Stow, Suff., 129, 276n117
Weston under Penyard, Here. *See* Ariconium, Here.
Wiltshire, 24, 65, 86, 92, 98–99, 101, 104, 106
Winchester, Hants., 24, 26–27, 30, 42, 145, 167

Wolverton Mill, Bucks., 42
Worcester, 77, 256n30
Worgret, Dor., 56–57, 135
Wykeham, N. Yorks., 65, 237n117, 238n125

York, 23, 26–27, 37, 43, 88–89, 128, 131, 142–43, 147, 167; Wellington Row, 88–89, 222n49, 236n102
Yorkshire, 26–27, 30, 58, 65–68, 87–88, 111–12, 114, 124, 128, 135, 139, 142–43, 146, 148, 153, 165, 168, 171

Zosimus, 19

ACKNOWLEDGMENTS

Although I had been thinking for some time about writing about the transition from the Roman to the medieval period in Britain, this book's true genesis is marked by the day, in September, 2013, when I got "the phone call," and along with it the life-altering news that I had been awarded a MacArthur Fellowship. The fellowship has allowed me to devote *much* more time to thinking through and researching this book than I would have otherwise had, but it has done more—it has pushed me to be bolder and to grapple with the impact of big events on both ordinary people and the everyday. A simple thank-you and a book about people who have been left out of history seems like a poor acknowledgment of what I owe to the MacArthur Foundation, but thank you nonetheless.

My university, Boston College, has also been generous in its support of my project, providing me with crucial research funds and research semesters, and allowing me to liberate myself from my duties as chair of the History Department a year early. Patricia De Leuuw, vice provost for faculties (now retired), especially, made sure that I got all that I needed, and Provost David Quigley and Dean Gregory Kalscheur helped smooth the way as well. The two chairs of my department during the period I wrote this book, Kevin Kenny and Sarah Ross, also supported my research in fundamental ways. I also want to acknowledge the librarians and staff at Boston College's O'Neill Library, especially those in Interlibrary Loan, whose hard work I rely on and whose efforts have been nothing short of heroic.

The burdens of writing history have been made easier by my extraordinary department, colleagues, graduate students, and undergraduates, and I am grateful, every day, for the intellectual community in which I labor. All have contributed in one way or another to this book, but my everyday conversations with a number of the department's premodernists have been especially helpful, in particular with Prasanna Parthasarathi, Virginia Reinburg, and Dana Sajdi. The stimulating company of the doctoral students who participated in my research seminar during this period—Christine Bertoglio, Rachel Brody, Richard Ford

Burley, Nicole Ford Burley, Alexander D'Alisera, Matt Delvaux, Regan Eby, Kathleen Forste, Janet Kay, Austin Mason, Christopher Riedel, Carolyn Twomey, and Sharon Wofford—has also made thinking and writing much easier. Undergraduates in various iterations of my "Romans and Barbarians" and material culture classes, as well as the seniors who have written undergraduate theses under my direction, have inspired me to think harder about how to articulate not just what I know, but how I know. A book takes a village: I am lucky in mine.

It is also a pleasure to acknowledge the invitations to speak and the audiences who have listened to and questioned me during the years I was writing this book, all of whom have helped me refine my questions and ideas: the Bard Graduate Center; Boston University; Carleton College; Florida State University, Tampa; Fordham University; Harvard University; Juniata College; the MacArthur Fellows Forum; the Medieval Academy of American's annual meeting in Boston; Ohio State University; the New York Botanical Gardens; Rutgers University; Shippensburg University; St. Andrews University; Stanford University; United States Naval Academy; University of Ghent; University of Kansas, Omaha; University of Liverpool; University of Miami; University of Missouri; University of North Carolina, Chapel Hill; University of North Carolina, Greensboro; University of Notre Dame; University of Oxford; Whitman College; and Yale University.

The same is true for invitations to and the participants in a number of projects, workshops, and conferences I have had the pleasure of attending: the Boston College McMullen Museum's and Yale University Art Gallery's "Rome and the Provinces" exhibit workshop; the "Thing of the Past" workshops at the Radcliffe Institute for Advanced Study and the University of Michigan; the "Aliens, Foreigners, and Strangers in Medieval England" conference at the British Academy; the "Listening to Silence: Sounding the Experiences of Rural Women and Children in Late Antiquity" workshop at Brown University; the "Transformations of Romanness" workshop at the University of Vienna; the "Material World of the Early Middle Ages" conference at Pacific University; the Diet Group at the University of Oxford; the "Recycling and the Ancient Economy" conference at All Souls College, Oxford; the "Ancient Britain and Classical Art" Workshop at the Classical Art Research Centre at the University of Oxford, and the many stimulating meetings of the Haskins Society and the "Archaeologies of the Norman Conquest" group.

Wendy Davies, Caroline Goodson, Ben Jervis, and Naomi Sykes have all generously read, commented on, and improved individual chapters of this book. Kit

French, Kate Gilbert, and Martin Millett have labored through the whole manuscript, and it is much improved because of their hard work and sound advice.

I am grateful to Noreen O'Connor-Abel, Managing Editor at the University of Pennsylvania Press, for coordinating the editing and proofing of this book and to Kathleen Kageff for copyediting the manuscript. Two of my Ph.D. students have also helped in the preparation of this book. Rachel Brody lent a hand with the bibliography and the notes and Alexander D'Alisera has produced the index.

My last and greatest debt is to Stavros Macrakis, who has had to live with me and my book and put up with my many absences; my periods of blank-eyed, book-writing incoherence; and daily conversations about hobnail boots, sand-tempered pots, and little corpses.

Lightning Source UK Ltd.
Milton Keynes UK
UKHW010954070922
408435UK00003B/74/J